JAPANESE FILMS

JAPANESE FILMS

A Filmography and Commentary, 1921–1989

by

Beverley Bare Buehrer

St J

St James Press

Chicago and London

Published in the United Kingdom by
   St. James Press
   2-6 Boundary Row
   London SE1 8HP
   England

Originally published in the United States by
   McFarland & Co., Inc., Publishers,
   Jefferson, North Carolina

ISBN 1-55862-163-6

For my husband Carl,
who has supported me
in so many ways

Table of Contents

Preface

It is a world of arranged marriages and loyalty beyond death. A world where suicide is not a cowardly act, but a heroic one. A world where social obligations can be so burdensome as to crush the individual's heart. Or a world where life's sadness can be echoed in the falling petals of cherry blossoms. It is a world which is simultaneously exotic but also universal in appeal. It is the world of Japan, and it can be reflected beautifully in its films.

Hidden from Western eyes for centuries, Japan opened up to the world only in the mid–1800s. Similarly, the Japanese film industry, from its inception one of the world's most prodigious, began to send its product to U.S. shores only in the 1950s. Even today, unless one lives near a large metropolitan area, a Japanese community or a university, it has always been difficult to find these films. And even when found, there was always the possibility that a viewer might dislike what he or she saw because of a lack of understanding of Japanese culture and film style.

The purpose of this book is to reveal the fascinating world of Japanese films. It is not meant to be a theoretical or critical volume. Instead, it is hoped that it will provide readers/viewers with helpful background information and add to their enjoyment of films already seen or yet to be viewed. It is also hoped that this book will help stimulate Western audiences to see more Japanese films which, in turn will increase demand, which will then make even more films available.

Deciding which films to include in this book was a very difficult process. Choosing more than 80 films to represent an equal number of years of Japanese filmmaking, and more than 50 directors, involved many challenges. While Ozu may be the most revered director in Japan, cultural differences make his films less appealing to mainstream American audiences than those of Kurosawa. So how many of Ozu's films should be included? Mizoguchi's name may be more recognizable than Naruse's but each is a respected, talented and important director. But should Mizoguchi take precedence over Naruse?

In choosing the films, the following questions about each were considered. Is it indicative of a certain period of Japanese history and filmmaking? Does it display a specific phase of a director's career or is it a good example of the type of film he is known for? Has the film received critical attention, won international film awards, been a landmark in any way or garnered high grosses at the box office? Sometimes when a film was chosen to satisfy one of the above criteria it meant excluding another that might have been more well known or received more critical acclaim. Sometimes preference was given to a film because of its availability to audiences in the United States. When a title is available through film rental or videotapes, this means it may be more easily found and seen by an interested reader.

Preference to those films which have been distributed in the West in some ways accounts for the quantity of films by directors like Akira Kurosawa. Kurosawa, probably the Japanese director most well known in the West, has the largest body of films readily available for viewing, but including all of his films would make for a lopsided presentation. But which to leave out? Whichever it is, it is bound to be someone's favorite.

For ease of reading, Japanese names are given in Western order, first name first, surname last, instead of the reverse, which is the Japanese norm. Anglicized spellings of Japanese words and names, which are ideographic, often vary from source to source. The *Bunraku* puppeteers, for example, may be spelled *kuroko* in one source and *kurogo* in another, an actor named Nakamura in one listing may be Nagamura in another. I have tried to be as consistent as possible, following the lead of such authorities as Donald Richie to whom all Western Japanese film lovers owe so much — from his writings to the retrospectives he has put together.

There are many people who have helped with this book, from friends to video and film distributors. However, I especially would like to thank the following people and organizations. The Film Center of the Chicago Art Institute and its kind staff not only for being one of the few places to regularly show Japanese films in the Midwest, but also for allowing me to dig through their files. The staff and libraries in DeKalb and at Northern Illinois University — especially the indefatigable interlibrary loan personnel. Dennis Doros at Kino International for his help in viewing films and Michael Jeck at R5/S8 for his fascinating phone conversations. A special thanks of a different sort are due to my family, my friends in Wordrights, Jim Parish and Robbie Franklin.

Introduction

In 1897 Japan met the movies. That year, the Lumière brothers'
Cinématographe and Edison's Vitascope were shown for the first time just
40 short years after Japan was forced by Commodore Perry to terminate its
centuries of self-imposed isolation. Two years later Japan began production
of its own films.

These first efforts were basically filmed performances of Kabuki plays.
To compensate for the silence of the films, the Japanese invented the *benshi*. Sitting on the stage while the film was being shown, the *benshi*'s job
was to provide dialogue, explain actions and impart plot. The first
Japanese film stars were, more often than not, *benshis* instead of actors.

By 1903 the first permanent theatre was built in Tokyo for the express
purpose of showing films. Four years later, Osaka had one as well. Many
small production companies started making films for the constantly growing
audiences. The first of the five major Japanese film companies, Nikkatsu,
emerged in 1912, the second, Shochiku, in 1920. (The other three were
Toho, established in 1937, Daiei, in 1942, and Toei, in 1949.)

Soon production centered in the cities of Tokyo and Kyoto. Tokyo
tended to specialize in the *gendai-geki* (films about contemporary life) and
Kyoto in *jidai-geki* (historical, costume films). By 1921, Japan was creating
important films and major directors were emerging. By 1927, Japan's film
industry had grown to the point that it was producing 700 films a year. It
was on its way to being one of the world's most prolific film producing
countries.

Surprisingly, only a smattering of Japanese films were known in the
West. Considering the quantity produced, it is astonishing that it would
take until the 1950s for them to establish themselves in the American film
consciousness. The first shown were *jidai-gekis: Rashomon, Gate of Hell,
Ugetsu*. They were beautifully crafted, visually stunning, and more than a
shade exotic. They won critical acclaim and international film competitions. Initially the Japanese were as surprised by the foreign acceptance
of these films as the West was of their quality. But we still knew little

of the _gendai-gekis_ and even less about what was produced before
Rashomon.

Just as the West was awakening to the wealth and excellence of
Japanese films, other elements within the Japanese film industry were also
awakening, namely atomic monsters like Godzilla, Mothra and Rodan. For
many American moviegoers (especially the baby-boomers growing up on
Saturday matinées and late-night television fare), these represented the
entire output of Japanese films. Except for an occasional showing of films
like _The Seven Samurai_ on a PBS channel or at a college campus film club,
Japanese films were limited viewing—limited in distribution and audience.

When they were found, some viewers felt the vehement acting style in
some Japanese films too overdone. Others objected to what they felt were
excruciatingly long takes, the lack of Western narrative structure, the
intrusive digressions to scenes of nature and the seemingly illogical actions
of characters. With only an occasional film to view, it became difficult to
put these apparent negatives into a cultural perspective. With only one
film from a director, it was difficult to judge the overall quality of his
work. There _is_ a reason for elements like the long take and the use of
nature, and when they are understood better, the films can be seen with
more enjoyment.

Problems with the Japanese film industry, compounded by haphazard
distribution, left Americans in the sixties and seventies with few _Rashomon_
equivalents to whet their appetites. News occasionally leaked out about the
works of Oshima and other Shochiku "new wave" directors—such as the
time the United States Customs seized prints of the "pornographic" _In the
Realm of the Senses._ But having these films actually reach U.S. theatres
was another problem. Instead, the West was more likely to be shown the
latest Kurosawa _jidai-geki._

Martial arts films would come to earn a degree of popularity and also
renewed interest in samurai films, but on the whole, new Japanese films
were restricted to those of tried-and-true popular directors like Kurosawa
and were confined to art house theatres in the larger cities.

The decade of the eighties wasn't much better when it came to
theatrical distribution of Japanese films in the United States—with one
exception: Juzo Itami's _Tampopo._ Itami's delightfully entertaining and off-
beat film took America by storm in 1987. Because of this, his earlier film
The Funeral was dusted off and released. Audiences eagerly awaited his _A
Taxing Woman,_ which was also released in 1987, but its sequel, _A Taxing
Woman's Return,_ did not fare as well at the box office in 1989.

But on the whole, by the end of the eighties, few Japanese films had
made their way into theatres in the United States. There was the occasional
documentary such as _The Emperor's Naked Army Marches On_ or the
interesting animated feature such as _Laputa,_ but even they were difficult to
find. A telling example of the state of current American distribution of

Japanese films can be found in a film called *Milo and Otis*. Toho's *Kaneko Monogatari*, as the film was originally known in Japan, was 1986's biggest grossing film (approximately $36 million) in its home country. The film's writer and director, Masanori Hata, is a trained zoologist and celebrated author who writes under the pen name of Mutsugoro. He has written more than 100 books in many genres and lives on the eastern coast of Hokkaido with almost 300 animals in his private menagerie. Starting with more than 400,000 feet of film shot on his farm over a four-year period, Hata, with the help of Kon Ichikawa, who acted as associate director, created a film about the exploits of a young kitten and puppy. It was shown at the 1986 Cannes Film Festival as *The Adventures of Chatran*. Columbia Studios planned to distribute the film, and an original release date of August 1988 was scheduled. The film was recut (down to 76 minutes from 90), rescored and an English narration by Dudley Moore was added.

The summer of 1988 came and went, however, without *Chatran*. Then, in the summer of 1989, news of distribution of the film resurfaced; it was going by the name, *The Adventures of Milo and Otis*. It was released theatrically that summer, but in a very limited number of markets (such as Milwaukee, and a few cities in Minnesota and the Upper Peninsula of Michigan). For some reason, Columbia pulled the film and talk moved to a possible wide release during Thanksgiving of 1989. It never happened. Now Sony Corporation has bought out Columbia, and the last word was *Milo and Otis* might hit the screens in the summer of 1990.

However, three elements did emerge which would increase the availability of Japanese films to American audiences. Although still limited to larger cities, audiences could finally be treated to representative bodies of works when retrospectives such as those for Naruse or those with a theme like "Japan at War" traveled around the country.

Of more importance to those away from major cities was the development of the videocassette recorder. The VCR and the services of mail order videotape rental companies have brought Japanese films to even the most remote area of the United States. Ironically, even though the VCR owes its origins to Japan, in the beginning, only a handful of Japanese titles were available on videotape in the United States. But even this is changing as distributors look for new titles to print and innovative programs are attempted such as that undertaken by Sony and the Japan Society (see the Distributors appendix).

The third element was the development of cable television and rare cable channels like the impressive Bravo. Unfortunately Bravo is available only in limited areas, but its innovative schedule has included Japanese movies in series like "Samurai Summer" in 1988, while also sprinkling into their regular movie assortment contemporary films like Oguri's *Muddy River*, Shinoda's *MacArthur's Children*, Takita's *Comic Magazine* and the latest films of Juzo Itami.

Perhaps now that audiences have better access to Japanese movies, they will also discover that there is a great deal to be appreciated and savored in these films. From the action-packed samurai films of Kurosawa to the wistful slice-of-life films of Ozu to the entertaining comedies of Itami, the variety of Japanese films must be seen to be believed.

Souls on the Road (1921)
Rojo no reikon

1921 / Shochiku. 91 min. B&W. *Director:* Minoru Murata. *Producer:* Kaoru Osanai. *Screenplay:* Kiyohiko Ushihara. *Adaptation:* Based on the novel **Children on the Street** by Wilhelm Schmidtbonn and on the play **Lower Depths** by Maxim Gorky. *Cinematography:* Bunjiro Mizutani and Hamataro Oda.

Kaoru Osanai *as Yasushi Sugino.* Haruko Sawamura *Youko, his wife.* Koreya Togo *Koichiro, their son.* Mikiko Hisamatsu *Fumiko, their daughter.* Ryuko Date *Mitsuko, Koichiro's fiancée.* Yuriko Hanabusa *Peer's daughter.* Sotaro Okada *Caretaker of villa.* Kumahiko Mohara *Steward of villa.* Minoru Murata *Taro.* Komei Minami *Tsurikichi, a released convict.* Shigeru Tsutamura *Kamezo, a released convict.*

- In the first of two intertwined stories, a wealthy but prodigal son leaves his paternal home to study the violin in Tokyo. When he finally returns home, he is penniless and brings with him his wife and sick child. The reception he receives from his father is a hostile one.

  In the second story, two ex-convicts wander through the countryside, broke and hungry, searching for a way to make a livelihood. Unlike the prodigal son, they find understanding, kindness and help along the way, especially from an old caretaker at a peer's country villa. The two stories come together when the two wanderers, who set off full of hope and courage for the future, find the rejected son dead in the snow.

- Director Minoru Murata (1894–1937) was one of the early pioneers of the Japanese cinema. He found his way into the emerging industry by way of the Shingeki Theatre where he led his own acting troupe. Financial difficulties, among others, eventually found his theatrical troupe turning into one employed by the growing film industry. In 1920, Murata joined the new Shochiku studios. His first production, *Souls on the Road*, was one of the first outstanding Japanese films and one of the earliest to approach the subject of social criticism.

  Souls on the Road was one of the first Japanese films to break with the tradition of filming historical dramas, instead presenting a modern story. One reason it broke wih this tradition was because its story and method of storytelling were derived from basically Western sources, an accomplishment particularly attributed to Shochiku producer Kaoru Osanai.

1

The film's basic dramatic principle was one used by D.W. Griffith in *Intolerance*. Separate plots with parallel developments are interwoven to complement and counterpoint each other. The pessimism of the son's story is contrasted with the optimism of the convict's story.

Murata, who also appears in the film, tells a visual story in an obviously visual medium, often using settings to create or emphasize a scene's tone. One of the first films to be shot on location (in mountain country during early winter) instead of under controlled studio conditions, *Souls on the Road* used landscapes to further the stories' counterpunctuality. By presenting sunshine in one scene and overcast skies in another, for example, Murata's use of nature to reflect atmosphere and mood eventually would become one of the most distinctive characteristics of Japanese movies.

Souls on the Road, like most of Murata's successful pictures, focused on individuals and their place within Japanese social conventions. By adapting Western stories to Japanese expectations, and thereby going around convention, Murata helped develop an audience for contemporary storylines and bring a greater degree of realism to Japanese films.

The film company which produced *Souls on the Road,* Shochiku, started out as a Kabuki production company in 1902. It expanded into films in 1920 and was the second of what would become the five major Japanese film companies. (The other four were Toho, Daiei, Toei and Nikkatsu.) Shochiku strove to imitate American-style films, and came to specialize in *shomin-gekis,* or films about the everyday life of the common man, usually from the lower middle classes. This genre, at its best, subtly combines tragicomedy and melodrama. While the tone of a *shomin-geki* may be melancholic, there is still an underriding feeling of cheerfulness and acceptance.

Some of the best *shomin-gekis* were those of another Shochiku director, Yasujiro Shimazu (1897–1945) who worked as assistant director on *Souls on the Road.* While very few of Shimazu's films have been shown outside Japan, he has had a profound influence on many other Japanese directors, namely Gosho, Toyoda and Yoshimura.

A Page of Madness (1926)
Kurutta ippeiji

1926 / Kinugasa Productions. / a.k.a. "The Crazy Page." 60 min. B&W. *Director:* Teinosuke Kinugasa. *Screenplay:* Teinosuke Kinugasa and Yasunari Kawabata. *Cinematography:* Kohei Sugiyama and Eiichi Tsuburaya. *Art Director:* Chiyio Azaki. *Producer:* Teinosuke Kinugasa. Film Rental: Films Inc., New Line Cinema.

Masuo Inoue *as Custodian.* Yoshie Nakagawa *His wife.* Ayako Iijima *Their daughter.* Hiroshi Nemoto *The doctor.*

• An old man has taken on the job of custodian in an insane asylum where his wife is an inmate. She was committed there after suffering a nervous breakdown during which she drowned their baby son. She attempted to drown herself as well, but was prevented from doing so by their daughter.

The reason the old man has taken the job of custodian is so that he might be able to help his wife to escape. He has tried, unsuccessfully, several times. Now he has fallen into his own form of insanity. Eventually, his deteriorating state of mind leaves him resigned to his lowly job in the asylum where his wife continues to be an inmate.

• Director Teinosuke Kinugasa (1896–1980) began his career as an *oyama* (also called an *onagata*), a female impersonator. Because women were not allowed to act in the traditional Japanese Kabuki theatre, and consequently in films, female characters were played by men. When audiences and the law finally accepted women on the screen, Kinugasa became a director and even founded his own company, Kinugasa Motion Picture League, in Kyoto. His first production was the avant-garde *Page of Madness.* It was a complete commercial failure.

Although Kinugasa claimed that he had not seen any German expressionist films before making *Page of Madness,* its similarities in style have led many critics to question his claim. For Japan, it was the first feature film to have cinematic "devices" totally overwhelm the plot. Conventional techniques of narration were cast aside by Kinugasa in favor of more subjective techniques which emphasized state of mind over story. Without title cards, the film communicates in a fragmented and free-form manner. It fuses reality and delusion, and brings the viewer within the confines of the asylum both spatially and emotionally.

Page of Madness abounds with flash backs, quick cuts, fast camera movements, optical inventions, and symbolism. It does not, however, use these devices for their own sake. Kinugasa has skillfully woven them into the film so that they become equally as important as the film's subject matter. *Page of Madness* is an accomplishment which deservedly earns Kinugasa status as one of the first great innovators in the Japanese Cinema. Long thought to be a lost classic of the Japanese silent film age, it was rediscovered in the early 1970s when director Kinugasa found the negative in his garden store room.

Crossroads (1928)
Jujiro

1928 / Kinugasa Productions–Shochiku. / a.k.a. "Crossways" and "Shadows of the Yoshiwara." 60 min. B&W. *Director:* Teinosuke Kinugasa. *Screenplay:* Teinosuke Kinugasa. *Cinematography:* Kohei Sugiyama. *Art Direction:* Bonji Taira.

Junosuke Bando *as Rikiya.* Akiko Chihaya *Okiku, his sister.* Yukiko Ogawa *O-ume.* J. Soma *The fake policeman.*

• The setting is the Yoshiwara (entertainment) district of 18th century Tokyo. A young man, Rikiya, is desperately in love with the geisha O-ume. After a duel with his rival, Rikiya runs, wounded, to his sister, Okiku, believing that he has killed his rival. Okiku nurses her brother back to health. When he returns to O-ume, he finds his rival not only still alive, but with the geisha he loves. In a rage, Rikiya tries to kill him, but is stopped when ashes are thrown into his eyes.

Blinded, Rikiya again goes to his sister for help, but she cannot afford to pay a doctor. When it is suggested by a procuress that she can earn money by prostituting herself, she considers the option until a fake policeman tries to rape her. Okiku kills the "policeman" in self-defense and is now in need of help herself.

Rikiya, delirious from his illness, again goes to see his love O-ume. When he sees the rival he thought he had killed, Rikiya dies from the shock. His sister waits in vain at the crossroads for the brother who will never come.

• After the commercial failure of the avant-garde *Page of Madness*, Kinugasa turned to making more commercial films in order to pay his debts. In was a dark time for Kinugasa, and *Crossroads,* though made with a great deal of polish, reflects the director's depression. In fact, Kinugasa worked mostly at night and had the sets painted gray to heighten the mood of depression.

Kinugasa calls *Crossroads* a "samurai film without duels." While it might fall within the genre of the historical samurai drama, the *jidai-geki,* it does differ in several respects. Usually the *jidai-geki* samurai is an aristocratic and irreproachable hero, but in *Crossroads* he is tormented.

Told from Rikiya's point of view, the story is not presented chronologically, but is rather shown through a kind of expressionistic montage reflecting Rikiya's delirium. In this way Kinugasa retains some of the artistic style he explored in *Page of Madness* while still producing a commercially viable product. It was *Crossroads* which brought the Japanese film industry its first international attention when Kinugasa showed it in Paris and Berlin.

I Was Born But... (1932)
Umarete wa mita keredo

1932 / Shochiku. 89 min. (orig. 100 min.). B&W. *Director:* Yasujiro Ozu. *Screenplay:* Akira Fushimi and Geibei Ibushiya. *Adaptation:* From an idea by Yasujiro Ozu. *Cinematography and Editing:* Hideo Shigehara. *Set Design:* Takejiro Tsunoda and Yoshio Kimura. Film Rental: New Yorker.

Hideo Sugawara *as Ryoichi, the elder son.* Tomio "Tokkankozo" Aoki *Keiji, the younger son.* Tatsuo Saito *Yoshi, their father.* Mitsuko Yoshikawa *Their mother.* Takeshi Sakamoto *Boss.* Seiichi Kato *The boss' son, Taro.* Shoichi Kofujita *The delivery boy.* Seiji Nishimura *Schoolmaster.*

• A traditional Japanese worker moves to the suburbs with his family in order to be near his boss and advance his position. His two sons, eight and ten, however, do not adapt well to this change, especially since the other boys in the neighborhood pick on them. Not long after the move, the boys begin fighting with neighboring children, including the son of their father's boss.

The boys start skipping school and forging high marks on their papers which they then take home to their father. The schoolmaster, however, had already told their father of their absence. One day a delivery boy they have befriended overpowers a local bully and as a result the two boys are not only accepted by their classmates, but made leaders.

During a social occasion, the boys' father's boss shows home movies in which their father demeans himself by making faces and toadying to his boss. Later the boys demand an explanation. The father explains that if he doesn't please his boss then he'll lose his job and the family won't be able to eat. As a consequence, the boys decide to alleviate the embarrassment by promising never to eat again.

The morning after fighting with their father and going off in tears, the boys are persuaded to eat a breakfast of rice balls. Their father walks part of the way to school with the boys when they encounter the boss and his son Taro. After a moment of embarrassment it is Ryoichi who tells his father to greet his boss. As Yoshi and his boss drive off to work, the three boys walk on to school together.

• Yasujiro Ozu was born in 1903 in Tokyo. He graduated from middle school in 1921 and for a few years worked as a teacher. In 1923, his uncle introduced him to the manager of Shochiku Studios and he started to work there as an assistant cameraman. In 1924 he was called into the military reserves, but he avoided service by pretending to have consumption. The next year he was back at Shochiku. By 1926 he was promoted to assistant director, and in 1927 he made his debut as a director with *Sword of Patience.*

Although sound films had come to Japan by 1932 with Heinosuke Gosho's *The Neighbor's Wife and Mine* (1931), Ozu and many other established directors continued to regard film as a silent medium. One of the main reasons Japanese directors continued to make silent films longer than their Western counterparts was the tradition within the Japanese cinema of the *benshi.* Often more celebrated than a film's stars, *benshis* were film narrators who sat on the stage beside the running film and filled in dialogue, plot and motivation for Japanese audiences. In essence, the Japanese never really had "silent" films, and when sound was technologically introduced, there was no rush to use it.

I Was Born But... was one of the last great silent films. Like Chaplin, Ozu was capable of successfully combining sadness and comedy without becoming maudlin. The comedy in this film arises mostly from the children's charming innocence in light of the seemingly ridiculous protocols and actions of adults. The sadness comes at their (and the audience's) realization that there are illogical social inequities in the world and that they must accept them to survive.

Ozu tells this story with humor but not the kind that involves gags or set up jokes. Instead he lets the humor evolve naturally from within the situation. In the same way he also doesn't wring sadness from the story but leaves a viewer feeling the very typically Japanese thought "such is life."

Wife! Be Like a Rose! (1935)
Tsuma yo bara no yo ni

1935 / P.C.L. / a.k.a. "Kimiko." 74 min. B&W. *Director:* Mikio Naruse. *Screenplay:* Mikio Naruse. *Adaptation:* From a stage play by Minoru Nakano. *Cinematography:* Hiroshi Suzuki. *Music:* Noboru Ito.

Sadao Maruyama *as Shunsaku Yamamoto.* Tomoko Ito *Etsuko, his wife.* Sachiko Chiba *Kimiko, his daughter.* Yuriko Hanabusa *Oyuki, his mistress.* Setsuko Horikoshi *Shizuko, Oyuki's daughter.* Kaoru Ito

Kenichi, Oyuki's son. Kamatari Fujiwara *Shingo, Etsuko's brother.* Chikako Hosokawa *Shingo's wife.*

● A young woman, Kimiko, lives alone with her mother. Her father abandoned the family several years earlier. Finances are tight for the two women even though the father occasionally sends money and Kimiko works in an office. Kimiko's mother teaches and publishes poetry, usually about loneliness.

Kimiko is a very modern woman. She has a boyfriend and would like to proceed with wedding plans, but that would be difficult without her father's help. At her uncle's suggestion, Kimiko searches out her father not only to urge him to come home, but also to berate him for having left in the first place.

Her father, Yamamoto, now lives in the country where he has become involved in a gold-prospecting enterprise and lives with his mistress, Oyuki, and her two children, Shizuko and Kenichi. Kimiko, who had always thought of her father's mistress as a wicked and evil geisha, now finds that she is a hard-working, virtuous woman who supports the whole family by working as a hairdresser. In fact, it was she who sent money to Kimiko and her mother, not Yamamoto. By doing so she has denied her own children, even preventing her daughter from getting an education. As further proof of her selflessness, Oyuki gives Yamamoto the money saved for Shizuko's wedding dress to buy a gift for Kimiko's wedding instead.

Yamamoto is finally convinced to travel to Tokyo to act as go-between for his daughter's marriage arrangements. Having seen her father in both settings, Kimiko now makes discoveries about him. Instead of the dishonorable sinner she has thought him to be, she finds a man who has a great deal of difficulty just communicating with a wife who is his intellectual superior. And the mother she has always lived with is now seen to be cool and distant. He is basically a simple man, and the family he has found in the country is much nearer to what he wants. Although her mother's poetry indicates her feeling of loss at Yamamoto's departure (she even sheds silent tears as she writes), she is too genteel to put up with him. Eventually Kimiko understands and concedes her father's choice.

● Mikio Naruse (1905–1969) had a very difficult childhood. Orphaned when he was 15, he left school early to find work but continued to educate himself at local libraries.

In 1926 he joined Shochiku Studios as an assistant director to Yoshinobu Ikeda. Using the pen name "Chihan Miki," Naruse wrote comedy scripts. With the help of his friend, fellow director Heinosuke Gosho, Naruse was given the chance to direct his first film in 1930, *Mr. and Mrs. Swordplay* (Chambara Fufu).

In 1934, after frustration at Shochiku's low pay and their reluctance to expand into sound films, Naruse left the studio for P.C.L. (Photo

Chemical Laboratories) which in the 1930s developed the producer system of filmmaking as opposed to the then current director system. (Also against tradition, P.C.L. hired people on a short-term contract which meant that instead of working in a protected family atmosphere, employees' work was reviewed when their contracts came up for renewal. P.C.L. would, in 1936, become Toho.) Here Naruse's talents bloomed, for the very next year he made one of Japan's best films, *Wife! Be Like a Rose!* This was Naruse's most successful prewar film and was the first Japanese sound film to be distributed in the United States.

The subject matter of most of Naruse's films is the family. Usually they are working-class poor, and usually they center around a woman. Like Yasujiro Ozu, Naruse is more interested in letting drama evolve out of his characters than in following a set plot. As a consequence, again like Ozu, his films have a steady flow to them. They have no real highs and lows and also seem devoid of endings. For the characters in Naruse's films, life simply goes on, just as it does in reality.

Disillusionment and disappointment are a way of life for Naruse's characters. They are tied into traditional situations but seem unable to find happiness in them. And while they may be smoldering and fighting internally about their plight, they are also resigned to it and consequently present an external veneer of calm acceptance.

In 1937 Naruse married the actress who played Kimiko in *Wife! Be Like a Rose!,* Sachiko Chiba. Their marriage, however, only lasted until 1942. Unfortunately, the fifteen years after his marriage, in addition to being a time of military control of the film industry, also produced a collapse in Naruse's career. With a few exceptions, namely *The Whole Family Works* and *Hideko the Bus Conductor* (Hideko Takamine's first starring picture for Naruse), which apparently were made begrudgingly as "national policy" films, his career slipped into a series of nondescript films. It would take several years for Naruse to come out of this slump, but when he did it was with a classic, 1951's *Repast.*

Osaka Elegy (1936)
Niniwa hika

1936 / Daiichi. / a.k.a. "Naniwa ereji." 89 min. (There are also versions with shorter running times.) B&W. *Director:* Kenji Miziguchi. *Screenplay:* Kenji Mizoguchi and Yoshikata Yoda. *Adaptation:* Based on the magazine serial *Mieko* by Saburo Okada. *Cinematographer:* Minoru

Miki. *Music:* Koichi Takagi. Film Rental: Films Inc., Janus. Video: Sony.

Isuzu Yamada *as Ayako.* Seiichi Takegawa *Junzo, her father.* Chiyoko Okura *Sachiko, her younger sister.* Shinkachiro Asaka *Hiroshi, her elder brother.* Benkei Shiganoya *Sonosuke Asai.* Yoko Umemura *Sumiko.* Kensaku Hara *Susumu Nishimura.* Eitaro Shindo *Fujino.* Kunio Tamura *The physician.* Shizuko Takizawa *Apartment maid.*

• Ayako, a young woman who works as a telephone operator, is propositioned by Asai, the well-to-do owner of the pharmaceutical company where she is employed in modern Osaka. He tries to take advantage of the fact that Ayako needs money to keep her father out of jail, but Ayako still refuses him. She is in love with a young executive employee at the company, Nishimura. When she tells Nishimura about Asai's actions, he doesn't seem to care.

Ayako's father, Junzo, is a drunken embezzler who cannot provide the money her brother, Hiroshi, needs for school. After a family argument, Ayako is kicked out of the family home. When Nishimura comes to her home, he is told that she has left forever. Later, it becomes evident that Ayako has become Asai's mistress. He has rented an apartment for her and has taken care of her family's debts. One day at the theatre, Asai and Ayako run into Sumiko, Asai's wife. The couple are only just protected when Ayako's ex-boss, Fujino, steps in and pretends to be her boyfriend.

At a department store, Ayako and Nishimura bump into each other. He asks her to marry him, but she puts him off. She doesn't want him to know about her arrangements with Asai. Sumiko discovers the truth about her husband and Ayako when a doctor who has been phoned to come and see Asai goes to his home instead of to Ayako's apartment. Sumiko goes to Ayako's apartment and reclaims her husband. Now rid of Asai, Ayako is determined to marry Nishimura.

While on the way to Nishimura's, Ayako runs into her sister Sachiko. She tells her that their brother, who is ashamed of Ayako, now needs 200 yen in order to graduate from college. Although she wants to lead her own life, she is coerced into becoming a prostitute. The money she makes in this unsavory way for her brother, though, is taken by her father to indulge his drinking.

Ayako is employed in a geisha house where, one day, her services are asked for by her ex-boss Fujino. Ayako takes his money, but runs away to her apartment. There she has arranged to meet Nishimura. Just as she is telling him everything, Fujino bursts in demanding either his money back or the services he has paid for. Ayako manages to get Fujino out of her apartment, but the police quickly come and arrest both her and Nishimura.

Nishimura refuses to stand by her and Ayako is forced by the police to submit to humiliation before she is released to her father. Her family, who have forced her into her current situation, think of her as a disgraceful and neglectful person and want nothing to do with her. Once again Ayako must leave her home.

• Director Kenji Mizoguchi, along with Akira Kurosawa and Yasujiro Ozu, is not only one of Japan's best known filmmakers in the West, but is also considered one of the world's great directors. A director of immense talent and productivity, Mizoguchi was a major force in Japanese and world films.

Mizoguchi was born in Tokyo in 1898 and grew up in poverty. He was the son of a carpenter who had to sell his oldest daughter, Suzu, to a geisha house. This event was witnessed by the seven-year-old Mizoguchi and it affected him greatly.

At 13 he had to quit school and go to work at first in a hospital and then as an apprentice to a textile designer. Mizoguchi's mother died when he was 17 and he left home to live with Suzu who by then had become the mistress of a wealthy nobleman.

Mizoguchi was always interested in "graphic arts." In 1914 he enrolled at the Aohashi Western Painting Research Institute, an art school specializing in Western-style painting. After being out of work for awhile, Mizoguchi's sister found him a job in 1916 at a newspaper in Kobe where he worked as an advertising illustrator.

In 1920 Mizoguchi entered Nikkatsu as an actor but was soon put to work transcribing scripts and quickly became assistant director to Haru Wakayama. Mizoguchi also worked with Eizo Tanaka who recommended the young man be given his own opportunity to direct. In 1922 Mizoguchi got his chance and debuted with *The Resurrection of Love (Ai ni yomigaeru hi)* a film the censors cut severely because of its "proletarian ideology."

Oddly enough, his first "hit" was a quasidocumentary fluke. In 1923, when the Great Earthquake hit, Mizoguchi grabbed a cameraman and started shooting pictures. He sent some footage to the West as newsreels and used the rest in *In the Ruins (Haikyo no naka)* which premiered only six weeks after the earthquake. In the aftermath, Mizoguchi was sent to Nikkatsu's Kyoto studios where he churned out uninspired films demanded by the studio.

Mizoguchi lived in Kyoto and enjoyed the city very much. He started a relationship with Yuriko Ichijo, a jealous call girl who attempted to murder Mizoguchi with a razor in 1925. This event threw Mizoguchi into a period of unproductivity which lasted almost six months. When he started working again, he made *A Paper Doll's Whisper of Spring (Kaminingyo haru no sasayaki)* which won critical acclaim and marked Mizoguchi's road towards his mastery of film. Searching for perfectionism became an obsession Mizoguchi retained throughout his career.

In the late 1920s Mizoguchi made several leftist "tendency films" which again were severely cut by censors. While Mizoguchi made many films between 1922 and 1935 (he made approximately 55 films, of which only six are known to exist) it was a period marked by money troubles and a stormy marriage to Chieko Saga whom he met in 1926. In an attempt to gain artistic control of his films, Mizoguchi joined Daiichi Films. At first Mizoguchi continued to make the same type of Meiji era films he made before coming to Daiichi in 1934. By 1936, however, he had changed to more contemporary settings, but still retaining his preoccupation with accurate sets.

Osaka Elegy was shot in just 20 days and with a small budget, but it is considered a forerunner of Japanese film realism and indicative of themes which would become central to Mizoguchi's work: the oppression of women and their victimization at the hands of dominating males.

Osaka Elegy was critically praised when it was released but ran into financial trouble. Daiichi (which was an arm of Shochiku meant to increase competition against its major rival Nikkatsu) had trouble gaining distribution for the film partly because the censors were initially displeased at the movie's realistic treatment of a sensitive subject. In fact, so great were Daiichi's fiscal misfortunes that they were able to produce only one more film, *Sisters of the Gion.*

Sisters of the Gion (1936)
Gion no shimai

1936 / Daiichi. 69 min. B&W. *Director:* Kenji Mizoguchi. *Screenplay:* Kenji Mizoguchi and Yoshikata Yoda. *Adaptation:* From the novel *Yama* by Alexander Ivanovich Kuprin. *Cinematography:* Minoru Miki. Film Rental: Films Inc., Janus. Video: Balzac.

Isuzu Yamada *as Omocha.* Yoko Umemura *Umekichi.* Benkei Shiganoya *Shinbee Furusawa.* Eitaro Shindo *Kudo.* Taizo Fukami *Kimura.* Fumio Okura *Antique shop owner.*

• Furusawa is a bankrupt merchant whose merchandise is being auctioned off. When his wife continues to complain about their situation, he leaves the house. He goes to the Gion, the geisha section of the city, and seeks the company of his long-time lover, Umekichi.

Umekichi is the older of two sister geishas. Her younger sister, Omocha, berates Umekichi for the way she acts. Umekichi holds traditional values and offers comfort to Furasawa without making demands on him. Omocha, on the other hand, refuses to become emotionally involved with any of her clients and views her job strictly as a business. Using men is just a means to her ends of getting out of the Gion and working in Tokyo or getting married.

While the sisters are on the way to a Kyoto shrine, Omocha is approached and told that a young kimono shop clerk is enamored of her. Omocha smiles, but continues on to the head geisha's where she makes a case for recognition of Umekichi's beautiful dancing. The head geisha says Umekichi may dance at an upcoming event, but to do so requires that she wear an expensive kimono. To help her sister, Omocha goes to the kimono shop clerk, Kimura, and uses his liking of her to get him to procure the kimono.

At a party, Umekichi meets a wealthy antique shop owner who is a friend of Furusawa's. He has drunk too much, but agrees to meet Furusawa at the sisters' home. There he drinks more and after treating Furusawa in a patronizing manner, is accused by Furusawa of once having sold fake antiques. Omocha takes the drunken antiques dealer home, stays the night and hopes to make him her sister's new patron. When she returns home, she tells Furusawa to leave. When Kudo, the owner of the kimono shop where Kimura works, discovers the missing expensive kimono, Kimura runs to Omocha. Omocha treats Kimura derisively especially after Kudo comes to her house and fires him. Now Omocha makes a play for Kudo.

One day Kimura runs into Furusawa and uses the meeting as an excuse to go to the sisters' house. Omocha is not home, but Umekichi and the antique shop owner are. Kimura tells her that Furusawa is depressed and living with his old servant. Consequently she runs out, leaving the two men alone. While they are there, Omocha and Kudo return to the house. Kimura is surprised and upset that the two are together and threatens them. Kimura phones Kudo's wife and reveals his illicit affair to her.

Umekichi and Furusawa find each other and decide to live together, away from Omocha. Nothing Omocha says will persuade her sister to abandon Furusawa and return to their home. Late one night, a taxi comes for Omocha, supposedly sent by Kudo. After the driver becomes abusive and refuses to stop the cab, Kimura comes out of hiding in the front seat and attacks her in revenge for the way she has treated him.

Omocha is taken to the hospital where she is told she is lucky to be alive and will probably be crippled from being thrown from the cab. Umekichi comes to the hospital but offers her sister no comfort. To her, Omocha's fate was predetermined because of the way she had treated the men in her life. Umekichi promises to stay with her sister in the hospital, but when she returns home she finds that Furusawa has returned to his wife who now has a good job. Back at the hospital, the two sisters contemplate their fates.

• Mizoguchi was pleased with the results of *Osaka Elegy* and decided to make another film about a similar subject, only this time setting it in the appropriate location in Kyoto. The Gion district is the traditional site of geisha houses. It was a location Mizoguchi visited often and one he felt he could capture accurately on film. Mizoguchi sees beneath the surface of the world where women make a living entertaining and catering to the whims of men. Both films realistically portray a social problem and capture the atmosphere of the world where these women live.

A part of this meticulous portrayal is due to Mizoguchi's insistence upon realistic detail and part is due to scriptwriter Yoshikata Yoda. Yoda had been ill in the hospital when he went looking for a job with Mizoguchi at Daiichi. He had no experience in scriptwriting but was familiar with Osaka, Kyoto and Kobe and was able to write in the more vernacular, heavy accent used in those cities. This was just what Mizoguchi was looking for when he started *Osaka Elegy* and he hired Yoda. It was the start of a continuing partnership in which Yoda would write most of Mizoguchi's scripts. Yoda wrote and rewrote scripts many times for the demanding director he greatly admired. In many respects he was treated viciously by Mizoguchi, often being told that a script was terrible, but never mentioning what was wrong. Yoda was left to try and outguess Mizoguchi and suffering his wrath if wrong. However, the collaboration was an outstanding one and the two films brought Mizoguchi to fame and marked the true artistic start of a distinguished career.

Sisters of the Gion is considered a continuation of *Osaka Elegy* in theme, style and topic. Ayako, in *Osaka Elegy,* has, in effect, now slipped into the world of the two sisters living in the Gion. All three women are victims at the mercy of the men who control their fate, even Omocha who tries to control her own fate. (It is a similarity enforced by actress Isuzu Yamada who played both Ayako and Omocha.)

Isuzu Yamada was born Mitsu Yamada in Osaka in 1917. She intended to play the samisen, but her career was sidetracked when she joined Nikkatsu studios at 14 (she has also worked for Daiichi and Toho). Yamada reached the peak of her film popularity during this period. The actress married director Teinosuke Kinugasa and her daughter, Michiko Saga, also appears in films. Besides the work she did for Mizoguchi, Yamada is probably best known in the West for her electrifying Lady Washizu in *Throne of Blood* and as Sembei's wife in *Yojimbo*.

Like *Osaka Elegy, Sisters of the Gion* also received critical acclaim and also ran into trouble with the censors. In their hands the film was cut, and did not make money for Daiichi. Even though *Sisters of the Gion* was rated as the winner in Japan's top ten list for 1936 (and *Osaka Elegy* was rated number three), it effectively bankrupt Daiichi. In a time when Japan was gearing up for what would become World War II, love of country was the feelings of the hour. Films about social criticism were not viewed favorably.

Humanity and Paper Balloons (1937)
Ninjo kami fusen

1937 / Toho. 86 min. B&W. *Director:* Sadao Yamanaka. *Screenplay:* Shintaro Mimura. *Cinematography:* Akira Mimura. *Music:* Chu Ota.

Kanemon Nakamura *as Shinza, the barber.* Chojuro Kawarazaki *Matajuro Unno, a ronin samurai.* Shizue Yamagishi *Otaki, Matajuro's wife.* Sukezo Suketayaka *Chobei, the landlord.* Tsuruzo Nakamura *Genko.* Hisako Hara *Otetsu.* Choemon Bando *Yabuichi.* Noboru Kiritachi *Okoma.*

• The time is the 18th century Tokugawa period and the place is a poor section of Tokyo. A *ronin* samurai (a masterless samurai who is without a means of livelihood) who has been reduced to living in poverty, has committed suicide. At first the other people who live in the area wonder why he transgressed the samurai code of *bushido* and didn't perform the traditional and honorable means of samurai suicide, *seppuku.* Then someone points out that in his poverty, the ronin had sold his sword for rice.

At the funeral, several members of the tenement community are introduced, including a goldfish seller, a blind masseur, a gambler, a noodle seller and another ronin and his wife. This ronin, too, is without a steady means of making a living and has sold his sword for rice. Each day he goes out in search of work. His wife, in the meantime, continually makes paper balloons as toys for children. The ronin makes some money, not by nobly serving a master, but by selling these children's toys.

Desperate for money, the samurai aids a needy friend and becomes involved in an unsuccessful kidnapping. As a result of the humiliation of his attempt, the wife kills the samurai in his sleep and then kills herself. The next morning, the tenement neighbors find the woman's balloons blowing throughout the courtyard. Once more the impoverished community escapes their dreary lives with a drunken wake.

• *Humanity and Papers Balloons* was a unique film in its time in that instead of glorifying the samurai and his chivalric code of *bushido*, takes a

Humanity and Paper Balloons (Sadao Yamanaka, 1937). The promising career of director Yamanaka, whose humanist films such as this one starring Shizue Yamagishi (left) and Chojuro Kawarazaki were not endorsed by the military censors, was cut short when he was sent to fight on the Chinese front and was killed. (Photo courtesy of Toho Co., Ltd.)

critical look at this historic and pervasive legendary character. Yamanaka's ronin are reduced from the usual heroic images to a less mythical, and probably in many cases more realistic, status. These samurai are not looked-up-to knights but impoverished men who have been humbled not only economically but also emotionally because they cannot meet the basic samurai prerequisites.

The opening of *Humanity and Papers Balloons* is both similar and dissimilar from many opening scenes in typical *jidai-geki* (period dramas) films. Samurai death scenes are common, but usually they perish while taking at least 20 of the enemy with them during a heroic battle. By showing this sadly unheroic samurai's death, Yamanaka immediately sets a tone of upsetting historic and artistic expectations. This theme is continued by the simple introduction of the impoverished members of the Edo community during a period which most people associate with a Golden Age of artistic achievements in Japan.

Sadao Yamanaka (1909–1938) made his first film in 1932 at the age of 23. He immediately gained a reputation as a director who could handle dialogue without sacrificing visual style, and who used exceptionally fluid editing. His films were not so much concerned with historical accuracy and plot as with situations and his characters' reactions to them. In many respects, Yamanaka is the father of the humanistic Japanese film. Unfortunately, in searching for a humanistic truth, his films become more and more pessimistic.

At a time when films were coming under the purview of a nationalistic and militaristic Home Office that was waging and justifying a war of expansion, Yamanaka's film debunking a national myth was not appreciated. Filmmakers were supposed to use the past to glorify the actions of the present, and Yamanaka's samurai didn't achieve this goal. In 1937 Yamanaka was drafted into the army as a foot soldier (an unusual situation for filmmakers at that time). He was sent to the Chinese front as retribution for his "antipatriotic" sentiments and died there in 1938. Sadly, only two of the 12 films he made have survived, *The Pot Worth a Million Ryo (Hyaku-man ryono tsubo,* 1935) and *Humanity and Paper Balloons,* which was his last work.

The company under whose auspices *Humanity and Paper Balloons* was made, started out in 1933 as Photo Chemical Laboratories, or P.C.L. as it was commonly known. In 1936 P.C.L. combined with another studio to form Toho Motion Picture Distributing Company with the main objective of film distribution (especially of Nikkatsu films), not production. When their deal with Nikkatsu fell through and left Toho with few films to distribute, they began production, luring away talent from established companies. When they put Shochiku's Kazuo Hasegawa (see *A Story from Chikamatsu*) under contract, a bitter battle ensued between the two.

Five Scouts (1938)
Gonin no Sekkohei

1938 / Nikkatsu. 73 min. B&W. *Director:* Tomotaka Tasaka. *Screenplay:* Yoshio Aramaki. *Adaptation:* From the original story by Yashiro Takashige (Tasaka's pen name). *Cinematography:* Saburo Isayama. *Art Direction:* Takashi Matsuyama.

Isamu Kosugi *as Platoon leader Okada.* Bontaro Miake *Sergeant Fujimoto.* Ichiro Izawa *Private Koguchi.* Shiro Izome *Corporal Nakamura.*

• During the early years of World War II, at the front in Northern China, a company commander sends five soldiers out on a reconnaissance patrol which is more or less a suicide mission. The men scout the enemy's position. While returning to their base, the men are ambushed and one man is lost. Back at the camp, the four remaining men mourn the loss of their comrade only to have him straggle back to camp. He had become separated from the others in the darkness and confusion of battle.

Their mission complete, the men are ordered to move out for battle. But the men know that this time the chances of really losing comrades is very high.

• Tomotaka Tasaka was born in 1902 in Hiroshima. His mother died when he was very young and his father went bankrupt. Tasaka was forced to leave school and take a job as a newspaper reporter. In 1924 he was employed by Nikkatsu's Kyoto studios and by 1926 he had become a director.

Tasaka's films are distinguished by their precise depiction of period and location. The year 1938 saw Tasaka make two of his best films, *Five Scouts* and *A Pebble by the Wayside (Robo no ishi)*. The latter film was set in the early 1900s and tells the story of an unfortunate boy whose drunken and indebted father sends him out to work instead of allowing him the schooling he wants. His life is a miserable one until he is rescued by his teacher. It is considered to be one of the best movies about the Meiji period and Tasaka felt it was his best film.

Five Scouts was the first significant Japanese feature film to depict the undeclared war in China. The government, eager to have films made which exalted the war effort, turned to Nikkatsu Studios because of their experience and expertise in making action films—even though they were usually in historic settings. Consequently Nikkatsu and *Five Scouts* set the style for future films of that genre.

Oddly enough, Tasaka, the director chosen to direct the pioneering film, was more well known for his character dramas. But it was just this bias towards creating convincing and compelling characters which made *Five Scouts* the success it was. Each of the five soldiers central to the film is invested with a different personality. Where one is a brusque veteran, another is so irresponsible that he becomes lost from his troupe. The actors' characters work well together and honestly generate a feeling of camaraderie.

This film will surprise the average Western viewer for whom World War II films evoke images of nationalism and propaganda. There is no dogmatic nationalism in this film and it even lacks the heroic characters usually associated with traditional Japanese *jidai-geki* films. (In fact, the film is often compared more to such pacifistic, antiwar Western films as *All's Quiet on the Western Front*.) Tasaka's soldiers do not go to war inspired by a heroic sense of mission. More realistically, they are afraid of the impending battles.

Five Scouts was one of the first Japanese films to be shown at an international competition. When it played at the Venice Festival (the oldest of the international film festivals), it won the Ministry of Popular Culture

award. Just when it seemed that Japanese films might have made inroads
into a worldwide film network, the beginnings of World War II put a stop
to it. Tasaka was to have directed another legendary antiwar film, *Harp of
Burma,* but he was too ill. In 1945 he was unlucky enough to have been in
Hiroshima on the day the atomic bomb was dropped. Although he survived, he became very ill from the radiation fallout. He was in the hospital
until 1949 and died in 1974.

The company which produced *Five Scouts,* Nikkatsu, is the oldest of
the five major Japanese film companies. Founded in 1912, Nikkatsu made
both period films *(jidai-geki)* at its Kyoto studios, and contemporary films
(gendai-geki) at its Tokyo studios. In 1942, under government order, Nikkatsu's production facilities were merged with two other companies to form
Daiei, and Nikkatsu was left with just its theatres. In 1954 Nikkatsu again
began production of films, but eventually began to specialize in films
which appealed to a younger audience like *yakuza* (gangster) films and
"roman poruno" (softcore pornography).

Earth (1939)
Tsuchi

1939 / Nikkatsu. 92 min. B&W. *Director:* Tomu Uchida.
Screenplay: Ryuichiro Yagi and Tsutomu Kitamura. *Adaptation:* From the
novel by Takashi Nagatsuka. *Cinematography:* Michiio Midorikawa. *Music:*
Akihiro Norimatsu.

Isamu Kosugi *as Kanji.* Akiko Kazami *Otsugi, his daughter.* Donguri-
boya *Yokichi, his son.* Kaichi Yamamoto *Ukichi.* Bontaro Miake *Heizo.*
Reisaburo Yamamoto *Kane, a horse dealer.* Sanemon Suzuki *Gen-san.*
Masako Fujimura *Tami.* Chieko Murata *Landowner's wife.* Mieshi Bando
Katsu. Mari Koh *Ohume.* Kyosuke Sawa *Hikozo.* Chie Mitsui *Yoshie.*
Miyoko Sakura *Aki.* Isamu Yonekura *Kumakichi.* Toshinosuke Nagao
Village policeman.

• Although there is structure to *Earth,* there is minimal plot. Depicting the life of peasant farmers, the film follows one year in their lives.
What plot there is revolves around one farmer who becomes penniless. His
misfortune plunges him into deep despair but in the end he finds a renewed faith.

The film primarily paints, through documentary-like footage, the
daily joys and sorrows of the farmers. It shares their closeness with nature,
their dependence on it, and their struggle against it.

• Tomu Uchida (1898–1970) started working in films in 1920 as a comic actor with Thomas Kurihara's Amateur Club. After working in the theatre for a while, he joined Nikkatsu as an assistant director working under directors such as Murata and Mizoguchi. During his first years with Nikkatsu, Uchida made silent, satirical comedies. By the mid–1930s, however, he was actively involved in bringing a greater realism to films, especially the *shomin-geki* genre.

Earth, Uchida's masterpiece, was made in secret—unknown even to management of his own company. When he approached them with the idea for the film, they were uninterested. The producers indicated that people went to the movies for entertainment and not to see the problems of other people, especially peasants. In light of the growing wartime atmosphere, a realistic picture of an impoverished rural Japan was also not desirable.

Ushida went ahead with his film anyway, and rented a small piece of land in a poor village. His actors were metamorphisized into seemingly authentic peasants who used rudimentary methods to tend their fields. Films usually tend to idealize their subjects, but in *Earth* they are shown to be simple, uneducated and suppressed. The shooting lasted a year and followed the cyclical rhythm of nature. The result was a poetic film, filled with power and hope for man. When it was shown, Uchida disproved his producers' misgivings. The film was a success.

Uchida's career was interrupted by the war, and he was sent to Manchuria and China. He was taken prisoner and did not return to Japan until 1954. At that time he joined Toei and became a specialist in *jidai-gekis*, remaking many classic films.

The Story of Tank Commander Nishizumi (1940)
Nishizumi senshacho-den

1940 / Shochiku. 136 min. B&W. *Director:* Kimisaburo (Kozaburo) Yoshimura. *Screenplay:* Kogo Noda. *Adaptation:* From a story by Kan Kikuchi. *Cinematography:* Toshio Ubukata. *Art Direction:* Yoneichi Wakita and Tatsuo Hamada. *Music:* Ki Maeda. *Assistant Directors:* Keisuke Konoshita and Noboru Nakamura.

Ken Uehara as *Nishizumi*. Takeshi Sakamoto *Goto*. Shin Saburi *Hosoki*. Chishu Ryu *Osumi*. Tatsuo Saito *Officer, 18th Battalion*. Michiko Kuwano *Chinese woman*. Ichiru Kodama *Hosokawa*. Seiji Nishimura

Murayama. Katsumi Kubota *Yamabe*. Toshiji Kawara *Okada*. Akio Isono
Uematsu.

• Against a background of praise for the Japanese army, Nishizumi's
story is told. The village where he grew up, went to school and learned the
philosophy of Japanese life and traditions is presented in such a way as to
emphasize Nishizumi's preparedness for service in the military. With his
father, a veteran, as an example, Nishizumi goes off to military school and
is sent, in 1938, to fight in China when he is 24 years old.

After several battle scenes set in or near Shanghai, Nishizumi appears
from within his tank. He chain-smokes and jokes with his fellow soldiers as
they prepare for more battles. Back at camp, Nishizumi and his comrades
go about normal daily activities like eating and singing, when the reality of
the war is suddenly brought back by the flag-draped bodies of the battle
dead which are moved into camp.

More battle scenes are depicted which highlight the resolve of
Nishizumi's tank assaults. He is gaining respect and admiration from the
men in his unit. His bravery is shown when he risks being shot while
testing the depth of a stream (with a Japanese flag) which the tanks need
to cross. His compassion is evident as he holds a dying comrade. Soon
Nishizumi is promoted to the rank of commander. In another act of
bravery, Nishizumi leaps from his tank to save the life of a wounded
Japanese soldier lying in the tank's path. In the process Nishizumi is
himself wounded in the leg, but unflinchingly continues helming his tank
in the attack.

Back in camp, a letter arrives from the brother of a dead soldier which
Nishizumi shares with the rest of the unit. The letter emphasizes how the
soldier's mother was proud that her son was able to do his duty for his
country, even at the cost of his life. The soldiers weep at the mother's
courage, patriotism and commitment.

One day the Japanese soldiers find a Chinese woman and her newborn
child taking refuge in their camp. The woman is panicked by the soldiers;
after all, they are her enemy. Nishizumi tries to calm and befriend the
woman by speaking to her in Chinese which he learned while serving in
Manchuria. He sends for a doctor. The woman is grateful to Nishizumi
and tells him how her house was robbed by Chinese soldiers and that her
husband is dead. The next morning Nishizumi finds that the woman has
run away with her lover and left her baby who had died during the night.
The soldiers, led by Nishizumi, compassionately bury the baby.

As the army advances on Nanking, battle scenes are interspersed with
scenes of soldierly camaraderie in the camp. After the fall of Nanking,
Nishizumi comes out of his tank amid the rubble of the defeated city. He
unflappably lights a cigarette (something he has done throughout the film)
and again goes out to test the depth of a river his tanks must cross. A

wounded Chinese soldier sees Nishizumi and manages to shoot him. Nishizumi's soldiers fire on the Chinese soldier and kill him and quickly take their commander to help. He has been critically wounded.

While his soldiers try to help him stay awake, the courageous Nishizumi is instead thinking of the war and telling his men to cross the river and fight. At the camp, Nishizumi is treated by the same doctor who treated the Chinese woman while his loyal men stand by. One badly wounded soldier even indicates that he would gladly die in Nishizumi's place. Unfortunately, both men die. Nishizumi's last words were, "What I have done is for the Emperor."

Meanwhile, the Chinese continue to attack only now the battles are getting close to the camp. As his unit charges into the battle, Nishizumi's tank, with his ashes riding atop, guides their way.

• Kimisaburo (a.k.a. Kozaburo) Yoshimura (b. 1911) entered Shochiku Studios in 1929 with the help and influence of a relative. Soon he became an assistant director to Yasujiro Shimazu. He constantly seemed to get into trouble at the studio, making mistakes and alienating studio officials. In 1944 he was drafted by the army and sent to Thailand, serving in a machine gun unit and then as an information officer. After a year in prison and repatriation after the war, he continued his film career at Shochiku.

His film *A Ball at the Anjo House (Anjo-ke no butokai,* 1947*)* was inspired by events Yoshimura witnessed at a party. He had difficulty writing the script, however, until someone recommended Kaneto Shindo. Their relationship lasted many years, and it would be Shindo who would write many of Yoshimura's best scripts. The two men's partnership flourished, and in March of 1950, they broke with the studio to form the production company Kindai Eiga Kyokai (Association of Modern Art Cinema).

Yoshimura eventually came to specialize in period films which he used to express his feelings and thoughts on modern Japan and its problems. He was a technically innovative and extremely versatile director who could make virtually any genre of film. He had a facility for selecting a filmic style appropriate for whatever story he was making, and yet he found fresh ways to depict tried-and-true plots.

The Story of Tank Commander Nishizumi was made, in part, to answer the criticism levied against Japan for its cruel actions in China. It attempts to do so by stressing the prewar, humanistic Japanese values of compassion and loyalty as personified by the character Nishizumi. The commander fraternizes easily with his troops and is an admired leader who directs by example. By offering Nishizumi as a humanistic character who is fully realized on the screen, the film transcends the propaganda efforts of the day. *Nishizumi* is a fast-paced film which, surprisingly, contains many touches of humor. It was also one of the "national policy" films made under the auspices of Japan's military government. From the time the war between Japan and China broke out in 1937 up until the time of the Allied Armies' occupation of Japan in 1945, the film industry was subjected to severe censorship at the hands of the Japanese Home Ministry. The Motion Picture Law of 1939 set standards for the plots of Japanese movies. No longer could films center on the individual or urban life, now they had to promote proper thinking, prewar values and patriotism on the homefront.

Unlike American war propaganda films, however, those created in Japan did not vilify the enemy and make them into caricatures which were easy to hate. The subject matter of these films usually was not the hated adversary but how the war could be a time for spiritual strengthening, for developing devotion to the nation and for self-sacrifice in the name of the common good. The war-time government of Japan learned of Nazi Germany's Goebbel's control of motion pictures in his country and how he used them to advance state goals. Consequently, Japan enacted more regulations which would allow them, too, to manipulate the content and type of films that could be made in Japan. With the attack on Pearl Harbor, films with a much more strident nationalistic tone such as Kajiro Yamamoto's *The War at Sea from Hawaii to Malaya* (1942) became the norm.

In 1951, Yoshimura made the first film of the world's first novel, *A Tale of the Genji (Genji Monogatari)*. The original story was written in the 11th century by a lady-in-waiting at the Imperial Court. It was never used as the basis of a film before because prior to 1945 it was forbidden to set dramas in the Imperial Court. With a great deal of publicity from Daiei, which used it to celebrate its tenth anniversary, *A Tale of the Genji* became the company's top grossing film. (The film's cinematographer, Kohei Sugiyama, won a prize at 1952's Cannes Film Festival.)

In 1956 Yoshimura contracted with Daiei and came to make many films centering on women. Many considered him a successor to Mizoguchi, a director famous for his films about women. In fact, when Mizoguchi died in 1956, Yoshimura was called upon to do the film, *An Osaka Story,* from the script Mizoguchi was working on at the time of his death.

The Loyal 47 Ronin, Parts I and II (1941–1942)
Genroku Chushingura

1941–1942 / Koa Productions–Shochiku. / a.k.a. "The 47 Ronin of the Genroku Era." 220 min. B&W. *Director:* Kenji Mizoguchi. *Screenplay:* Kenichiro Hara and Yoshikata Yoda. *Adaptation:* From the play by Seika

Mayama based on the popular legend. *Cinematography:* Kohei Sugiyama. *Art Direction:* Hiroshi Mizutani. *Set Direction:* Matsuji Ono. *Music:* Shiro Fukai. *Executive Producer:* Shintaro Shirai. Videotape: Sony. Film Rental: Films Inc., Janus.

Chojuro Kawarazaki *as Kuranosuke Oishi.* Yoshizaburo Arashi *Takuminokami Asano.* Mantoyo Mimasu *Kozunosuke Kira.* Kanemon Nakamura *Sukeimon Tomimori.* Utaemon Ichikawa *Tsunatoyo Tokugawa.* Isamu Kosugi *Denpachiro.* Mitsuko Miura *Yosenin.* Seizaburo Kawazu *Etchumori Hosokawa.* Tsuruzo Nakamura *Denuemon Horiuchi.* Kunitaro Kawarazaki *Jurozaemon Isogai.* Mieko Takamine *Omino.*

• **Part I:** On March 14, 1701, Lord Asano, lord of Ako Castle, is attending formal ceremonies at Edo Castle. It was customary for visitors to receive etiquette instructions at times like this, and for the "pupil" to give extravagant payments in return. Lord Asano is unfamiliar with this custom and slights his instructor, Kira. As a consequence, Kira takes every opportunity to disparage and insult the innocent Asano.

Finally, losing his patience at Kira's insults, Asano draws his sword upon Kira within the castle walls. This is an offense which carries the penalty of death. Although Kira is only minimally hurt, he does not step in on Asano's behalf to show that the lord was provoked, and Asano makes no attempt to defend himself. Asano is ordered to commit seppuku. His lands and possessions are confiscated, his family disinherited and his retainers discharged, his samurai are turned into ronin, masterless men. And no action is taken against Kira.

Many of Asano's vassals are upset that the lord's chief retainer, Oishi, seems to be acquiescing to the Shogun's demands. They want to defend the castle and take revenge on Kira. Oishi, however, quietly goes about making preparations to turn over Ako Castle and its estates. When Oishi learns that the Emperor agrees that the Shogun has committed an injustice, Oishi finally discloses the reason behind his actions. He has realized that they have two choices: defend the castle and die, or abandon the castle and live to have revenge on Kira. Realizing Oishi's wisdom, the men band together and sign a pact to die, if necessary, to avenge Lord Asano. In the meantime, Kira has hired many retainers for his protection and seems to have found favor with the Shogun.

As time goes by it would appear that the ronin, especially Oishi, have forgotten their plans. Oishi has fallen into dissolution, spending all his time and money on sake and women. He has however, sent petitions to the Shogun to restore the Asano family. Many of the ronin become discouraged by Oishi's seeming lack of loyalty to their lord. When they come to demand that he do something, Oishi points out that if the Shogun is considering the petition, then revenge is impossible and not justifiable. Even Oishi's wife and her family feel that he has abandoned his

The Loyal 47 Ronin (Kenji Mizoguchi, 1941–1942). Possibly one of the most frequently filmed stories, this tale of 47 ronin samurai (also called *Chushingura*) as adapted by Mizoguchi is one of the least violent and most poetic. (Photo courtesy of Sony Video.)

lord and not acted like a true samurai. She asks him for a divorce, which he grants, and she returns to her family.

Part II: Tomimori, one of Lord Asano's ex-vassals, weary of Oishi's lack of action, decides to kill Kira while he attends a Noh play. However, magistrate Tsunatoyo Tokugawa, who will appear in the play, hears of Tomimori's plans and stops him. Although he wants justice done, he doesn't want Tomimori's brash actions to cause the entire plan to fail.

It is revealed to Tomimori that Oishi's drunkenness is really a ruse used to lull Kira into a false sense of security. Oishi knows there is no legitimate way he can get revenge and he must resort to extraordinary methods. When word arrives that the petitions have been turned down and there is no chance of the Asano estates being returned to his family, the ronin activate their plans.

Oishi visits Asano's widow, Yosenin, to ask permanent leave of the family. While Yosenin hopes to get word that vengeance will soon be exacted, Oishi departs without a hint of his intentions. Later Yosenin receives a letter telling her that on the 15th year of Genroku (January 30, 1703), 47 ronin attacked Kira's castle and killed and beheaded Kira. The ronin take Kira's head to Asano's grave and vow to wait for the legal system to mete out their punishment.

For committing the obviously illegal act of killing Kira, the 47 ronin spend months at Lord Hosokawa's manor awaiting the decision of the Daimyos who will decide their fate. The ronin finally find out the Daimyos' decision when Yosenin sends Oishi two vases of flowers, a sign that they will be allowed the honorable samurai death of seppuku instead of an ignoble execution.

Isolated in Hosokawa's castle, the 47 ronin spend the next two months preparing and awaiting their deaths. Most of the men face their self-execution with acceptance, but it proves difficult for some of the younger ronin, especially Isogai whose fiancée, Omino, has disguised herself as a boy and sneaked into the castle to see him again.

Omino wants to find out if Isogai's proposal to her was just a part of the revenge plan, or if he really loves her. Initially Oishi refused to let Omino see Isogai fearing it would break the young man's resolve. When they do meet, however, Omino realizes Isogai's true feelings when she discovers he sentimentally has kept her *koto* pick close to him all this time. After he leaves, Omino also commits seppuku in the hopes of being with him in the next life.

As the ronin prepare to commit their final act of loyalty to their lord, they hear the unofficial message that the Shogun has deprived Kira's son of his estates and that his house has been abolished. In some way vindicated, as their names are announced, one by one they perform seppuku.

• As the Japanese government found itself more and more involved in the events of World War II, they mandated that studios produce films which would enhance the public's "fighting spirit." These so-called "national policy" films were not of great interest to Mizoguchi nor to Shochiku. With the government not concerned about films which raised social awareness and featured topical issues like *Osaka Elegy* and *Sisters of the Gion,* Mizoguchi turned to Japan's past to find topics which the government would approve of. He found a subject which fit the country's militaristic aims in the well-known legend, *Chushingura.* Mizoguchi's *The Loyal 47 ronin* not only glorified Japan's past, it also showed some of Japan's most historically admired heroes sacrificing themselves for a noble cause. Just what the government wanted, a film meant to inspire the spirit of self-sacrifice of the 47 ronin in the people of Japan who were becoming more and more deeply involved in war.

There have been many theatrical and written versions of the classic Japanese legend of the *Chushingura*. They, in turn, have inspired dozens of films. This story of the lengths heroes must go to in order to retain their honor in Japanese society is probably most familiar to U.S. audiences through Hiroshi Inagaki's color spectacle made for Toho in 1962. Inagaki, who is a master of the action-packed *chambara*, as can be imagined, made a film quite different from the more literary-minded Mizoguchi's.

Basing his film on the original records of the event instead of the Kabuki play used by Inagaki, Mizoguchi's film is more thoughtful and much less action-oriented (with the exception of the slight initial wounding of Kira and aftermath of Omino's suicide, no scenes of violence or battle are even seen in the film). It was still, however, an enormous production for Mizoguchi. He, as usual, insisted on authenticity to historic epoch in actions, sets, props and costumes. Full-scale sets were constructed, accurate in every detail.

Shochiku, which was being pressured by the government to make more films with patriotic messages, created a subsidiary company, Koa, which was responsible for special productions such as Mizoguchi's version of the *Chushingura*. Costs mounted for the first part of the film, eventually totaling more than five times what was normal for a *jidai-geki*. The film broke Koa. Committed to the project, however, the second part was filmed at Shochiku studios in Kyoto, again at great costs.

Part I opened in Tokyo on December 8, 1941, the day after Pearl Harbor; Part II in February of 1942. The film didn't recoup at the box office Shochiku's expenditures, but it was greatly liked by the government. The entire film was given a special prize from the Minister of Education.

Horse (1941)
Uma

1941 / Toho. 129 min. B&W. *Director:* Kajiro Yamamoto. *Assistant Director:* Akira Kurosawa. *Screenplay:* Kajiro Yamamoto. *Cinematography:* Hiromitsu Karasawa (Spring), Akira Mimura (Summer and studio), Hiroshi Suzuki (Autumn), Takeo Ito (Winter). *Music:* Shigeaki Kitamura. *Editor:* Akira Kurosawa. Film Rental: R5/S8.

Hideko Takamine *as Ine.* Keita Fujiwara *Jinjiro, her father.* Chieko Takehisa *Saku, her mother.* Kaoru Futaba *Ei, her grandmother.* Takeshi Hirata *Toyo, her brother.* Toshio Hosoi *Kinjiro, her youngest brother.* Setsuko Ichikawa *Tsuru, her little sister.* Sadao Maruyama *Mr. Yamashita, the*

Horse (Kajiro Yamamoto, 1941). There was nothing as important in Ine's (Hideko Takamine) life as horses in this film which combines fictional narrative and documentary film footage to tell a compelling story. (Photo courtesy of R5/S8 and Toho Co., Ltd.)

teacher. Sadako Sawamura *Kikuko, his wife.* Yoshio Kosugi *Zenzo Sakuma.* Tsuruko Mano *Mrs. Sakuma.* Shoji Kiyokawa *Mr. Sakamoto.*

• Ine, a young farm girl, attends a horse auction and watches as Zenzo's horse is sold to soldiers for 450 yen. Zenzo is slightly drunk, but elated, for the soldier's bid was 100 yen better than the previous bid. When she returns home, Ine is reprimanded by her mother. The family makes straw mats to augment their meager living and Ine has not been around to help them move the mats into the stable before the rain started. In the stable Ine brings up a subject very dear to her heart—the fact that the family, unlike their neighbors, doesn't have a horse. Her mother, exasperated at Ine's harping on the subject, reminds her of how they once tried raising a horse but it died and the family is still in debt from it. Ine constantly calls her mother "mean."

Arrangements are soon made, however, for Ine's family to feed and care for the pregnant mare, Hanakaze, throughout the winter in exchange for the colt when it comes. Her brother, Toyo, however, hates horses but has had a special bath mat he has made accepted for showing at a Tokyo Folk Craft exhibition.

One day Ine's father is injured when a cart gets caught in the rocks and, in trying to free it, he is run over by it. Her father blames Hanakaze for his accident, but Ine reminds him that he had been drinking at a wedding party. When the doctor comes to treat her father, Ine takes the other children outside to distract them. The family's plight worsens while the father slowly mends. In a yearly union assessment, the family must pay 300 yen, and soon Ine is feeding the mare while the family must limit its own food intake. The union representative, seeing the family's plight, brings them some eggs and puts off collecting the assessment for awhile. At the same time, Toyo gets a registered letter from a company in Tokyo which saw his bath mat and wants to handle sales for him. They have also enclosed an advance of 30 yen.

Although it seemed that things were improving for the family, bad fortune strikes again when Hanakaze becomes ill. Her breathing is difficult and she hasn't eaten in ten days. Even though still strapped financially, the family must call in the veterinarian, Sakamoto. He diagnoses Hanakaze as being ill with strangles, a gut disease. It is an ailment common to horses in the winter as a result of their not getting enough green grass and sunlight. To help the horse, Ine walks ten kilometers in a blinding snowstorm to the hot springs at Yunosama. At the springs Ine digs through the snow until she finds green grass which she collects for the mare. When she returns home, Ine is cold and exhausted, but her diligence has touched her mother's heart.

As spring arrives, Hanakaze recovers and gives birth. It is a difficult delivery caused by the foal's leg becoming bent and stuck. Ine's family cheers on the foal and the father who is assisting the delivery. When the foal is safely born, it is dawn and the family goes off to bed. During the spring and summer, the colt grows strong under Ine's care. A postponed problem, however, comes back to haunt them; the union representative wants the family's dues paid. The only way the family can come up with the money is to sell Ine's colt even though it doesn't bring in as much money as it would if it were older. Both Hanakaze and Ine are distraught at the colt's loss and Ine goes to work in a spinning mill in order to earn enough to buy it back.

Two years later, Ine returns home for a visit during the summer Bon festival. As she walks past a herd of horses she looks for her colt but cannot find him. She walks on and soon finds she is being followed by a large horse — her fully grown colt. After her vacation, Ine decides not to return to the mill since her horse is to be sold soon at the fair. At the horse auction, bidding is slow on Ine's horse. She needs at least 500 yen in order to buy the horse back. Just as it seemed that the horse would only fetch 410 yen, the army steps in and bids 550 yen. Ine, now free from the mill, still cries at the loss of her horse. Ine's mother and sister both suggest that the family raise another horse next year. But Ine's heart is still with this horse. As she listens for the last whinnies from her horse, she breaks down and cries once again.

• Kajiro Yamamoto (1902–1973) taught economics at Keio University until he quit to join Minoru Murata's theatrical troupe. In 1920 he joined Nikkatsu and worked as an actor, scriptwriter, assistant director and finally director. During the 1930s he moved to P.C.L. and specialized in comedies.

Yamamoto got the idea for *Horse* while he was listening to a horse auction on the radio. In the background he could hear the sobbing of a young girl; a young girl who would eventually become Ine. *Horse* is an outstanding example of a semidocumentary film. It weaves together the best of dramatic fiction techniques and the verisimilitude which can only be achieved by filming actual events. The result is a poetically honest film which set new standards for filmmakers in Japan. Yamamoto's effort took three years to plan and another year to film. It is almost hard to believe that such a pastorally attractive film was released in the same year that Japan bombed Pearl Harbor. The only adjustment the film seemed to make for the war effort was the fact that it was the Japanese army which was buying the horses at both the beginning and end of the film.

Horse was filmed at several locations throughout northern Japan and beautifully captures nature, the environment and seasons which are so important to the Japanese. Yamamoto often commuted from the mountain shooting locations to Tokyo to film a money-making comedy. When he did so, he left production in the hands of an assistant director. This assistant turned out to be extremely capable not only in creating a masterpiece in Yamamoto's absence but in his own later career. The assistant who learned the trade under Yamamoto was Akira Kurosawa.

During the war Yamamoto made "national policy" films such as *The War at Sea from Hawaii to Malaya (Hawaii-Marei oki kaisen,* 1942*).* In essence, it used the same style of documentary approach he used in the film *Horse.* So realistic was Yamamoto's use of cinematic special effects, that when *Hawaii to Malaya* was viewed by the Occupation forces they had great difficulty distinguishing real scenes from "created" scenes. After the war Yamamoto, who was a political conservative, refused to make films supporting the views of the Occupation forces. Instead Yamamoto spent the rest of his directorial career making comedies in the tradition of those found in Japanese music halls.

Sanshiro Sugata (1943)
Sugata Sanshiro

1943 / Toho. / a.k.a. "Judo Saga." 80 min. B&W. *Director:* Akira Kurosawa. *Screenplay:* Akira Kurosawa. *Adaptation:* From the novel by

Tsuneo Tomita. *Cinematography:* Akira Mimura. *Art Director:* Masao Tot-
suka. *Music:* Seichi Suzuki. *Sound:* Tomohisa Higuchi. *Lighting:*
Masayoshi Onuma. *Editor:* Akira Kurosawa and Toshio Goto. *Assistant
Director:* Toshio Sugie. *Producer:* Keiji Matsuzaki. Videotape: Sony,
Balzac. Film Rental: Films Inc., R5/S8 (also part 2), Janus.

Susumu Fujita *as Sanshiro Sugata.* Denjiro Okochi *Shogoro Yano.*
Takashi Shimura *Hansuke Murai.* Yukiko Todoroki *Sayo, his daughter.*
Yoshio Kosugi *Saburo Momma.* Ranko Hanai *Osumi, his daughter.*
Ryunosuke Tsukigata *Gennosuke Higaki.* Akitake Kono *Yoshima Dan.*
Soshi Kiyokawa *Yujiro Toda.* Kunio Mita *Kohei Tsuzaki.* Akira Nakamura
Toranosuki Niiseki. Sugisaku Aoyama *Tsunetami Iimura.* Kuninori Kodo
Priest. Ichiro Sugai *Police Chief.*

• In 1882 a young man, Sanshiro Sugata, comes to Tokyo to find an
instructor to teach him the art of jujitsu. He first goes to the house of
Hansuke Murai but the instructor is out. He sits with Murai's students and
listens to them talk about the despised new form of jujitsu, judo, as
taught by Shogoro Yano. Since their school has been awarded the contract
to teach the police jujitsu, they consider the new judo a threat.

When someone tells them that Yano is coming down the road, the
students of the Shinmei school go out to attack him. Unfortunately for
them, Yano easily defeats them, throwing each in turn into the river.
Sugata, who was watching this impressive battle, throws himself at Yano's
feet and asks to study with him. Sugata soon excels at judo but it becomes
obvious that he has not understood the spiritual philosophy upon which it
is based. After he gets into a fight with peasants, he is brought before his
teacher. Yano scolds him saying, "Teaching judo to someone who doesn't
know life is like giving a sword to a lunatic." Sugata is angered by Yano's
accusations and says he would die for his teacher. At this point he thrusts
open a door and jumps into the pond just off the porch. Yano refuses to
apologize to Sugata and the stubborn Sugata seems condemned to hang
onto a post in the pond all night. Suddenly, when he sees a white flower,
he understands the error of his ways.

One day Gennosuke Higaki, a man dressed in western clothes, comes
to Yano's school demanding a lesson. He injures one of Yano's students,
but when Sugata asks to be allowed to fight him, he is refused because
Yano does not allow him to compete. An invitation is issued for each
school to send its best to a police tournament. The winner will get the
contract to teach at the academy. Sugata will fight Morai. Hansuke Morai
is an older man, used to drink, but who has stopped just to train to fight
Sugata. Murai's daughter, Sayo, fearing for her father's life, tries to kill
Sugata but is stopped by Sugata's friends and fellow students.

Sugata and Yano come upon Sayo praying at a temple. He is attracted
to her and goes back several times and one day fixes Sayo's sandal for her.

Neither initially knows who the other is but soon they find out. Sayo deeply affects Sugata and makes his fighting her father very difficult. He must fiight, however, and eventually wins. In keeping with his new-found understanding of life, though, he visits the injured Murai who, along with his daughter, likes Sugata's visits. Higaki, however, does not. He issues a challenge to Sugata to a fight to the death. On the wildly blowing hillside where they meet, the two fight in the tall grass. Sugata is almost choked by Higaki until the clouds in his vision stand still and become the white flower he saw in the pond. He now wins the fight.

• Akira Kurosawa is perhaps the Japanese director most well known in the West. It was through his films that many moviegoers experienced their first taste of Japanese films, and found them very palatable. Kurosawa was born in 1910 in Tokyo, the youngest of seven children. His strict father was an army officer who became a physical education instructor. Kurosawa showed a talent for painting early in his life and enrolled at the Doshusha School of Western Painting at the age of 17. After graduation he worked as an illustrator for popular magazines. He soon discovered, however, that he couldn't make a living as a commercial artist.

In 1936 Kurosawa saw a recruiting ad for P.C.L. Studios (Photo Chemical Laboratory, which later became Toho Studios). They were looking for assistant directors. Kurosawa submitted the required essay on "the problems with Japanese films and their solutions," and was called in with about 500 other people for further interviews. His next assignment was to write a script treatment based on a newspaper clipping. This eliminated many of the candidates, and the few left went on to an oral interview. Finally, Kurosawa was accepted for employment.

It was while working as an assistant to Kajiro Yamamoto that Kurosawa's love of and education in film really developed. Kurosawa's training under Yamamoto included cutting his directorial teeth by doing whole scenes in films like *Horse*. Like most assistant directors working their way up within the Japanese film industry of the period, Kurosawa spent a great deal of his time writing scripts. When he read Tsuneo Tomita's novel, *Sanshiro Sugata*, Kurosawa found the story he wanted to use for his first film.

In Japan of 1943, the military government had strict control over the types of films which could be made. It was not an especially conducive atmosphere for creativity. Kurosawa chaffed under the military mandate to make "national policy" films but managed to get his script past the censors. After seven years of apprenticeship, Kurosawa finally made his first film at the age of 33. *Sanshiro Sugata* is a surprisingly mature first film both in its technical style and as a personal statement. Amazingly, Kurosawa was able to combine his own personal convictions with the requirements imposed by the government to come up with a film that honored the samurai spirit (which the military relished) while still being entertaining.

Sanshiro Sugata (Akira Kurosawa, 1943). **The final battle between Sanshiro (Susumu Fujita, right) and Higaki (Ryunosuke Tsukigata, left) on a windblown hillside gave great evidence of the power and accomplishment of a young Kurosawa on his first film. (Photo courtesy of Toho Co., Ltd.)**

The accomplishment of showing passing time by focusing in on an abandoned shoe which is rained upon, chewed by puppies and finally impaled on a fence is masterful for a debut effort. Similarly, there is a sophistication in the means of imparting Sanshiro's enlightenment not by having him say so, but by economically symbolizing it in a white flower (a scene not in the original novel, but improvised by the young director). In Kurosawa's hands, *Sanshiro Sugata* becomes a story of achieving personal enlightenment and internalizing moral principles which would become a favorite theme in many of his films to come.

In March of 1944, *Sanshiro Sugata* was shortened by 1856 feet in compliance with the Japanese censors. Even though an attempt to reconstruct the film was made in 1952 for a re-release, the film's original pieces were lost in the destruction and confusion of the war's aftermath. As can be imagined, Kurosawa argued often with the military censors about his other wartime scripts. Eventually he was able to make a sequel to *Sanshiro Sugata (Part Two)* as well as the documentary-like *The Most Beautiful* (1944). This last film is also notable because the actress who played Tsuru, Yoko Yaguchi, was married to Kurosawa in 1945 and remained his wife and close companion and coworker until her death in 1984 while Kurosawa was filming *Ran*. The third script Kurosawa managed to get approved before the end of the war in 1945 was *The Men Who Tread on the Tiger's Tail.*

The Men Who Tread on the Tiger's Tail (1945)
Tora no o o fumu ototachi

1945 (released in 1952) / Toho. / a.k.a. "They Who Step on the Tiger's Tail." 58 min. B&W. *Director:* Akira Kurosawa. *Screenplay:* Akira Kurosawa. *Adaptation:* From the Kabuki play **Kanjincho.** *Cinematography:* Takeo Ito. *Art Direction:* Kazuo Kubo. *Lighting:* Iwaharu Hiraoka. *Music:* Tadashi Hattori. *Sound:* Keiji Hasebe. *Assistant Director:* Jin Usami. *Producer:* Motohiko Ito. Videotape: International Historic Films. Film Rental: Filmic Archives / Reel Images, Films Inc., Janus, Kit Parker, R5/S8.

Denjiro Okochi *as Benkei.* Susumu Fujita *Togashi.* Masayuki Mori *Kamei.* Takashi Shimura *Kataoka.* Aritake Kono *Ise.* Yoshio Kosugi *Suruga.* Dekao Yoko *Hidachibo.* Hanshiro Iwai *Yoshitsune.* Kenichi Enomoto *The porter.*

• In the 12th century, a time of clan warfare, General Yoshitsune of the Genji clan flees from his brother, Yoritomo. Yoshitsune is accompanied by five loyal retainers and Benkei, his bodyguard, all of whom are disguised as traveling monks. Along the way they are joined by a talkative porter who gradually comes to realize who the monks really are.

As they approach the border crossing for Kaga Province, Yoshitsune disguises himself as a porter. At the border the monks claim to be canvassing the country for funds to rebuild Todai Temple, but the provincial magistrate, Togashi, sees them and is suspicious of them. He wants to arrest them but Benkei asks permission to perform a last prayer. Togashi grants this request, but then asks Benkei to read the decree indicating that they are collecting money for a temple. Benkei proceeds to "read" the decree which is actually a blank scroll.

Togashi, however, is still not convinced these men are real monks. While he grills them on things like why they carry swords, the comic porter becomes more and more nervous. Finally Togashi agrees to let the group cross the border. Suddenly, one of Togashi's aides thinks he recognizes Yoshitsune. In an attempt to thwart the identification, however,

Benkei shoves Yoshitsune and beats him with a stick when he falls. Now Togashi is confounded. If the porter really is Yoshitsune, he should be arrested, but if he is a nobleman, no vassal like Benkei would dare lift a hand and strike him. Togashi allows them to pass.

Later, the group laughs about the incident. Everyone, that is, but Benkei who is weeping because he cannot forgive himself for striking his lord. Yoshitsune, however, forgives Benkei. Then a messenger from Togashi arrives bearing sake as an apology. The men proceed to get drunk, the porter dances, and Benkei sings a song. Soon the porter is fast asleep. Later, when he wakes up, he is alone. But "the monks" have laid a fine kimono over him while he slept. Happy, the porter dances off.

• In 1944 the Japanese military government asked Kurosawa to make a movie based on the well-known story *The Men Who Tread on the Tiger's Tail* (it forms the basis of the Kabuki *Kanjincho* and the Noh *Ataka*). The story emphasized the feudal values of loyalty which the government liked, while still providing a high level of entertainment.

When Kurosawa was originally approached to film this famous story, the director was initially more interested in doing a costume film titled *Dokoi kono yari* (The Lifted Spear). But during the war he could not obtain the horses he needed for that film. Instead, he agreed to make *Tiger's Tail*. Kurosawa wrote the script in one night and constructed the story so that only one stage set was needed and the rest of the film could be shot on location and thereby save the company a lot of money.

The largest portion of *Tiger's Tail* takes place at the border crossing. What could have been a very static episode is turned into an energetic and imaginative screen presentation through Kurosawa's developing mastery of filming techniques. For a film made during a time when standards were low and propaganda demands high, Kurosawa managed to create his shortest masterpiece. He also proved that he was a master of the dramatic narrative.

When the censors saw the film, which incorporated Kurosawa's changes including the addition of the comic porter, they refused to release it. This was a serious classical Kabuki drama, and it was considered heretical to add a comic character which gave the story an irreverent humor and decreased its propagandistic value.

After Japan's defeat in World War II, the country was governed by the American army of Occupation, headed by General MacArthur. His headquarters, called SCAP (Supreme Commander for Allied Powers), now took the place of the Japanese military censors and imposed their own set

The Men Who Tread on the Tiger's Tail (Akira Kurosawa, 1945). Benkei (Denjiro Okochi, left), disguised as a traveling monk, discusses the situation with his lord, Yoshitsune (Hanshiro Iwai) in the Kurosawa film, which was denied distribution first by the wartime Japanese censors and later by the Occupation forces. (Photo courtesy of Toho Co., Ltd.)

of film standards. Under the Occupation, all scripts had to be cleared by the CIE (Civil Information and Education Section). Also affected were pre- and postproduction from January 1946 to June 1949 (although postproduction control continued until April 1952).

Under the authority of the CIE and SCAP, themes such as militarism, nationalism, and subject matter like the *zaibatsu* (families which owned and ran large businesses) were not allowed. Other subjects which were not approved of were suicide, prejudice or the degradation of women. What they wanted to promote were the ideals of democracy, especially as they could apply to Japan.

While reviewing films made prior to the war, many were found to be completely unsuitable and were banned. One sad result of the zealousness with which SCAP and CIE carried out their censorship was the complete destruction of many of these films. A major part of Japanese film history was now completely lost.

Because the authorities also disapproved of feudalism, it became very difficult to make a *chambara* or a *jidai-gekis* since they are inevitably set during Japan's feudal period. When the censors saw Kurosawa's *The Men Who Tread on the Tiger's Tail*, they felt its feudalistic setting and story were opposed to the democratic standards they were trying to impart to the Japanese movie-going public. The film was again prevented from reaching the screens, and was only finally released in 1952 when the Occupation ban on period films was lifted.

Drunken Angel (1948)
Yoidore tenshi

1948 / Toho. 98 min. B&W. *Director:* Akira Kurosawa. *Screenplay:* Keinosuke Uegusa and Akira Kurosawa. *Cinematography:* Takeo Ito. *Art Director:* So Matsuyama. *Lighting:* Kinzo Yoshizawa. *Music:* Fumio Hayasaka. *Producer:* Sojiro Motoki. Videotape: Balzac. Film Rental: Filmic Archives/Reel Images, Films Inc., Janus, Kit Parker.

Takashi Shimura *as Sanada, the doctor.* Toshiro Mifune *Matsunaga, the gangster.* Reisaburo Yamamoto *Okada, the gang boss.* Chieko Nakakita *Miyo, the nurse.* Michiyo Kogure *Nanae, Matsunaga's mistress.* Noriko Sengoku *Gin, the bar girl.* Eitaro Shindo *Takahama, the doctor's friend.* Choko Iida *The old servant.* Yoshiko Kuga *Schoolgirl.*

• Matsunaga, a gangster in one of 1948 Tokyo's poorer neighborhoods, comes to Dr. Sanada to have a wound taken care of. He says he has a nail in his hand, but it is really a bullet. Dr. Sanada, whose office is near a community cesspool filled with debris and bubbling gasses, tries to take care of the impoverished people, but is angered by their poverty-caused disease and the postwar corruption which fosters it. Sanada's only source of refuge from his dismal surroundings is alcohol.

While treating Matsunaga, Sanada discovers that the gangster probably is also suffering from tuberculosis. The doctor wants him to get an x-ray and warns him to change his lifestyle, but Matsunaga just runs off to the nearby Noi Cabaret. Sanada follows him and the two men drink together. Although Matsunaga is tough on the outside, he is lonely on the inside. Matsunaga finally gets an x-ray taken and reluctantly returns to Sanada's office for treatment. Matsunaga has been controlling the area normally run by Okada who is now in jail for slashing a man's face beyond recognition. But now Okada has been released. Okada retakes control of his territory and also takes over Matsunaga's girlfriend who has left him after he suffered a lung hemorrhage.

Matsunaga goes to live with Sanada. Miyo, Dr. Sanada's nurse, is also an ex-mistress of Okada's. To protect her and in retaliation for Okada's interference in his life, Matsunaga returns to his girlfriend's rooms and attacks Okada. The two men fight amid buckets of spilling paint until Okada finally stabs Matsunaga. Matsunaga staggers out onto the roof and falls to his death. Gin, a sake bar girl, who has been cured of tuberculosis by Sanada, has always loved Matsunaga. She has paid for the gangster's funeral and is now carrying his ashes back to her mountain home. She stops to talk with Sanada who is still bitter about life but is heartened by Gin's recuperation and selflessness.

• When Kurosawa and Keinosuke Uegusa wrote the original script for *Drunken Angel* the main character was to have been Dr. Sanada. Initially he was a very positive character, a real "good guy." But Kurosawa found him to be too good to be interesting. Consequently, the character was given a weakness, alcoholism, which made him a more intriguing, conflicting character. Similarly, the "bad guy," the gangster Matsunaga, was also given an underlying goodness. It was the ambivalence of these characters which made for a film of psychological depth and a benchmark in presenting realistic characters in Japanese films.

As can be seen in the title, Takashi Shimura's Dr. Sanada was supposed to be the central character, but despite the script, it was Matsunaga who emerged on top. The reason for this is a simple one, Toshiro Mifune. Mifune, born to Japanese parents in Tsing-tao, China, in 1920, served in the Imperial Air Force during World War II. He entered films almost by accident. With a little experience in photography, Mifune heard of an opening for an assistant cameraman at Toho in 1946. Along with hundreds of others, he submitted an application. When he was called to Toho's studios a little later, he was interviewed by a panel which asked that he laugh. An odd thing to request of someone who will be a cameraman. As it turned out, Mifune's application had been misrouted to the studio's "new faces" talent search. Mifune became hostile and was about to leave when an elderly panel member called him back. He was asked to act drunk, and Mifune, thinking he is being made a fool of and still angry, pulled out all the stops. Impressed, the panel had Mifune hired—one of only 16 out of thousands of applicants.

The panel member who recognized Mifune's inherent talent was Kajiro Yamamoto, the director under whom Akira Kurosawa worked. Kurosawa, who was working nearby, walked into the talent search while Mifune was "performing." Also impressed by what he saw, Kurosawa would soon be using Mifune in *Drunken Angel* (it was only his third film), and it would be the start of a relationship that would include 16 films, many of them masterpieces of world cinema.

Mifune's appearances in these masterpieces and his powerful screen presence has made him probably the Japanese screen personality most well known abroad. He has appeared in many international productions such as *Grand Prix* (1966) and *Shogun* (1980), but it was *Drunken Angel* which initially made him a star. Kurosawa has often said that Mifune brought such energy, magnetism and originality to the basically no-good character of Matsunaga that he couldn't hold him back. As a result, Matsunaga's role kept getting larger until it eclipsed Shimura's title character.

While Mifune's angry brashness provided a bold performance, it could also have easily typecast him in the postwar "angry young man" parts. However, Kurosawa had the foresight to cast Mifune in a wide variety of roles. He played a strictly ethical doctor in *The Quiet Duel*, an earnest young detective in *Stray Dog*, a vengeful painter in *Scandal*, a variety of samurai and even an old grandfather in *Record of a Living Being*. For Kurosawa, having an actor like Mifune who could quickly and competently convey his ideas on the screen proved to be an asset. In many instances, the fast pace of a Kurosawa film can be credited directly to Mifune's performance.

In *Drunken Angel*, Mifune's vitality overwhelmed the title character (while taking nothing from Shimura's performance) and caused Kurosawa to rewrite the story. Now not only would it reflect contemporary problems, but would also focus on the growing relationship between the two men. The gangster and the doctor, seemingly on opposite sides of the human spectrum, are drawn to each other and eventually come to respect each other.

In 1948, Toho underwent a strike when the company tried to fire many union members (especially those suspected of being Communists). Union supporters occupied company buildings and were only dispersed after the police and the U.S. Army drove them out. That was the year

Drunken Angel **(Akira Kurosawa, 1948). Although the eponymous Dr. Sanada was to have been the main character in this film, the energy of a young Toshiro Mifune (left) as Matsunaga soon had Kurosawa rewriting the script. (Also seen is Michiyo Kogure as Nanae.) (Photo courtesy of Toho Co., Inc.)**

Kurosawa left Toho to form the Film Art Association (Eiga Geijutsuka Kyokai) production company with his mentor, Kajiro Yamamoto and directors Mikio Naruse and Senkishi Taniguchi. His first projects under this banner were *The Quiet Duel (Shizukanaru ketto,* 1959) which was handled by Daiei, and *Stray Dog (Noru inu,* 1949) handled by Shin-Toho. The company was short-lived, however, and soon Kurosawa was again working for the major companies. But not before making a film he had wanted to make for some time. It was a film Daiei could not or would not comprehend, but which Kurosawa was determined to make. It was also a film which would change the course of the Japanese film industry as perceived in the world market. That film was *Rashomon*.

Late Spring (1949)
Banshun

1949 / Shochiku. 108 min. B&W. *Director:* Yasujiro Ozu. *Screenplay:* Yasujiro Ozu and Kogo Noda. *Adaptation:* From the novel ***Father*** *and Daughter,* by Kazuo Hirotsu. *Cinematography:* Yuharu Atsuta. *Art Director:* Tatsuo Hamada. *Lighting:* Haruo Isono. *Music:* Senji Ito. *Editor:* Yoshiyasu Hamamura. Videotape: Balzac. Film Rental: New Yorker.

Chishu Ryu *as Professor Shukichi Somiya.* Setsuko Hara *Noriko, his daughter.* Haruko Sugimura *Masa Taguchi, Somiya's sister.* Hohi Aoki *Katsuyoshi, her son.* Jun Usami *Shoichi Hattori.* Yumeji Tsukioka *Ayako Kitagawa.* Kuniko Miyake *Akiko Miwa.* Masao Mishima *Professor Onodera.* Yoshiko Tsubouchi *Kiku Onodera.* Yoko Katsuragi *Misae Onodera.*

• Twenty-seven-year-old Noriko lives with her widowed father, a college professor. Professor Somiya often works in his home on scholarly research with his assistant, Hattori. Noriko has put aside all thoughts of marriage in order to take care of her father.

Noriko meets one of her father's old friends, Professor Onodera. They go to an art show, a walk in the park and to a restaurant and Noriko discovers that Onodera has remarried. Noriko finds distasteful the idea of this widowed man remarrying and tells him so. When Noriko returns home, Onodera comes with her to visit with her father. While the two men visit, it is uncovered that Noriko has been ill from labor she was forced to perform during the war. They also discuss the possibility of Noriko marrying.

Noriko and her father's assistant, Hattori, seem to get along together well, going for bicycle rides and generally looking like good friends. Their compatibility makes Noriko's aunt and her father wonder if Hattori would be a good match for her. When Professor Somiya approaches Noriko with their idea, she just laughs, for Hattori is already engaged to someone else. Later, Noriko's aunt finds another possible match in Mr. Satake. But Noriko insists that she has all she can handle taking care of her eccentric father. When her aunt chastises that with that kind of an attitude she'll never get married, she also poses the idea of her father marrying a friend, Mrs. Miwa. The idea of her father remarrying like Mr. Onodera upsets Noriko. At a Noh performance, Noriko sees her father smile at Mrs. Miwa, and she again becomes upset.

At home, Professor Somiya informs Noriko that her aunt has arranged for her to meet Mr. Satake. Noriko replies with the fact that she must stay and take care of him, but he insists that he has been taking advantage of her and that it is time she marry. Noriko is concerned about who would take care of him if she left, and he brings up Mrs. Miwa. Noriko runs upstairs, but her father pursues her and again asks if she'll meet Mr. Satake. Noriko finally gives in. Several weeks after Noriko and Mr. Satake meet, her aunt asks for her decision. At first Noriko doesn't answer, but eventually she gives in and agrees to marry him.

Noriko and her father go to Kyoto to visit Professor Onodera and his family. When she sees how nice his family is, Noriko apologizes to him for

Late Spring (Yasujiro Ozu, 1949). The constantly changing relationships between family members (especially between parents and children) is one of the sadder facts of life depicted by Ozu. Professor Somiya (Chishu Ryu), who is taken care of by his daughter Noriko (Setsuko Hara, center), realizes that she must soon marry and leave him.

her initial judgment against him. Back at their inn, Noriko and her father again discuss why she should marry. Noriko is happy with things the way they are, but her father tells her that it is the way life is and that she must work to make her marriage a happy one.

Noriko is now dressed in the traditional wedding costume and drives off to her wedding. Later, Professor Somiya meets Noriko's friend Aya in a restaurant. While talking, the professor confesses that he never intended to marry again and that it was the only way he could get Noriko to marry. Back at his home, the professor sits alone, peeling an apple.

• One of Ozu's favorite themes is the opposing desires of and friction between members of a family even though they feel deep affection and loyalty to each other. Inevitably, these interactions within a family, and particularly the problems which arise between parents and children, will result in some sort of separation. For Noriko it is the separation of marriage, in other Ozu stories it may mean being employed away from home or death. While Ozu is saddened by these events, he also recognizes that they are unavoidable. This awareness of the inherent transience and sadness of human existence is what the Japanese call *mono no aware,* and it is what Ozu's films excel in communicating.

One of the ways which Ozu communicates this feeling of *mono no aware* is through the use of the prolonged take. When a viewer sees the professor in his home at the end of the film, it is quickly and easily understood that he is alone. By holding the scene on the screen, however, Ozu forces the viewer to go beyond mere intellectual understanding to internalize the professor's feelings and reach a greater degree of compassion. With a longer take, a viewer can take the time to emotionally identify.

With the release of *Late Spring,* Ozu would primarily come to focus on the lives of middle class families. (Something which in the 1960s and 70s would help to give rise to criticisms that Ozu was a bourgeois director.) *Late Spring* was the first postwar collaboration of Ozu and his favorite scriptwriter and best friend, Kogo Noda. It is considered in many respects a prototype of the films they would come to make together in the 1950s and 60s.

Oftentimes Ozu would use scenes of nature to cinematically punctuate his films and provide transition between scenes. This reflection of human experience in nature is also expressed in the titles of his films in this period which are named for seasons. Besides *Late Spring,* Ozu also had films titled *Early Summer, Early Spring, Late Autumn, The End of Summer* and *An Autumn Afternoon.* For some, it becomes difficult to connect the right title to the right film. Indeed, it can be complicated even more when basic plots and themes repeat themselves as they do in *Late Spring* and Ozu's last film, *An Autumn Afternoon.* Ozu didn't use this labeling system to be purposefully confusing, but employed seasons which corresponded to a primary emotion or a stage of life of a major character. Late spring, for example, could refer to Noriko's age in life — just past the spring when young women normally marry.

Setsuko Hara, who so completely fleshes out the stubborn Noriko who is reluctant to leave the serenity of her father's household, was one of several performers Ozu used over and over again. She has appeared in *Early Summer* and *Tokyo Story* among many others for Ozu and in Naruse's *Repast* and *Sounds from the Mountains.* Born Masae Aida in Yokohama in 1920, Hara joined Nikkatsu in 1935 and went on to become one of Japan's most popular and perennial stars from the 1930s through the 1960s. Known as "the eternal virgin," she was an actress who depicted spirited and decent women other women could identify with.

When Ozu died in 1963, Hara suddenly decided to retire from acting at the age of 43. The circulated reason for this unexpected resignation was that Hara had only acted to support her large family and that she never really enjoyed doing it. She lives the life of a recluse, using her original name, in Kamakura.

Rashomon (1950)

1950 / Daiei. 88 min. B&W. *Director:* Akira Kurosawa. *Screenplay:* Shinobu Hashimoto and Akira Kurosawa. *Adaptation:* "In a Grove" *("Yabu no naka")* and "Rashomon," two short stories by Ryunosuke Akutagawa. *Cinematography:* Kazuo Miyagawa. *Art Direction:* So Matsuyama. *Music:* Fumio Hayasaka. *Producer:* Jingo Minoru (with later titles produced by Masaichi Nagata). Videotape: Embassy Home Entertainment. Film Rental: Film, Inc., Janus. Laserdisc: Criterion Collection, The Voyager Company.

Toshiro Mifune *as The bandit.* Masayuki Mori *Takehiro, the samurai.* Machiko Kyo *Masago, the samurai's wife.* Takashi Shimura *The woodcutter.* Minoru Chiaki *The priest.* Kichijiro Ueda *The commoner.* Kaisuke Kato *The police agent.* Fumiko Homma *The medium.*

• In a torrential thunderstorm, a woodcutter, a priest, and a commoner take shelter in the ruined Rashomon gatehouse of Kyoto. It is the 12th century, a period of civil war, fires, epidemics, and bandits. While waiting for the storm to pass, the woodcutter and the priest recount to the commoner the story of a recent police inquest in which both took part.

The tale they tell is of a samurai and his wife who, while traveling on the Sekiyama-Yamashina Road, were waylaid by the infamous bandit, Tajomaru. Tajomaru, who desired the samurai's wife, lures the husband off into the forest by offering to sell him swords and mirrors found in a nearby tomb. After tying up the samurai, the bandit then forces the wife into following him into the forest on the pretense that her husband has been bitten by a snake.

Once in the forest, Tajomaru rapes the wife after she has attempted to fight him off with her dagger. During the events that follow, the husband is killed. During the inquest, however, "the events that follow" become obscured by conflicting accounts of the story. According to the captured Tajomaru, the wife easily gave in to his sexual advances, then told him to kill her husband because she could not stand to be disgraced in the eyes of two men. The bandit unties the samurai and in the ensuing swordfight the samurai is killed by Tajomaru and the wife runs away.

The wife is the next witness at the inquest. According to her, after she was raped, Tajomaru ran away and her husband could only stare at her in hatred. She cuts his bonds and offers him her dagger so he may kill her, but in her emotionally distraught state she faints. When she awakens she sees her husband's body with her dagger in his chest. She admits to the court that she must have killed him.

The third account of events comes from the dead samurai speaking through a medium. In this version, Tajomaru begs the samurai's wife to marry him after he has raped her. When she says he must kill her husband, though, Tajomaru is shocked and instead asks the husband what he should do with her—kill her or spare her? She runs off and Tajomaru chases after her. Later the bandit returns, cuts the samurai's bonds and leaves again. Because the samurai has been disgraced, he takes his wife's dagger and commits suicide. But from the darkness that is his death, he hears footsteps approach and the expensive dagger is pulled from his chest.

Although these are the three stories given at the inquest, there is one more version to be divulged, that of the woodcutter who found the body. According to the woodcutter's story, after the rape the shrewish wife belittles each man's manhood and cajoles them into fighting a duel over her. In the comically inept contest which follows, the samurai falls into a thicket and the bandit runs him through with his sword.

After recounting these conflicting sides of the same event, both the priest and the woodcutter are dismayed at the state of man which could have brought about all this lying. The commoner, however, laughs it all off. Nearby in the ruins, a baby is heard crying. When the three men go to investigate, the commoner quickly starts to steal the baby's few belongings. He is chastised by the woodcutter for being selfish, but in his own defense, the commoner points out that he has seen through the woodcutter's story. He knows the woodcutter was the one who stole the valuable dagger from the samurai's corpse. With this the commoner runs off leaving the woodcutter with his guilty conscience and the priest with the abandoned baby.

When the rain ends, the woodcutter tries to take the baby from the priest whose entire faith in man has been shattered. Angrily, the priest berates him for trying to take what little the child has left. But he has misunderstood the woodcutter's motives. He already has six children of his own, he tells the priest, one more won't make it any more difficult. As he walks into the now sunny day, he has restored the priest's faith in man.

• Of all the films produced in Japan by 1950, perhaps no other is as responsible for waking up Western audiences to the treasures available there than *Rashomon*. Although it was not the first film exported to the West, it was the first to garner international awards after World War II. There is a popular myth about *Rashomon* which paints it as an underappreciated film in its homeland. That was not the case. Although it did not receive very favorable reviews when it was released, it did have box office appeal. In fact, it was the fourth largest grosser for Daiei studios in 1950 and theatre managers chose it as the eighth ranking commercial hit for the same year.

Daiei, which was formed in 1942 (partially from the production facilities taken from Nikkatsu by the government), was headed by Masaichi Nagata. Nagata, perhaps the producer of more Japanese films distributed

Rashomon (Akira Kurosawa, 1950). The film that opened up the West to Japanese films, *Rashomon* challenged the nature of the truth reflected in a cinematic style of clashing shadows and light. Here Takehiro (Masayuko Mori, left) clashes swords with the bandit Tajomaru (Toshiro Mifune). (Photo courtesy of Toho Co., Ltd.)

abroad than any other, had started with Nikkatsu studios in 1925. He started as a page, and worked his way up, eventually heading Daiichi, a company founded by Shochiku to, it was hoped, deal a death blow to its major rival and Nagata's first employer, Nikkatsu. Under Daiichi's banner Nagata helped Mizoguchi, who would become a close friend, to make *Osaka Elegy* and *Sisters of the Gion*. Daiichi didn't last long, however, and Nagata moved on to head Daiei. Temporarily purged from the industry during the U.S. Occupation, Nagata was quickly "rehabilitated," returned to work at Daiei and began to produce films like *Rashomon*.

Rashomon, however, was not the type of film Japanese audiences were used to. A movie which had no real solution, that offered the idea that reality was relative, was alien to the Japanese who preferred their stories neatly wrapped up. In many Japanese theatres, when *Rashomon* was shown, interpreters similar to the old *benshis* were employed to offer insight into the movie's meaning.

At the same time, what struck most Western audiences as odd is that in telling their version of what happened, each of the three main characters did not do what Western audiences would expect in this kind of a mystery, deny guilt. In fact, all claim to have committed the killing. They do not conceal guilt, only the truth. What each does do is tell the story in such a way as to portray themselves in the best possible light in view of accepted Japanese social traditions. Retaining a proper self-image was the motive for bending the facts. In Japanese culture, honor, as reflected through actions, must be preserved at any cost. Consequently, the bandit's story is filled with boastful bravado, the samurai's with tormented and injured honor, and the wife's with frenzied hysteria.

The proud samurai in *Rashomon* was intelligently played by Masayuko Mori (1911–1973). Born Ikumitsu Arishima, Mori was the son of novelist Takeo Arishima. He studied philosophy at Kyoto University but left to become a stage actor. While continuing to act on the stage, Mori was invited to join Toho in 1942 and quickly established himself as a talent in both arenas. Known for his perceptive portrayals of men undergoing mental and emotional confusion, Mori was in great demand as a performer, and much admired by his legion of women followers.

There is a cinematically beautiful awareness of nature in *Rashomon*. Nature is a common and often haunting theme in Japanese art, and especially in its films. The torrential rains cascading off the ruined gate contrast with the sunlight piercing through the forest's canopy. The rain seems to symbolize the chaos of the period and the dark and evil outlook on life adopted by men living then. The sunlight attempts to penetrate these shadows, but in doing so, it uncovers a world created not of concrete events, but of subjective views of reality. A world so imbued with subjectivity could be one of bleakness (as was attested to by *Rashomon*'s priest), but Kurosawa is not a director of hopelessness. The epilogue-type ending in which the baby is found is typical of the way in which Kurosawa seeds hope into a movie. Compassion has become a hallmark of Kurosawa films.

After World War II, Japan eagerly investigated and pursued options to increase its prestige abroad. Films were an obvious ambassador, and film festivals seemed like the clearest way to gain wider distribution. When an invitation to participate finally came from the Venice Film Festival, the question of what film to send arose. Guilliana Stramigioli, the head of the Italifilm branch in Japan, screened several possible candidates and took a liking to *Rashomon*. She suggested it be sent to represent Japan. Daiei, however, had been continually baffled as to what the movie was about, and was extremely reluctant to send it. They were afraid of failure at the competition, and the consequent loss of face. The Japanese studios felt that Western audiences would only understand films which were made specifically for export abroad. *Rashomon* did not fall into this category.

Stramigioli's views, however, were very influential. When *Rashomon* won the coveted Lion of St. Mark first prize in 1951, it came as a surprise to everyone involved. (Kurosawa hadn't even known that it was entered!) And the film continued to garner awards. That same year it was listed as the best foreign film in the *New York Times* annual ten-best list, won a special Board of Governor's Award for most outstanding foreign-language film from the Academy of Motion Picture Arts and Sciences, and Kurosawa was chosen the best director by the National Board of Review.

The Japanese need not have worried. Western audiences loved *Rashomon*. In fact, because of its powerful story and intricate characters, it was to undergo a transformation which was to become a common fate for several of Akira Kurosawa's films—it was remade by a Western director. *Outrage*, released in 1964, was directed by Martin Ritt and starred Paul Newman as the bandit (from Mexico), Claire Bloom as the woman he allegedly rapes, Laurence Harvey as her husband, and Edward G. Robinson as the narrator. Western audiences were and still are drawn by *Rashomon's* exotic appeal. They are fascinated by the foreign images on the screen and enjoy the intellectual puzzle. With its unprecedented Western reception, *Rashomon* primed Western markets for Japanese films.

Early Summer (1951)
Bakushu

1951 / Shochiku. 135 min. B&W. *Director:* Yasujiro Ozu. *Screenplay:* Kogo Noda and Yasujiro Ozu. *Cinematography:* Yuharu Atsuta. *Music:* Senji Ito. *Editor:* Yoshiaku Hamamura. *Producer:* Takeshi Yamamoto. Film Rental: Janus. Videotape: Sony.

Setsuko Hara *as Noriko*. Chishu Ryu *Koichi*. Kuniko Miyake *Fumiko*. Chikage Awashima *Ayako*. Chieko Higashiyama *Grandma*. Ichiro Sugai *Grandpa*. Haruko Sugimura *Mrs. Yabe*. Kan Nihonyanagi *Kenkichi Yabe*. Shuji Sano *Mariko*. Kuniko Igawa *Takako*.

• Noriko Mamiya lives with her brother, Koichi, his wife, Fumiko, their two young sons, Isamu and Minoru, and her mother and father. Noriko is 28 years old and has never been married. She commutes daily to downtown Tokyo where she works in an office. Noriko has three main friends. One, Ayako, is unmarried like Noriko, while the other two, Mariko and Takako, are already married. When the four get together, there is always a friendly argument about whether it is better to be married or single.

Mr. Satake, Noriko's boss, has a friend, Manabe, who he feels would be a good match for Noriko. He gives her Manabe's photographs and asks her to show them to her family. Noriko is hesitant about marrying an unknown man who also has the added disadvantage of being 40 years old. Noriko's brother, Koichi, is a doctor and is eager to have his sister married.

Early Summer (Yasujiro Ozu, 1951). **A typical scene composition and shooting angle for Ozu is seen in this family meal featuring Setsuko Hara, Chieko Higashiyama, Kuninori Miyake, Ichiro Sugai, Kuninori Kodo and Chishu Ryu. (Photo courtesy of Sony Video.)**

Noriko begins to accept the idea of being married, especially after her two married friends fail to show up at a party at Noriko's house. Kenkichi Yabe, a widower neighbor who lives with his small daughter and his mother, works at the hospital with Koichi. He is an old family friend, having gone to school with Norika's other brother, Shoji, who went to war and was never heard from again and is presumed dead. Kenkichi is offered a job in Akita in northern Japan. The move upsets Kenkichi's mother and one evening, just before Kenkichi is to leave, she tells Noriko that it is her dream that her son would marry Noriko. Mrs. Yabe is overjoyed when Noriko accepts.

At first Noriko's family is upset that she is turning down the successful but unknown Manabe and marrying a widower with a child, but eventually they come to accept her decision. The family has a final group photo taken before Noriko goes off to Akita and her parents move to another town to live with her elderly uncle.

• To attempt to describe the plot of an Ozu film never does it justice. They appear to be nothing more than a simple telling of everyday things that happen. But the "telling" is done with such symmetry, artistry and sharpness that there is a deceptive refined simplicity to his films. By focusing on the same seemingly mundane themes like the desires for a happy family life, Ozu's films are not steeped in drama which makes plots "move." Instead they are extremely even films (some call them "slow") which find interest in the daily events in life. The audience never sees Manabe, never sees Chako's wedding, never even sees Noriko's wedding.

This is Ozu's way. It is not the high points in a person's life that interest Ozu, but the daily routines of life. These are the days that contain happiness and where family relationships are truly created, not during special occasions.

Ozu is considered the most Japanese of directors and export of his films, at first, was thought to be out of the question. Who but a Japanese would be interested in or understand the daily life of other Japanese? Foreigners wanted exotic costume dramas, not Ozu's contemporary non-dramas, officials thought. But once Western audiences did have a chance to see and judge Ozu's films they were touched by the universality of his themes and the compelling nature of his characters.

As if to tie all his films together, Ozu often repeats character names. Setsuko Hara plays a Noriko in *Late Spring, Early Summer* and *Tokyo Story*. Similarly, Chishu Ryu plays a Kichi in both *Early Summer* and *Tokyo Story*. And the unseen son, Shoji, in *Early Summer* is also an unseen son in *Tokyo Story,* but now we meet his widow, Noriko. Even the grandchildren in *Early Summer* and *Tokyo Story* have the same names, Minoru and Isamu. This is not to imply that these are the same characters from film to film, but that they are character types carried over from one film to another.

Ozu also used the same themes over and over again, just as he used the same actors to play similar characters. However, each movie is distinct and carries within it scenes of telling beauty and feeling. When Noriko's older brother, Shoji, is mentioned, we learn that he went to war and was never heard of again. His mother has never given up hope that someday he will return. At this point she longingly looks out a window and Ozu cuts to a carp windsock flying from a pole in a gentle breeze. These carp are the symbol of male children flown on the traditional "boys' day" holiday on May 5th, a day when she had certainly flown carp for Shoji.

The transience of life and the inevitability of change symbolized by a family which once had a son and no longer does is Ozu's reason for asking his audience to enjoy daily moments of happiness. Ozu has no real need for dramatic conflict between his characters because it is enough that their intertwined lives will constantly touch each other by just being there, or not being there.

Ozu himself never married. He lived most of his life with his mother. According to Chishu Ryu, one of Ozu's favorite actors, Ozu's best friend was probably cowriter Kogo Noda, and working with Noda provided Ozu with some of his most happy times. Noda worked with Ozu on most of his scripts, and the two would usually finish the writing in about four months. At that point Ozu had pretty well already shot the film in his mind. When he went to actually film the story, the script was never changed. Like many of Ozu's films, *Early Summer* leaves a viewer with an affecting moviegoing experience. His movies also require that viewers involve themselves with his films; give themselves over to the experience. Ozu cannot really be judged by watching only one film. His themes and style become more obvious and more appreciated when more films are seen.

Repast (1951)
Meshi

1951 / Toho. 97 min. B&W. *Director:* Mikio Naruse. *Screenplay:* Sumie Tanaka and Toshiro Ide. *Adaptation:* From the novel by Fumiko Hayashi. *Cinematography:* Masao Tamai. *Art Direction:* Satoshi Chuko. *Music:* Fumio Hayasaka.

Ken Uehara as *Hatsunosuke Okamoto.* Setsuko Hara *Michiyo, his wife.* Yukiko Shimazaki *Satoko Okamoto.* Kan Nihonyanagi *Kazuo Takenaka.* Hisako Takibana *Sumi Takenaka.* Eitaro Shindo *Yuzo Takenaka.* Haruko Sugimura *Matsu Murata, Michiyo's mother.* Yoko Sugi *Mitsuko Murata, Michiyo's sister-in-law.* Keiju Kobayashi *Shinzo Murata, Michiyo's brother.* Ranko Hanai *Koyoshi Dohya.* Akiko Kazami *Seiko Tomiyasu.* Mitsue Tachibana *Katsuko Suzuki.* Cheiko Nakakita *Keiko Yamakita.*

• In Osaka, a childless couple, Michiyo and Hatsunosuke, have been married for five years. Instead of the traditional arranged marriage, theirs was one of love and of which their families disapproved. The routines of married life are causing them to gradually drift apart. While the husband, a stockbroker, seems complacent enough about their situation (he has no qualms about indulging in a new pair of shoes for himself and ignoring his wife's desires), the wife's resentment and frustration grows.

One day Hatsunosuke's niece, Satoko, arrives. She has run away from her home in Tokyo because of her impending arranged marriage. She is a scheming young woman and manages to finagle an invitation to stay with them. While a pouting Michiyo stays home and cleans her house, Hatsunosuke and Satoko go on a sightseeing tour. Later, at her school reunion (to which she is embarrassed to wear a very old suit), Michiyo meets an old friend, Dohya, a single woman who envies Michiyo's married life. When she returns home, she suspects that the conniving niece has been consorting with neighborhood people of questionable character and has possibly tried to seduce Hatsunosuke. Finally Michiyo tells her husband of her pent up animosity and emptiness. As a result she returns to her own family in Tokyo.

Michiyo's stay with her mother, brother and sister-in-law is marked by

Repast (Mikio Naruse, 1951). Family members taking each other for granted is a common theme for Naruse. Here Michiyo (Setsuko Hara, left) silently endures the routine of her marriage to Hatsunosuke (Ken Uehara). (Photo courtesy of Toho Co., Ltd.)

inactivity and depression. Finally, her brother confronts her with the way she has made life more difficult for their mother and his wife. Even her mother tells her to return to her husband before he finds someone else. Seeking advice and companionship, she spends an evening with her friend and cousin, Kazuo. Michiyo is attracted to Kazuo, but when he makes faint overtures towards her, she is insulted. After all, she is still married. Michiyo then meets another friend, Keiko, a widow with two young children to support. Keiko's unemployment money has run out and she must sell newspapers just to get by. Their meeting further depresses Michiyo. The "new" life she had hoped for in Tokyo totally eludes her.

Hatsunosuke arrives in Tokyo on a business trip. Husband and wife meet again, and the two reconcile, even though nothing is really resolved. Michiyo returns with Hatsunosuke to Osaka. On the train back, Michiyo tears up a letter she has written her husband but never mailed. The pieces are set adrift out the train window.

• It took almost 15 years for Naruse to again make the same quality of film as *Wife! Be Like a Rose!* which brought him fame in 1935. With *Repast,* his stature as one of Japan's finest filmmakers was restored. Perhaps part of his revival was due to Naruse's utilization of the writings of Fumiko Hayashi. In Naruse's subtle hands, popular writer Hayashi's stories took on a dimension which made them more universal than the simple character studies they seemed. *Repast* was Naruse's first adaptation of a Fumiko Hayashi work, and it was her last novel. It was unfinished when she died, and Naruse, Toshiro Ide and Sumie Tanaka added an ending which was in keeping not only with Hayashi's philosophy, but also with Naruse's filmic themes. Naruse would continue this successful collaboration with Hayashi's works when he filmed *Lightning, Late Chrysanthemums,* and *Floating Clouds* and her autobiographical *A Wanderer's Notebook.*

With *Repast* Naruse began a series of films centered on domestic disharmony, usually between husband and wife and from the woman's point of view. Naruse's women feel their lives to be incomplete and their situations to be hopeless. (Ozu's women, on the other hand, acquiesce to their places in life while Mizoguchi's try to rise above it.) Naruse's women are basically strong and even stubborn but because they are unable to sacrifice the protection of the socially sanctioned marriage, they are overcome in the end.

Repast heralded a period in which Naruse made some of his best films. It also marked a revival of the *shomin-geki,* films about everyday family life. As successful as *Repast* was, it would be a film he made a year later, a basically atypical film, which won him international recognition, 1952's *Mother.*

Vacuum Zone (1952)
Shinku chitai

1952 / Shinsei Eiga. 129 min. B&W. *Director:* Satsuo Yamamoto. *Screenplay:* Yusaku Yamagata. *Adaptation:* From the novel by Hiroshi

Noma. *Cinematography:* Minoru Maeda. *Art Direction:* Yasuzo Kawashima. *Music:* Ikuma Dan.

Takashi Kanda *as Troop Commander Mine.* Yoshi Kato *Lt. Hayashi.* Eiji Okada *Okamoto.* Yoichi Numata *Duty officer of the week.* Koichi Nishimura *Sgt. Osumi.* Isao Kimura *Kitani.* Asao Sano *Ikeno.* Isao Numazaki *Hikoza.* Tsutomu Shimomura *Soda.* Toshio Takahara *Some.* Kiyoshi Nonomura *Uchimura.* Kenji Susukita *Uchimura's father.* Harue Tone *Hanayei.*

• The time is January 1944, "just before the destruction of Japan." Kitani, who has just been released from military prison, is being reassigned to his old unit, the 112th Regiment where he used to work in the paymaster's office. Kitani served a two-year, three-month sentence for stealing the wallet of another officer, Lieutenant Hayashi. Because of his time in prison, Kitani is one of the few four-year army men in the barracks, the rest having been shipped off to the China front. Normally that would entitle him to a high degree of status and authority, but it is precisely because of his prison term that he is not awarded that position and he is reluctant to take it.

In Kitani's barracks are new recruits who, like Private First Class Soda, are university graduates and despised by the other men who are not as well educated, but have been in the army longer. Soda, who was a history teacher in the secondary schools, is not inclined to abuse his position of authority to harass the recruits and also befriends Kitani. One of the recruits, Anzai, is particularly singled out for beatings and humiliation. When Anzai spills two buckets of bean soup, he and all the new recruits are punished by being forced to crawl and beg forgiveness from all the other men in the barracks.

Through flashbacks, we learn Kitani's history. He is in love with a debt-ridden geisha, Hanayei. One day, he finds a wallet. Not knowing who it belongs to, Kitani takes the money and throws the wallet away. He wants the money to pay Hanayei's debts and free her. Lieutenant Hayashi, whose wallet it was and who also works in the paymaster's office, brings charges against Kitani and has him arrested and tried. The other two officers in the paymaster's office tell Kitani not to worry. During the trial Kitani's notebook and the letters he wrote to Hanayei are brought into evidence. The court finds his writings antimilitaristic and believes he was telling military secrets to Hanayei. Kitani has not heard from Hanayei since the trial, and later finds out that the military police have taken her away.

During his trial, Kitani tries to tell the prosecutor about the rampant corruption in the paymaster's department, but the prosecutor doesn't seem interested in this information. To the military, Kitani showed no repentance while in jail and was insubordinate. At one point he lashed out at his brutal jailers and was punished by being chained out in the rain. To

Kitani, he has been unjustly imprisoned. At the barracks, Kitani finally breaks when the other soldiers call him a jailbird and Hanayei a whore. He lashes out at all the men in the barracks, hitting and punching them as he describes the brutal treatment he underwent in jail.

The sergeant under whom Kitani worked when assigned to the paymaster's department, Kaneko, is still on the camp. He tells Kitani how sorry he was that he couldn't help him at his trial and tries to help him now. Behind his back, however, Sergeant Kaneko is bribing other officers to get him out of the camp and sent to the front. When Kitani suddenly finds himself posted to the front, an assignment that means sure death, he finds Lieutenant Hayashi, who is in the camp hospital, and tries to kill him. Only then does he find out that the corrupt corporal and Sergeant Kaneko in the paymaster's office had used Kitani's trial to push him out. Hayashi, thinking Kitani was one of the corrupt ones, had falsely testified against him. Hayashi had been pushed out of the department and sent to Manchuria.

Kitani now realizes that the corporal and Sergeant Kaneko had gotten him assigned overseas to get rid of him. That night, with Soda's help, Kitani sneaks out of the barracks and tries to escape. When the soldiers are aroused to hunt for him, however, he is discovered trying to climb a fence and caught. The next day, Kitani is on board a ship bound for the southern war front.

• Like many directors, Satsuo Yamamoto (1910–1983) got his theatrical start as an actor. He dropped out of school in order to join a drama group and in 1933 entered Shochiku and became an assistant director working under Naruse among others. When Naruse moved to Toho, Yamamoto went too. He made his theatrical debut there in 1937 with *Young Miss.* The next year he directed the first cinematic version of Andre Gide's *La Symphonie Pastorale* and went on to translate several literary works to the screen. But Yamamoto's real interest came to be in films with a social message. During the war Yamamoto served in the Imperial army and was sent to Manchuria. It was these experiences which gave *Vacuum Zone* its authenticity and Yamamoto his beliefs about military corruption and abuse of authority. The power of his film, and the antiwar pictures of others made at this time, had a great influence on pacifist feelings in postwar Japan.

Yamamoto's attack on the system goes beyond the desire for a more humanistic approach to life, for his films are deeply permeated with political ideology. When a book on *Social Methodology* is found hidden among one recruit's belongings, he is condemned as a socialist. When another soldier is unnecessarily imprisoned, he innocently passes time by reciting passages from *The Communist Manifesto* which were taught to him by his brother, a mechanic, now in prison for being a Communist. It was this abuse of authority and power which was Yamamoto's central theme. In *Street of Violence (Boryoku no machi,* 1950) the subject was gangsters. It was ruthless strike-breaking managers in *Street without Sun (Taiyo no nai machi,* 1954) and politicians in *Uproar over a Typhoon (Taifu sodoki,* 1956).

Under the influence of the post-war SCAP (Supreme Commander for the Allied Powers) administration, trade unions quickly flourished in the Japanese film industry. As a result, the largest company, Toho, had its unions go out on strike three times between March 1946 and August 1948. SCAP felt that their early leniency towards labor groups had allowed them to become centers for Communist activity and had fostered the development of Communism in Japan. Consequently, they banned the first nationwide general strike which was set for February 1, 1947. During Toho's third strike, the management fired 1200 employees, especially singling out Communists and those most active in the unions.

Among those fired were directors Fumio Kamei, Tadashi Imai and Satsuo Yamamoto who (along with actress Isuzu Yamada and director Teinosuke Kinugasa) then founded their own production company. Independent production companies thrived for a very short period in the 1950s, but they were not long-lived. The large companies quickly moved to drive them out of business. *Vacuum Zone* was one of the films produced by the leftist-backed independent production company, Shinsei Eiga.

Although the leftist independent companies were virtually gone by the 1970s, Yamamoto was still able to produce films in keeping with his personal philosophy. In 1974 he made *The Family (Kareinaru ichizoku)* about misuses within the banking business and in 1975 he made *Solar Eclipse (Kinkanshoku)* centering on election fraud. *The Barren Zone (Fumo chitai,* 1976) was a telling account of the Lockheed scandal which impacted both the U.S. and Japan.

Ikiru (1952)

1952 / Toho / a.k.a. "Living" or "To Live." 130 min. (orig. 143 min.). B&W. *Director:* Akira Kurosawa. *Screenplay:* Shinobu Hashimoto, Hideo Oguni and Akira Kurosawa. *Cinematography:* Asakazu Nakai. *Art Direction:* So Matsuyama. *Lighting:* Shigeru Mori. *Music:* Fumio Hayasaka. *Sound:* Fujio Yanoguchi. *Editor:* Akira Kurosawa. *Producer:* Shojiro Motoki. Videotape: Media. Film Rental: Films Inc., Janus.

Takashi Shimura *as Kanji Watanabe.* Nobuo Kaneko *Mitsuo Watanabe.* Kyoko Seki *Kazue Watanabe.* Miki Odagiri *Toyo.* Kamatari

Fujiwara *Ono*. Makoto Kobori *Kiichi Watanabe*. Kumeko Urabe *Tatsu Watanabe*. Yoshie Minami *Maid*. Nobuo Nakamura *Deputy Mayor*. Minosuke Yamada *Saito*. Haruo Tanaka *Sakai*. Bokuzen Hidari *Ohara*. Minoru Chiaki *Noguchi*. Shinichi Himori *Kimura*. Kazuo Abe *City Assemblyman*. Masao Shimizu *Doctor*. Yunosuke Ito *Novelist*. Ko Kimura *Intern*. Atsushi Watanabe *Patient*. Yatsuko Tanami *Hostess*. Fuyuki Murakami *Newspaperman*. Seiji Miyaguchi *Gang-boss*. Daisuke Kato *Gang member*. Ichiro Chiba *Policeman*. Toranosuke Ogawa *Park Section Chief*. Akira Tani *Old man in bar*. Kin Sugai, Eiko Miyoshi and Fumiko Homma *Housewives*.

• Kanji Watanabe is a 30-year civil servant who is now the Chief of the Citizen's Section. He has stagnated within the bureaucratic system for years, filling hours with useless activity and shifting blame and work to other departments. This is what happens to a group of concerned mothers who want a vacant lot cleaned up and made into a park. But the passive Watanabe has his whole world shaken when he discovers that he has stomach cancer and only about six months left to live. He tries to tell his son, Mitsuo, of his situation, but Mitsuo is too selfish and uncaring to take notice of the man's agony. Instead he is more interested that his father doesn't dissipate his savings, mistakenly jumping to the conclusion that his father has a mistress.

Watanabe takes money out of his bank account to spend on a good time, but he doesn't know how. At a sake bar he meets a writer of cheap novels who, when he discovers Watanabe's plight, takes him under his wing and shows him a night on the town. The novelist takes him to a pachinko parlor, bar hopping, a strip show, and dancing. When an aggressive prostitute "steals" Watanabe's hat, the novelist advises him to just buy a new one, which he does, an untypically jaunty one.

One of the workers in Watanabe's department is Odagiri, a young woman who comes to his house so he can stamp her resignation. The two spend a nice day together and Watanabe wants to keep seeing her. It's not that he's in love with her, but that he is attracted to her youthful love of life. One night over dinner, Watanabe finally tells Odagiri about his impending death. He is feeling hopeless until he comes upon the idea of how to give meaning to his remaining days. He will push through the park that local residents want by forcing all the sections involved to work together instead of passing the problem on.

Five months later, his park completed, Watanabe dies. At his funeral the Deputy Mayor and other section officials take credit for the park—an act which makes the residents angry because they know that it was Watanabe who really saw that it was created and he was completely slighted at the opening ceremony. Watanabe's coworkers can't understand why he changed about six months ago, and Mitsuo says his father can't

Ikiru **(Akira Kurosawa, 1952). A final scene in *Ikiru* is one of the most touching ever captured on film. Having fought the system to erect a park for neighborhood children, a dying Watanabe (Takashi Shimura) swings in the snow while singing a favorite song, "Life Is Short." (Photo courtesy of Toho Co., Ltd.)**

have known he had cancer because he never told him. When a policeman returns Watanabe's hat, which he found in the park, the mourners find out that he spent his final hours happily swinging on a park swing singing "Life Is Short" to himself as snow gently began to fall. Recounting Watanabe's drive to create the park, his coworkers gradually discover that he did know of his impending death. Inspired, and drunk, the men vow to fight the system in his honor. The next day, however, things are just as they usually are in the bureaucracy.

• Akira Kurosawa is often called one of the most humanistic directors ever to have worked in films. In *Ikiru* he presents a compassionate and moving story of one man's personal determination in the face of death, to overcome seemingly insurmountable opposition in order to leave behind something of value. Through Watanabe's efforts on behalf of the unfortunate neighbors who want to change an unhealthy lot into a park, he not only produces the park, but also finds his own enlightenment, fulfillment and redemption. For Kurosawa, these personal "good deeds" are the road to accomplishment and one of the most valuable commodities in modern society.

What is amazing is that Watanabe is not a superheroic samurai, but an average man. We may admire the samurai fighting against overwhelming odds, but we can empathize with the ordinary man desperately struggling to help others and give his life meaning. Watanabe's quiet dignity, his perseverance in the face of death and officials who abuse their power, is Kurosawa's homage to men who make a difference. In *Ikiru,* just one man's efforts brought about a small respite in a world of indifference and injustice. It was a thankless job, unappreciated until after his death (and even then only shortly), but one which changed a neighborhood. In essence, Watanabe turned his bad luck (his disease) into good works, and others benefited.

Kurosawa paints Watanabe with a compassionate brush. We first see him in his office. His past efforts are indicated by a file long buried in his desk drawer: "A Plan to Increase Office Efficiency Submitted by Kanji Watanabe, November 7, 1933." It never amounted to anything more than the scrap paper Watanabe now uses it for. He has been "dead" for 25 years, and now that he really gets a death sentence, he finally learns to live. Though Kurosawa's script tenderly addresses the problems of old age, death and the purpose of life, it is the acting of Takashi Shimura which undoubtedly elicits audience compassion.

Takashi Shimura, like Toshiro Mifune, is an actor often used by Kurosawa. Born in 1905 with the real name of Shoji Shiazaki, Shimura didn't enter the world of films until the relatively late age of 30. Not often playing the lead (*Ikiru* and *Seven Samurai* being exceptions), Shimura appeared in almost all of Kurosawa's films through 1965. He also appeared in several of Inoshiro Honda's science fiction films including *Godzilla,* but it was under Kurosawa's direction that his talents blossomed. His controlled, inconspicuous acting style brought great strength to his parts whether they filled the screen as did Watanabe or were smaller as was his woodcutter in *Rashomon.* When he died in 1982, he left behind many screen characters who, while not handsome, usually imparted strength and inward nobility.

Ikiru is often named in top ten film lists. No one who has seen Shimura's Watanabe sitting on a swing in his finished park, the snow gently falling while he sings his favorite song, "Life Is Short," can ever forget it.

The Life of Oharu (1952)
Saikaku ichidai onna

1952 / Shin Toho. 133 min. (orig. running time 148 min.). B&W.
Director: Kenji Mizoguchi. *Screenplay:* Yoshikata Yoda and Kenji Mizo-
guchi. *Adaptation:* From the novel *The Life of an Amorous Woman
(Koshoku Ichidai Onna)* by Saikaku Ihara. *Cinematography:* Yoshimi
Hirano. *Art Direction:* Hiroshi Mizutani. *Music:* Ichiro Saito. *Editing:*
Toshio Goto. *Producer:* Hideo Koi. *Executive Producer:* Isamu Yoshii.
Videotape: Video Yesteryear.

Kinuyo Tanaka *as Oharu.* Tsukue Matsuura *Tomo, Oharu's mother.*
Ichiro Sugai *Shinzaemon, Oharu's father.* Toshiro Mifune *Katsunosuke.*
Toshiaki Konoe *Lord Harutaka Matsudaira.* Hisako Yamane *Lady Mat-
sudaira.* Jukichi Uno *Yakichi Ogiya.* Eitaro Shindo *Kabee Sasaya.* Akira
Oizumi *Fumikichi, Sasaya's friend.* Masao Shimizu *Kikuoji.* Daisuke Kato
Tasaburo Hishiya. Toranosuke Ogawa *Yoshioka.* Hiroshi Oizumi *Manager
Bunkichi.* Haruyo Ichikawa *Lady-in-waiting Iwabashi.* Kikue More *Myokai.*
Kiyoko Tsuji *Landlady at the inn.* Yuriko Hamada *Otsubone Yoshioka.*
Kyoko Kusajima *Lady-in-waiting Sodegaki.* Noriko Sengoku *Lady-in-
waiting Sakurai.* Sadako Sawamura *Owasa.* Masao Mishima *Taisaburo
Hishiya.* Eijiro Yanagi *Counterfeiter.* Chieko Higashiyama *Old nun
Myokai.* Tozen Hidari *Clothes rental store owner.* Takashi Shimura *Old
man.* Benkei Shiganoya *Jihei.*

● Oharu, a 50-year-old prostitute long past her prime, seeks refuge in
a temple where the statues remind her of a past love and cause her to
reflect on her past. In 1686, Oharu had been the beautiful daughter of a
rich merchant who served in the Imperial Palace in Kyoto. She is wel-
comed at the local manor where she is looked upon favorably by the young
lord. One day, a minor samurai, Katsunosuke, stops the young Oharu as
she visits a shrine. He tells her that his lord would like to see her and takes
her to a nearby house. When she gets there, however, the lord is not
there. It is Katsunosuke who has wanted to see her and now he tells her of
his love for her. At first she is put off by his improper attentions, but
eventually she succumbs to his appeals for she has secretly been enamored
of him all along. Before the two can consummate their love, the police
come and arrest the two.

As a result of their illegal activity (Oharu has committed misconduct
with a person of inferior rank), Katsunosuke is beheaded and Oharu and
her family are cast out of the Palace and exiled from Kyoto. Her family
berates her for ruining their life of comfort. When Oharu hears that Katsunosuke's last words were a petition for a time when true love can be

fulfilled, she attempts suicide. But the act is stopped by her mother. Later, a royal appeal reaches the village where Oharu and her family live. Lord Matsudaira's wife cannot have children and is now looking for a mistress who can give him a son. Oharu is hired to fill the position for 100 ryo and an allowance. When Oharu finally produces a son for Lord Matsudaira and his clan's future is secured, she is denied access to the child and promptly returned to her family with a 5 ryo payment.

Oharu's father, who had expected a 300 ryo bonus and thought they were in favor with the clan, has gotten himself deeply into debt. He takes out his anger by beating Oharu and selling her to a geisha house at Shimabara, the red-light district of Kyoto. Oharu interests many clients, especially a wealthy country man who wants to purchase Oharu's contract. She not only refuses to be bought, but also refuses to service him. He demands her termination, but he is discovered not to be a wealthy man but a counterfeiter. Again Oharu is forced to return to her parents.

Soon Oharu is sold to a merchant as a hairdresser to his jealous wife, Owasa. Owasa has been very ill and has lost a lot of hair. It is Oharu's job to keep this loss from her husband. One day the counterfeiter visits the merchant and reveals Oharu's past life as a courtesan. Learning this, the merchant rapes Oharu and when his wife finds out, she demands that Oharu's hair be cut and that she be fired. That night, Oharu exposes the wife's baldness and returns to her parents. Eventually Oharu achieves a degree of happiness when she marries a fanmaker she had known from her days with the merchant. Unfortunately, she is again plunged into desperation when her husband is killed by robbers.

Seeking respite from her downward-spiraling life, Oharu attempts to join a convent. In this she is helped by a servant, Bunkichi, of the merchant she was employed by and who has silently admired her. He gives Oharu the cloth she needs for a nun's kimono, but when Jihei, the merchant's chief clerk, learns of Bunkichi's actions, he goes to the convent to get the cloth back. Once there, however, he is struck by Oharu's beauty and when she tells him the cloth has already been made into a kimono she is forced to disrobe to return the cloth. A nun witnesses Oharu's actions and interprets them as sexual. She sends Oharu away in humiliation. Bunkichi, pitying and loving Oharu, steals 50 ryo from the merchant and runs away with her. He is quickly caught and Oharu is left with no recourse but begging and prostitution.

One day Oharu sees her son passing by with members of the Matsudaira clan. She cannot present herself, however, because of the embarrassment she would cause him and the disgrace her past would bring to the clan. She leaves and resumes her life as a beggar/prostitute. When Oharu awakens back at the temple from the beginning of the film, she is ill. Her mother, who has been looking for her, nurses her through the sickness and tells her that Lord Matsudaira has died and that Oharu has been summoned

The Life of Oharu (Kenji Mizoguchi, 1952). Mizoguchi, one of the foremost directors of films about the plight of women, depicted Oharu (Kinuyo Tanaka, right)
through an uncontrollable life which began with affluence and beauty and ended
with poverty and degradation. (Photo courtesy of Toho Co., Ltd.)

to the palace. Hoping for the best at the castle, Oharu is disillusioned and
disappointed to find that clan advisers have demanded her exile, far from
the castle and her son, where she can never be a threat to them. Before
they can take her away, however, she escapes. But there is no hope for
Oharu who has now become a wandering nun, begging for alms.

   • After the war, Mizoguchi fell into a slump, even though his films
with women-sensitive themes pleased the Occupation forces. His working
relationship with longtime scriptwriter/collaborator Yoda was starting to
strain as was the one with his favorite actress Kinuyo Tanaka with whom
he was linked romantically. (Mizoguchi's wife had gone insane and was
committed to an asylum while he was working on part II of *The Loyal 47
Ronin*. Afterwards he secretly lived with his wife's sister and her children.)
To compound Mizoguchi's problems, his movie heroines and filmmaking
style were starting to look old-fashioned to postwar audiences.

   For years Mizoguchi had wanted to make *The Life of Oharu* and this
was the project he chose to help fight the downturn in his career. When
presented with the idea, Shochiku refused and Mizoguchi quit. He moved
to Toho where he made several *josei eigas* (women's films). But it took
several years for him to find a backing studio, Shin Toho, for *Oharu*. It
was while Mizoguchi was making the film that a momentous event took
place for Japanese films: Akira Kurosawa's *Rashomon* won the top prize at
the Venice Film Festival. Upset by the young director's success, Mizoguchi

became obsessed with creating a masterpiece, especially one which would be appreciated by the West. This obsession brought out Mizoguchi's usual demands for perfection, but also met with problems because of the conditions under which the film was made. Shin Toho "studios" turned out to be an abandoned arms factory and a bombed-out park between Kyoto and Osaka where trains ran often and their contemporary noise disrupted the historic film.

With an outstanding performance by his favorite actress, Kinuyo Tanaka *(Where Chimneys Are Seen, Sandakan 8), The Life of Oharu* created a film genre closely associated with Mizoguchi. Most of the films he made in the last part of his career were dramas centering on one representational character set against an historical backdrop recreated with typical Mizoguchi detail and inspiration. *Oharu* is a masterful period film which not only captures the many different social environments of the Tokugawa Edo period but also is possibly the best treatment of Mizoguchi's favorite theme, the victimization of women, especially in feudal Japan. This was a time when women were treated as chattel property by fathers and husbands. They were not allowed to determine the fate of their own lives but lived committed to the rigid responsibilities thrust upon them.

Many dramatic plots revolve around these social responsibilities, especially when they clash with personal desires. The social duties and obligations *(giri)* faced by women and men often conflicted with their personal feelings *(ninjo)*. Oharu is responsible for and to her parents, her lord and her social position, even though her heart was with the lowly retainer, Katsunosuke. By defying, even if only in spirit, these social codes, Oharu is punished (and by extension, her family also). She cannot fight, and personal justice has no place in this society.

The Life of Oharu was a very long and expensive film. It was not well received by Japanese audiences even though it did create a stir among critics. When it was chosen to represent Japan at Venice in the 1952 Film Festival, however, it astounded audiences. Mizoguchi ended up sharing the International Prize with John Ford's *The Quiet Man*. The prize not only won worldwide recognition for Mizoguchi, it also caused a re-evaluation of his position back in Japan. With the success of *Oharu*, Mizoguchi was given carte blanche from Daiei Studios.

Mother (1952)
Okasan

1952 / Shin Toho. 98 min. B&W. *Director:* Mikio Naruse.
Screenplay: Yoko Mizuki. *Adapation:* From the prize-winning girls' school

essay "My Mother." *Cinematography:* Hiroshi Suzuki. *Music:* Ichiro Saito. *Art Director:* Masatoshi Kato. *Sound:* Kihachiro Nakai. *Editing:* Hidetoshi Kasama. *Producer:* Ichiro Nagashima. Videotape: Sony.

Kinuyo Tanaka *as Masako Fukuhara.* Kyoko Kagawa *Toshiko, her daughter.* Eiji Okada *Shinjiro.* Masao Mishima *Ryosuke Fukuhara, her husband.* Akihiko Katayama *Susumu Fukuhara, her eldest son.* Daisuke Kato *Uncle Kimura.* Chieko Nakakita *Aunt Noriko.* Keiko Enonami *Chako, her second daughter.*

• The Fukuhara family lives in the outskirts of Tokyo in 1950. During the war, the family's laundry business was destroyed in a fire. Masako and her daughter, Toshiko, make and sell hot cakes in the winter and ice candy in the summer. Masako's husband, Ryosuke, works at a factory. Their only son, Susumu, used to work at an upholstery shop until the dust made him ill and he had to go to a sanatorium. After working hard, the family finally has saved enough money to reopen their laundry business. One day, Susumu runs away from the sanatorium. He has come home to be near his mother, and to die.

The family is helped in the laundry by "Uncle" Kimura, who was Ryosuke's apprentice and who has just recently been released from a Soviet prisoner of war camp. Things seem to go well for the family and Toshiko dreams of going to dressmaker's school. She is also developing a serious relationship with Shinjiro, the very modern baker's son who sings Italian songs and makes arty "Picasso" bread. Unfortunately, Mr. Fukuhara has worked so hard to open the laundry that he becomes ill. He refuses to go to the hospital and, that autumn, he too dies. The family keeps working hard at the laundry with Uncle Kimura's help. Soon, however, Toshiko hears unsettling gossip about her mother and her "uncle" indicating that they will be married.

Also living with the Fukuharas is Tetsuo, the son of Masako's sister, Noriko. Noriko has been repatriated from Korea and is going to school to learn to be a hairdresser. She visits the Fukuharas often and practices on the two girls. In one session she cuts Chako's hair short, and in another she practices on Toshiko for a contest, dressing her in a formal kimono and combing her hair into a traditional wedding arrangement. When Shinjiro sees her dressed like this, he assumes she has entered into a traditional arranged marriage and races home to protest to his parents. He later finds out the truth, and is surprised when the woman he has just seen dressed so traditionally, now winks at him.

Times are hard for the family, and it is decided that the youngest daughter, Chako, will go to live with her aunt and uncle whose only son has died. The family has a farewell picnic at an amusement park, and the next day Chako sadly departs from her beloved mother. When Masako hears about the gossip, it is decided that it would be best for "Uncle"

Mother (Mikio Naruse, 1952). Toshiko (Kyoko Kagawa, left) has her hair styled in the manner of a traditional bride by her aunt (Cheiko Nakakita) while her cousin (Takashi Ito) and mother (Kinuyo Tanaka) watch. (Photo courtesy of Sony Video and Toho Co., Ltd.)

Kimura to move on. He finds a new, and cheaper, apprentice to replace him at the laundry, a 16-year-old farm boy, and mother and daughter are left to run the laundry together.

• Naruse's *Mother* belongs to a popular film genre in Japan known as the *haha-mono* or "mother picture" (see *A Japanese Tragedy*). Unlike most of the entries in this genre, however, Naruse's mother is not mistreated by unappreciative children. Although she suffers through the war, poverty, the death of her son and husband, and the loss of her youngest daughter, this mother remains cheerful and fills the movie with hope. *Mother* is told not from the point of view of the mother, Masako, but through the eyes of her loving eldest daughter, Toshiko. It is her voice-over which is heard at the film's end saying, "Dear Mother, whom I love very much, are you happy? Stay with us forever."

While Naruse presents his characters' stories as simply as possible, he is not above a bit of cinematic manipulation. At one point "the end" flashes across the screen and it appears that the film is over before the characters' problems are resolved. Before disappointment can set in, however, Naruse shows that "the end" really belonged to *The Tragic Love,* a film the aunt has taken the family to (a scene sadly missing from the currently available videotape version).

Mother was the first major film for young actress Kyoko Kagawa (b.

1931) who played the 18-year-old Toshiko. She was often c?
well, the "traditional" young Japanese woman. She also ar
Mizoguchi's *Sansho the Bailiff* and *A Story from Chikamaw.*
released in Europe the year after it appeared in Japan and brought ι.
a degree of international recognition. The film went on to win a Silver
Lion at the 1952 Venice Film Festival.

A Japanese Tragedy (1953)
Nihon no higeki

1953 / Shochiku. 116 min. B&W. *Director:* Keisuke Kinoshita. *Assistant Director:* Yoshio Kawazu. *Screenplay:* Keisuke Kinoshita. *Cinematography:* Hiroyuki Kusuda. *Art Direction:* Kimihiko Nakamura. *Music:* Chuji Kinoshita. *Producer:* Takashi Koide and Tyotaro Kuwata.

Yuko Mochizuki *as Haruko Inoue.* Yoko Katsuragi *Utako, Haruko's daughter.* Masami Taura *Seiichi, Haruko's son.* Keiji Sada *Tatsuya.* Ken Uehara *Masayuki Akazawa, the English teacher.* Sanae Takasugi *Mrs. Akazawa.* Keiko Awaji *Wakamaru.*

• A background of newsreel footage of war trials, strikes, riots and disasters of the period is the setting for the story of Haruko Inoue. Haruko has lost her husband in the war and now must raise her two children alone. She earns a paltry living acting as a maid in the seaside resort town of Atami. Her daughter Utako works as a seamstress and studies English. Her son, Seiichi, is in Tokyo attending medical school.

Haruko has made many sacrifices to support her children, including hoarding black-market goods and descending into prostitution, but they see her as neglecting them. Because of her work, Haruko believes it would be better for her children to be raised by her brother-in-law, but while living with him, they are bombarded with negative input about their mother from his wife. Through the years they have grown into hateful and grasping young adults.

Because Utako was raped, she distrusts and resents men. She flirts with her English teacher, Akazawa, and plans to run away with him. When Akazawa's wife confronts Utako, she insults his wife and returns to her mother. Alarmed by the incident, Haruko goes to Tokyo to see what her son thinks they should do. Seiichi, however, is not really interested in his mother and her problems. In the hopes of being adopted by a wealthy man who has lost his own son, Seiichi can only talk about changing the

A Japanese Tragedy (Keisuke Kinoshita, 1953). This famous entry in the *haha-mono* (mother film) genre starred Yuko Mochizuki (left) as the typical mother who does her best for her children but is eventually spurned by them, as in this scene with her son played by Masami Taura. (Photo courtesy of Shochiku Co., Ltd.)

family records. Haruko, distraught by her son's rejection, starts to return to Atami. As she reflects back on her life and her sacrifices for her ungrateful children, she hurls herself in front of an oncoming train. Back in Atami, only Tatsuya, a street musician, and Wakamaru, a geisha, sing of her memory.

• Even though he is not well-known outside Japan, Keisuke Kinoshita (b. 1912) is considered to be one of that country's greatest postwar directors. He is also one of the most popular with Japanese audiences.

Kinoshita loved films early in his life but, as was his parents' desire, studied at the Hamatsu Engineering School. His family eventually resigned themselves to his desire to become a filmmaker and they helped him apply at Shochiku's Kamata Studios. He was told, however, that he needed either a university education or he could enter their photography department. As a consequence Kinoshita eventually studied at the Oriental Photography School in 1932. In 1933 he returned to Shochiku which put him to work as an assistant in the film processing lab. He worked his way to be Yasujiro Shimazu's camera assistant then his assistant director. Kinoshita tried his hand at writing screenplays and wrote in every genre possible trying to advance himself. He was just about to make a test film when he was drafted into the military in 1940. He continued to write scripts during his term of service in the Pacific war and upon his return to Shochiku, was assigned as assistant director to Kozaburo Yohimura. Finally, in 1943, he was promoted to director.

Kinoshita is a very prolific filmmaker who does so many different types of films so well that he defies categorization. For some critics this means that there seems to be no "Kinoshita style," while for others it is indicative of just what a genius he was. His first film, *The Blossoming Port (Hana saku minato,* 1943) was an unusual production for Japan, a social satire, and one of the best of Japan's wartime comedies. (Oddly enough, later it was banned and confiscated by the Occupation authorities.)

When he made *Army* (1944), the story of a mother who emotionally struggles with the idea of her son going off to war, it was labeled an antiwar film by the Information Ministry. He wanted to make a film on the Kamikaze troops, but because the Ministry disliked *Army,* they refused. Kinoshita's personal philosophy, which saw beauty in innocence, spilled over into his films and made it difficult for him to make movies in keeping with "national policy" film standards. Like Kurosawa after him, he ended up sitting out the rest of the war and not making films.

In 1951 Kinoshita made *Carmen Comes Home (Karumen kokyo ni kaeru),* the humorous story of a Tokyo stripper who returns to her hometown, shocks local residents, then proceeds to raise money for the local school. It was Japan's first color film and was followed by the sequel, one of Japan's best social satires, *Carmen's Pure Love* in 1952.

With *A Japanese Tragedy* Kinoshita returned to the realm of drama and produced one of his masterpieces. Set against a time of postwar turbulence and the changing social values which seem to corrupt the innate goodness of those it touches, *A Japanese Tragedy* has fast-paced editing which not only compares the past to the present, but also lends depth and believability to the characters. When Utako and Seiichi insist on more money from their mother one day while eating, there is a quick flashback to their mother desperately trying to buy rice on the black market to feed her children. The connection of the past to the present is further enhanced by Kinoshita's use of newsreel footage of actual events juxtaposed to the story contained in the film. Kinoshita's characters are a product of the society they live in. Like the children in Ozu's *Tokyo Story,* the children of *A Japanese Tragedy* are forsaking old ways and duties in favor of the new.

Like Naruse's *Mother, A Japanese Tragedy* is another example of the *haha-mono* or mother picture. It centers on a character who is a mother, but unlike Naruse's film, *A Japanese Tragedy* is a more typical example. As is usual for the genre, the mother is very self-sacrificing and her efforts are almost always unappreciated by her ungrateful children, especially her sons. It is an extremely popular style of film with Japanese audiences.

Actress Yuko Mochizuki, who plays the mother in *A Japanese Tragedy,* was born in Tokyo in 1918 and became a specialist in *haha-monos.* She worked for many years on the stage, as both a dancer and actress, before moving into films. Although she is a truly versatile actress, she has come to be known as *Nihon no haha* (mother of Japan). Instead of fighting this type of typecasting as Western actresses might, Mochizuki used it to her advantage. After retiring from films, she capitalized on her mother image and successfully ran for the Japanese House of Councilors in 1971. Another actor of note in *A Japanese Tragedy* is Keiji Sada. Born in Kyoto in 1926 (his real name is Hiroshi Nakai), Sada graduated from Wasedo University and not long afterward joined Shochiku. His debut in Kinoshita's *The Phoenix (Fushicho,* 1974) established the young actor as a romantic leading man. Sada went on to appear in Ozu's *Equinox Flower (Higambana,* 1958) and *An Autumn Afternoon (Samma no aji,* 1962) as well as portraying Tatsuya Nakadai's friend in *The Human Condition.* His career, unfortunately, was cut short when he was killed in an auto accident in 1964.

The Crab-Canning Ship (1953)
Kanikosen

1953 / Gendai Productions. 112 min. B&W. *Director:* So Yamamura. *Screenplay:* So Yamamura. *Adaptation:* From the novel by Takiji Kobayashi. *Cinematography:* Yoshio Miiyajima. *Art Direction:* Motoshi Kijima. *Music:* Akira Ifukube. *Producer:* Tengo Yamada.

So Yamamura *as Matsuki.* Masayuki Mori *The doctor.* Akitake Kono *Shibaura.* Kow Mihashi *Asakawa.* Akira Tani *Suda.* Mikizo Hirata *Foreman.* Rosak Kawarazaki *Boy.* Shin Morinawa *Kurasa.* Sumiko Hidaka

Whore. Sanaye Nakahara *Natsu.* Haruye Wakahara *Dancer.* Shisuye Yamagishi *Mother.* Yasushi Mizura *Young man.*

• In 1926, a crab-canning ship belonging to a Japanese fishing business exhaustively fishes for crab in the North Pacific off the Kamchatka Peninsula. Most of the sailors on the ship have been recruited from the ranks of workers and farmers. They are treated brutally on the ship and must work under the worst possible conditions. Finally, pushed to the brink, the sailors mutiny and take control of the ship. Their victory is short-lived. A boarding party from an Imperial Navy warship bloodily puts down the workers' rebellion.

• So Yamamura (b. 1910) started in films as an actor. He has a composed and masterful acting style which makes him stand out in scenes. He has appeared in films by Mizoguchi, Ozu *(Tokyo Story)*, Kobayashi *(The Human Condition)* and others.

In 1953 he made his directorial debut with *The Crab-Canning Ship.* Made after the American Occupation forces left Japan and limitations on film topics were lifted, *The Crab-Canning Ship* was an indictment of the exploitation which existed in prewar Japan. The film was based on a popular proletarian novel. It was written by Takiji Kobayashi, a leading leftist activist who died in prison in 1933. While Yamamura converted the novel to film without losing its distinctive character, it didn't seem to have the sting which leftist films would come to have. The ship's workers, struggling for their rights, took on the nature of a collective hero while the "villains" of the film were blackly drawn and overly stereotyped.

More than Yamamura's topic was revolutionary, so was his style of filming. Greatly influenced by Eisenstein's *Battleship Potemkin* and the Soviet silent cinema from which it emerged, the imagery Yamamura used (a close-up of an anchor chain, a blood-stained flag covering the sailors' corpses) was very forceful. In the end, however, the film elicited more of a compassionate response in the viewer than the solidarity usually aimed at by leftist directors. Nonetheless, it was still a fundamental advance in the branch of Japanese cinema which worked for enlightenment and reform.

Where Chimneys Are Seen (1953)
Entotsu no mieru basho

1953 / Studio Eight–Shin Toho. / a.k.a. "Four Chimneys" and "Chimney Scene." 108 min. B&W. *Director:* Heinosuke Gosho. *Screenplay:*

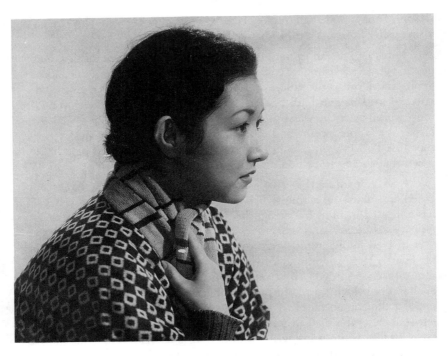

Where Chimneys Are Seen (Heinosuke Gosho, 1953). Hideko Takamine as the resentful Senko had been an actress from an early age who, in her early career, was referred to as the Shirley Temple of Japan. She became one of Japan's most versatile and accomplished actresses.

Hideo Oguni. *Adaptation:* From the novel ***The Good People*** by Rinzo Shiina. *Cinematography:* Mitsuo Miura. *Art Direction:* Tomoo Shimogawara. *Music:* Yasushi Akutagawa. *Sound:* Yuji Dogen. *Editor:* Nobu Nagata. *Producer:* Yoshishige Uchiyama.

Ken Uehara *as Ryukichi Ogata.* Kinuyo Tanaka *Hiroko.* Hiroshi Akutagawa *Kenzo Kubo.* Hideko Takamine *Senko Azuma.* Chieko Seki *Yukiko Ikeda.* Ranki Hanai *Katsuko Ishibashi.* Haruo Tanaka *Chuji Tsukahara.*

• Ryukichi and Hiroko live in a poor, industrial area of Tokyo. The couple have no children until they are suddenly left with one, the child of Hiroko's worthless first husband and his mistress. Hiroko had assumed that her husband was dead and now finds that he lives on waste land near a desolate river bank eking out a living.

The baby's constant crying puts a considerable strain on the couple as well as upon Kenzo and Senko, the tax collector and his war-embittered mistress who have rented the room above Ryukichi and Hiroko. With constant tension between Hiroko and Ryukichi from the incessant and unbearable crying, Hiroko attempts suicide. Luckily, her attempt is unsuccessful.

Eventually, like the view of the four chimneys which changes in number depending on where one stands, the couple changes their outlook and becomes accustomed to the baby. As Ryukichi says, "Life is whatever you think it is. It can be sweet or it can be bitter, whichever you are yourself."

• Heinosuke Gosho (1902–1981) was the son of a geisha (his father's mistress) and a descendent of nobility and the emerging Japanese middle/ merchant class. Upon his graduation from a commercial-technical school, Gosho joined Shochiku Studios in 1923 and worked as an assistant director to Yasujiro Shimazu. He made his first film as a director in 1925. It was Gosho who made Japan's first talking picture, *The Neighbor's Wife and Mine (Madamu to nyobo)* in 1931. The film is acclaimed for not using sound for sound's sake. Instead of exploiting the novelty of sound, Gosho expertly crafted it into his movies. The silence needed by a pressured writer in *The Neighbor's Wife and Mine* is eloquently subverted by a neighbor who plays noisy jazz records, for example.

Gosho contracted tuberculosis around 1935 and continually fought bouts of illness. During the three years he was ill he developed his theory of *junbungaku* or "pure literature." Normally the relationship between literature and film is one of popularity and commercial value. Gosho (and Shiro Toyoda and Mikio Naruse) fought against this commercialism in favor of filming better works and is considered a leader in the pure literature movement.

After his illness and the end of World War II, Gosho went to work at Toho. He was an ardent supporter of the Toho Employees Union during the heated labor disputes which occurred there. Organized unions were virtually unknown in Japan until the Occupation forces had encouraged them. The unions, seeking control as well as higher wages, and especially under Communist leaders, struck Toho several times. Discouraged by the strikes and Toho's policy of controlling its films, Gosho left. In 1951 he started an independent production group, Studio Eight, where he made *Where Chimneys Are Seen.*

The problems faced by ordinary people are Gosho's primary concern. This made him, along with Naruse and Ozu, one of the leading *shomin-geki* directors. He depicts his characters with great understanding and compassion. Like the writer's annoying jazz music of *The Neighbor's Wife and Mine* and the crying baby of *Where Chimneys Are Seen,* the disruptions of daily life become Gosho's focus. Some critics believe his movies to be overly sentimental, but the combination of humor and poignancy which Gosho brings to his subjects gave rise to the critical term "Goshoism": a blend of sentimentality and humor, the desire to laugh and cry at the same time. According to Gosho, life is what we make of it. It should be accepted with its joys and sorrows. Technically, he is a superior director. He takes painstaking care about the locations and sets where he shoots and about lighting and camera angles. He is known for taking many shots of a scene (and unlike Ozu, Gosho moves his cameras often). He painstakingly edits together these shots to further enhance the film's atmosphere and to create a usually quick but simple tempo.

Actress Kinuyo Tanaka, who plays Hiroko in *Chimneys*, was one of the most popular movie stars in Japan during the 1930s. Born in 1924, Tanaka first worked with a musical troupe before joining Shochiku in 1924. She has starred in Gosho's *The Neighbor's Wife and Mine*, Mizoguchi's *Sansho the Bailiff* and *Life of Oharu*, Kinoshita's *The Ballad of Narayama*, as well as in films directed by Naruse, and her husband, Hiroshi Shimizu (Tanaka is a also a cousin to Masaki Kobayashi). Among her most memorable roles was that of the potter's wife in *Ugetsu* and as the outcast karayuki-san in *Sandakan 8*. In 1953 she became the first woman in Japan to direct a film *(Love Letter)* and has done many since. At the time of her death in 1977, she was appearing in a television serial.

Chimneys won the International Peace prize at the 1953 Berlin Film Festival.

Ugetsu (1953)
Ugetsu monogatari

1953 / Daiei. / a.k.a. "Tales of the Pale Moon After a Rain." 95 min. *Director:* Kenji Mizoguchi. *Screenplay:* Matsutaro Kawaguchi and Yoshi-kata Yoda. *Adaptation:* From two stories *"Asaji ga yado"* (The Inn at Asaji) and *"Jasei no in"* (Serpent of Desire) from the collected stories of Akinari Ueda (1768) and Guy de Maupassant's "La Décoration." *Cinematography:* Kazuo Miyagawa. *Music:* Fumio Hayasaka. *Sound:* Iwao Otani. *Art Director:* Kisaku Ito. *Lighting:* Kenichi Okamoto. *Editor:* Mitsuji Miyata. *Producer:* Masaichi Nagata. Videotape: Embassy, Discount Video Tapes, Video Yesteryear. Film: Filmic Archives/Reel Images, Films Inc., Janus, Kit Parker.

Machiko Kyo *as Lady Wakasa*. Masayuki Mori *Genjuro*. Kinuyo Tanaka *Miyagi*. Mitsuko Mito *Ohama*. Sakae Ozawa *Tobei*. Sugisaka Koyama *The high priest*. Royosuke Kagawa *The village master*.

Ugetsu (Kenji Mizoguchi, 1953). When Genjuro (Masayuko Mori) attempts to profit from war, he falls under the spell of the beautiful but ghostly Lady Wakasa (Machiko Kyo) and ends up sacrificing his family for his own desires.

• Genjuro, the potter, and his brother-in-law, Tobei the farmer, decide that the civil wars of the 16th century which rage around them offer a perfect opportunity to attain their fondest desires: Genjuro to become wealthy and Tobei to become a samurai. Along with their wives, they start the perilous boat journey to the city, Oziwa, on the other side of Lake Biwa. Along the way they find a dying boatsman who warns them of pirates who will steal the women. Genjuro decides to put his wife, Miyagi, and son ashore for safety while the remaining three continue the trip.

In Oziwa, Tobei abandons his wife, Ohama, while he attempts to gain fame as a fierce warrior. Ohama is soon set upon and raped, eventually becoming a prostitute just to survive. Meanwhile, Genjuro's pottery is much admired by the Lady Wakasa who asks that he bring them to her mansion. Once there, Genjuro falls under the Lady's spell and forgets everything. One day, a Buddhist priest Genjuro meets tells him that Lady Wakasa is a ghost and that he must flee for his life and return to his own family. With Sanskrit incantations written on his body, Genjuro confronts Lady Wakasa and her nursemaid and slashes at them with a sword until he falls exhausted in the garden. When he awakens the next morning, the mansion is nothing more than an old ruin.

Tobei, who has lied his way into being thought of as a great warrior by stealing the head of an opposing lord, has been made a samurai and given retainers. As he parades into town, he and his men partake of the services of a geisha house. It is the same house where his wife now works. Realizing what a high price has been paid for his dreams, Tobei frees Ohama and returns to being a farmer.

Genjuro also returns home, but his house is in a shambles. Eventually he finds his wife cooking supper and patiently awaiting his return. He falls asleep quickly, but is surprised the next morning to discover Miyagi has disappeared. Genjuro is told that his wife had died, attacked by starving men, and that it was just her spirit that met him, and now watches over him.

• When *Ugetsu* won the silver prize at the 1953 Venice Film Festival, it became the next major film after *Rashomon* to focus worldwide attention on the Japanese film industry. Several of the talented people responsible for *Rashomon*'s success were also among those who worked on *Ugetsu* including the producer, Masaichi Nagata, who delighted in being called the Darryl Zanuck of Japan, photographer Kazuo Miyagawa, and actors Masayuki Mori and Machiko Kyo.

Cinematographer Miyagawa (b. 1908), whose legendary career would extend well into the 1980s, graduated from the Kyoto Commercial School and went to work for Nikkatsu in 1935. He has worked for many important Japanese directors from Kurosawa to Ichikawa. He has built up an international reputation for his mastery of both standard and Scope framing and both color and black-and-white film. Working on more than 100 films, Miyagawa is often the one responsible for lifting an ordinary film into the realm of the extraordinary with his camerawork.

Many Westerners think *Ugetsu* is a perfect example of what a Japanese film should look like — even though the Japanese feel that designation belongs to the films of Yasujiro Ozu. It is thought by many critics to be Mizoguchi's best, and one of the most perfect films ever made. *Ugetsu* is often found on top-ten lists decades after it was first released.

There are many reasons why *Ugetsu* rates such high critical acclaim. There was Mizoguchi's insistence on dialogue, action and set design authentic to the 16th century story setting. There is the undeniable visual excellence created by the film's high production values. And there is the almost hypnotic mood created by Mizoguchi's craftsman-like direction and camera work.

At the center of Mizoguchi's technical cinematic style is the use of a camera which, unlike Ozu's, is highly mobile. In Mizoguchi's films, the actors will perform a scene without interruption, preserving its emotional integrity, while the camera — usually in a long or medium shot — actively weaves around the action, changing background details as it moves, but never breaking the scene's continuity.

The mood Mizoguchi creates in *Ugetsu* is remarkably evoked in several memorable and famous scenes such as the picnic in Lady Wakasa's garden and the night boat journey across fog-enshrouded Lake Biwa in which a slowly beating drum and the chant-like singing of Ohama heighten the haunting atmosphere and foreshadow eerie events to come. This scene carries more than just the two families from one side of the lake to the other, for it also carries them from their actual poverty to their hoped for prosperity, from Genjuro's family ties to his phantom lover and also transports the viewer from a film that could have been just an historical story of two men's dreams to that of an allegorical tale.

Like other films from Japan's "Golden Age" of the 1950s, historic settings were often used to make modern points. *Ugetsu* showed how people survive amid the violence and anarchy of war and at the same time advocates the very traditional Japanese idea that social or economic ambition, which could put the good of the individual above that of society, could easily lead to disaster. It should be noted that the 16th century was a time which allowed for upward mobility. A farmer could win a reputation in battle and be made a samurai as Tobei wanted, unlike centuries later when class distinctions were much more rigid, and mobility virtually impossible.

Ugetsu also provides Mizoguchi with the perfect story in which to champion his favorite subject: the role of women in maintaining an orderly world and redeeming men through unselfish love. The Lady Wakasa's love of Genjuro is selfish in that it asks him to stay with her forever and forsake those to whom he has made a commitment. Genjuro's wife's love, on the other hand, transcends her own death for the sake of her husband. When the movie comes full circle—from Mizoguchi's opening shots of the village; through Genjuro's fall, repentance and acceptance of his potter's life; and back to the closing shots of the same village—it is the voice-over of Miyagi's spirit who indicates that she never wanted them to be wealthy but who paid the high cost of Genjuro's greed, that softly says "now at last you have become the man I wanted you to be."

The ending of *Ugetsu* is one of the best cinematic examples of the Japanese philosophy of *mono no aware*. As much a feeling as a philosophy, *mono no aware* is the traditional Japanese acceptance of the inherent sadness of life and the transcience of all things. Genjuro's realization of the folly of his dreams of wealth have led him to the simple but virtuous life which his wife knew all along was best. To flow peacefully with life instead of fighting against it is a basic zen principle and it is the heart of *mono no aware*. It is an underlying current often found in Japanese films (especially those of Ozu) and, although it may be difficult for Westerners to understand, by the end of *Ugetsu,* in the hands of master-director Mizoguchi, even the most logical mind can have a feeling for it.

Gate of Hell (1953)
Jigokumon

1953 / Daiei. 90 min. Color. *Director:* Teinosuke Kinugasa. *Screenplay:* Teinosuke Kinugasa. *Adaptation:* From a story by Kan Kikuchi. *Cinematography:* Kohei Sugiyama. *Art Direction:* Kisaku Ito. *Music:* Yasushi Akutagawa. *Costume Design:* Sanzo Wada. *Producer:* Masaichi Nagata. Videotape: Embassy, Video Yesteryear. Film Rental: Films Inc., Janus.

Kazuo Hasegawa *as Moritoh*. Machiko Kyo *Lady Kesa*. Isao Yamagata *Wataru Watanabe*. Yataro Kurokawa *Shigemori*. Kotaro Bando *Rokuro*. Jun Tazaki *Kogenta*. Koreya Senda *Kiyomori*. Tatsuya Ishiguro *Yachuta*. Kenjiro Uemura *Masanaka*. Gen Shimizu *Saburosuke*. Kikue Mohri *Sawa*.

• It is the 12th century; a period of war between rival clans. While Lord Kiyomori is away, the rival Minimoto clan starts a rebellion at the Imperial Palace. They plan on setting fire to the palace, capturing the Emperor and overthrowing the Taira Regime. In an attempt to divert the rebels' attentions, Lady Kesa is sent out by the Emperor's troops as a decoy. She is escorted by Moritoh, a brave samurai who is responsible for many clan victories.

Moritoh not only protects the Lady Kesa but also acts as a courier to bring back Lord Kiyomori. When the war has been won, Moritoh asks Lord Kiyomori for Kesa as his reward for services rendered. Although Kiyomori has promised to give Moritoh whatever he wants, Kesa is already married to Wataru. Kiyomori tries to dissuade Moritoh from his request, but Moritoh stands firm. In an attempt to resolve the dilemma, Kiyomori allows Moritoh a chance to see Kesa and persuade her to go with him. When Kesa refuses, Moritoh becomes enraged. He threatens to kill Wataru, Kesa and her aunt if she does not submit.

Kesa is now faced with an impossible dilemma. She cannot let her loved ones die, but she also cannot dishonor her husband by going with Moritoh. She finds only one way out of the situation. The night when Moritoh plans on murdering Wataru in his sleep, Kesa arranges to sleep in her husband's bed. She sacrifices herself to save her husband's life and honor, and to prevent any further killing. Moritoh kills Kesa and when he realizes what he has done, begs Wataru to kill him to put him out of his misery. But Wataru is not a vindictive man. Moritoh is so remorseful and impressed by Kesa's nobility of spirit that he becomes a monk.

• Following his acclaim as a director of unconventional films in the 1920s like *Page of Madness,* Kinugasa turned his hand to more traditional films. After World War II, he came to specialize in extravagant costume dramas as well as remakes of his earlier films.

What set *Gate of Hell* apart from its *jidai-geki* counterparts at this time was its exquisite yet subtle use of color. Using a modified Eastman-color process, *Gate of Hell* would go on to win many awards and set a standard of color use which Kinugasa later used in films like *The Snowy Heron* (1958).

Kinugasa directed *Gate of Hell* with great skill. The battle scenes are fluidly choreographed. The film is highlighted by the movement of actors and garments and the elegance of each scene's composition. He also brought out a purposefully stiff acting style from Machiko Kyo as the Lady Kesa which worked well with the almost overly-emotional style of Kazuo Hasegawa as Moritoh, the samurai who thought he could capture a woman's heart by force.

Kazuo Hasegawa, who played Moritoh, was born in Kyoto in 1908. After apprenticing as a Kabuki actor, Hasegawa joined Shochiku in 1926. He has appeared in many Kinugasa films, often receiving billing under the name "Nagamaru" or "Chojiro Hayashi." He also appeared in Mizoguchi's *A Story from Chikamatsu*. It was Hasegawa who became the center of fierce fighting between Shochiku and Toho when the later studio hired him away from the former. That year, Hasegawa was attacked by a razor-wielding Korean (later discovered to be a hired hit man) which left the actor with a scar on his left cheek. Hasegawa went on to work for Daiei and later turned to directing.

Machiko Kyo (b. 1924), who played the demure Kesa, is one of the premier actresses of Japanese films. Born in Osaka (her real name is Motoko Yamo), she has appeared in many of the classics. She played the samurai's wife in *Rashomon,* the ghost princess in *Ugetsu,* the young wife in *Odd Obsession* and has even appeared in the American production of *The Teahouse of the August Moon.* Kyo joined Daiei in 1949 after getting her start as a dancer with the Osaka Shochiku Girls' Opera in 1936. When she signed with Daiei, she underwent a makeover at the hands of producer Masaichi Nagata. In his hands, she was turned into Japan's first sexy "glamour girl." Along with Toshiro Mifune, Kyo was one of the Japanese stars best known in the West.

Very few of Kinugasa's works are known outside of Japan even though he was quite productive in the 1950s. Although he made two or three films a year, they were mostly standard melodramas and *chambaras.* After *Rashomon* (1950) and *Ugetsu* (1953), *Gate of Hell* was the next important Japanese film to receive critical acclaim and commercial success in the West. It won the Grand Prix at the Cannes Film Festival; two Academy Awards, one for Best Foreign-Language Film and one for Costume Design (Sanzo Wada); and the Best Foreign Film Award from the New York Film Critics.

Gate of Hell (Teinosuke Kinugasa, 1953). The forceful nature of Moritoh (Kazuo Hasegawa), who will take what he wants, in this case Lady Kesa (Machiko Kyo), is shown by the callused way he breaks her musical instrument to get her attention.

Tokyo Story (1953)
Tokyo monogatari

1953 / Shochiku. 139 min. B&W. *Director:* Yasujiro Ozu. *Screenplay:* Kogo Noda and Yasujiro Ozu. *Cinematography:* Yuharu Atsuta. *Art Direction:* Tatsuo Hamada. *Lighting:* Itsuo Takashita. *Music:* Kojun Saito. *Editor:* Yoshiyasu Hamamura. *Producer:* Takeshi Yamamoto. Film Rental: New Yorker. Videotape: New Yorker.

Chishu Ryu *as Shukichi Hirayama.* Chieko Higashiyama *Tomi Hirayama.* Setsuko Hara *Noriko.* So Yamamura *Koichi.* Haruko Sugimura *Shige Kaneko.* Kyoko Kagawa *Kyoko.* Kuniko Miyake *Fumiko.* Nobuo Nakamura *Kurzao Kaneko, Shige's husband.* Eijiro Tono *Sanpei Numata.* Hisao Toake *Hattori.* Shiro Osaka *Keizo.* Zen Murase *Minoru.* Mitsushiro Mori *Isamu.*

• Shukichi and Tomi Hirayama are an elderly couple who live in Onomichi, a port town near Hiroshima, with their youngest daughter, Kyoko. Because the couple is elderly, they decide to travel to Tokyo to see their other children and grandchildren. Their son, Koichi, is a busy pediatrics doctor and their daughter, Shige, runs a beauty salon. Both are too busy to visit much with their parents and feel inconvenienced by them. Noriko, the self-supporting widow of their son Shoji who was killed in the war, is the only one who manages to take a day off to show them the town. In the meantime, their own children decide to send the couple off to Atami, a hot-springs resort, rationalizing that it would be a treat for them.

The Hirayamas do not enjoy their "vacation" at the noisy spa and return to Tokyo. Inconvenienced by their early return, the children seem to have no room for their parents. Consequently, Tomi spends the night in Noriko's cramped apartment while Shukichi gets drunk with friends.

The couple decides to return to Onomichi. When Tomi falls gravely ill on the train, the couple briefly stops in Osaka where their other son, Keizo, lives. Their children are sent for, but by the time they reach Onomichi, their mother is already in a coma and dies soon afterward. Immediately after the funeral, all the children return to their own lives except for Noriko who spends a few days visiting with Kyoko. Shukichi gives Noriko Tomi's watch in recognition of the fact that she had been kinder to them on their visit than their blood children. Noriko returns to Tokyo by train, and Kyoko can hear the train's whistle from the classroom where she teaches. Shukichi now sits alone in the empty house.

• *Tokyo Story* is probably the most popular of all of Ozu's films. It is also one of the few shown outside Japan with any frequency. For many people, Ozu's reputation lies almost entirely with the viewing of this one film. Luckily, it is Ozu's best and one of his personal favorites. Except for a retrospective of Ozu's work organized by Donald Richie in the early 1960s for the Museum of Modern Art, Ozu's works are rarely seen in the West, and *Tokyo Story* only opened theatrically in New York in 1972, 19 years after its initial release. A sorry situation for what, to many critics, is the greatest of all Japanese motion pictures.

Like most Ozu films (and Japanese haiku poetry), the simplicity of the plot belies the film's depth. *Tokyo Story* continues Ozu's favorite themes of loneliness, the breakdown of tradition and authority, the disintegration of families and the rifts which can exist between the generations. Also like many of Ozu's films, there is an inherent sadness at the transience of life *(mono no aware)* which permeates the story. The Hirayamas' children did not take the time to love their parents until it was too late, and even then they quickly forgot the lesson, returning to their own self-centered worlds.

While Ozu's characters are undergoing difficult times personally, they rarely vocalize their feelings. That is one of Ozu's stylistic strengths. An audience doesn't need to be told of a character's sadness, for they have lived it with him. The last scene of *Tokyo Story* tells it all. Shukichi sits alone in a room in his empty house thinking about a life now filled with loneliness but also accepting it with a calm serenity.

Tokyo Story (Yasujiro Ozu, 1953). In an Ozu film rarely do characters sit across from one another. As in this scene with Kyoko (Kyoko Kagawa, left) and Noriko (Setsuko Hara), Ozu has his characters sit side-by-side, with his camera lens positioned at their eye level.

Chishu Ryu, who plays Shukichi, has appeared in all but two of Ozu's films. Born in 1906, Ryu joined Shochiku studios as an actor in 1925 (Ozu became director there in 1927). His first feature role was in Ozu's *I Flunked But... (Rakudai wa shita keredo,* 1930*)* and his first big role was in *College Is a Nice Place (Daigaku yoi toko,* 1936*).* Ryu has also appeared in films by Keisuke Kinoshita including *Carmen Comes Home (Karumen kokyo ni kaeru,* 1951*)* and most recently played the Buddhist priest in Juzo Itami's *The Funeral* (1984). He is a very low-key actor, perfect for Ozu's films.

Ozu's cinematic style is very unusual and very recognizable. His camera is invariably positioned at a low angle, about three feet from the floor (for this reason his sets were usually constructed with ceilings). In this way he can not only keep a scene's composition stable, but it also controls the point of view, making it similar to that of an audience at a theatre, say, or at a tea ceremony or a guest seated on a tatami mat in the home of one of his characters. His camera was not only low, but also stationary, rarely dollying, tracking or panning. He rarely used transitions indicating time lapses or location changes and rarely used fades or dissolves. His usual method of cinematic transition is to cut to a seemingly unrelated shot of buildings, shorelines or fields.

Many scenes seem static and long-lasting, and the relatively unmoving people inside them seem artificially posed. If two people are talking, they are often seated side by side facing in the same direction. Characters and locations are repeated frequently through a picture fostering a feeling of familiarity which leads to identification. Dialogue, while polished in Ozu's script, nonetheless still sounds as if it is natural conversation and thus carries on the feeling and significance of everyday life.

This film is Ozu at his best. *Tokyo Story* is an extremely moving and powerful film presented in a masterfully understated and economical manner.

Wild Geese (1953)
Gan

1953 / Daiei. / a.k.a. "Mistress." 104 min. B&W. *Director:* Shiro Toyoda. *Screenplay:* Masashige Narusawa. *Adaptation:* From the novel by Ogai Mori. *Cinematography:* Mitsuo Miura. *Supervising Art Director:* Kisaku Ito. *Art Director:* Takeo Kimura. *Music:* Ikuma Dan. *Lighting:* Tsurekichi Shibata. *Editor:* Masanori Tsuji. *Producer:* Yuji Hirao and Kenji Kuroiwa. Videotape: Embassy. Film Rental: Films Inc., Janus.

Hideko Takamine *as Otama.* Hiroshi Akutagawa *Okada.* Eijiro Tono *Suezo the moneylender.* Jukichi Uno *Kimura, Okada's friend.* Choko Iida *Osan.* Eiza Tanaka *Zenso, Otama's father.* Kumeko Urabe *Otsune, Suezo's wife.* Miko Odagiri *Oume, Otama's maid.* Kuniko Miuake *Osada, the sewing mistress.*

• Otama, a young and beautiful woman, lives in poverty with her ailing father who sells candy from a pushcart. She has already made one mistake in her life when she lived with a man who, unbeknownst to her, was already married and had a child. When she found out, Otama tried to kill herself.

As a way out of her poverty, an old lady arranges for Otama to become the mistress of a dry goods widower who owns a store in Hamacho. Otama and her father meet the widower, Suezo, at Matsugen where there is also a student party going on. Before meeting Otama, Suezo goes to the students' party to collect on money he has loaned to Okada Ishihara, a handsome medical student. In reality, Suezo is not a drygoods store owner but a money lender. He is also not a widower but has a shrewish wife and children. The old lady has lied in order to have her own debt with Suezo canceled.

Wild Geese **(Shiro Toyoda, 1953). Using nature to parallel a film's mood or story is typical of Japanese films. In Toyoda's sad tale of Otama's (Hideko Takamine, left) unrequited love for Okada (Hiroshi Akutagawa) there is a beautiful final scene of two wild geese.**

One of Suezo's clients is a poor woman, Oshige, with five children who supports herself by selling kimono goods. She pays off part of her debt with cloth she doesn't own. Suezo doesn't care, as long as he gets paid. He was once a school janitor, bossed around by students, who saved his money and opened a business. Suezo puts Otama and her father in new but separate houses. Otama's house is next door to the sewing mistresses. Otama first discovers something is wrong with her relationship with Suezo when a fish seller won't sell fish to Oume, her maid, because she works for the mistress of a usurer. Later, Suezo lets slip about his wife. Vowing never to be fooled again, Otama seeks a degree of independence by learning to sew from her neighbor.

One day, while walking in the rain, Otama meets a woman with an umbrella identical to her own. She guesses that it belongs to Suezo's wife, Otsune. The other woman recognizes the material Otama's kimono is made out of as that which Oshige used to pay on her loan. Oshige is now reduced to being a streetwalker.

On her way home, Otama discovers Okada playing with a pet bird Suezo has given her. They are immediately attracted to each other. Later Okada saves the bird by killing a snake attacking it. Otama invites him in to wash his hands. As he leaves, it starts to rain and Otama runs after him and lends him an umbrella. She follows him only to find that he has gone to Suezo's place of business for a loan.

If Okada passes his exams, he can become the assistant to a German doctor and study in Europe. Suezo only finds him half of the money he needs so Okada sells his medical book. Otama purchases back the book and plans on giving it to him when he returns her umbrella. When he does come to Otama's, Suezo also drops in. Suezo is suspicious, and now Okada knows who Otama's patron is. On an evening when Suezo is supposed to be out of town, Otama prepares a special thank-you dinner for Okada. When he passes by, however, it is an uncomfortable moment in which nothing is said and he continues on with his friend. They are on their way to a farewell party; Okada is going to Germany.

In an attempt to catch her with Okada, Suezo unexpectedly shows up at her house. Although Okada is not there, Otama's interest in him is obvious. She fights with Suezo and tells him she won't be in bondage to him any more. She runs off after Okada only to see him riding off into the fog with the German doctor. Sadly, she wanders to a nearby pond and watches as one of two wild geese takes off and flies away.

• Shiro Toyoda (1906–1977) was born in Kyoto and originally wanted to become a playwright. After being encouraged to write screenplays by director Eizo Tanaka, he entered Shochiku Studios in 1925 as a screenwriter and as an assistant to Yasujiro Shimazu whose original assistant, Heinosuke Gosho, had been promoted to director. In 1936 he moved with many other ex–Shochiku people to the independent company of Tokyo Hassei Eiga. There Toyoda made *Young People* (1937) which was a commercial hit. In 1941 the small company failed. Toyoda later joined forces with Heinosuke Gosho and cameraman Mitsuo Miura to form Studio Eight Productions which was terminated in 1954 and turned out Gosho's *Where Chimneys Are Seen.*

Wild Geese is a melancholy tale of a love which can never happen. The beautiful black and white cinematography of Mitsuo Miura, with whom Toyoda would often work, greatly enhanced the late 1800s period atmosphere of the film. For many critics, *Wild Geese* is considered among the best *Meiji-monos*. Many of his screen images linger in the memory just as do the plots steeped in *mono no aware*. When Otama and Otsune meet in the rain, their spiral-patterned umbrellas are seen from above; as Otama follows Okada, a single pagoda is reflected in a rain puddle; when Otama realizes her one chance at true love has just left in a carriage, it is symbolized by the lone goose flying off into the night. (Expressing emotions through nature is a compelling and beautiful tradition in Japanese films.)

Toyoda is known as an actor's director. This is probably partially due to his early desire to work in the theatre and partly because he chooses stories with but a few main characters, casting each one with great care.

Reluctant to dissipate spontaneity on rehearsals, Toyoda allows his actors freedom with just a hint of careful direction. Much of the poignancy of *Wild Geese* is directly attributable to the performance of Hideko Takamine whose acting is as controlled as is the life of the woman she is portraying.

Many of Toyoda's films are about women and the freedom (or lack of same) which they usually sacrifice because of the demands of a society which traditionally limits them. While Toyoda doesn't openly promote an end to these traditions, which usually stifle the young, he does manage to elicit a great deal of sympathy for them. Hideko Takamine as Otama turned in a touching performance; Hiroshi Akutagawa's understated Okada also adds depth to the film. The son of the famous author Ryunosuke Akutagawa who wrote *Rashomon*, Hiroshi is a celebrated stage actor whose talents transferred well to the screen in such films as *Where Chimneys Are Seen* and Inagaki's 1958 *Rickshaw Man*. Although he has made few films, those parts he has undertaken he infuses with quiet strength and intelligence.

Sansho the Bailiff (1954)
Sansho dayu

1954 / Daiei. 132 min. B&W. *Director:* Kenji Mizoguchi. *Screenplay:* Yoshikata Yoda and Fuji Yahiro. *Adaptation:* From the novel by Ogai Mori. *Cinematography:* Kazuo Miyagawa. *Art Direction:* Hiromoto Ito. *Lighting:* Kenichi Okamoto. *Music:* Fumio Hayasaka. *Sound:* Iwao Otani. *Editor:* Mitsuji Miyata. *Producer:* Masaichi Nagata. Videotape: Sony. Film Rental: Filmic Archives/Reel Images, Balzac, Films Inc., Kit Parker.

Yoshiaki Hanayagi *as Zushio*. Kyoko Kagawa *Anju*. Kinuyo Tanaka *Tamaki, their mother*. Eitaro Shindo *Sansho*. Akitake Kono *Taro*. Masao Shimizu *Taira no Masauji, their father*. Ken Mitsuda *Prime Minister Fujiwara no Mitsuzane*. Chieko Naniwa *Ubatake*. Kasuhito Okuni *Normiura*. Kimiko Tachibana *Namiji*. Ichiro Sugai *Nio*. Masahiko Kato *Zushio as a boy*. Naoki Fujima *Zushio as a little boy*. Keiko Enami *Anju as a girl*. Ryosuke Kagawa *Donmo*. Kanji Koshiba *Kuranosuke Koto*. Shinobu Araki *Satao*. Reiko Kongo *Shiono, the maidservant*. Shozo Nabu *Taira no Masatomo*. Ryonosuke Higashi *Manager of the brothel*. Bontaro Miake *Yoshitsugu*. Sabaura Date *Kanahira*. Sachiko Aima *Sugano*. Sachio Horikita *Jiro Sako*. Hachiro Okuni *Saburo Miyazaki*. Ikkei Tamaki *Peacekeeping officer*

Masayoshi Kikuno *Jailer.* Sumao Ishihara *Old graveyard keeper.* Tomino-
suke Hayama *Old priest.*

● In 11th century Japan, Tamaki, her daughter Anju, her son Zushio
and the family's old nursemaid walk through a forest remembering the
events seven years earlier which have caused them to live in exile. Their
husband/father was the governor of the province and supported the
masses in their battle against feudal corruption by refusing to have more
soldiers sent to his area. Their presence would mean further hardship for
his peasants. As a consequence of refusing orders from higher up, Taira no
Masauji is sent into exile. Just before he leaves, he gives his son a family
heirloom, a statue of the goddess of mercy, and tells him to remember
that "without mercy, a man is a beast. Be sympathetic to others. Men are
created equal and everyone is entitled to happiness."

When Tamaki and her children camp in a secluded area of the forest,
the nurse, Ubatake, tries to find them hot food and lodging. An old nun
comes upon the family in the forest and offers them food and a place to
stay. The next morning, however, the nun has betrayed them to robbers
who drown Ubatake and kidnap Tamaki to the far island of Sado. Anju
and Zushio are sold to the notorious bailiff Sansho who runs the minister
of justice's manor in Tango. Like many manors of this period it uses slave
labor to work the land, and Sansho's cruel and ruthless methods have made
the manor very productive. When Sansho's son, Taro, who loathes the
labor camp, hears the children's story he is so upset that he leaves home.

After ten years working for the manor, Zushio has abandoned his
father's credo. Now he works as one of Sansho's overseers and is as cruel as
Sansho, uncaringly branding the forehead of an escaped slave, for example. One day Anju hears a new slave girl from the island of Sado singing a
sad song with the refrain, "Zushio, Anju, where are you?" She demands to
know where she heard this song and, while listening to it, their mother's
fate is told.

On Sado Island, Tamaki had been turned into a prostitute named
Nakagami. One day she tried to escape but was caught and her heel ten-
dons cut as punishment and to keep her from trying to escape again.

When one of Anju's friends, an old woman, Namiji, is dying, Zushio
is told by Sansho to dump her in the forest. Anju convinces Zushio to at
least make a shelter for her friend. As the two collect branches and grass,
they remember that day camping in the forest. Suddenly Zushio proposes
that they run away. Anju, however, realizes that she must stay behind to
keep the guards at bay. Zushio escapes carrying Namiji and finds refuge in
a mountain temple where he finds Taro. Anju, in the meantime, has
delayed the guards as long as possible and then, to escape Sansho's
wrathful torture to discover where Zushio has gone, peacefully commits
suicide by drowning herself in a pond.

disgrace, but it is soon apparent that he is cosmetically sacrificing his rank in order to impersonate a monk and save a kidnapped child. Takeshi Shimura's heroic Kambei is in stark contrast to his incredibly moving Watanabe in *Ikiru* and it is to Shimura's and Kurosawa's credit that both characters are equally believable. Kambei's relationship to Katsushiro, that of master/disciple or teacher/pupil, is one often emphasized by Kurosawa. It appears as early as *Sanshiro Sugata* and forms the core of *Read Beard*. This is the way the skill and the code of the samurai is passed on, it is also the way people learn to be accomplished and humane.

As much a hallmark as Kurosawa's humaneness is the technical expertise he brings to his films. The unselfconscious acting was greatly aided by the use of the telephoto lens, a rarity at the time, which not only removed the camera from the actors but also managed to throw the viewer into the midst of the battle scenes. This was also the first film in which Kurosawa used a multi-camera technique. By filming the uninterrupted action from several vantage points he was able to sustain the continuity and level of performance then later reconstruct the action scene-by-scene in the editing room. It is in the editing that Kurosawa really controls the intensely fast pace for which *Seven Samurai* is known. (It has often been noted that Kurosawa only photographs so as to have something to edit.)

While one remembers distinct scenes, like framed pictures, from a film like Mizoguchi's *Ugetsu*, one will recall *Seven Samurai* for scenes which overflow with movement. Through tight editing, Kurosawa also manages to compact events. When the farmer, Rikichi, throws himself at Kambei's feet to ask for his help the film would be slowed down by a retelling of village problems. Instead, Kurosawa films it thus: Rikichi: "Please." Wipe to medium shot inside the farmer's inn where they are seated, heads bowed and Kambei is staring through the window at the street. Kambei: "No, it's impossible." In four words and just several seconds, Kurosawa has told all.

It should be no wonder that *Seven Samurai* won a silver prize at the Venice Film Festival in 1954, the Academy Award for Best Foreign Film in 1955 and, like *Ugetsu*, frequently shows up on ten-best film lists.

A Story from Chikamatsu (1954)
Chikamatsu monogatari

1954 / Daiei. / a.k.a. "The Crucified Lovers." 102 min. B&W. *Director:* Kenji Mizoguchi. *Screenplay:* Yoshikata Yoda. *Adaptation:* From Matsutaro Kawaguchi's

adaptation of Monzaemon Chikamatsu's *Bunraku* play "Daikyoji Sekireki."
Cinematography: Kazuo Miyagawa. *Art Direction:* Hiroshi Mizutani.
Lighting: Kenichi Okamoto. *Music:* Fumio Hayasaka. *Sound:* Iwao Otani.
Editor: Kanji Sugawara. *Producer:* Masaichi Nagata.

Kazuo Hasegawa *as Mohei*. Kyoko Kagawa *Osan*. Yoko Minamida
Otama, the servant. Eitaro Shindo *Ishun*. Sakae Ozawa *Sukeemon*. Ichiro
Sugai *Genbee*. Haruo Tanaka *Doki*. Chieko Naniwa *Oko*. Tatsuya Ishiguro
Isan. Kimiko Tachibana *Umetatsu Akamatsu*. Hisao Toake *Chamberlain
Morinokoji*. Shinobu Araki *Nobleman's major-domo*. Koichi Katsuragi
Priest. Hiroshi Mizuno *Kuroki, the Chief State Councilor*. Ikkei Tamaki
Jushiro Umegaki. Keiko Koyanago *Okaya*. Kanai Kobayashi *Otatsu*. Shiro
Miura *Worker*. Nobuko Tanei *Little girl*. Soji Shibata *Worker*. Tadashi
Iwata *Chushichi*. Ichiro Amano *Blind musician*. Seishiro Hara *Dock
worker*. Sachio Horikita *Dock worker*. Reiko Kongo *Boat maidservant*.
Sumai Ishihara *Innkeeper*. Shiro Osaki *Chestnut seller*. Midori Komatsu
Old lady of the tea house. Jun Fujikawa *Village official*. Fumihiko
Yokoyama *Village chieftain*.

• The time is 1683, the place Kyoto. Ishun is a court printer who has
landed the very desirable contract to print the ruler's calendars. This job is
supervised by Mohei, Ishun's designer. Mohei is very ill, partly from a cold
and partly from exhaustion. He is tended by Otama, a house servant who
is in love with him. The beautiful Osan, whose family is in dire need of
money, has been married to the rich Ishun. Her worthless brother, Doki,
comes to Osan asking for a large sum of money as does her mother, Oko.
They have three days to pay off debts and the house mortgage to save the
family name.

Ishun tries to seduce Otama but she falsely claims to be engaged to
Mohei, who later tells her he cannot go along with her ruse. Ishun is a very
hard man and refuses to help Osan's family by lending them money.
Mohei, however, who is secretly in love with Osan, overheard her conversation with her brother and offers to try and help her. When Mohei asks
Ishun for the seal to stamp some receipts, he, at the same time, secretly
stamps a blank page which he will use to obtain the money Osan needs.
His deed is soon discovered by Sukeemon, Ishun's overseer, who, instead
of reporting him to Ishun, demands a share of the money. Mohei, a very
good person, confesses everything to Ishun. Immediately Osan and Otama
beg Ishun for mercy for Mohei. Otama even tells Ishun that Mohei was
stealing the money to buy her out of servitude. Ishun believes this and
locks Mohei in a storeroom.

When Osan thanks Otama for lying to save her family, Otama tells
her of Ishun's attempts to seduce her. One night Osan tries to catch her
husband in adultery by changing bedrooms with Otama. Her plan runs
into terrible trouble, however, when Mohei, who has escaped, comes to see

A Story from Chikamatsu (Kenji Mizoguchi, 1954). Ishun (Eitaro Shindo) spies on his wife Osan (Kyoko Kagawa) while she is in the company of Mohei (Kazuo Hasegawa) in a tale that attacks not only the inhumanity of feudal society but also the emerging power of the merchant class.

Otama. He is soon followed by Ishun who accuses Osan of being Mohei's mistress. Mohei escapes and when Osan is given a knife by the hypocritical Ishun so she can commit the honorable act of seppuku, she too runs away. When Mohei comes across her in the streets, he agrees to take her with him to Osaka. The two travel incognito but in complete propriety.

In the meantime, Ishun has tried to cover up the entire situation and is basking in praise from the court for his calendar. When noblemen come to him for loans, he is unable to refuse them because of his new and slightly precarious standing at court. Isan, one of Ishun's rival printers, has learned of Mohei and Osan's running away. Isan approached Sukeemon with a proposition. A samurai whose wife becomes involved in an illicit love affair is put in the position of either killing them or losing his ranking and assets. If Sukeemon could help Isan catch Mohei and Osan together and prove that Ishun was concealing the situation, the court would take away his business and Isan would get it. He in turn would make Sukeemon the proprietor of Ishun's shop.

Mohei and Osan are almost captured on the road and are starting to believe there is no hope for them. As a consequence, they decide to commit suicide. They take a boat out onto Lake Biwa where Mohei binds

Osan's legs. Before she is set into the lake, though, Mohei finally confesses his love for her. As she collapses in his arms, her will to live is renewed. They become lovers on the run, pursued by Sukeemon. Eventually they make their way to Mohei's father's house in a remote area. The old man reluctantly lets them stay in a hut on his property. Soon the couple are discovered and, with Mohei being turned over to his father's custody, Osan is returned to Kyoto. There she "recovers" at her mother's, refusing to return to Ishun.

Mohei runs away from his father and makes his way back to Kyoto. He goes to Osan's house to find her but while her mother pleads with him to leave, Osan's worthless brother reports them to Ishun. When Ishun's men arrive, the two are gone. If they cannot live together, they will die together. They will commit *shinju,* double suicide. By the next day the two are again recaptured. Because Ishun has been covering up their affair his assets are confiscated and he is banished. As is the custom of the day, the two lovers are bound together and led through the town to a site where they will be crucified.

• Mizoguchi's approach to film is almost always a literary one. Something he reads will inspire him and from it will be born one of his films. In the case of *A Story from Chikamatsu,* the origins are in a story by one of Japan's most famous dramatists, Monzaemon Chikamatsu. His 17th century writings have formed the foundations for many Japanese films including Masahiro Shinoda's similar *Double Suicide* (1969).

The story's theme of tragic love is typical of Mizoguchi's attraction to those characters (especially women) who have been wronged and suffer the consequences of what to him was an unjust society. The stifling morality and traditions of feudal Japan are favored targets for Mizoguchi's filmic ire and *A Story from Chikamatsu* is possibly the best illustration of this protest.

Although Mohei and Osan are social "criminals," Mizoguchi endows them with a high level of dignity and nobility. Yet while pity is the emotion one might expect these characters to elicit, in reality it is something more akin to respect. While one might sympathize with them for the society in which they are trapped, their love seems to transcend it. For the Japanese, the suicide for love *(shinju)* they want to commit is considered one of the highest forms of protest allowed against constraining laws and traditions. It is also a manifestation of the highest form of spiritual bonding the lovers can achieve.

A Story from Chikamatsu attacks both the ruling class and the merchant class. Ishun exploits his employees and treats them unfairly. The ruling class takes advantage of their position of power over Ishun to borrow money from him and then eagerly justifies condemning him so they can cancel their debts and confiscate his assets. For Mizoguchi, money has replaced virtue and consequently the truly virtuous are condemned. Among Japanese critics, *A Story from Chikamatsu* is perhaps Mizoguchi's best-liked film. While it did not win the Western accolades that *Ugetsu* and *Life of Oharu* did, it was awarded the prestigious art recognition citation from the Japanese Ministry of Education.

Twenty-Four Eyes (1954)
Nijushi no hitomi

1954 / Shochiku. 154 min. B&W. *Director:* Keisuke Kinoshita. *Screenplay:* Keisuke Kinoshita. *Adaptation:* From the novel by Sakae Tsuboi. *Cinematography:* Hiroyuki Kusuda. *Art Direction:* Kimihiko Nakamura. *Music:* Chuji Kinoshita. Videotape: Sony. Film Rental: Films Inc., Janus.

Hideko Takamine *as Hisako Oishi.* Eisei Amamoto *Hisako's husband.* Shizue Natsukawa *Hisako's mother.* Chishu Ryu *Teacher.* Toyo Takahashi *Woman teacher.* Ushio Akashi *Schoolmaster.* Takahiro Tamura *Isokichi Isoda.* Hideki Goko *Isokichi in lower class.* Hitobumi Goko *Isokichi in upper class.* Rei Miura *Takeichi Takeshita.* Yukio Watanabe *Takeichi in lower class.* Shiro Watanabe *Takeichi in upper class.* Yasukuni Toida *Yoshitsugu Tokuda.* Makoto Miyagawa *Yoshitsugu in lower class.* Jun'ichi Miyagawa *Yoshitsugu in upper class.* Giichi Otsuki *Tadashi Morioka.* Takero Terashita *Tadashi in lower class.* Takaaki Terashita *Tadashi in upper class.* Tatsuo Shimizu *Jinta Aizawa.* Kunio Sato *Jinta in lower class.* Takeshi Sato *Jinta in upper class.* Yumeji Tsukioka *Masuno Kagawa.* Hiroko Ishii *Masuno in lower class.* Shisako Ishii *Masuno in upper class.* Toyoko Shinohara *Misako Nishiguchi.* Yasuyo Koike *Misako in lower class.* Akiko Koike *Misako in upper class.* Kuniko Ikawa *Matsue Kawamoto.* Setsuko Kusano *Matsue in lower class.* Sadako Kusano *Matsue in upper class.* Toshiko Kobayashi *Sanae Yamaishi.* Kaoko Kase *Sanae in lower class.* Kayoko Kase *Sanae in upper class.* Yumiko Tanabe *Kotsuru Kabe in lower class.* Naoko Tanabe *Kotsuru Kabe in upper class.* Ikuko Kambara *Fujiko Yamashita in lower class.* Toyoko Ozu *Fujiko Yamashita in upper class.* Yoshiko Nagai *Kotoe Katagiri.* Hiroko Uehara *Kotoe in lower class.* Masako Uehara *Kotoe in upper class.*

• Hisako Oishi is the new first-grade teacher at the local school on the island of Shodoshima in 1928. The students attend the first through fourth grades at this school before going off to the consolidated school for fifth

Twenty-Four Eyes (Keisuke Kinoshita, 1954). Miss Oishi (Hideko Takamine, center) stands among the 12 students (or 24 eyes) of her class as Kinoshita tellingly traces the children's story from prewar to postwar Japan. (Photo courtesy of Shochiku Co., Ltd.)

grade. Miss Oishi must travel nine miles from her home to school and does so most economically on a bicycle. Her bicycle, however, along with her Western style suit, makes her the object of gossip among the provincial islanders.

There are 12 students in Miss Oishi's class, and her friendly manner easily wins them over. One day, while at the beach, Miss Oishi falls into a hole some of her students dug in the sand. As a result her tendon is cut and she must stay at home to recuperate. The students, not realizing how long a walk nine miles is, decide to slip off and visit her. Soon, however, they begin to get tired and hungry and a few start to cry. When Miss Oishi returns from the doctors, she sees them from the bus, takes them home and gives them something to eat. She sends them home by bus but first the class has a picture taken on the beach.

Miss Oishi's leg will take a long time to heal and reluctantly she transfers to the closer consolidated school where she will be waiting for her students when they get to the fifth grade. Five years pass by. The Japanese have started their Pacific war campaign, Miss Oishi has gotten married and several of Miss Oishi's students, who are now in the sixth grade, have also started to face the problems of adulthood. One girl, Matsue, has to drop out to take care of her baby sister after her mother dies. When the baby, too, dies, she is sent off to live with relatives. Another student, Fujiko, whose family once were prominent in the village but are now bankrupt, will also soon move away.

Most of Miss Oishi's boys want to be soldiers because they think it will

used near the Marshall Islands. Tanaka's film was to feature a giant octopus. It was given the working title of *The Big Monster from 20,000 Miles Beneath the Sea* until someone suggested it be named after a burly man on the set nicknamed Gojira (a combination of "gorilla" and "kujira" or whale).

The monster, as sketched by Iwao Mori, soon became a hybrid of a prehistoric Tyrannosaurus and an Allosaurus with a dragon-like set of plates along its spine. The monster's special effects were turned over to Eiji Tsuburaya, the Ray Harryhousen of Japanese film. Inspired by *King Kong,* Tsuburaya (1901–1970) constructed two rubber suits which were worn alternately by Haruo Nakajima or Tetsuka Katsumi. (Nakajima would go on to play Gojira in at least 11 sequels.) Their scenes were filmed at high speed to achieve a slow-motion-like effect. Besides men in suits, Gojira was also represented by half-suits (a set of legs worn like pants on suspenders), a "radiation" breathing puppet head and torso, and a small-scale full-length remote control puppet used for long shots. Gojira's distinctive roar was the result of running a pair of rough leather gloves over a string bass. Beside special effects, another technical factor which should be singled out for mention is the elegantly haunting music of Akira Ifukube. In many scenes this is what helped to make *Godzilla* more than just the horror film some people view it as. Ifukube was also responsible for the music in *Harp of Burma, Night Drum, Buddha* and *Sandakan 8.*

The original *Gojira* took approximately six months to complete and cost about 30 times more than the average Japanese film of the time. Of course, it also broke all box office records during its premiere. It was this success which caused Toho to cash in and churn out 16 Godzilla sequels (although in later reincarnations Godzilla, having become a folk hero to the Japanese, protects instead of attacks the island nation) and a cornucopia of science fiction and fantasy films over the next 15 or so years. Most of these films, although directed by someone other than Honda, were actually controlled by Tsuburaya who, in 1963, started his own special production company.

The titles of these monster flicks have become staples of the television movie matinees and late night showings. *Rodan, Mothra, Ghidrah, Veran, Gamera,* and 1968's epic *Destroy All Monsters* which featured Rodan, Spiga, Manda, Mothra, Godzilla and his son Minya (in another movie he has a son named Godzooki!) peacefully living on Monster Island until Ghidrah shows up to set them off on a worldwide stampede. Also of interest is 1962's *King Kong vs. Godzilla,* in which King Kong emerges victorious in the versions released in Europe and America,

Godzilla (Inoshiro Honda, 1954). The special effects of Eiji Tsuburaya may look primitive by today's standards, but in their day they proved to be the equal of anything achieved by Hollywood. (Photo courtesy of Toho Co., Ltd.)

and Godzilla in the Japanese release. The cycle of monster movies petered out when production costs finally surpassed box office receipts.

King Kong vs. Godzilla was not the only time a Gojira movie was changed for American consumption. Eighteen months after *Gojira* premiered in Japan, Joseph E. Levine bought the film (reportedly for less than $20,000) and hired director Terry Morse to shoot additional footage and re-edit the film so that not only was it dubbed but also had all-new scenes containing Raymond Burr's character. All Burr's scenes were shot in a studio in one day. When prepublicity for the American distribution started, the title was mistranslated and changed giving it a more reptilian sound to Occidental ears. (The original Japanese version of *Gojira* was not released in the United States until the summer of 1982.)

Another very important change between *Gojira* and *Godzilla* was that the original theme of the dangers of nuclear weapons was de-emphasized. *Gojira* is more than just the product of indiscriminate use of nuclear technology; it also kills randomly and dispassionately, just as did the two bombs dropped on Hiroshima and Nagasaki. Even in its altered form, the Japanese attitude towards the atomic power unleashed on them is obvious. As is often the case in Japan's monster films, the creature is the result of nuclear reactions and is defeated by the unselfish work of a Japanese scientist. In many of these films—especially in those of a later cycle when the threats come from outer space—Japan seems to play the part of peacemaker. In 1985 producer Tanaka decided to dust off his prehistoric creation and made *Godzilla 1985*, a terrible retread of the original. It was directed by Kohji Hashimoto and even went so far as to have Raymond Burr make another "inserted" repeat appearance for American audiences, who also had a chance to enjoy Godzilla rampaging through New York City in Dr. Pepper commercials on television. Godzilla, or Gojira if you prefer, has attained the status of Mickey Mouse in Japan. Even today, it often makes appearances at store openings and is still heavily merchandised.

Director Inoshiro Honda (b. 1911) graduated from the arts department of Nippon University and entered the PCL Studios in 1933. He worked as a second assistant director under Yamamoto, and Yamamoto's first assistant director, Akira Kurosawa. Honda went on to work with Kurosawa doing second-unit shooting on *Stray Dogs* and later as production director on *Kagemusha* and *Ran*.

Of all the actors in *Godzilla*, Takashi Shimura is the one with the most recognizable and legitimate claim to fame. A member of Akira Kurosawa's often used group of actors, Shimura also starred in *The Seven Samurai, Rashomon, Yojimbo,* and the heart-breaking *Ikiru*.

Samurai (Trilogy) (1954–1955)
Miyamoto Musashi; Ichijoji no ketto; Ketto Ganryujima)

1954–1955 / Toho. Part I: Samurai; Part II: Duel at Ichijoji Temple; Part III: Duel on Genryu Island, a.k.a. "Musashi and Kojiro." 92 min. (Part I), 104 min. (Part II), 105 min. (Part III). Color. *Director:* Hiroshi Inagaki. *Screenplay:* Tokuhei Wakao and Hiroshi Inagaki. *Adaptation:* From Hideji Hojo's adaptation of Eiji Yoshikawa's novel *Miyamoto Musashi. Cinematography:* Jun Yasumoto (Parts I and II), Kazuo Yamada (Part III). *Art Direction:* Makoto Sono (Parts I and II), Hiroshi Ueda and Kisaku Ito (Part III). *Lighting:* Shigeru Mori (Parts I and II), Tsuruzo Nishikawa (Part III). *Music:* Ikuma Dan. *Sound:* Choshichiro Mikami (Parts I and II), Masanobu Miyazaki (Part III). *Producer:* Kazuo Takimura. Videotape: Embassy. Film Rental: Films Inc., Janus.

Toshiro Mifune *as Musashi Miyamoto (Takezo).* Rentaro Mikuni *Matahachi (played by Sachio Sakao in Part II).* Kaoru Yachigusa *Otsu.* Mariko Okada *Akemi.* Kuroemon Onoe *Priest Takuan.* Mitsuko Mito *Okoh, Matahachi's mother.* Eiko Miyoshi *Osugi.* Koji Tsurata *Sasaki Kojiro.* Akihiko Hirata *Seijuro.* Yu Fujiko *Denshichiro.* Daisuke Kato *Toji.* Ko Mihashi *Koetsu.* Kenjin Iida *Jotaro.* Michiyo Kogure *Yoshino Dayu.*

• **Part I:** In 1600 Takezo and Matahachi watch armies parade through their village of Miyamoto as they go off to war. Takezo dreams of a soldier's glory and decides to join the army. Matahachi, who must take care of his mother and is engaged to the orphaned Otsu, shouldn't go, but he sneaks off anyway. At the great battle of Sekigahara, Takezo and Matahachi are not fighting but digging a ditch. When their troops are routed, they do not run, but stay to fight. When the battle is over, Matahachi is wounded.

The two men take refuge in the house of Oko and her daughter Akemi. Oko's husband has been killed and the two women live by stripping dead samurai of their possessions. As Matahachi heals he falls in love with Akemi, but she has fallen in love with the wild Takezo. When brigands attack Oko they are defeated by Takezo. Oko makes a play for Takezo but he runs away. Oko tells Matahachi, however, that he tried to rape her. Matahachi then leaves with Oko and Akemi, eventually marrying Oko.

Takezo tries to return to Miyamoto, but when guards attempt to stop him, he ends up killing one. The officials recruit villagers to go into the hills and look for him and his relatives are arrested as their hostages. The villagers are unsuccessful, but a priest, Takuan, goes into the mountains with Otsu. There Takezo is attracted to the aromas of Takuan's cooking food and Otsu's calming bamboo flute music. The priest captures Takezo and takes him back to Miyamoto but, recognizing Takezo's exceptional abilities, refuses to turn him over to the authorities. Takezo is bound and hoisted high into a tree where the priest lectures him and lets him think about his ways.

Otsu's heart goes out to Takezo and she lets him down from the tree. They run away briefly, but Otsu is captured and taken to Himeji Castle. When the priest offers to take Takezo to Otsu, he tricks him and locks him in a room filled with books. Three years pass and through the priest's intervention, Takezo is to begin moral training for service to Himeji Castle. In recognition of his new samurai status, he is named Musashi Miyamoto. Musashi sets out to travel and train himself for service. As he crosses the Hanada bridge, he sees Otsu, who has been working nearby just to watch for him. Otsu goes to collect her possessions in order to travel with him, but when she returns to the bridge, Takezo is gone. Scratched into the bridge rail is written "forgive me."

Part II: Musashi Miyamoto has been traveling the countryside with a young boy, Jotaro, whose parents died during the great battle of Sekigahara. He is searching for knowledge and skill. He fights a duel with Old Baiken who uses a chain and sickle. Although he wins, a priest tells him that he is strong, but not mentally relaxed and is not a samurai yet. For the samurai, swordsmanship means chivalry.

In Kyoto, the capital city of medieval Japan, Akemi lives with Matahachi and Oko and is to be offered to Seijuro, the heir of the famed Yoshioka family, in exchange for money. Akemi is not happy about this since she is in love with Musashi. One day she meets Otsu who is selling fans by a bridge waiting for Musashi. Without realizing both are in love with the same man, they talk about how they hope to see their samurai again.

Musashi, trying to make a name for himself, has called upon the Yoshioka school of swordfighters, asking to duel the master, Seijuro. Seijuro is not there so Musashi leaves a challenge to meet at the Sanju bridge. At the bridge, however, Musashi, whose skill has impressed and scared the pupils of the Yoshioka school, is ambushed by Seijuro's men. Musashi wins the battle while another accomplished, unemployed samurai looks on, Sasaki Kojiro.

Denshichiro Yoshioka, Seijuro's brother, seeking to cleanse the family name of his brother's cowardly act, duels with Musashi in the Rengein Temple yard and is killed. In the meantime, Seijuro, who has raped Akemi, now buys her from her mother Oko and Oko's companion, Toji. With his brother's death, it becomes his turn to meet Musashi at five in the morning at the lone pine treees of the Ichijoji temple. However, Seijuro's men keep him from the battle and again ambush Musashi. With the

Samurai (Trilogy) (Hiroshi Inagaki, 1954-1955). Musashi Miyamoto (Toshiro Mifune, right) starts out Inagaki's trilogy as a brash young man searching for glory, but by the third part he has discovered the "true way" of the samurai. (Photo courtesy of Toho Co., Ltd.)

odds eighty to one and with Seijuro's men even using bows and arrows and guns against him, Musashi still wins even though he is wounded. When Seijuro finally shows up, Musashi easily defeats him. As he is about to deliver the death blow, Musashi remembers the many people who have tried to temper his strength. As a result, he does not kill Seijuro and walks away. Otsu finds Musashi and cares for him. When he is healed, he makes an abrupt pass at her. Otsu is flustered and pushes him away. Hurt, Musashi walks off renouncing the love of women.

Part III: Sasaki Kojiro is unhappy because his vast talents have gone unrecognized while those of Musashi have become legendary. In Edo, the shogun's political and military headquarters, Kojiro performs a swordfight for the shogun to try to win an appointment with him. Although he wins the duel, he cripples his opponent, which is not looked upon favorably. After Kojiro skillfully kills four swordsmen of the Obana school, Musashi finds and takes them back to the school for burial. The disgraced Obana master, however, refuses their bodies. Musashi buries them and while in the cemetery meets Kojiro. Kojiro challenges Musashi but he is put off until the next evening. While eating later that day, Musashi and Jotaro's meal is disrupted by the loud gambling in the next room. When Jotaro tells them to be quiet, Kumagoro, a tough horse dealer, tries to pick a fight with Musashi. When he sees the samurai removing live flies

Floating Clouds (Mikio Naruse, 1955). The disillusionment of love within postwar Japan is the theme of Naruse's story of Tomioka (Masayuki Mori, left) and Yukiko (Hideko Takamine). (Photo courtesy of Toho Co., Ltd.)

Hideko Takamine *as Yukiko Koda*. Masayuki Mori *Kengo Tomioka*. Mariko Okada *Osei Mukai*. Daisuke Kato *Sekichi Mukai, Osei's husband*. Cheiko Nakakita *Kuniko Tomioka, Kengo's wife*. Isao Yamagata *Sugio Iba*. Akira Sera *Kinasku Ohta*. Roy H. James *American soldier*. Mayuri Mokusho *Bar girl*.

• In November of 1946 Yukiko Koda, who had served as a clerk in a forestry camp in Indochina during World War II, is repatriated back to Japan. After she disembarks from the ship, she wanders aimlessly. She has no family and no real place to go. Before the war she had lived with her ex-brother-in-law, but he had sexually abused her. She searches out Tomioka, the forestry boss she had worked under during the war. The two had an affair, and Tomioka had promised to divorce his wife after the war. At Tomioka's home, however, the door is answered by his wife.

Tomioka and Yukiko go to a hotel and make love. Tomioka has become remote and resigned. He has no job and lives off his wife's modest income even though she is ill with tuberculosis. Tomioka tells Yukiko that now he is back in Japan things are different and he has no intentions of divorcing his wife. Tomioka offers Yukiko money, which she rejects.

Yukiko returns to her ex-brother-in-law's to get bedding, which she sells to buy an overcoat, but again has to put up with his sexual advances. She tries to get work as a secretary but gives up because she is turned down for not knowing English. In desperation, she writes to Tomioka asking for money, but before he can answer she has become a prostitute and takes up with an American soldier. Her brother-in-law catches up with her and tells Yukiko that he will not press theft charges against her for taking the bedding if she becomes his mistress. Although she lives as a prostitute, she will not accept the shame of his offer.

Tomioka has tried unsuccessfully to establish himself in business and comes to Yukiko when his wife is admitted to a sanatorium. Like the soldier and her ex-brother-in-law, Tomioka's interest in Yukiko is only sexual. To recapture moments of past happiness, however, Yukiko is willing to submit to Tomioka. The two go off to a hot springs together and meet another veteran of Southeast Asia, Sekichi, and his wife Osei. Tomioka is attracted to Osei and makes no secret of it. The humiliated Yukiko leaves Tomioka and later discovers that she is pregnant. She again goes to Tomioka and finds that Osei has left her husband and now lives with Tomioka. As a consequence, Yukiko has an abortion. While recovering, Yukiko sees a newspaper article about Osei being murdered by her jealous husband. She visits Tomioka but finds him flirting openly with a bar girl.

Yukiko decides to finally let her ex-brother-in-law take care of her. He has joined up with an old army buddy and is now the leader of a questionable religious order, the Congregation of the Believers in the Sun. As she begins to rise above the poverty she has known she finds out that Tomioka's wife has died. Yukiko steals money from the church and again searches out Tomioka. He has been offered another job with the forestry service on a secluded island in southern Japan. He has decided to take the job and reluctantly agrees to take Yukiko with him. On the island, an already ill Yukiko finds herself weakened further by the incessant rain. When Yukiko dies, a distraught Tomioka finally reveals his love for her. As he applies lipstick to Yukiko's corpse, there is a flashback to Indochina where the two found a time of happiness.

• *Floating Clouds* is the most popular film in Japan by Mikio Naruse, an almost overlooked director in the West. It is possibly his darkest and most pessimistic film, and contains almost none of the comic touches he allows in his other films. Once again his subject matter is marital disharmony and the exploitation of women who, although strong and determined in their own right, are nonetheless destined to succumb to the demands of Japanese society.

The dramatic situations in which Naruse characters find themselves involved aren't those of fighting terrible villains or life-threatening circumstances. Rather they are daily struggles which constantly threaten to overwhelm. As a result, there are rarely victories but often compromises. Sometimes the efforts of Naruse's characters provide no forward motion but just help them maintain their present position and prevent them from declining further.

In *Floating Clouds* there is a special regard and infatuation with the past. Scenes of Tomioka and Yukiko's life in Indochina are revealed in flashbacks that present the time as a golden and romantic one. In contrast to the war-devastated Tokyo, Indochina is exotic and beautiful. The depressed and indifferent Tomioka of the present is opposed to the handsome and reserved one in Indochina. Yukiko, who wanders from man to man in a spiraling descent into poverty and prostitution in Tokyo, was attractive and spirited when they fell in love during the war. The movie, like the Japanese of the early 1950s, could find comfort in an idealized past while having to live in a relatively uncertain and unattractive present. The Japanese, also like a typical Naruse heroine, faced that present with a great deal of stoicism.

The Burmese Harp (1956)
Biruma no tategoto

1956 / Nikkatsu. / a.k.a. "The Harp of Burma." 116 min. B&W. *Director:* Kon Ichikawa. *Screenplay:* Natto Wada. *Adaptation:* From the novel by Michio Takeyama. *Cinematography:* Minoru Yokoyama. *Art Direction:* Takashi Matsuyama. *Lighting:* Ko Fujibayashi. *Music:* Akira Ifukube. *Sound:* Masakazu Kamiya. *Editor:* Masanori Tsujii. *Producer:* Masayuki Takaki. Videotape: Connoisseur. Film Rental: Films Inc.

Rentaro Mikuni *as Captain Inouye.* Shoji Yasui *Private Yasuhiko Mizushima.* Tatsuya Mihashi *Defense commander.* Tanie Kitabayashi *Old woman.* Yunosuke Ito *Village head.* Takeo Naito *Kobayashi.* Jun Hamamura *Ito.* Shunji Kasuga *Maki.* Akira Nishimura *Baba.*

• Private Mizushima is assigned to a Japanese unit stationed in Burma at the close of World War II. He is an accomplished, self-taught player of a handmade native instrument, the Burmese harp. The unit's leader is a graduate from a music school, and he has taught his men to sing their way through trying times. By July 1945, the Japanese army is virtually defeated and the unit is making its way by foot over the Burmese mountains towards Thailand. When the unit approaches a threatening forest, Mizushima, who speaks a little Burmese and could easily pass as a native, dresses in native clothing in order to scout ahead. When he has secured an area, he signals the rest of his unit by playing the "all clear" on his Burmese harp. Mizushima comes to be greatly respected by his fellow soldiers.

One night, after seeking food and shelter in a village, the soldiers notice that the Burmese natives have disappeared. The soldiers fear an ambush. To divert the enemy's attention, they sing while they prepare to fight. One of the songs they sing is "Hanyu no yodo," a moving song which is very similar to the British song "Home Sweet Home." When the Japanese soldiers have finished their song, the British soldiers acknowledge the Japanese by singing the English version. With this, the two sides come together only for the Japanese to learn that three days earlier, the war had ended. In a bloodless surrender, the unit is sent to a prisoner-of-war camp in Mudon. Everyone, that is, but Mizushima. Mizushima is recruited to try to persuade another unit of the Japanese army hidden in the mountains that the war is over. Believing that they can never surrender, however, the unit decides to fight on. After the British bombardment, the only one left alive is Mizushima who was knocked unconscious.

In Mudon, Mizushima's comrades ask an old Burmese woman whom they have befriended to find out about the friend they left behind. She tells them about the fight in the mountains and that there were no survivors. But Mizushima is not dead. For five days he lay unconscious, nursed by a Burmese Buddhist monk. One day while the monk is bathing, Mizushima steals his clothes and starts on the long journey to Mudon disguised as a monk. He soon collapses from hunger, however, and nearby villagers, believing him to be a monk, give him food. As he travels, he comes across body after body of dead Japanese soldiers. Mizushima is greatly affected by this sight. He cremates several bodies, makes a funeral mound and prays for their souls. When Mizushima reaches a river battlefield he again comes upon the monk who had earlier saved his life. The monk comments upon the number of unburied bodies of foreigners, then offers Mizushima his boat to take him to Mudon so he can rejoin his unit.

Mizushima reaches the camp late at night and sleeps at a nearby monastery. The next morning he hears a young native boy playing a harp and begging for money from the British soldiers. When he hears how well Mizushima plays, the boy asks him for lessons. The two happen upon a British funeral for the dead Japanese and a tomb for the unknown

The Burmese Harp (Kon Ichikawa, 1956). Reunited after months apart, Mizushima (Shoji Yasui, left) listens to his conscience against the pleas of his comrades in a scene set against a reclining Buddha, the symbol of Mizushima's compassion and spiritual quest. (Photo courtesy of Connoisseur Video.)

Japanese soldier. Memories of the carnage he has seen flood back to Mizushima and he runs away. Haunted by the memory of the dead bodies he has seen, he cannot bring himself to face his fellow soldiers when he finally encounters them on a bridge. Instead he returns to the river battlefield and begins digging graves. Joined by several natives, Mizushima discovers a Burmese ruby while digging. One of the natives suggests that it is the soul of the dead he is burying.

When Mizushima's unit returns to camp, they hear the little boy playing Mizushima's unique arrangement of "Hanyu no yodo," but the British prevent them from questioning the boy. Later, when the unit attends a memorial service for British soldiers who died in the war, they again see, among the monks, one who resembles their friend. He is the only one carrying a white box like those used for ashes of the cremated dead in the Japanese Buddhist ceremony. When the captain is given the job of removing the urns containing the ashes of the British dead, he discovers among them the white box the monk carried. He opens it and finds Mizushima's symbolic offering, the ruby.

One day the unit is singing near a statue of a reclining Buddha. Mizushima, who is sleeping inside the statue hears them and automatically begins playing along on his harp. The excited soldiers rush to him, but the guards call them away. Mizushima, who has been holding the door shut against them, recognizes their voices and sadly watches as they leave. Back at the camp the unit discovers that they only have three days before returning to Japan. In one last attempt to communicate with Mizushima, the soldiers have trained a parrot to say "Mizushima, let's go home." It is the brother to the parrot they had seen perched on the monk's shoulder. They ask the old lady to give their parrot with his important message to the monk. Just before they are to leave, Mizushima, with both parrots on his shoulders and the little boy at his side, stands apart from the POW camp fence. He does not approach and his comrades sing the familiar "Hanyu no yodo." When Mizushima plays along, they finally know he is alive. He still refuses to approach and instead plays the Japanese "Song of Farewell." When finished, he bows and walks away.

Just before leaving, the unit is given a message by the old lady. It is Mizushima's other parrot which he has trained to say he cannot return. There is also a letter for the captain which he reads to the unit. In it Mizushima says that although he misses his homeland very much and wants to return, the war has left him with many doubts and a personal mission. He explains how he could not recognize them because it would have lead to being put in the POW camp and prevented him from carrying out his task of burying the war dead. Mizushima has now assumed the life of a Buddhist monk. As the parrot repeats Mizushima's message in the background, the captain's voice breaks as he finishes reading the letter.

• Kon Ichikawa was born in 1915 and got his start in film in the animation department of J.O. Studios in 1933. His first film, a puppet story titled *Dojoji musume* which he made for Toho Studios, was confiscated by the Occupation authorities because it contained forbidden "traditional feudal remnants." Ichikawa has worked for Shin Toho and Nikkatsu Studios as well, and from 1956 he worked mainly for Daiei. After doing a series of light-weight comedies like those based on the Pu-san character, Ichikawa made *The Heart (Kokoro, 1955)*, his first psychological melodrama.

Often working with his wife, scriptwriter Natto Wada, Ichikawa has evolved into perhaps one of Japan's most versatile directors. (Ichikawa also writes his own screenplays, but usually under the name of "Christie" which he borrowed from his favorite writer, Agatha Christie.) Although, as is the case for most directors in Japan, his movies are those to which he has been assigned and not necessarily those he would choose to do himself, he has always brought a personal quality to the work whether it be a comedy or a drama. His films are sparked by elements of black humor, and a visual style which can find a rueful beauty in the most forlorn of settings.

As early as 1946 (Keisuke Kinoshita's *Osone-ke asa* / *A Morning with the Osone Family*), Japan was producing antiwar films. Under the close watch of the American Occupation authorities, these films were restricted to a more emotional approach. They reached a peak in the mid–1950s through the early 1960s with Ichikawa's *The Burmese Harp* and *Fires on the Plain* (1959) as well as Masaki Kobayashi's *The Human Condition* trilogy (1959–61).

The 1946 novel on which Ichikawa based *The Burmese Harp* was written by Michio Takeyama. It won literary awards and was also adapted for the stage in Japan. Incredibly, it was intended originally as a children's story. The spiritual quest of Mizushima is the heart of the story, but it is couched in an infrastructure filled with tension. Ichikawa masterfully composes his scenes in a lyrical and often symbolic manner. The film employs a leisurely but nonetheless powerful tempo and an effective use of flashback. It is an excellent example of the Buddhist philosophy that an ideal follower is one who is motivated by compassion to perform deeds which cultivate the six Buddhist virtues of generosity, morality, patience, zeal, concentration and wisdom.

When *The Burmese Harp* was shown at the Venice Film Festival and won the San Giorgio Prize, Ichikawa, like Kurosawa, Kinugasa and Mizoguchi before him, immediately received international recognition. Thirty years later Ichikawa remade *The Burmese Harp*. It became Japan's top box-office hit for 1985 and was selected as an official entry for the Venice International Film Festival where it was warmly received.

Street of Shame (1956)
Akasen chitai

1956 / Daiei. / a.k.a. "Red-Light District." 94 min. B&W. *Director:* Kenji Mizoguchi. *Screenplay:* Masashige Narusawa. *Adaptation:* From the short story "Susaki no onna" by Yoshiko Shibaki. *Cinematography:* Kazuo Miyagawa. *Art Direction:* Hiroshi Mizutani. *Settings:* Kiichi Ishizaki. *Music:* Toshiro Mayuzumi. *Sound:* Mitsuo Hasegawa. *Editor:* Keiichi Sakane. *Producer:* Masaichi Nagata. Videotape: Embassy. Film Rental: Films Inc., Janus.

Machiko Kyo *as Mickey*. Aiko Mimasu *Yumeko*. Ayako Wakao *Yasumi*. Michiyo Kogure *Hanae*. Kumeko Urabe *Otane*. Yasuko Kawakami *Shizuko*. Eitaro Shindo *Kurazo Taya*. Kenji Sugawara *Aoki*. Bontaro Miake *Policeman*. Hiroko Machida *Yorie*. Toranosuke Ogawa *Mickey's father*. Daisuke Kato *Policeman Miuazake*.

• The Yoshiwara has been Tokyo's red-light district for more than three centuries. One of the many houses of prostitution there is Dreamland, owned by the Tayas. For many years, the government has been proposing, debating and defeating an antiprostitution bill. Once again the bill is up for a vote.

Yasumi is Dreamland's "#1 girl." One of her patrons is Aoki, the owner of a quilt and bedding shop who has given Yasumi so much money that his shop is on the verge of failure. Aoki says she wants to be with Yasumi but she puts him off. Upstairs she has another customer waiting for her, a salesman who wants to pay off Yasumi's debts and marry her. Mickey is a very Westernized young woman who has been brought to Dreamland for a job. Her father owns a business in Kobe, but she has run away from home. She accepts a job with the Tayas, receiving 40 percent of the money she brings in. Yumeko, whose real name is Sayo Kadowaki, is a widow supporting her son, Shuichi, who lives with her in-laws in the country. One day Shuichi comes to visit his mother, but she is embarrassed and sends him away. He leaves and Yumeko energetically starts soliciting customers on the street — an act she undertakes with renewed vigor to earn even more money for her son so she can give him a good life. Shuichi, however, sees her and leaves in shame. Hanae, who also works at Dreamland, is married, but her husband is unemployed. They have a baby and her husband has tuberculosis. Hanae can only intermittently afford his medicine, but he is worsening and needs to go to a sanatorium. For the baby's sake, they have rejected the idea of a double suicide. Yorie is also in debt to Dreamland and has been proposed to. She wants to accept, but the debt seems to make it impossible. When the government declares that debts of prostitutes are invalid, Yorie decides to marry and the girls have a small party for her.

Yumeko travels to the country to see her son but discovers that he has moved to Tokyo and now works in a toy factory. She constantly tries phoning him where he works until finally he calls to tell her to leave him alone. They arrange a brief meeting. Yumeko hopes she will be able to quit her life in the Yoshiwara and come to live with her son. But this is not to be. Shuichi instead disowns her, driving her mad. Back at Dreamland, Yumeko drifts into insanity and must be taken away to an asylum. A thin, haggard and disillusioned Yorie returns to the Yoshiwara after discovering that her husband is impoverished and only married her to get free labor. Mickey's father comes to Dreamland to bring her home. Her sister cannot arrange a good marriage nor her brother get a good government job as long as she continues in her lowly profession. She is shocked to learn her mother has died but then berates her father, who quickly married the mistress he taunted her mother with during her life. Angered, she throws him out.

Yasumi, who has ruined the quilt shop owner, is now getting money from the salesman. Upon her latest request, he has even gone so far as to

Street of Shame (Kenji Mizoguchi, 1956). Mickey (Machiko Kyo), a young girl who has run away from home, entertains a customer in Mizoguchi's documentary-like story of prostitution and the lives of five women.

embezzle funds from his company in order to buy off her debts and marry her. He has bought tickets to the spa at Beppu for them so he can escape the police. Yasumi has no intentions of marrying him and refuses. Her bluntness causes a fight in which she is knocked unconscious. Over the radio it is announced that the antiprostitution bill has again been defeated. Taya patronizingly justifies the victory by claiming that it is a good thing. Businesses like his fill the gaps in the welfare system and the owners are really social workers.

Outside Dreamland, Hanae's ill husband and son are waiting. They have been evicted from their apartment. Now they must live on the streets. Belying Taya's claims, Hanae quits and goes with them. Yasumi initially had needed money for her father who had been taken to prison. Now she uses the money she has extracted from men to buy the quilt and bedding shop and open her own business. Even though Dreamland has been losing its employees, a new young girl is being forced into the same life. Her father was a miner hurt in an accident. Since her mother continued to borrow from the Tayas, she must now start to repay by becoming a prostitute.

• For what would be his final film, Mizoguchi returned again to the contemporary setting of the *gendai-geki*. The story goes that when

Mizoguchi saw the first draft of Narusawa's script about the red-light district of Tokyo he was extremely upset and demanded that the young writer go and get some firsthand experience. (He had not used long-time collaborator Yoshikata Yoda because he wanted a more current Tokyo feel in the film. Yoda was at the time working on what would have been Mizoguchi's next script, *Osaka Story*.)

The mid–1950s was a time when there was a massive popular campaign to ban prostitution. Mizoguchi wanted his film about the lives of prostitutes to be semidocumentary in tone, but because of the political climate, the brothels kept him from the Yoshiwara and the authentic settings he required. Mizoguchi previously had made a film set in a brothel, *A Woman of Rumor* (1954) about an owner and her daughter in the Shimabara district of Kyoto. In both films the potentially titillating subject matter is treated matter-of-factly with no sensationalism. For Mizoguchi, a brothel is just a business. However, it is also one which exacts a high price from those it exploits.

There are several problems with *Street of Shame*. To some, the film contains too much melodrama, too much conspicuous crusading on behalf of good intentions. (Some even believe that the movie was responsible for the ban on prostitution which took effect in 1957.) But perhaps more questionable was Mizoguchi's controversial use of arty electronic music which, for Western ears, gives parts of the film the feel of a science fiction film. Still, the film is fascinating. It is enhanced by fine acting on the part of the actresses who play the five central, and very different, prostitutes. Like his *Utamoro and His Five Women* (1946), Mizoguchi expertly weaves together the separate and complicated stories of his main characters. While Mizoguchi recreates the feel of the Yoshiwara, he has to some extent sacrificed that "atmosphere" which Western audiences admired so in his other films in favor of delineating his characters.

Ayako Wakao (b. 1933), who plays the business-like Yasumi, was inspired to become an actress after seeing Kazuo Hasegawa in a stage performance while she was in high school. She joined his acting troupe and later was recruited by Daiei's Masaichi Nagata for the company's acting school. Initially typecast as the empty-headed ingenue, her talent and beauty helped her to move into more challenging roles like that of Yasumi.

Machiyo Kogure (b. 1918), who plays the married Hanae, graduated from Nippon University with a degree in theatre arts. She went to work for Shochiku and made her first film in 1937. She took a hiatus from her career during the war when she married and moved to Manchuria, but returned afterwards to both Japan and her career. Also appearing in Kurosawa's *Drunken Angel*, Kogure is a talented and intelligent actress.

With the talents of this ensemble acting, Westerners went to see *Street of Shame*, making it the first film about contemporary Japanese life to attract a large audience abroad. The film also achieved a great deal of success at the box office and, unlike the studios Mizoguchi had virtually bankrupt early in his career, helped to bail out the strapped Daiei Studios. Mizoguchi's career spanned 34 years, in which he made more than 80 films. He had a passionate relationship with his chosen artistic medium and presented many compassionate themes in a masterfully aesthetic milieu. The films Mizoguchi made before dying of leukemia at age 58 in 1956 will reward anyone who watches them.

Throne of Blood (1957)
Kumonosu-jo

1957 / Toho. / a.k.a. "Cobweb Castle" or "Castle of the Cobwebs." 110 min. B&W. *Director:* Akira Kurosawa. *Screenplay:* Shinobu Hashimoto, Ryuzo Kikushima, Hideo Ogune and Akira Kurosawa. *Adaptation:* From the William Shakespeare play **Macbeth**. *Cinematography:* Asakazu Nakai. *Art Direction:* Yoshiro Muraki and Kohei Ezaki. *Music:* Masaru Sato. *Sound:* Fumio Yanoguchi. *Producer:* Shojiro Motoki and Akira Kurosawa. Videotape: Media, International Historic Films. Film Rental: Films Inc., Janus.

Toshiro Mifune *as Taketoki Washizu*. Isuzu Yamada *Asaji, Lady Washizu*. Takashi Shimura *Noriyasu Odagura*. Minoru Chiaki *Yoshiaki Miki*. Akira Kubo *Yoshiteru*. Takamaru Sasaki *Kunimaru*. Chieko Naniwa *Witch*.

• In medieval Japan, a series of messengers arrive at Forest Castle to report on the status of an ongoing border battle. At first it would seem that Lord Kunihara's troops are losing the battle, but successive messengers report a change as commanders Washizu and Miki fight back the rebels. Kunihara calls for Washizu and Miki to come to the Forest Castle, but the two men become lost in the forest labyrinth which surrounds the castle. The two men believe they are being held within the forest by evil spirits and soon come upon a ghostly hut. Inside is an even more ghostly woman, singing softly and spinning. She predicts that Washizu will become the master of the North Castle and eventually will become master of the Forest Castle itself. For Miki she prophesizes that he will become commander of the first fort and that his son will become lord of the Forest Castle. Then, as mysteriously as she appeared, she disappears. Washizu and Miki try again to reach Forest Castle, eventually leaving the forest, but emerging into a thick fog which again impedes their progress.

Throne of Blood (Akira Kurosawa, 1957). Adapting Shakespeare's *Macbeth* brought about one of the most visually stunning films to come out of Japan. Here Washizu (Toshiro Mifune) is attacked by his own men because the prediction that he will fail when the forest approaches the castle has come true. (Photo courtesy of Toho Co., Ltd.)

At the castle, the first half of the old woman's prediction comes true. Now in command of the North Castle, Washizu's life would seem on a good path, but his wife, Asaji, thinks otherwise. She plants in his mind the idea that his friend Miki will betray him. Should Miki tell Lord Kunihara of the prophecy, Kunihara, feeling threatened, undoubtedly will kill Washizu. Convinced that she is right, Washizu kills Lord Kunihara when he visits North Castle on a hunting trip. Now Washizu becomes the ruler of Forest Castle. He gives a celebration at which Miki and his son are to be the guests of honor, but Asaji has already convinced him to get rid of the two men in order to insure that their son (she is pregnant) will rule next.

While Miki is killed en route to the celebration, Miki's son escapes. Asaji's son is stillborn and Asaji is deathly ill. Washizu again goes into the forest to consult with the old woman and she tells him he will never lose a battle until the forest approaches the castle. At first his men are assured by the prediction, but when the besieging troops cut down trees and use them as camouflage to march on the castle, they revolt against Washizu, finally killing him with their own arrows.

• Many readers and viewers will immediately recognize the plot of *Throne of Blood* as being that of Shakespeare's *Macbeth*. What they may not realize if they've never seen the film is the overwhelming atmosphere it creates. This is a visually stunning film which superbly captures the tale's gloom and oppressiveness. It is reflected in dark forests, rooms with low ceilings (one with blood on the floors and walls which won't be washed away), and obscuring fog. Eerie scenes such as the one where birds invade the castle just before Washizu's death provide cinematic omens of the preordained tragedy. When Miki's horse refuses to allow itself to be saddled to take its rider to the ill-fated celebration, it later returns home riderless.

While *Throne of Blood* is Shakespeare translated to medieval Japan, it also incorporates many elements of the traditional Noh theatre. Lady Asaji's mask-like makeup; her stiff, stylized actions; and her monotone speech reflect that of an actress in the Noh theatre. The film's settings, music and use of a chorus also have their foundations in Noh, as does the supernatural element of the ghost prophetess who is filmed in shimmering white, her voice a lifeless monotone, and who moves and sounds like a Noh actor.

Throne of Blood is the most visually handsome of all Kurosawa's black and white films. Always a perfectionist (something which would later cause Kurosawa many woes in trying to find a studio to produce his increasingly expensive films), Kurosawa built a castle from scratch on the slopes of Mount Fuji for exterior shots. There the director found the ideal landscape with Fuji's black volcanic ground and enough natural fog to fit his images. Demanding a low, squat castle be built, Kurosawa faced problems with finding enough manpower to build it until help came from a nearby United States Marine base. Interior and courtyard shots were done in Tokyo, but Kurosawa insisted that the volcanic soil be imported from Fuji to make the sets match exterior shots.

Throne of Blood was not the only time Kurosawa turned to Western literary works as a basis for his films. He has also filmed Dostoevsky's *The Idiot (Hakuchi)* in 1957, and Shakespeare's *King Lear* under the title of *Ran* in 1985.

Snow Country (1957)
Yukiguni

1957 / Toho. 120 min. B&W. *Director:* Shiro Toyoda. *Screenplay:* Toshio Yasumi. *Adaptation:* From the novel by Yasunari Kawabata.

Cinematography: Jun Yasumoto. *Art Direction:* Kisaku Ito and Makoto Sono. *Music:* Ikuma Dan. *Sound:* Masao Fujiyoshi. *Editor:* Hiroichi Iwashita. *Producer:* Ichiro Sato. Videotape: Sony. Film Rental: East-West Classics.

Keiko Kishi *as Komako.* Ryo Ikebe *Shimamura.* Kaoru Yachigusa *Yoko.* Hisaya Morishige *Yukio.* Chieko Naniwa *Head maid.* Maruo Tanaka *Porter.*

• Shimamura is an artist from Tokyo who has come on the train to the snow country of northern Japan. It is December and the snow creates beautiful mountain scenery. This is not Shimamura's first visit to the inn. He was there previously. During that visit he had a brief affair with a young geisha in training, Komako, who is the stepdaughter of the local music teacher. Her teacher also has another stepdaughter, Yoko, and a son, Yukio. Yoko and Yukio are also on the train with Shimamura this December. Yukio had been in Tokyo working in a watch shop and going to night school until he contracted tuberculosis. Yoko has escorted him home where he will soon die.

During Shimamura's absence, Komako has become a fulltime geisha in order to pay Yukio's hospital bills. According to the blind masseur Shimamura meets, Komako and Yukio were engaged, it was their mother's wish. Komako has an older man as a patron, as does the artist Shimamura. In fact Shimamura also has a wife and children. When Shimamura is just about to leave again for Tokyo, Yoko comes looking for Komako because Yukio is so much worse. Komako, however, seems to have no feelings for Yukio and refuses to leave Shimamura.

Later, in a letter to Komako, Shimamura writes that he will return for the Torioi Children's Festival in February—"without fail." Komako, who has come to believe she is pregnant with Shimamura's child, spends the festival meeting every train at the station, but Shimamura is not on any of them. Komako leaves her patron who completely withdraws his support of her, even forcing her to vacate her house. Her teacher dies, Yoko takes on a job as a maid at the inn, and Komako's debts continue to mount. She is not, however, pregnant.

Once again Shimamura returns to the inn. Komako tries to show him that she has become a callused, hard-working geisha, but it soon becomes obvious that she still loves him. Yoko, who loved Yukio, both hates Komako for the way she treated Yukio, and is indebted to her because Komako supports her. Yoko asks Shimamura to take her back to Tokyo with him, partly to make Komako jealous and partly to diminish her responsibilities. Shimamura tells Komako about Yoko's request and that he is planning on taking her. At the same time a fire breaks out at the storehouse where Yoko has gone to see a movie. A frantic Komako unthinkingly tries to rush into the storehouse and is very upset when she

sees Yoko on a stretcher, her face severely burned. Shimamura returns to
Tokyo without Yoko, probably never to return to the snow country.
Komako and Yoko are destined to live on together with just the memories
of the men they loved.

• *Snow Country* is a film of vast visual beauty which is based on a
novel by Yasunari Kawabata, the only Japanese novelist to receive a Nobel
Prize for literature. Like Kawabata's novel, Toyoda's film captures a rich
atmosphere of emptiness, loneliness and love never realized. Kawabata,
who also wrote the novel on which Naruse based his *Sound of the Mountains (Yama no oto,* 1954*)*, wrote *Snow Country* in the 1930s, the period in
which the story is set.

This was the same decade that gave rise to the *junbungaku* film movement, with which Toyoda is closely associated. Translated as "pure literature," directors who subscribed to this doctrine based their films on written
works that are not necessarily popular. In fact, they are usually anything
but. The stories they chose were those of a classic nature. This movement,
which also owes a lot to Gosho (see *Where Chimneys Are Seen*) and
Shimazu, was popular until the outbreak of World War II and was often
used to circumvent prewar censorship, the logic being that the stories were
already well known to viewers so there was no point in censoring them.

The main characters in a Toyoda film are usually fairly passive. Just as
they seem to allow events to flow around them and never question or fight
their fate, so Toyoda is more interested in just revealing a character's personality instead of concentrating on plot and action. *Snow Country* is more
wordy than is usual for a Toyoda film, for he more often shows what a
character is feeling by what is seen on the screen than spoken on the
soundtrack. Because of his emphasis on character, Toyoda tends to gravi-
tate to scripts which feature just a few roles. Consequently, casting these
parts became a very important process and Toyoda insisted on the right to
choose the actors and actresses he used. One actor which Toyoda often
used was Ryo Ikebe.

Ikebe (b. 1918), who plays Shimamura, originally entered Toho
Studios as an apprentice scriptwriter. However, Director Yasujiro Shimazu
"discovered" the handsome actor and put him in front of the camera.
Specializing almost entirely in films with a contemporary setting, Ikebe
won acclaim for his role in Ozu's *Early Spring (Soshun,* 1956*)*.

Another Toyoda regular is Hisaya Morishige (b. 1913) who played the
ill Yukio. Morishige is much better known for his comic roles such as that
of *Marital Relations (Meoto zenzai,* 1955*)* and *A Cat, Shozo, and Two
Women (Neko to Shozo to futari no onna,* 1956*)*. Not only is Morishige an
accomplished actor in Toho's stables, but he is also well known as a radio
disc jockey and comedian, and is a gifted practitioner of the Japanese art
of storytelling known as *naniwa-bushi.*

Snow Country (Shiro Toyoda, 1957). The coldness of the winter snow seems to echo Shimamura's (Ryo Ikebe, left) restrained heart, especially when it comes to dealing with geisha Komako (Keiko Kishi). (Photo courtesy of Sony Video and Toho Co., Ltd.)

Bcause Toyoda plans out each scene in great detail, his films are invariably tightly constructed. *Snow Country* originally ran just over two hours, but when Toho decided to send the film to the Cannes Film Festival, they made many changes to it. Fearing that foreigners wouldn't sit through a long film, let alone a long Japanese film, they not only cut scenes but added a running commentary and titles. Toyoda's cinematic pace and even the film's meaning were sacrificed.

Ballad of Narayama (1958)
Narayama bushi-ko

1958 / Shochiku. 98 min. Fujicolor and Tohoscope. *Director:*
Keisuke Kinoshita. *Screenplay:* Keisuke Kinoshita. *Adaptation:* From the
story by Shichiro Fukuzawa. *Cinematography:* Hiroyuki Kusuda. *Art Direction:* Kisaku Ito. *Music:* Rokuzaemon Kineya and Matsunosuke Nozawa.
Sound: Hisao Ono. *Editor:* Yoshi Sugihara. *Producer:* Masaharu Kokaji
and Ryuzo Otani. Film Rental: Kino.

Kinuyo Tanaka *as Orin, the grandmother.* Teiji Takahashi *Tatsuhei.*
Yuko Mochizuki *Tamayan.* Danko Ichikawa *Kesakichi.* Keiko Ogasawara
Matsuyan. Seiji Miyaguchi *Matyan.* Yunosuke Ito *Matayan's son.* Ken Mitsuda *Teruyan.*

• In a mountain village 69-year-old Orin is a healthy and alert old
woman who must soon depart on her last journey. The trip is one all old
people in the village must make. She will be taken by her son to the top
of Mount Narayama where she will wait to die. Orin is eager to make the
journey, but first she must put her family in order. Orin lives with her
son, Tatsuhei, and his children. Tatsuhei is a widower and Orin needs to
find him a new wife before she can leave. She finds a widow, Tamayan, in
a nearby village and has the woman come to live with them. Orin likes the
woman and helps her to feel at home, even showing her a favorite spot to
catch fish.

Tatsuhei loves his mother and is very reluctant to take her to Narayama. Orin, however, is very aware of the social censure which will befall
her if she doesn't go. When her grandson brings his pregnant girlfriend to
live with the poor family it means another mouth to feed and the public
disgrace of Orin seeing her great-grandson. She is also aware of how her
healthy teeth make it seem as if she has eaten well for an old woman in
lean times. To help convince her son that she must go, Orin breaks her
teeth on a grinding wheel.

When Orin feels all is ready, she and Tatsuhei visit the village elders
for instructions for going to Mount Narayama. The next morning, carrying
Orin on his back, Tatsuhei makes the difficult trip. After leaving his
beloved mother on the mountain, Tatsuhei starts to return to his village.
He comes upon another villager and that villager's father, Matayan,
fighting on the path. Matayan had clung to life and refused to make the
trip to Narayama. As a consequence, his miserly son refused to feed him
and Matayan had to beg food from Orin. Now, in disgrace, the son has
tied up Matayan and is forcing him to go. During the struggle on the
mountain path, Matayan is pushed over the edge by his son. Tatsuhei,

The Ballad of Narayama (Keisuke Kinoshita, 1958). Stylized settings highlighted Kinoshita's version of the popular story of sons who must carry their parents to and abandon them on Mount Narayama. (Photo courtesy of Shochiku Co., Ltd.)

witnessing this, rushes forward and in the struggle which follows, the son accidentally falls down the mountain.

In the quiet of the hillside, it begins to show—a portent of good luck. Tatsuhei, concerned for his mother, runs back to her. Orin, however, will not speak to him and the son returns to the village. Outside his home he nears his new wife and his children singing.

• Director Keisuke Kinoshita has always seemed to delight in experimenting with the technical methods of making films. In *Carmen Comes Home* he made the first color film, in *A Japanese Tragedy* he used newsreel footage to enrich his theme, in *She Was Like a Wild Chrysanthemum* the old man's memories are misted and framed in old-fashioned ovals. In *The Ballad of Narayama* Kinoshita used highly artificial sets, strong colors and a Kabuki influenced style of acting, music, lighting and commentator's narrative to emphasize the legendary character of the story.

The Ballad of Narayama is a pseudofolk tale which is told in many forms throughout Asia. (It was remade in 1983 by Shohei Imamura and won the Cannes Grand Prix.) To Westerners it may seem like a gruesome custom fit only for a horror film, but in Kinoshita's able hands the story becomes one of the most powerful illustrations of Japan's national character in the cinema. He captures a poetic feel for scenery and rhythm and evokes an intense feeling of mood through the combined use of images, music and settings.

There is a deeply human treatment of characters in *The Ballad of Narayama* which bespeaks Kinoshita's interest in traditions, the demands they make on people and the links between people—especially family members. During the 1960s, when the film industry was undergoing a decline in business, and movies progressed into more explicit realism, Kinoshita's type of film became less popular. Kinoshita was an uncompromising director who wanted to make only the movies he believed in. Consequently, in the '60s, this master of the post–World War II Japanese cinema, was forced to transfer his talents to television. A change which was a loss for films, but which he did very successfully.

The Hidden Fortress (1958)
Kakushi torideno sanakunin

1958 / Toho. / a.k.a. "Three Bad Men in a Hidden Fortress." 139 min. (many U.S. prints are only 126 min.). Color and Tohoscope. *Director:* Akira Kurosawa. *Screenplay:* Shinobu Hashimoto, Ryuzo Kikushima, Hideo Ogune and Akira Kurosawa. *Cinematography:* Kazuo Yamasaki. *Art Direction:* Yoshiro Muraki and Kohei Ezaki. *Music:* Masaru Sato. *Sound:* Rumio Yanoguchi. *Producer:* Masumi Fujimoto and Akira Kurosawa. Videotape: Media. Film Rental: R5/S8 (139-min. version), Janus.

Toshiro Mifune *as General Rokurota Makabe.* Misa Uehara *Princess Yukihime.* Minoru Chiaki *Tahei.* Kamatari Fujiwara *Matakishi.* Susumu Fujita *General Hyoe Tadokoro.* Toshiko Higuchi *Girl.* Eiko Miyoshi *Old lady-in-waiting.* Takashi Shimura *General Izumi Nagakura.* Kichijiro Ueda *Slaver.* Koji Mitsui *Soldier.*

• Tahei and Matakishi are two 16th century farmers who have sold their homes in order to buy arms to fight in one of the many civil wars which mark the period. They thought they were going to get rich, but they were on the losing side. Now all they want to do is to get to friendly territory. While traveling they try to boil down some stolen rice only to find one of the sticks they are using contains a hidden gold bar. They frantically search for more until they are followed by a mysterious man.

The man tells them the gold is his and that it is stolen war funds. He offers to split it with them if they will help him smuggle it into Hoyakawa territory. The man turns out to be Rokurota Makabe, a famous Akizuki general. The money belongs to the defeated Akizuki clan, and it is Makabe's job to see that it and Princess Yuki survive the defeat and re-establish the clan. Makabe takes them behind some hills to a hidden fortress where the princess is hiding. They see her and find a comb with

The Hidden Fortress (Akira Kurosawa, 1958). The relationship between the two peasants, Tahei and Matakishi (standing, Minoru Chiaki, left, and Kamatari Fujiwara), is said to have inspired George Lucas when he created C3PO and R2-D2 for *Star Wars*. (Toshiro Mifune as Rokurota, seated.) (Photo courtesy of R5/S8 and Toho Co., Ltd.)

the Akizuki crescent on it. One of the farmers goes to town to collect the reward for turning in the princess only to discover she has already been executed. The woman Yamana's men have executed, however, is Kofuyu, Makabe's sister, who has sacrificed herself for the princess.

The real princess is rather tomboyish, raised like a boy because her father had no male heir. Dressed manishly, the princess is convinced to pretend to be a mute in order to pass by Yamana's men and not have her speech give her away. The three men and the princess set out with two horses, carrying the sticks containing the clan's fortune. At one point they are almost discovered, but Makabe chases down Yamana's men—right into a Yamana encampment. There Makabe meets an old adversary, Hyoei Tadokoro. The two men fight a duel with lances and Makabe wins, but spares Hyoei's life and rides away.

The Akizuki entourage meets with several adventures, but after being separated from the two farmers, the princess and Makabe are captured by Yamana's men. They are visited by Hyoei who now bears a terrible facial scar given by his lord to shame him for suffering a defeat and not dying. The three talk for a while and the princess tells him that what you make of another's kindness is up to you. She then sings a touching song she had heard on her trip when they stumbled onto the Yamana fire festival. The next day, as the princess and Makabe are being taken away with the gold, Hyoei starts to sing the fire festival song. He frees the captives and defects to the Akizuki clan.

The horses carrying the clan's gold are set running and finally stop near Tahei and Matakishi. Thinking they are rich, the farmers once again fight over the size of the shares. They are quickly seized by Hoyakawa's men, however, and taken to Makabe and the princess who are now in friendly hands. The two are rewarded for their efforts with one gold bar and the princess orders them not to fight over it.

• *The Hidden Fortress* is similar to Kurosawa's earlier *The Men Who Tread on the Tiger's Tail*. Both involve a flight from capture, both have members of nobility disguised as commoners, and both have comic overtones. In *Hidden Fortress*, most of the humorous moments evolve out of the characters of the farmers Tahei and Matakishi. American director George Lucas has said that these two characters struck him as so funny that he incorporated them into one of his own movies. Of course he changed them from farmers to robots and gave them the names R2-D2 and C3PO, but the seeds for their constant squabbling and enduring friendship found in his *Star Wars* trilogy is easily seen in *Hidden Fortress*.

All the characters in *Hidden Fortress* are drawn in an expressive and entertaining manner. From the stubborn princess to her heroic guard, each character comes to life fully on the screen and is used to maximum effect in Kurosawa's hands. Set against a backdrop of the difficult period of a civil war, Kurosawa's characters reflect the values of loyalty and sacrifice on the part of Makabe and avarice and ambition on the part of the farmers.

The characters' progress through the story is a highly enjoyable and exciting one. Just when the authorities know how the princess is traveling, fate intervenes and changes their situation. When they are discovered to be three men, three horses and a girl, fortune has them selling the horses and buying one of the princess' female subjects who had been sold into slavery. Now they are passed up by soldiers who see three men, two women, no horses and a cart. The cart is loaded down with the sticks into which Makabe has hidden the clan's gold, and when their situation is again discovered, they only escape by "disappearing" into a crowd of people, all carrying sticks, to the local fire festival. When celebrators want to throw the whole cart into the fire, Makabe helps. The next morning they pick out the gold from the fire's ashes and again have changed their traveling appearance.

All this is told through scenes which vary in their editing pace. Kurosawa is a master editor (starting with his early training with Kajiro Yamamoto) and he edits almost all of his own films. (In fact, having final editorial control is extremely important to Kurosawa. When it was denied

Edo, but also told her that her husband had a mistress there. Otane was very grateful to the drum instructor but also feared he would talk. Otane admits to Hikokuro that she became drunk on Peach Festival Day while in the teacher's company and was seduced by him.

With this revelation, Hikokuro, who still loves Otane, is forced to have her commit suicide. When she tries, she is unable to perform the act, and Hikokuro stabs her himself. Hikokuro now must go to Kyoto and hunt down and kill the drum teacher. Hikokuro is a man possessed. He finds Miyaji during the Gion Festival and runs him through with his sword. Hikokuro has done what society has demanded and not what he has wanted. He has followed the rules and committed a legally registered revenge, and he is left with nothing.

• Tadashi Imai was born in Tokyo in 1912, the son of a priest. He studied at Tokyo University but did not graduate. While at the university, Imai adopted the Communist ideology, joined a Communist youth league, and was arrested twice. In 1935 he joined J.O. Studios as a continuity writer and later as a director after the studio merged with Toho in 1937. After the war, Imai joined the Japan Communist Party. When the strikes hit Toho in the 1940s, Imai was blacklisted during the "red purge" which followed.

When he became a victim of the anticommunist movement in the Japanese film industry, it was difficult if not impossible for him to make films within the mainstream studio system. In 1950 Imai produced the first Japanese film made without institutional financing, *And Yet We Live (Dokkoi ikiteiru)*. This broke new ground for independent filmmakers, and not just for its means of financing. *And Yet We Live* was greatly influenced by Italian neorealism, especially Vitorio de Sica's *The Bicycle Thief.* In 1963 Imai's *Bushido* was a hit at the Berlin Film Festival and from then on his films became decidedly more commercial.

With this ideological background, it should come as no surprise that Imai is not known so much for the style of his films (which is of the realist school) as for their thematic content. Often contemporary stories, his films tend to depict and argue on behalf of the poor and exploited. Imai's directing style is notoriously spontaneous and his films are rarely planned out, making them inconsistent in quality. He was, however, one of the favorites of Japanese film critics.

Night Drum is one of the best films directed by Imai. Adapted from a play by famed author Monzaemon Chikamatsu, the film, in Imai's hands, is a devastating condemnation of feudal social codes. Set in the 18th century, during the height of the Tokugawa Shogunate, the plot not only analyzes and attacks the abuse of women under feudalism, but also sees how the entire system denies human feelings. Otane is not the only victim of this restrictive code. Hikokuro is a loving husband, even after he

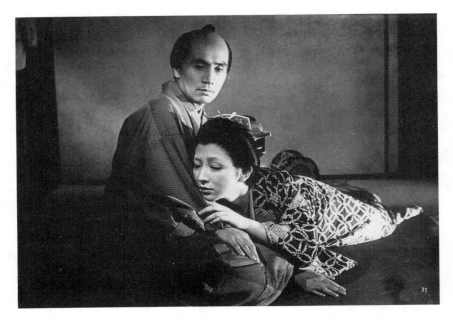

Night Drum (Tadashi Imai, 1958). The feudal system of 18th century Japan was condemned by Imai in this film, which centered on the machinations behind protecting one's honor; here Otane (Ineko Arima) pleads with Miyaji the drum teacher (Masayuki Mori). (Photo courtesy of Shochiku Co., Ltd.)

learns of his wife's infidelity, but society will not allow him to forgive his remorseful wife.

Rentaro Mikuni, who plays Hikokuro, was born Masao Sato in 1923. He did stage work before joining Shochiku in 1951. He made his film debut in Kinoshita's *Good Fairy* and took his stage name from the character he played in that film. Mikuni is an intense, intelligent and versatile actor who can excel in either period or contemporary, serious or comic films. He has played the captain in Ichikawa's *The Burmese Harp,* the lord in Kobayashi's *Harakiri,* Musashi Miyamoto's friend in Inagaki's *Samurai,* and the father of the murderer in Imamura's *Vengeance Is Mine,* and has appeared in many Naruse films.

Fires on the Plain (1959)
Nobi

1959 / Daiei. 108 min. B&W and Daieiscope. *Director:* Kon Ichikawa. *Screenplay:* Natto Wada. *Adaptation:* From the novel by Shohei

Ooka. *Cinematography:* Setsuo Kobayashi. *Art Direction:* Tokuji Shibata. *Music:* Yasushi Akutagawa. *Editor:* Kon Ichikawa. *Producer:* Masaichi Nagata. Videotape: Embassy. Film Rental: Films Inc., Janus, Kit Parker.

Eiji Funakoshi *as Tamura.* Osamu Takizawa *Yasuda.* Micky Curtis *Nagamatsu.* Mantaro Ushioi *Sergeant.* Yoshihiro Hamaguchi *Officer.* Kyu Sazanaka *Army surgeon.* Asao Sano, Hikaru Hoshi, Masaya Tsukida and Yasushi Sugita *Soldiers.*

• It is the winter of 1945. The war in the Philippines is virtually over. On the island of Leyte the Japanese army, which has been told to fight to the end and commit suicide before surrendering, is being overrun by American forces.

Private First Class Tamura, a gentle man who suffers from tuberculosis, has been sent back to his unit by a hospital which "cured" him in three days, keeping Tamura's five-day supply of rations. His unit officer, however, refuses to let him rejoin his starving troop because he is too ill to forage for his own rations. He is told to return again to the hospital or die in the attempt using a hand grenade. Placing the grenade in his haversack with his few potatoes, he again treks back to the hospital.

At a fork in the road, Tamura lets fate—in the form of a dropped twig—determine the path he takes. On the path through the dense jungle chosen by the stick, he sees the first of the fires used by the Filipino guerrillas to communicate over the vast plains. Tamura stumbles onto a Filipino who is cooking outside his hut. The Filipino offers Tamura some of the foul-smelling food, then runs away. When Tamura leaves, he again sees a fire and, upon emerging from the jungle at the hospital, murmurs that he is saved. Once more the hospital rejects him, however. Tamura is told he may rest there only if he has food. Tamura meets other "cured" patients outside the hospital and they conjecture about surrendering, believing the Americans take good care of their POWs. In the distance, another guerrilla fire burns. American artillery fire blows up the hospital and everyone inside is killed.

Once again Tamura takes to the hills in his attempt to survive. In an abandoned village he comes upon a church, its steeple filled with crows. Inside the church Tamura discovers heaped corpses of massacred Japanese soldiers which are being eaten by the birds. Clues, such as a Lucky Strike cigarette carton, indicate that the village was occupied by American troops.

He tries to befriend a young Filipino couple who arrive in the village by boat, but when the girl starts screaming, he panics and shoots her. The boy runs away when Tamura's gun jams. Saddened at his act, Tamura decorously straightens the dead woman's skirt only to discover a cache of salt hidden in the floorboards under her. Brusquely he shoves the woman's body aside and fills his haversack with salt. On his way out of the village, Tamura throws his rifle into a stream.

While wandering, Tamura meets three other Japanese soldiers at a potato field. They have plenty to eat and are planning to make their way to the town of Palampon where Japanese soldiers will be evacuated to Cebu. This route, however, requires that they cross the American-guarded Ormoc highway. The soldiers do not share their food with Tamura, but divide up Tamura's salt. On the trek to the highway, they see many dead and dying Japanese soldiers. From one Tamura is given another rifle. One soldier comes upon a pair of boots which he immediately exchanges for his own. A second soldier, coming upon the first soldier's discards, exchanges his worse boots for these. Finally, Tamura, coming upon these castoffs, looks down at his own soleless boot shells, takes them off, and walks on barefoot.

Eventually the soldiers come upon the highway but are warned that if any of them are considering surrendering, they will be shot. That night, the soldiers attempt to cross the road, only to be caught in mid-try by tanks which chew up their ranks. The next morning, Tamura sees American soldiers searching among the Japanese dead for survivors. He decides to surrender, but as he is about to do so, another soldier attempts to do the same thing and is shot down by a Filipino guerrilla with the Americans. There is nothing left for Tamura but to wander on.

Tamura becomes delirious with hunger and thirst and is on the verge of collapse when he comes across Nagamatsu, a soldier he met outside the hospital, and his companion Yasuda. They tell Tamura that they have survived on monkey meat, but Tamura has seen a severed human hand nearby and is suspicious. They offer some to Tamura, but because of his weakened condition and bad teeth, he cannot eat it. Yasuda and Nagamatsu are extremely suspicious of each other and Yasuda cons Tamura out of his grenade so he will have protection against the rifle-armed Nagamatsu. When Nagamatsu discovers Yasuda has the grenade, he ambushes him and proceeds to butcher him for dinner. Tamura, revolted by the scene, takes Nagamatsu's gun and shoots him. Tamura staggers off towards the fires on the plain. All he wants is to see people leading normal lives. He wants to surrender but is shot down. He falls, his hands raised in submission.

• Ichikawa's fame reached the West when his *The Burmese Harp* won the San Giorgio Prize at the Venice Film Festival in 1956. With the gruesome poetry of *Fires on the Plain*, which parallels the motifs of *The Burmese Harp*, his reputation was assured. The main characters in Ichikawa's works, like Tamura in *Fires on the Plain* and Mizushima in *Harp*, are outsiders. They want nothing more than to escape the world which they, in all their innocence, must live. Armed with only their personal ethics, Ichikawa's heroes fight the misery created by their fellow men. Often, though, they seem like nothing more than insects on the landscape, caught up in situations beyond their control.

Fires on the Plain (Kon Ichikawa, 1959). The savagery of war causes more than death on the battlefield in Ichikawa's films. The fight for survival is oftentimes waged even against one's own comrades, as it is here for Tamura (Eiji Funakoshi, right).

Ichikawa does not explain or analyze his characters. By creating a complete world in which they live, Ichikawa absorbs viewers into his films and compels them to empathize with his heroes. Ichikawa is a humanist who is attracted to the devastating elements of society but who also, as represented in the visual style of his films, can still find compensation in beauty. He is often condemned for being an aesthete. His characters are not just mortal men trying to survive impossible situations like war. They are people dominated by personal ideals and visions. While some strive for life at any cost, Ichikawa's heroes also seek beauty and harmony.

Ichikawa finds poetry even in the most unexpected situations. In large part this is due to his highly visual style. Marked by austere but handsome compositions, Ichikawa is a master at the use of the large screen. Often using an abrupt style of editing and startling sound effects, Ichikawa effectively alternates his scenes of violence with those typical of an Ozu-like tranquility.

Even though *Fires on the Plain* is a war film, it is not a fast-paced action film. The narrative is leisurely (in fact, about half the film is devoid of dialogue) and reflective, allowing the viewer to succumb to the fascinating world he is witnessing. The screenplay, written by Ichikawa's wife,

Natto Wada, is very faithful to the original novel—with one exception. The novel, written by Shohei Ooka, who was himself a POW during the war, ends with Tamura in a mental hospital where he meditates on the meaning of his experiences, on the God who guided him, and on his triumph in not succumbing to eating human flesh.

Besides finding a melancholy beauty in Tamura's story, Ichikawa also manages to find humor. Most of Ichikawa's films are infused with irony and moments of black humor. To many Western viewers, Ichikawa's combination of humor and tragedy can be a bit disconcerting. For the Japanese, however, the two can be complexly intertwined. In humor there can be tragedy, and in tragedy one can find humor.

Floating Weeds (1959)
Ukikusa

1959 / Daiei. 119 min. Color. *Director:* Yasujiro Ozu. *Screenplay:* Yasujiro Ozu and Kogo Noda. *Adaptation:* From Tadao Ikeda's script for Ozu's film *Tale of Floating Weeds* (1934). *Cinematography:* Kazuo Miyagawa. *Art Direction:* Tomo Shimogawara. *Music:* Takanori Saito. *Producer:* Masaichi Nagata. Videotape: Connoisseur. Film Rental: Films Inc., Janus, Kit Parker.

Ganjiro Nakamura *as Komajiro Arashi.* Machiko Kyo *Sumiko.* Haruko Sugimura *Oyoshi.* Hiroshi Kawaguchi *Kiyoshi.* Ayako Wakao *Kayo.* Mantaro Ushio *Sentaro.* Haruo Tanaka *Yatazo.* Koji (Hideo) Mitsui *Kikinosuke.* Tadashi Date *Sensho.* Chishu Ryu *Owner of the theatre.*

• On a hot summer day, a traveling troupe of actors arrive in a small harbor down in the Wakayama peninsula in southern Japan. The troupe performs Kabuki plays, but not of the most classic sort nor with the most talented of actors. The troupe is headed by and named for Komanjuro Arashi. Arashi has a special incentive for coming to this area because his former mistress Oyoshi and their son Kiyoshi live in the town. Kiyoshi, however, does not know that Arashi is his father. To him, his father died when he was a baby, and Arashi is just his uncle.

Another person who doesn't know about Arashi's secret life is his current mistress, Sumiko, who is also an actress in the troupe. Sumiko finds out about Arashi's past mistress and son and calls at Oyoshi's house while Arashi and Kiyoshi are there. She makes allegations, but Arashi manages to get rid of her before she can tell Kiyoshi that his uncle is really his

Floating Weeds (Yasujiro Ozu, 1959). Kiyoshi (Hiroshi Kawaguchi) goes fishing with his "uncle" Arashi (Ganjiro Nakamura), who, in this more light-hearted Ozu film, turns out really to be his father.

father. Angered by Sumiko's actions, Arashi tells her it is over between them. In retaliation, Sumiko plots a vengeful act. She pays Kayo, a pretty young actress in the troupe, to "vamp" Kiyoshi. Kayo does this, but she soon falls in love with the boy.

Gradually the troupe finds itself in trouble. Turnouts for the shows are low, their manager never returns, and a troupe member runs off with all the company's cash. As a result, the troupe must break up, train fare being raised by selling their costumes.

Oyoshi wants Arashi to settle down with her and admit his relationship to their son. Arashi considers this until Kiyoshi, who had run away with Kayo, returns home and an argument ensues. Oyoshi tells Kiyoshi the truth and he is angered by the deception played on him. Realizing he could never lead a happy life with the boy now, Arashi leaves. At the train station, he runs into Sumiko. At first he ignores her, but eventually the two make up and travel to a new city where they will try to join another troupe.

• The later works of Yasujiro Ozu were often remakes, to one degree or another, of his previous films. *Late Autumn* (and to some extent *An Autumn Afternoon*) reflects much which is in *Late Spring* just as *Ohayo* resembled *I Was Born, But....* *Floating Weeds* is a much more obvious remake, even retaining much of the original silent film's title *A Story of Floating Weeds (Ukigusa monogatari,* 1934).

Producer Masaichi Nagata of Daiei Motion Picture Company had wanted Ozu to make a picture for them, but his Shochiku contract had always kept him busy. When Ozu finished *Ohayo* early, he got Shochiku to agree to loan him to Daiei. Originally Ozu had wanted to remake *A Story of Floating Weeds* in a snowy setting, and called his working script "The Ham Actor." Unfortunately his plans were thwarted when little snow fell that year in the area he wanted to shoot in. Consequently Ozu changed the season and setting—dramatically—to a steamy hot port town in southern Japan.

The intervening 25 years had mellowed Ozu and this later film is much less harsh than the original. While *Floating Weeds* embodies much which is within Ozu's thematic style—a family torn apart, the generation gap, the inevitability of changes in everyday life—it is also untypically Ozu in that it has one of his most dramatic plots. Ozu has often said that plot bores him and as has been said before, describing an Ozu storyline is completely to under-represent the experience of an Ozu film. *Floating Weeds,* however, has more than the usual amount of dramatic moments and machinations: Sumiko plotting against Arashi, Kayo seducing Kiyoshi, the confrontation between father and son.

Even though the story may seem more active than normal for Ozu, his camera is not. It is still stationary, about three feet from the floor, and without pans, tracking or zoom shots. However, *Floating Weeds,* which was photographed in color by Kazuo Miyagawa *(Rashomon, Ugetsu),* is a strikingly beautiful film. There is something very approrpriate about Ozu's use of vibrant colors. It amplifies the story of this troupe of "colorful" itinerant Kabuki performers.

Among the actors portraying the Kabuki performers is Koji (Hideo) Mitsui. In the original 1934 version of this film, Mitsui played the son. In the 1959 film, coming full circle (like most of Ozu's films), Mitsui plays one of the actors in the troupe, Kikinosuke, who steals the company's funds after shaming two other actors out of doing the exact same deed the night before. Humorous moments like this one are often present in Ozu's films, although some are blacker than others. *Floating Weeds* contains many lighthearted moments, perhaps none as amusing as when one of the actors in the troupe tries to pick up a pretty young barber by going to the shop to get a shave he doesn't need. But the young woman will have nothing to do with his advances and calls out her protective and sizable mother to shave him. The looks shared by mother and "seducer" as she strops the razor raise a smile surpassed in the next scene when the actor appears with a bandage on his cheek.

Ozu's last films, though not necessarily typical of Ozu's style and theme, are still the most light-hearted since his very early films. His characters' problems are the same as in his other films, but in the later films they seem to endure them with more humor and a bit less melancholy. Ozu would go on to make only three more films, *Late Autumn (Akibiyori,* 1960), *The End of Summer (Kohayagawa ke no aki,* 1961) and *An Autumn Afternoon (Samma no aji,* 1962). During this period, the Japanese film industry was undergoing dynamic changes. Directors like Kon Ichikawa, Kaneto Shindo and Nagisa Oshima were altering the face of Japanese films. Ozu was starting to be associated with a bourgeois, formal style which many in the younger cinematic set felt was out of date. Ozu died of cancer at the age of 60 in 1963. The tombstone of this director of films that have proved to be universal and enduring does not bear his name. Instead it is inscribed with one character, *mu.* Translated, *mu* means "nothingness," but it is a Zen nothingness which implies everything.

The Human Condition (1959–1961)
Ningen no joken

1959–1961 / Shochiku. Part I 200 min.; Part II 180 min.; Part III 190 min. B&W. Part I: No Greater Love. Part II: Road to Eternity. Part III: A Soldier's Prayer. *Director:* Masaki Kobayashi. *Screenplay:* Zenzo Matsuyama and Masaki Kobayashi. *Adaptation:* From the novel by Junpei Gomikawa. *Cinematography:* Yoshio Miyajima. *Art Direction:* Kazue Hirataka. *Music:* Chuji Kinoshita. *Sound:* Hideo Nisizaki. *Lighting:* Takashi Kato (I), Akira Aomatsu (III). *Editor:* Keiichi Uraoka. *Assistant Director:* Yuguro Imai (I), Koichi Inagaki (III). *Producer:* Shigera Wakatsuki. Videotape: Sony. Film Rental: Films Inc., Janus.

Tatsuya Nakadai *as Kaji.* So Yamamura *Okishima.* Michiyo Aratama *Michiko, Kaji's wife.* Chikage Awashima *Jin Tung Fu.* Ineko Arima *Yang Chun Lan.* Keiji Sada *Kageyama.* Akira Ishihama *Chen.* Shinji Nambara *Kao.* Seiji Miyaguchi *Wang Heng Li.* Toru Abe *Sergeant Watai.* Masao Mishima *Kuroki.* Eitaro Ozawa *Okazaki.* Koji Mitsui *Furya.* Kyu Sazanka *Cho Mei-san.* Nobuo Nakamura *Chief of head office.* Hideo Kisho *Kudo.* Jun Tatara *Warrant Officer Hino.* Kei Sato *Shinjo.* Taketoshi Naito *Tange.* Kunie Tanaka *Obara.* Kokinji Katsura *Sasa.* Kaneko Iwasaki *Nurse Tokunaga.* Keijiro Morozumi *Hironaka.* Yusuke Kawazu *Terada.* Kyoko Kishida *Ryuku.* Reiko Hitomi *Umeko.* Fijio Suga *Captain Nagata.* Nobuo Kaneko *Kirihara.* Tamao Nakamura *Girl refugee.* Hideko Takamine *A woman in the settlers' village.* Chishu Ryu *Village elder.*

• **Part I:** In South Manchuria of 1943, Kaji works for the South Manchuria Steel Company, worries about being drafted and wants to marry Machiko. His company profits and supports the war effort by exploiting Chinese and Manchurian labor. Kaji is a humanist and makes out a report theorizing that if the men are treated more humanely, the company will get better production. The company decides to give Kaji a chance to prove his theories and sends him to the Loh Hu Liong mines in the hinterlands of Manchuria as a labor supervisor. This assignment also provides a military deferment for Kaji and he and Michiko are married.

At the mines the main problem is a labor shortage. The men are treated badly since ore is more important than men and the Japanese overseers think harsh treatment is the only way to make them work at their capacity. When the army sends the mines 600 north Chinese prisoners to use as labor, Kaji is put in charge of them. The prisoners arrived stuffed into hot cattle train cars where they have had no food or water for days. The army officer in charge tells Kaji that he doesn't care if the POWs die, as long as they don't escape.

Kaji tries to win the trust of the POWs, but the mine executives make it extremely difficult, demanding a 20 percent increase in output and refusing to prosecute a Japanese leader who kills a POW. The Japanese pit bosses, who treat their laborers harshly, and the Manchurian bosses who skim money off the laborers, want Kaji to fail. They plan an escape for the Chinese prisoners. When the Kempeitai (military government) finds out, Kaji is in trouble. Later, 18 more men escape and the especially cruel pit boss, Okazaki, sets up seven POWs as trying to escape to get Kaji in even more trouble. Without benefit of a trial, the seven Chinese prisoners are to be executed, including Kao, a militant prisoner.

The army forces Kaji to witness the executions, but after three men have been beheaded Kaji revolts. The officer in charge threatens to kill Kaji until the Chinese prisoners who have been watching start chanting "murderer" and advance on the military. Outnumbered, the army officer calls off the remaining executions. Kaji is taken away by the military and his house searched. Kaji is beaten and tortured while in the hands of the army and eventually released, but back at the mine Kaji receives notice of his emergency call to military service.

Part II: In the army, the treatment of the recruits is as bad as the treatment of the mine laborers. The veteran soldiers and those of higher rank seem to delight in the army-endorsed, face-slapping discipline used on new men and men of lesser rank. If a man is weak, like recruit Obara, then he is especially singled out for this abuse.

Obara wears glasses, can't hit the target during rifle practice and is troubled by problems at home (his wife and mother don't get along). Kaji tries to protect him, but usually his efforts are futile. Kaji makes friends with Private First Class Shinjo, who, like Kaji, is also blacklisted by the

The Human Condition (Masaki Kobayashi, 1959–1961). Part I. Kaji (Tatsuya Nakadai) attempts to carry his moral principles for the humane treatment of employees into a mine in war-torn Manchuria. (Photo courtesy of Sony Video.)

Kempeitai. Both men have communistic leanings and are considering deserting across the Russian border, which lies just beyond the swamplands.

On a forced march maneuver, Obara is on the verge of collapse. Kaji helps carry a part of his pack, but in the end Obara must ride home. To the army, this is a disgrace, and the vets beat Obara and force him to humiliatingly act the whore. As a result of all this, Obara commits suicide. Kaji demands of his superiors that Superior Private Yoshida, who was most responsible for Obara's treatment, be punished. Kaji's demands, however, are ignored.

When Shinji lets an innocent Chinese civilian escape at the border front, he is arrested. During a prairie fire he makes a run for the border. Both Kaji and Yoshida chase after Shinjo, but Kaji pushes Yoshida in the swamp. Shinjo escapes, and Kaji rescues Yoshida, but both end up in the hospital where Yoshida dies. In the hospital, Kaji meets another sympathetic soldier, Tange, and a friendly nurse. When Nurse Tokunaga is found fraternizing with Kaji, both are sent to the front.

At the front, Second Lieutenant Kageyama, who knows and likes Kaji from his days as a recruit, is in charge. He makes Kaji a superior private and puts him in charge of the new recruits. Once again Kaji is in the position of trying to win trust and obedience by treating people with kindness

The Human Condition (Masaki Kobayashi, 1959–1961). **Part II. Sabotaged by the inhumanity of those who profit from and love war, Kaji is drafted into the army, where even more inhumane treatment is found. (Photo courtesy of Sony Video.)**

instead of brutality. When the vets can't get at Kaji's men to beat them up, they instead beat up Kaji. To prevent friction among his troops, Kageyama sends Kaji and some of his men out to dig trenches. It seems like a peaceful respite until Russian tanks attack Kaji and his men who have nothing to defend themselves with but their rifles. After the battle has raged around them, just a few men are left. They hide from the Russian soldiers but their position is about to be given away by a soldier who has gone insane. To protect the ones left, Kaji must kill one of his own soldiers.

Part III: Kaji and the two surviving men from his unit, Terada and Hironaka, make their way south through the Manchurian countryside looking for other units. Along the way they run into a party of starving civilians and a small band of army men headed by Captain Nagata who refuses to give them any supplies because "they survived" instead of dying in battle. Later, one of Nagata's men deserts and brings them food. It turns out to be Tange whom Kaji had met in the hospital.

The straggling band of people must not only fight the Russian soldiers as they make their way south, but also Chinese villagers who are now armed and forming militias. When the men reach the road, they split into two parties. Three soldiers, led by Kinihara, offer to see one young woman and her brother to their home nearby. Tange has finally had enough and goes off to surrender to Russian soldiers.

Kaji and his men reach a settlement populated by women and one old man. The settlement is ten kilometers from the railroad, and beyond

The Human Condition (Masaki Kobayashi, 1959–1961). Part III. Reaching the final stage of human degradation, Kaji (center) now finds himself a prisoner of war in a Russian camp where personal standards are sacrificed for survival. (Photo courtesy of Sony Video.)

that is a POW camp. The men stay for a night but the next day Russians march into the village. Just as they are about to be ambushed by Kaji and his men, one woman rushes out and asks them not to shoot. Kaji and his men finally surrender. Life at the POW camp is worse than Kaji expected at the hands of the Communists he had idealized. One problem is that the worst men in the Japanese army seem to be in charge of the prisoners. One of them is Kinihara, whom Kaji had sent away after discovering that he had raped and possibly murdered the young girl he was supposed to have been escorting. Even the interpreter purposefully misinterprets Kaji's words for his own benefit.

The work, salvaging scrap metal, carrying sacks and logs, is very hard and the Russians take very little care of their prisoners. Food is scarce and Kaji tells Terada to scavenge food from the garbage to help keep their strength up. When Kaji is sent to perform hard labor on the railroad lines, Kinihara catches Terada scavenging. Kinihara beats the young and very ill Terada and puts him on latrine duty. After collapsing, Terada dies. When Kaji returns, he beats Kinihara and throws him in the latrine where he drowns. Disillusioned by everyone but his wife, Michiko, Kaji escapes from the camp to make his way to her.

For days Kaji walks through the cold and snow. He begs for food, but is given none. Starving, exhausted and suffering from exposure in his ragged clothes, Kaji "talks" to Michiko in his mind. "Michiko I'm home with you at last," Kaji says as he falls, unable to walk another step. There, as the snow drifts over him, he dies.

• Masaki Kobayashi was born in Hokkaido in 1916 and studied philosophy and Oriental art at Waseda University. In 1941 he joined Shochiku's Ofuna Studios, but was drafted into the army in January of 1942. He served in Manchuria but, in protest to the war, refused to be promoted above the rank of private. In 1944 he was transferred to the Ryukyu Islands until the war was over and then was in a detention camp on Okinawa. In 1946 he returned to Shochiku and became an assistant director to Keisuke Kinoshita for whom he also did some script work. Kinoshita's lyrical style of scene composition with its detailed control of atmosphere and appearance greatly influenced Kobayashi. In 1952 he made his first film as a director, *My Son's Youth (Musuko no seishun)*.

In 1953 he made *Thick-Walled Room (Kabe atsuki heya)* which was based on the diaries of Japan's "war criminals." The film, which examined the guilt of those in and out of jail so soon after war, angered the studio and Shochiku did not release it until three years after its completion.

Attacking corruption and social problems became a trademark of Kobayashi's films. In *I'll Buy You (Anata kaimasu,* 1956*)* he took on the commercialization and corruption of Japanese baseball and in *Black River (Kuroi kawa,* 1957*)* he tackled the organized crime and prostitution which surrounded the American army bases in Japan. The culmination of this period was *The Human Condition.* Kobayashi began work on the film in 1957. He made it independently with backing from the Ninjin Club and it took four years. Because he was actually sent to Manchuria, Kobayashi's film greatly parallels Gomikawa's best-selling six-volume novel just as in many ways Kaji's experiences parallel Kobayashi's. *The Human Condition* is extremely critical of the military's authoritarian mentality and became one of Japan's most successful and controversial antiwar films. The more than nine-hour-long epic is painstakingly drawn, well-acted and very intense.

After Part I of the film was released, Kobayashi received many letters asking him not to let Kaji die. But Kobayashi's heroes are idealists who refuse to conform to traditions which are inhuman. Because he rejects military customs, Kaji is called weak, but Kobayashi vividly shows otherwise. Kaji is a superior soldier, he is the unit's best marksman, not only carries his own pack on the grueling forced march, but also that of his friend. In his own way, he provides a great deal of needed leadership. As one soldier tells him, "You're probably alive today because you drag others up to your level of ability."

Kaji's problem, like that of so many of Kobayashi's heroes, is that it is difficult if not impossible to retain one's humanity under inhuman conditions. Kaji objects to the system, fights against it, but is finally killed by it. It is the poignant, heart-breaking story of a humanist living in an inhuman time. It is not good triumphing over evil, for it is the struggle which is really the story.

Tatsuya Nakadai, who perfectly captures Kaji's descent from the lofty levels of compassion to the lower depths of sheer survival, was "discovered" by Kobayashi and became his favorite actor. He was born in Tokyo in 1932 and joined the Haiyuza (Actor's Theatre) Drama Institute in 1952. His first movie role was a small one in Kurosawa's *Seven Samurai*. In 1958 he had a lead in Kon Ichikawa's *Conflagration* and his reputation was incontrovertibly established in *The Human Condition*. Nakadai has an intense acting style which lends itself to both period and contemporary films as well as providing the versatility of playing hero or villain convincingly. The haunted, lost look Nakadai used for many of Kaji's heroic scenes worked just as well when playing Okamoto's bedeviled samurai villain in *Sword of Doom* (Nakadai made 10 films with Okamoto). Nakadai has also appeared in Akira Kurosawa's *Yojimbo* (which he made, among others, during the three-year *Human Condition* shooting), *Sanjuro, High and Low,* and starred in *Ran* and *Kagemusha*. He plays the lead in Gosha's *Goyokin* and appears in Naruse's *When a Woman Ascends the Stairs,* Ichikawa's *Odd Obsession,* and Kobayashi's *Rebellion* and *Kwaidan.*

The Human Condition won the San Giorgio Prize at the Venice Film Festival.

Odd Obsession (1959)
Kagi

1959 / Daiei. / a.k.a. "The Key." 107 min. orig. (U.S. version 96 min.). Color. *Director:* Kon Ichikawa. *Screenplay:* Natto Wada, Keiji Hasebe and Kon Ichikawa. *Adaptation:* From the novel by Jun'ichiro Tanizaki. *Cinematography:* Kazuo Miyagawa. *Art Direction:* Tomoo Shimogawara. *Music:* Yasushi Akutagawa. *Editor:* Hiroaki Fuji and Kon Ichikawa. *Sound:* Ken'ichi Nishii. *Lighting:* Tatsui Ito. *Assistant Director:* Masunari Nagamura. *Executive Producer:* Hiroaki Fuji. *Producer:* Masaichi Nagata. Videotape: Embassy. Film Rental: Films Inc., Janus.

Machiko Kyo *as Ikuko Kenmochi*. Ganjiro Nakamura *Kenji Kenmochi*. Tatsuya Nakadai *Kimura*. Junko Kato *Toshiko Kenmochi*. Tanie Kitabayashi *Hana*. Ichiro Sugai *Masseur*. Jun Hamamura *Dr. Soma*. Mantaro Ushio *Dr. Kodama*. Kyu Sazanaka *Curio dealer*.

• Kenmochi, an older man with a young wife, Ikuko, gets stimulant shots from his doctor in an attempt to keep young. Kenmochi is an expert on classical art, but has no regular source of income. An internist, Kimura,

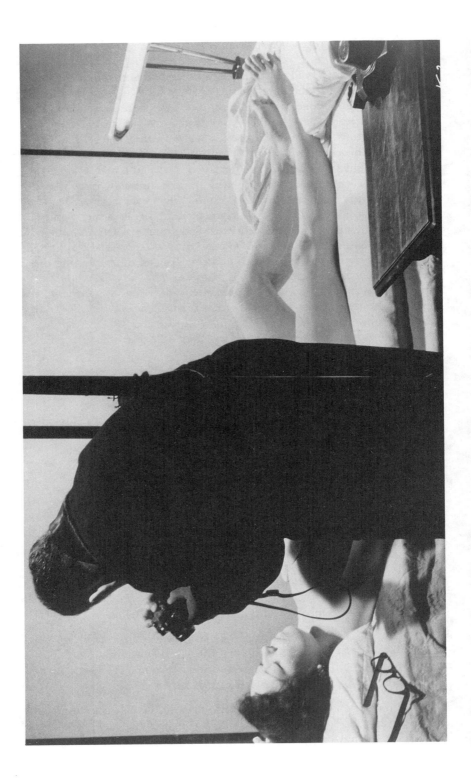

is seen as a possible suitor for Kenmochi's daughter, Toshiko. Kimura is invited to visit the Kenmochis that evening. After drinking several drinks, Ikuko goes off to bathe and passes out in the tub. Her husband, daughter and Kimura carry her to her bedroom and Kenmochi encourages the intern to touch his wife. He admits that jealousy makes him feel younger.

Kimura loans his Polaroid camera to Kenmochi who returns it but asks Kimura to develop film from his other camera. It turns out to be nude photos of Ikuko taken after she has passed out from drinking. Kimura and Toshiko make love in a room in Osaka near a train yard even though Kimura thinks Toshiko is plain and Toshiko does not care much for Kimura. Hana, the Kenmochi's elderly housekeeper, accidentally confuses a green can of cleanser and a red can of roach poison. She switches contents of the cans thinking it will keep her from being confused. When Toshiko discovers her father photographing her unconscious mother and realizes he's trying to push her into a relationship with Kimura, she moves out of the house.

Ikuko cannot handle liquor but her husband is "training" her to drink and insists on it. Ikuko says, "No matter what, a wife must submit to her husband's wishes." Kenmochi plays voyeur to see Ikuko and Kimura together and soon Ikuko is sneaking out to see Kimura. One night when Ikuko gives in to Kenmochi and they make love, he has a paralyzing stroke. When Kimura stops by to visit, Ikuko gives him the key to the back entryway.

One night, while feeding Kenmochi, Ikuko undresses in front of him. The excited Kenmochi dies and Ikuko stifles a smile behind her kimono sleeve. Later, at a meal, Toshiko tries to poison her mother's tea but uses the wrong can. Hana, however, upset at the goings-on in the house, poisons the salad which Ikuko, Toshiko and Kimura will eat. Although Hana confesses, the police say it is suicide brought about by the obviously impending financial ruin—a fact that is confirmed by newspaper headlines.

• By 1959, Ichikawa had proved himself to be a director of great versatility. Best known in the West for his antiwar films *The Harp of Burma* and *Fires on the Plain,* the darkly satirical *Odd Obsession* came as a bit of a surprise. The movie is loosely based on a book by Jun'ichiro Tanizaki, which caused quite a stir when it was released in Japan. Ichikawa's film, however, departs from the book in several ways. In the book both Kenmochi and Kimura are professors, and Kenmochi is afraid that his bad health could lead to his dismissal. The plot, which is told in a diary-like fashion through both Ikuko and Kenmochi's points of view, indicates that Ikuko is physically repulsed by her husband while Kenmochi believes his

Odd Obsession (Kon Ichikawa, 1959). Ikuko (Machiko Kyo) helps her elderly husband, Kenmochi (Ganjiro Nakamura), indulge in his odd obsession, photographing her while she is naked and unconscious.

wife to be over-sexed. But the most important Ichikawa addition to the story is the final death scene which does not appear at all in the book. It is as if Ichikawa wants to have nothing to do with these characters and consequently kills them all off. Indeed, the four main characters of *Odd Obsession* are not people an audience (Western or Eastern) can easily identify with or feel sympathy for. They are very self-centered but inflict themselves only on one another. In a way, the story takes on the appearance of being an amoral tale because there is no one to "root" for.

There is a decided lack of love within the Kenmochi family. The daughter loathes her authoritarian father, Kenmochi exploits his wife for his own sexual pleasure, and Ikuko submits while at the same time enjoying the game she is being "forced" into. Even the major outside character, Kimura, is painted as a social climber ready to use mother and daughter to gain money and position. The only relationship which hints at caring is the one between Ikuko and her daughter who sympathizes with how she is being used by her father. However, even this relationship is "poisoned" when the mother willingly takes up a relationship with Kimura, the daughter's fiancé.

The idea that people will not willingly grow and accept the limitations of aging but will fight it with every psychological and medical tool they can find, may not seem illogical to Western audiences where this is the norm, but in Japan where elders are traditionally held in great regard, this plot could be construed as heresy.

The plot takes on the appearance of a melodrama except that there is no suspense. The audience is never waiting for one person to discover what the other is doing. Each character is aware of the other's antics. The plot could also be seen as a dark comedy except there are no really funny scenes. Even the implied pornographic element is missing. While cameraman Miyagawa's expert lensing enhances and even eroticizes many scenes, Ichikawa never lets the movie arouse the viewer. Instead Ichikawa delicately balances all three elements, never making one dominate the other. Jokes are sprinkled subtly throughout the film. Even death does not escape. At the meal table several days after Ikuko has "murdered" her husband by excessively exciting him after his stroke by feeding him while she was naked, the family discusses how lucky it was that Kenmochi didn't die alone. Kimura innocently states, "At least he died peacefully with you in his eyes." Ichikawa has no problem equating sexuality with illness and death and, in fact, finds them perfect fodder for satire.

The film effectively uses color and composition — thanks to the craftsmanship of both cinematographer and director — and more than one critic has noted that the Kenmochi house, as filmed, makes for a crushingly claustrophobic set. Conversely, every time the action shifts to outside, the scenes are always devoid of people other than the main characters thus imparting a feeling of isolation.

With *Odd Obsession* Ichikawa shows yet another side of his directorial skills. They would be skills easily stretched even further with films such as *Tokyo Olympiad*. *Odd Obsession* won a special prize at the 1960 Cannes Film Festival for "the courage of its approach." It also received a Golden Globe Award for Best Foreign Film in 1960.

Cruel Story of Youth (1960)
Seishun zankoku monogatari

1960 / Shochiku. / a.k.a. "Naked Youth" and "Story of Cruelty." 96 min. Color. *Director:* Nagisa Oshima. *Screenplay:* Nagisa Oshima. *Cinematography:* Takashi Kawatama. *Art Direction:* Koji Uno. *Music:* Riichiro Manabe. *Editor:* Keiichi Uraoka. *Producer:* Tomio Ikeda. Film Rental: New Yorker Films.

Yusuke Kawazu *as Kiyoshi Fujii.* Miyuki Kuwano *Makoto Shinjo (his girlfriend).* Yoshiko Kuga *Yuki Shinji (her sister).* Jun Hamamura *Masahiro Shingo, their father.* Fumio Watanabe *Akimoto, the doctor.* Kei Sato *Akira Matsuki, the gangster.* Kan Nihonyanagi *Keizo Horio.* Toshiko Kobayashi *Teruko Shimonishi, the teacher.* Shinji Tanaka *Ito.* Shinjiro Matsuzaki *Terada.* Shinko Ujiie *Masae Sakaguchi.* Aki Morishima *Yoko Ishikawa.* Yuki Tominaga *Toshiko Nishioka.* Asao Sano *The inspector.*

• When teenage Makoto is offered a ride home from the Ginza strip by an older man, she soon finds herself being attacked by him. She is "saved," however, by Kiyoshi, a university student, who savagely beats the older man and, before letting him go, demands hush money from him. When Makoto and Kiyoshi next meet, it is while a demonstration is going on in the street. They then go to an industrial waterfront area where, after Makoto slaps Kiyoshi, he pushes her off the logs they'd been standing on. Although Makoto can't swim, Kiyoshi takes his time about helping her up. When he finally does, he seduces her.

Back on the Ginza, several pimps try to recruit Makoto but again Kiyoshi comes to her rescue. Makoto's sister, Yuki, tries to stop her young sister's romance, but it results in Makoto's leaving home and moving in with Kiyoshi. Eventually Makoto becomes pregnant. She has an abortion, which is performed by the drunken doctor who was once her sister's big romantic interest. To get money, the couple continues their profitable scam of getting older men to pick up Makoto and attempt to rape her when Kiyoshi comes in, beats them up and obtains more hush money.

After the abortion, Makoto and Kiyoshi are arrested for intimidation.

Makoto is released after she repents, but Kiyoshi is only released after he tells them about the doctor who performed the abortion. His bail money is paid by the older married woman who had once kept him. Because Kiyoshi had used a stolen motorbike to follow Makoto during their scam, he ends up in trouble again with the pimps. They beat him up and strangle him. At the same time, Makoto, who had again resorted to her game of being picked up by older men, leaps out of a car, gets her foot caught in the door and is dragged and killed. The film ends with a split screen of two bodies.

• Nagisa Oshima was born in Kyoto in 1932. His father, a government employee at a fishery experimentation station, died when Oshima was six. A young teenager when World War II ended and the American occupation of Japan began, Oshima enthusiastically took to the democratic ideals imposed by the new government. By the time he had entered law school at the University of Kyoto, however, these ideals had begun to tarnish under the reality of the Cold War. Oshima became a leader of the campus student movement and after graduation had difficulty finding a job because he was branded as "a red."

In 1954, knowing virtually nothing about films, Oshima took the entrance exams (along with 2,000 others) at Shochiku's Ofuna Studios. He placed first and was hired as an apprentice assistant director. During this time, Oshima was not only assisting and writing scripts, but he was also writing film criticism. It was traditional in the Japanese film industry for directors to come up through the ranks and undergo long apprenticeships under the reigning studio directors. After the late 1950s, however, exceptions were being made to this rule.

At Shochiku, Yoshishige Yoshida, Masahiro Shinoda and Nagisa Oshima, all in their late twenties, began directing relatively quickly in the studio's attempt to attract a younger film-going audience. As a result, films with a new approach in content and style blossomed at Shochiku giving rise to the Shochiku (or "Japanese" or "Ofuna") *Nouvelle Vague* (or "New Wave") which was named for and paralleled a similar movement in France.

Oshima directed his first film in 1959, *A Town of Love and Hope (Ai to kibo no machi)*, for which he also wrote the screenplay. Like most of his early Shochiku films, it fell into the genre of the teenage juvenile delinquent films known as *taiyozoku* or "Sun Tribe" films, a name originating from writer Shintaro Ishihara's "culture of youth" novel *Season of the Sun (Taiyo no kisetsu)*. Without the obligatory "happy ending," Oshima's film was not well-received at Shochiku. It was given a very minimal release and Oshima found himself without work for six months. Fortunately, the critics liked Oshima's first film and eventually Shochiku had to give him another chance.

The result was *Cruel Story of Youth*, his second film for Shochiku. It

Cruel Story of Youth (Nagisa Oshima, 1960). Kiyoshi (Yusuke Kawazu) and Makoto (Miyuki Kuwano) escape on a stolen motorcycle in Oshima's *taiyozoku* film about Japan's alienated youth.

was made on a restricted budget and employed many of the techniques which are associated with the Japanese New Wave, especially the "newsreel look" of the hand-held camera. Oshima has said that he chooses the style of his films according to their theme, and the jerky, hand-held camera of *Cruel Story of Youth* perfectly matches the film's chaotic story of two people defiantly out of sync with society. Oshima also employs jump-cuts, dutch tilt angles, alienating long shots and peculiar close-ups of objects to intensify their symbolism.

Many of these techniques, while ruining that perfectly realized technical film image viewers had come to expect of a polished theatrical release, instead heightened the emotional realism of the story. However, Oshima's story of alienated youth trapped in a compassionless society, is also devoid of sympathetic characters in which to invest one's emotions. Kiyoshi and Makoto commit their crimes with a frighteningly cold indifference. They become both renegades against and casualties of the system while at the same time evoking neither good nor evil.

Set against the backdrop of the demonstrations against the Japan U.S. Mutual Security Pact, *Cruel Story of Youth* presents the disillusionment and lack of dreams of Kiyoshi and Makoto's generation and the unfulfilled dreams of the slightly older generation of Makoto's sister. In a way the story reflects Oshima's own political voyage for the period. Twenty-eight

years old when he made this second film, it became his first major box
office hit in Japan. (*Cruel Story of Youth* premiered in the U.S. in 1961,
but on the west coast only. It wasn't until 1984 that it finally ran
theatrically in New York City.)

Shochiku was eager to capitalize on the popularity of its New Wave,
but it perpetrated its own kind of censorship on Oshima's films such as
changing titles or pulling his films from theaters as it had with *A Town of
Love and Hope* (which had originally been titled "The Boy Who Sold His
Pigeon"). Oshima went on to make a third and fourth film for Shochiku,
The Sun's Burial (Taiyo no hakaba) and *Night and Fog in Japan (Nihon
no yoru to kiri),* both released in 1960. This last film was a daring story
about the revision of the Ampo Treaty. When the conservative Shochiku
realized what it had on its hands, it quickly withdrew the film from
Japanese theaters after only a four-day run. An angry Oshima, finally
pushed too far by the confines of traditional studio strictures, quit. He
made television documentaries for a while and eventually set up his own
production company, *Sozosha* (Creation Company), with his wife, the
popular actress Akiko Koyama.

When a Woman Ascends
the Stairs (1960)
Onna ga kaidan o agaru toki

1960 / Toho. 110 min. B&W. *Director:* Mikio Naruse. *Screenplay:*
Ryuzo Kikushima. *Cinematography:* Masao Tamai. *Art Direction:* Satoshi
Chuko. *Music:* Toshiro Mayuzumi. *Editor:* H. Ito. *Costumes:* Hideko
Takamine. Film Rental: East-West Classics.

Hideko Takamine *as Keiko Yashiro.* Masayuki Mori *Nobuhiko Fujisaki.* Reiko Dan *Junko Inchihashi.* Tatsuya Nakadai *Kenichi Komatsu, the
bartender.* Eitaro Ozawa *Minobe.* Keiko Awaji *Yuri.* Ganjiro Nakamura
Goda. Daisuke Kato *Matsukichi Sekine.*

• Keiko Yashiro is a young, childless widow. She has been a "mama-
san," a proprietress, in a bar in Tokyo's Ginza district for the past five
years. It is her responsibility to take care of her mother, divorced brother
and his son, who has polio. She has always remained faithful to her
deceased husband and has never encouraged any of her customers or taken
on a patron as is common in her business. Business is very competitive and

Keiko, who is around 30 years old, realizes that life for a single woman is difficult. Her only real hope is to either marry again or attain independence by owning her own bar.

Yuri, a young girl who used to work for Keiko, has taken on Keiko's wealthiest customer, Minobe, as her patron. He, in turn, has set her up in her own bar. The owner of Keiko's bar berates her for not having slept with Minobe to keep his business, but she would never do that. The manager of her bar, Komatsu, respects Keiko for her conduct and is in love with her himself. Keiko starts a contribution book in order to buy her own bar, the Conga. In the meantime, Yuri has run into financial difficulties at her own bar. In an attempt to put off her creditors she plans on pretending to commit suicide. She mixes sleeping pills with brandy, but her plans go awry and she dies.

When Keiko rejects the advances of another rich customer, he sets up another one of her girls, Junko, with her own bar. Junko also manages to lure away Keiko's bartender. Because of all the stress, Keiko develops ulcers. Hope seems to come when one of her customers, Sekine, brings her her favorite perfume, Black Narcissus, and proposes to her. Unfortunately, it turns out that Sekine is not only poor and a bit feeble-minded, but also already married. While raising money for her bar (as well as for her nephew's operation and to find money to pay her brother's lawyer to keep him out of jail), Keiko falls for one of her customers, a banker, Fujisaki. The night she spends with him she dreams of her husband. He visits her by ship and brings her presents of vegetables. Unfortunately, Fujisaki is to be transferred to Osaka. As a parting gift he gives her stocks worth 100,000 yen, but he will not leave his family for her. She, however, cannot keep his money and returns the stocks to him at the train station where she sees him with his homely wife. Once again Keiko returns to her life as a "mama-san" and climbs the stairs to her bar on the second floor.

• Director Mikio Naruse came close to being "discovered" in the West twice. His *Wife! Be Like a Rose!* was the first Japanese sound film to be shown in New York. While it attracted attention, it was usually compared to French films and dismissed. In the 1950s, when the world was clamoring for more Japanese films because of the acclaim given films like *Rashomon* and *Ugetsu,* Naruse again attracted attention with *Floating Clouds.* Unfortunately, he seemed unable to sustain his presence in the West as did Kurosawa and Mizoguchi.

Some interest was stirred in 1970 when a retrospective of his films was sponsored by the Japan Film Library Council. In 1984, 15 years after Naruse's death, the efforts of the Japan Society in New York, critic/historian Audie Bock and the 25-film touring retrospective they put together, started to achieve for Naruse the recognition he deserved.

While Naruse was a director more comfortable with dialogue than

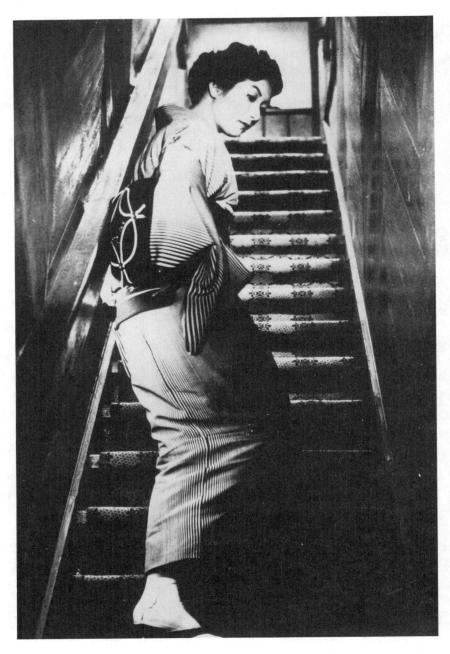

When a Woman Ascends the Stairs (Mikio Naruse, 1960). Symbolic of the loneliness of her character, Hideko Takamine as Keiko despises her nightly climb up the stairs to wait on the customers in her bar. (Photo courtesy of Toho Co., Ltd.)

plot, he was also a master of the unspoken dialogue. In his films a gesture, a glance, a subtlety of movement could say more than lines of spoken words. He was said to be an uncommunicative director who rarely gave his actors directions. Possibly for this reason, he often worked with the same actors over and over again. These actors understood what was expected of them and delivered it to Naruse's satisfaction. Among the stock company players he created was his perennial favorite, Hideko Takamine, and Daisuke Kato, who plays the simple-minded suitor, Sekine, in *When a Woman Ascends the Stairs*. The rotund Kato is often a source of lightness among otherwise heavy actors. He played the helpful "uncle" in *Mother* and the jilted husband in *Floating Clouds*. He is probably more well known to Western audiences for his appearances in *Yojimbo* (as the ugly feudal gangster, Inokichi) and in *The Seven Samurai* (as Shichiroji, one of the seven heroes).

While Naruse may have virtually ignored his actors, he paid minute attention to his sets. His directing was austere and so were the sets he used. He liked them to be claustrophobic and basically devoid of distracting details. He would remove a vase of flowers if he felt it would take an audience's attention away from his characters. Naruse's films may sound depressing, but there is something very emotionally satisfying about his characters and the acceptance of life their stories project. Sadly, only about half of the 88 films he made have survived. It is also a shame that so many of the films he made were those the company compelled him to do instead of those which he wanted to do and could do so well.

The Island (1961)
Hadaka no shima

1961 / Kindai Eiga Kyokai. / a.k.a. "The Naked Island." 92 min. B&W. *Director:* Kaneto Shindo. *Screenplay:* Kaneto Shindo. *Cinematography:* Kiyoshi Kuroda. *Music:* Hikaru Hayashi. Videotape: Discount Videotapes, Video Yesteryear. Film Rental: Kit Parker.

Nobuko Otowa *as Toyo, the mother.* Taiji Tonoyama *Senta, the father.* Shinji Tanaka *Taro, the elder son.* Masanori Horimoto *Jiro, the younger son.*

• From morning until night, a mother and father and their two young sons try to eke a living out of a very small island. Before dawn the mother and father row to the mainland to obtain precious water from a spring and bring it back in buckets to their island. While their two sons rush around feeding the family's goat and ducks and collecting firewood and cooking breakfast, the mother and father carefully wend their way up the island's steep and precarious stone steps to the house.

The eldest son must be rowed to the mainland for school and while there the mother fetches more water and rows back to the island. The precious water is carefully doled out a scoopful at a time on the family's crops. Daily events rarely vary throughout the seasons—seaweed is gathered in the rain for fertilizer, for example—but there is a trip to the city occasioned by one son's catching a large fish which they sell and celebrate with dinner in a restaurant.

One morning while the parents are acquiring water on the mainland, their eldest son becomes seriously ill. By the time they row back and discover him sick, row back to the mainland for the doctor and row him back to the island, their son has died. After the funeral, which is attended by the son's classmates and teacher, the mother and father return to scraping out a living on the island's harsh soil. But the mother succumbs to her grief and purposefully empties a bucket of the hard-won water—an accidental spilling earlier had earned her a slap from her husband. Her husband watches impassively as she tears up their meager crops. Soon, her grief spent, she again starts watering the plants. Their life must go on.

• Born in 1912 near Hiroshima, Kaneto Shindo's family were one time wealthy landlords who went bankrupt and became farmers. He first found work in film with Shochiku's Kyoto Studio's film developing laboratory in 1934. He moved on to the studio's art department, and, after winning two scenario competitions, moved into screenwriting, studying under Kenji Mizoguchi while working as his assistant director. He successfully teamed with director Kimisaburo Yoshimura as his screenwriter and wrote practically all of that director's films. Dissatisfied with Shochiku's control over their films, Yoshimura and Shindo left to form their own company, Kindai Eiga Kyokai (Society of Modern Film), with a few others including Nobuko Otowa, the actress who plays the mother in *The Island* and who married Shindo in 1978 after having lived with him for 20 years.

Otowa, who was born Nobuko Kaji in Osaka in 1924, was a graduate of the Takarazuka Girls Opera School—a school which has given Japanese films many fine actresses. In 1950 she went to work at Daiei, usually being cast in lighter roles. When she joined Shindo's Kindai Eiga Kyokai, she was given more serious roles which she handled skillfully, bringing an understated strength to her realistic portrayals.

In 1951 Shindo made his first film as a director, *Story of a Loving Wife (Aisai monogatari)*, an account of Shindo's first wife who died in 1940. Many of his early films were criticized for being overly sentimental, but he was also becoming known as a director who brought realism to his

stories. Having gained a reputation for films with themes of social criticism, in 1952 Shindo was asked by the Japan Teachers Union to film Arata
Osada's bestselling novel *Children of the Atom Bomb*. When the Union
saw his finished film, *Children of Hiroshima (Gembaku no ko)*, they
objected to the way Shindo had sentimentalized the story and sacrificed
the political significance. The film has, however, often been cited for its
touching scenes, idealism and pictorial beauty. Nonetheless, the union
took the project away from Shindo and gave it to Hideo Sekigawa who
produced the more scathing *Hiroshima* (1953). (A hardline, anti–American
film, *Hiroshima* was nonetheless successful in starting a national antibomb
movement within Japan.) In 1963, Shindo abandoned films with a social
message and started to direct films highlighted by eroticism such as
Onibaba and *Lost Sex*. By the later part of that decade, he had again
changed his primary filmic theme, making thrillers like *Heatwave Island*.

To make *The Island*, Shindo used his own money and had to resort to
many cost-conscious maneuvers. The island he used was "rented" from a
hermit for a few bags of rice. The actors and crew were offered no wages
but daily expenses and a percentage of the film's profits. The entire project
ended up costing about $15,000. The result is a most unusual film, and
one which may not appeal to every viewer. Using a semidocumentary style,
it is unrelenting yet visually poetic in its depiction of the family's hard life
and startling in its use of no dialogue. The only sounds used in this film
are those few which are appropriate to the scene: water running, a hoe
pounding the earth, sounds from a marketplace, students singing a song, a
mother's laughter or sobs. *The Island* won the grand prize at the Moscow
Film Festival in 1960.

Buddha (1961)
Shaka

1961 / Daiei. 154 min. orig. (some releases 139 min.). Color. *Director:* Kenji Misumi. *Screenplay:* Fuji Yahiro. *Cinematography:* Hiroshi
Imai. *Art Direction:* Kisaku Ito, Akira Naito. *Music:* Akira Ifukube. *Lighting:* Ken'ichi Okamoto. *Sound:* Masao Osumi. *Editor:* Kanji Suganuma.
Executive Producer: Masaichi Nagata. *Producer:* Akinari Suzuki.

Kojiro Hongo *as Siddhartha*. Raizo Ichikawa *Kunala*. Shintaro Katsu
Devadatta. Hiroshi Kawaguchi *Ajashartu*. Keizo Kawasaki *Upali*. Katsu-
hiko Kobayashi *Ananda*. Ganjiro Nakamura *Ashoka*. Machiko Kyo *Nan-
dabala*. Tamao Nakamura *Auttami*. Charito Solis *Yashodara*. Junko Kano

Buddha (Kenji Misumi, 1961). This Japanese entry into the Cecil B. DeMille religious epic contest acted more as a vehicle for Daiei's top stars; it was Japan's first 70mm film.

Matangi. Fujiko Yamamoto *Usha.* Isuzu Yamada *Dalidevi.* Yumeji Tsu-keioka *Takshakara.* Haruko Sugimura *Vaidehi.* Mieko Kendo *Amana.* Tokiko Mita *Sari.* Hironi Ichida *Naccha.* Machiko Ai *Kalika.* Matsaburo *Sonna.* Reiko Fujiwara *Child's mother.* Gen Misumura *Shariputra.* Joji Tsurumi *Arama.* Shiro Otsuji *Kalodayl.* Yoshiro Kitahara *Kaundinva.* Jun Negami *Mahakashyapa.* Toshio Chiba *Graha.* Ryuichi Ishii *Bandhu.* Yoichi Funaki *Madugaliputra.* Sanemon Arashi *Rayana.* Osamu Maryuama *Jivaka.*

• A young Prince Siddhartha fights a duel and wins an archery contest against Devadatta. As a result, he is entitled to marry Yashodara. Prince Siddhartha, however, is weary of the opulent life which comes with his position. Instead he is concerned about the poverty and human degradation he sees around him. When he approaches his advisors about this problem, they all tell him to ignore it. As a consequence, Prince Siddhartha travels to see the oracle who will help him. On his journey he sees even more human suffering and resolves that people must learn to take control over their own lives. Prince Siddhartha, seeking enlightenment, becomes a monk.

After a previously unsuccessful attempt to take Yashodara away from Siddhartha, Devadatta once again makes an attempt several years later. Devadatta threatens Yashodara's maid, pretends to be the Prince and rapes Yashodara. As a result, she commits suicide.

Prince Siddhartha continues to struggle against temptations of the flesh and of wealth and searches for spiritual enlightenment. As he wanders the countryside preaching and performing miracles, he gathers many disciples. In the meantime, Devadatta has been seeking supernatural powers with which he will fight Prince Siddhartha who by now has been "reborn" and become the Buddha ("the Enlightened One"). With miracles such as ending a drought and stopping an elephant who was about to trample one of his priests, Buddha gains many converts.

Takshakara, stepmother of Kunala and wife of King Ashoka, has made advances towards her stepson. He spurns her because he is in love with Usha. To punish him she tells the king that Kunala attacked her. The king sentences Kunala to be banished and Takshakara, who has gone on to seduce the captain of the guard, further punishes him by having him blinded. Kunala and Usha travel to see Buddha and are strengthened by his teachings. They return to the palace, forgive Takshakara, and discover that his father did not order the blinding. Takshakara jumps from the palace wall to her death and Kunala's eyesight is miraculously restored.

Devadatta, who has been proclaiming a return to the old religion, tries to gain power by manipulating Prince Ajashatru into being a follower. He tells Ajashatru that his mother and father tried to kill him as a child. Ajashatru has his father imprisoned and starves him to death. His mother, Vaidehi, is forced to explain the truth of the situation to Ajashatru. He is really an illegitimate child and his parents have been trying to keep him from finding out. Ajashatru orders his father's release, but it is too late; he has died. Devadatta, meanwhile, has been rounding up Buddhist converts and having them killed. (He crushes them under the feet of an elephant.) He starts a rebellion and attempts to have Ajashatru and all Buddha's priests killed. His plans are thwarted, however, when an earthquake occurs. He cries out for help and is rescued by Buddha. As Buddha lies dying, many people gather around him to watch his ascent into the heavens.

• Kenji Misumi (1921–1975) was born in Kyoto and graduated from Ritsumeikan University. In 1941 he entered Nikkatsu Studios and then went on to work at Daei. Almost all Misumi's films have been *jidai-geki* (period dramas) films. He is probably most well known as the original director for most of the early entries in the popular Zatoichi series.

The religious epic is one genre of film which the Japanese never seemed to be interested in. After the release of Cecil B. DeMille's *The Ten Commandments,* however, suddenly there was an incentive for making one. The result was *Buddha,* the first 70mm film to be produced in Japan. It is as colorful and spectacular as any DeMille epic.

Happiness of Us Alone (1961)
Namonaku mazushiku utsukushiku

1961 / Tokyo Eiga Co. for Toho. / a.k.a. "Nameless, Poor, Beautiful." 114 min. (orig. 131 min.). B&W. *Director:* Zenzo Matsuyama. *Screenplay:* Zenzo Matsuyama. *Cinematography:* Masao Tamai. *Art Direction:* Satoru Nakakao and Takeshi Kano. *Music:* Hikaru Hayashi. *Sound:* Kenji Nagaoka. *Editor:* Y. Sabura. *Producer:* Sanezumi Fujimoto and Kenichiro Tsunoda.

Hideko Takamine *as Akiko Katayama.* Keiju Kobayashi *Michio Katayama.* Izumi Hara *Akiko's mother.* Yoichi Numata *Akiko's brother.* Mitsuko Kusabue *Akiko's sister.* Yuzo Kayama *Akira.*

• In 1945, Akiko, a deafmute, returns home to live with her mother because her husband has died. While living there, she attends a reunion of the alumni of her old school. There she meets Michio Katayama who is also a deafmute. Michio falls in love with Akiko and, despite her reservations, she is persuaded to marry him. He convinces her that through love and compassion they can overcome their handicaps. Unfortunately, their life together is not happy. Akiko and Michio desperately eke out a living shining shoes. Their first child dies and Akiko's good-for-nothing brother sells his mother's house, forcing her to move in with Akiko and Michio.

When Akiko again becomes pregnant, her mother gives her a gold ring. She wants her to buy a sewing machine and start a small business for the family. Akiko buys the machine, only to have her brother turn around and sell it. Akiko runs away in desperation; she intends to commit suicide. Michio runs after her and uses his power of persuasion to convince her not to give up hope and the two return home.

The next spring, their son graduates from elementary school with honors. The same day he graduates, a young man comes to visit Akiko. When he was a child, he was orphaned and rescued by Akiko during an air raid in the war. Akiko finally comes to realize that she can and has been a good mother and wife, despite her handicap.

• Zenzo Matsuyama was born in 1925 and made a name for himself in Japanese film history as a screenwriter before turning his hand to directing. He joined Shochiku Studios as an assistant director in 1948 and also worked in the script department. He worked under Keisuke Kinoshita and later wrote scripts for several directors. He also wrote scripts in collaboration with Masaki Kobayashi. With Kobayashi he wrote the famous trilogy *The Human Condition* (1959–1961). It was also Kobayashi who organized Matsuyama's marriage to Kobayashi's favorite actress, Hideko Takamine.

In 1960 Matsuyama made his directorial debut with *My Hobo.* Matsuyama favors films which deal with social problems. His characters are often those who suffer injustices at the hands of other people or society in general. They may be victims of an illness such as polio in *Could I But Live* (1965) or a physical limitation as in *Happiness of Us Alone,* but they are almost always misunderstood and their stories told with a high degree of compassion and melodrama.

Yojimbo (1961)

1961 / Kurosawa Films for Toho. a.k.a. "The Bodyguard." 110 min. B&W. *Director:* Akira Kurosawa. *Screenplay:* Ryuzo Kikushima and Akira Kurosawa. *Cinematography:* Kazuo Miyagawa. *Art Direction:* Yoshiro Muraki. *Lighting:* Choshiro Ishii. *Music:* Masaru Sato. *Sound:* Hisashi Shimonaga and Choshichiro Mikami. *Producer:* Tomoyuki Tanaka and Ryuzo Kikushima. Videotape: Discount, Embassy, Video Yesteryear. Film Rental: Filmic Archives/Reel Images, Films Inc., Janus.

Toshiro Mifune *as Sanjuro Kuwabatake.* Eijiro Tono *Gonji, the sake seller.* Kamatari Fujiwara *Tazaemon, the silk merchant.* Takashi Shimura *Tokuemon, the sake merchant.* Seizaburo Kawazu *Seibei, Tazaemon's henchman.* Isuzu Yamada *Orin, Seibei's wife.* Hiroshi Tachikawa *Yoichiro, their son.* Kyu Sazanak *Ushitora, Tokuemon's henchman.* Tatsuya Nakadai *Unosuke, Ushitora's younger brother.* Daisuke Kato *Inokichi, Ushitora's brother.* Ikio Sawamura *Hansuke.* Akira Nishimura *Kuma.* Yoshio Tsuchiya *Kohei, a farmer.* Yoko Tsukasa *Nui, his wife.* Susumu Fujita *Homma.*

• The time is 1860. It is the end of the Tokugawa Shogunate's period of influence and power and the emergence of the merchant class. Because there is no real role for samurai any more, they have become masterless and impoverished, forced to earn a living in any way they can. One such ronin samurai, Sanjuro Kuwabatake, comes into a small town only to be greeted

by a dog carrying a human hand. From an old sake seller, Gonji, he learns how the town is torn by two warring factions. On the one side is Seibei who runs the geisha and gambling house and works on behalf of the silk merchant, Tazaemon. On the other side is Ushitora and his two brothers, Inokichi and Unosuke, who work on behalf of the sake merchant, Tokuemon. Both sides have hired as many ronin, criminals and thugs as they can find and have terrorized the town to the point where the silk fair, the source of most of the town's income, cannot be held.

Intrigued (and a bit disgusted) by these warring parties, Sanjuro is inspired to pit each against the other until they wipe each other out. First Sanjuro goes to Seibei who, seeing his expert skill, hires him for 50 gold coins. But Sanjuro overhears Seibei's wife, Orin, plotting to use him and then kill him in order to not have to pay him. As Seibei's troops rally on the street to attack, Sanjuro quits their employ, leaving Seibei's men facing Ushitora's. Neither can back out and hesitantly they move closer to battle.

At the last minute, the battle is stopped when provincial inspectors come to town. They stay for a while and all is calm until they have to leave because a nearby magistrate has been killed. Sanjuro discovers that Ushitora has hired two men to kill the magistrate. He captures the men and takes them to Seibei—if he turns them in the government will take care of Ushitora. Sanjuro then goes and tells Ushitora that Seibei has captured the two killers. In an attempt to get the killers by trade, Unosuke captures Seibei's son, Yochiro. At the prisoner exchange, however, Unosuke, who has a gun, shoots the two men and keeps Yochiro. Seibei in turn captures Takaemon's mistress, Nui, the enslaved wife of a poor farmer. Sanjuro frees Nui, kills her guards, and blames Seibei.

Ushitora and his men burn down the silk house in retaliation. Then Seibei's men put holes in Tokuemon's sake barrels. But soon Sanjuro's trick is discovered, and he is savagely beaten by Ushitora's men. Ushitora burns down Seibei's house and kills his family as they escape the smoke. Sanjuro manages to escape Ushitora's men and he is sneaked out of town in a coffin. He recuperates in a nearby temple with food and medicine brought daily by Gonji. When Ushitora takes Gonji captive, Sanjuro comes to town and kills the rest of the gang. Life is once again peaceful, and Sanjuro strides out of town.

• Like many directors, Kurosawa established his own production studios. It was under the auspices of his Kurosawa Productions that he made *The Bad Sleep Well* (1960), a modern mystery centering around corporate and government corruption. His second film was *Yojimbo,* in which

Yojimbo (Akira Kurosawa, 1961). A popular hero in both the East and West, Toshiro Mifune's yojimbo, Sanjuro, creates havoc in a town split by two corrupt and warring families. (Photo courtesy of Toho Co., Ltd.)

he combines the two worlds of the samurai and the emerging modern merchant.

Of course the samurai, long past his historic use, is now a masterless ronin, an outsider wherever he goes, forced to make a living by performing odd jobs such as being a bodyguard *(yojimbo)*. And the merchants, instead of being pillars of the community, are evil and corrupt—forerunners of the *yakuza* (gangsters) Kurosawa purposefully wishes to denounce in this film.

Sanjuro Kuwabatake (his first name referring loosely to his thirtyish age, his second name inspired by mulberry trees he sees out a window and says he used to raise) is not the typical heroic samurai Western audiences expected after *Seven Samurai*. He seemed to have no code of ethics and followed no rules. He is unkempt, gruff and verging on antisocial. It is hard to tell why he stays in the town. Is it to earn money (he always seems to be giving it away or giving it back) or is it to rid the town of its corrupt factions? After all, what motive does he have for cleaning up this town? Perhaps he just enjoys pitting his wits against the warring sides, seeing them wear each other down. Or perhaps he truly has the seeds of the samurai within him. The latter seems very probable when judged in light of the risks he takes just to free a woman stolen from her husband and child.

The bodyguard Sanjuro Kuwabatake is a fascinating character, and the story Kurosawa gives him to play out is a highly entertaining one. It appealed to both Japanese and Western audiences and underwent the same fate as Kurosawa's earlier *Seven Samurai;* it was remade by a Western director.

In this case it was Italian director Sergio Leone who borrowed *Yojimbo*'s story and turned it into the spaghetti Western *A Fistful of Dollars* in 1964. Mifune's fascinating Sanjuro Kuwabatake evolved into "the man with no name" and made an international star out of Clint Eastwood.

Sanjuro would be borrowed and reincarnated once again in the West, when the character, as played by John Belushi, appeared on the television show "Saturday Night Live" in a continuing series of samurai skits. Sanjuro would also make a guest appearance in one of Japan's favorite series of films, that of the blind masseur, Zatoichi, in *Zatoichi Meets Yojimbo* (1970).

In *Yojimbo* Kurosawa again had the opportunity to work with expert cinematographer Kazuo Miyagawa, who filmed his *Rashomon*. Although the two made a cinematically dynamic pair, the difficulty in their working together lies in the fact that Miyagawa worked for Daiei while Kurosawa worked for Toho. *Yojimbo* was a very successful film for Kurosawa. So successful in fact, that it spawned a sequel, *Sanjuro*.

Sanjuro (1962)
Tsubaki Sanjuro

1962 / Kurosawa Films for Toho. 96 min. B&W. *Director:* Akira Kurosawa. *Screenplay:* Ryuzo Kikushima, Hideo Ogune and Akira Kurosawa. *Adaptation:* From the novel by Shugoro Yamamoto. *Cinematography:* Fukuzo Koizumi. *Art Direction:* Yoshiro Muraki. *Lighting:* Ichiro Inohara. *Music:* Masaru Sato. *Sound:* Wataru Konuma and Hisashi Shimonaga. *Producer:* Tomoyuki Tanaka and Ryuzo Kikushima. Videotape: Embassy, Discount. Film Rental: Films Inc., Janus.

Toshiro Mifune *as Sanjuro Tsubaki.* Tatsuya Nakadai *Hanbei Muroto.* Yuzo Kayama *Iori Izaka.* Akihiko Hirata, Kunie Tanaka, Hiroshi Tachikawa, Tatsuhiko Hari, Tatsuyoshi Ehara, Kenzo Matsui, Yoshio Tsuchiya *The samurai.* Takashi Shimura *Kurofuji.* Kamatari Fujiwara *Takebayashi.* Masao Shimizu *Kikui.* Yunosuke Ito *Chamberlain Mutsuta.* Takako Irie *Lady Mutsuta.* Reiko Dan *Chidori Matsuta.* Keiju Kobayashi *The spy.*

• While asleep in the back room of an abandoned house, the ronin samurai Sanjuro overhears nine young samurai discussing corruption within their clan. One, the leader Iori Izaka, took a petition to his uncle, the chamberlain, but was refused help. His uncle warns Izaka that since they have no idea who the most corrupt man in the clan is, they had better leave things alone. Instead, Izaka took his concern to Kikui, the superintendent. Kikui tells Izaka that he will help and that he should gather all his concerned friends at this abandoned house.

Sanjuro suddenly steps out of the darkness and confronts the samurai with something they had not considered—things are not always as they appear. After discussing several factors, Sanjuro convinces them that it is Kikui who is corrupt and that their assembly is an ambush. When Kikui's men, headed by Hanbei Muroto, surround the house, they find only Sanjuro there. He starts to fight, but Hanbei calls his men off. Sanjuro is obviously not one of the men they are looking for. Impressed by his skills, however, Hanbei offers Sanjuro employment. When the men leave, it is discovered that Sanjuro has hidden the nine samurai beneath the floor boards.

Sanjuro joins the samurai when he realizes they cannot protect the chamberlain by themselves. They go to the chamberlain's house only to find Kikui had already arrested him, and his wife and daughter are under guard. The men rescue the wife and daughter, but the chamberlain is no longer at this house. In an attempt to find the chamberlain's location, Sanjuro goes to Hanbei for a job. The samurai are split over whether he is helping them or defecting. His eccentric manner has confused them. Four

Sanjuro (Akira Kurosawa, 1962). Toshiro Mifune (far right) reprises his role as the popular *yojimbo,* Sanjuro. Here his help is requested by young samurai who are plotting what to do about clan corruption. (Photo courtesy of Toho Co., Ltd.)

samurai follow Sanjuro and are captured. Now Sanjuro must compromise his position to help them escape.

The samurai are hiding out in a house next door to the Camellia Mansion, home of one of the corrupt clan elders. There a stream begins which flows into the samurai's hideout. When a part of the petition is found in the stream, the samurai realize that the chamberlain is being held next door. Sanjuro tricks Hanbei into sending the army he has amassed at the Camellia Mansion to the Komyoji temple where he says he saw from the second floor, the rebel samurai gathering. The troops leave, but an elder suddenly realizes that there is no second floor at the Komyoji temple. Sanjuro is tied up, but he tricks the elders into giving the signal to attack, filling the stream with camellia blossoms. The young samurai then attack and free the chamberlain.

Kikui commits harakiri and the chamberlain is restored to his position. Sanjuro is offered a place within the clan, but he refuses and quietly leaves. The chamberlain orders the samurai to go after him. They find Sanjuro on the road, met by Hanbei. Hanbei insists on a final duel. Sanjuro tries to avoid it since the two are so alike, but Hanbei insists. The two stare each other down for a long time then each slashes his sword, once, simultaneously. Sanjuro kills Hanbei with the one stroke. The samurai are impressed, but Sanjuro sends them away and walks off down the road.

• The original script for *Sanjuro* was written by Shugoro Yamamoto, the author of the novel which Kurosawa adapted as *Red Beard* in 1965. At first the story's main character was to be someone who fought better with his head than with his sword. Kurosawa rewrote the script before *Yojimbo* was released, but after the success of *Yojimbo,* the script was rewritten again and made as a sequel. Although the characters have different names, there are many similarities between the two films. The scenes in which Sanjuro gives his name are parallel. In *Yojimbo* he says his name is Sanjuro (from his thirtyish age) and picks Kuwabatake (mulberry) from trees he sees outside a window. In *Sanjuro* he gives his first name the same way, but this time he is surrounded by camellia blossoms and chooses the last name Tsubaki (camellia).

The "two" Sanjuros are also similar in manner, abrupt, sarcastic and taciturn. Both are prone to chastising those who would "pretend" to be samurai—the nine young men in *Sanjuro* and the merchant gangsters in *Yojimbo.* Both Sanjuros are highly competent swordsmen with a samurais' souls, while presenting unmannerly exteriors clad in socks filled with holes, disheveled hair and the same kimono. Both films use intrinsic humor to great effect, and choose suitable locations and characters for the story. The grotesque gangsters (the worst of which is probably Daisuke Kato's Inokichi—and to think he was once one of the noble Seven Samurai!) in *Yojimbo* are set against a windswept, dusty town virtually decaying under the weight of their evil actions. In *Sanjuro,* however, the young samurai's hideout is a most pleasant mansion surrounded by blooming flowers.

Kurosawa thought about doing a color scene in *Sanjuro* but decided against it. (This is something he would save for *High and Low.*) What Kurosawa did try in *Sanjuro* was the spectacular and shocking effect used in the final fight between Sanjuro and Hanbei. Claiming it was the first time it was tried in Japanese films, Kurosawa had Sanjuro's lethal sword thrust so deeply into Hanbei that the blood gushes out. According to Donald Richie it was really chocolate syrup mixed with carbonated water and put under 30 pounds of pressure that created the cinematic explosion. A similar effect was used in *Ran* when Lady Kaede is beheaded. (The decapitation is hidden by Jiro, but her blood visibly spews over the wall.) When the young samurai who have witnessed this death compliment Sanjuro on his skill, he quickly and harshly reprimands them. As in all Kurosawa films, a deep humanism is always around to moderate the violence which surrounds his characters. With *Sanjuro,* Kurosawa Productions had another hit on their hands.

Harakiri (1962)

1962 / Shochiku. / a.k.a. "Seppuku." 135 min. B&W. *Director:* Masaki Kobayashi. *Screenplay:* Shinobu Hashimoto. *Adaptation:* From the

Harakiri (Masaki Kobayashi, 1962). The suicide Hanshiro Tsugumo (Tatsuya Naka-dai) has planned for himself is not the ritual one of harakiri, but one of dying valiantly while avenging the death of his son-in-law. (Photo courtesy of Shochiku Co., Ltd.)

novel *Seppuku* by Yasuhiko Takiguchi. *Cinematography:* Yoshio Miya-jima. *Art Direction:* Junichi Ozumi and Shigemasa Toda. *Music:* Toru Takemitsu. *Sound:* Hideo Nishizaki. *Editor:* Hisashi Sagara. *Producer:* Tat-suo Hosoya. Film Rental: Films Inc., Janus.

Tatsuya Nakadai *as Hanshiro Tsugumo.* Akira Ishihama *Motome Chi-jiiwa.* Shima Iwashita *Miho Tsugumo.* Rentaro Mikuni *Kageyu Saito.* Tet-

suro Tamba *Kikokuro Omodaka*. Yoshio Inaba *Jinnai Chijiiwa*. Masao
Mishima *Tango Inaba*. Ichiro Nakaya *Hayato Yazaki*. Yoshi Aoki *Umeno-
suke Kawabe*. Jo Azumi *Ishiro Shinmen*. Kei Sato *Masakazu*.

● In a notebook an entry is written. It is May 13, 1630, the weather is
fair, the heat is rising and no incidents worthy of note have happened;
however, around midday... Hanshiro Tsugumo, a former samurai with
the Geishu clan, has come to the manor of the Iyi clan. He is impoverished and asks for their help in committing seppuku. He is received by
Kageyu Saito who proceeds to tell him the following story.

Earlier that year, Motome Chijiiwa, another ronin came to the Iyi
manor asking to commit seppuku. The house retainers discussed the matter
and decide to insist that Motome perform the act, unlike other clans who
often give money or jobs to ronin approaching them in a similar manner.
The Iyi retainers feel this sort of begging besmirches the code of the
samurai and consequently they insist on his death. Their demand surprises
Motome, but he intends to do the only honorable thing. However,
Motome requests a few days' delay so that he can attend to a personal matter. The retainers refuse. They will make an example out of Motome even
though he has had to sell his original swords and now has only ones made
of bamboo. He will be disgraced by having to commit an extremely pain-
ful and difficult seppuku with bamboo blades. The act is so difficult that
he ends up biting off his own tongue, lodging his wooden sword in the
tatami mat and plunging himself upon it. Only then does his second,
Hikokuro Omodaka, traditionally complete the act by beheading him.

Upon hearing the story, Tsugumo is not deterred. He shows Saito his
samurai swords, refuses the traditional seppuku white robes and asks for
the assistance of the Iyi clan's three master swordsmen to act as his seconds.
However, each is away from the mansion and unavailable. The swordsmen
are sent for, and while Tsugumo waits, he tells his own life story.
Tsugumo, like Chijiiwa, was also a samurai for the Geishu clan. When the
clan was dissolved by the shogun for rebuilding Hiroshima Castle against
Tokugawa wishes, Tsugumo's best friend, Jinnai Chijiiwa, commits seppuku rather than live as a ronin. He prevents Tsugumo from doing the
same by asking that he take care of his son, Motome. After a while,
Motome falls in love and marries Tsugumo's daughter, Miho. Tsugumo
ekes out a meager living at the unsamurai-like task of making umbrellas,
Miho makes fans, and Motome tutors the children of a merchant. But des-
titution is always near.

When Miho and their son, Kingo, become ill, Motome must sell his
swords. Although both Tsugumo and Motome agree that ronins begging
from other clans discredits the samurai code, Motome is forced to do
exactly that, at the Iyi clan manor. It was to inform Tsugumo that Motome
had requested a few days' extension.

When Omodaka and two other Iyi retainers return Motome's body to Tsugumo (Miho and Kingo dying several days later), he discovers Motome's terrible death at the hands of the Iyi clan and the bamboo swords he was forced to perform it with. These three Iyi retainers are the ones Tsugumo is requesting as his seconds, and word has now reached the Iyi clan that each retainer is incapable of coming. Tsugumo, who is an experienced warrior, tells how he had challenged each retainer and disgraced them by cutting off their topknots instead of killing them. The Iyi clan's warriors have come up in a time of peace, and have not been tested in battle.

By now the Iyi clan realizes that Tsugumo is there to exact his revenge on the clan. He tells them of their hypocrisy, they spout the samurai code to Motome but don't live by it themselves. When he produces the retainers' topknots, Saito orders that Tsugumo be killed. A bloody battle ensues in which the Iyi clan even resorts to using muskets. In the end, Tsugumo does what he originally set out to do and commits seppuku just as he is shot.

In one last attempt to enshroud the clan in the samurai code, Saito orders the dishonored retainers to commit seppuku, those killed by Tsugumo are listed as having died of illness and Tsugumo's death is listed as just another ronin samurai's harakiri.

• The Edo period (1615–1867) was one marked by peace and an end to clan warfare. As a consequence, many of the samurai who had earned their livings defending the clans, were without jobs. Many became ronin, masterless samurai, men who no longer had a function within society but who still were expected to live by the samurai code, even though often trapped by poverty.

Many samurai went to clan manors asking permission to commit harakiri in the hopes that instead they would be given a few coins or, better yet, jobs. Because harakiri is not an especially effective or quick form of suicide, it became customary for one about to commit the act to have a "second" or "best man" who would, once the act was done, quickly bring on death by beheading him. Harakiri (literally "belly slitting") is a term known worldwide, but is not often used in Japan. Rather, they refer to the act as seppuku, a Chinese-derived, more aesthetic term for the noble act of ritual suicide.

The samurai code of honor, like the military code of *The Human Condition*, was used by director Kobayashi as symptomatic of those rigid social systems which subject human actions to inhuman conditions. In effect, the codes created by man, have grown out of control and now control man. Like many of Kobayashi's heroes, man can fight against these indifferent practices, but he cannot escape the fact that he is a part of them. Their rebellion against the system's injustices form the plot of the film, but ultimately their fight will be futile. They will be defeated, usually dying, but the system will go on. This has become Kobayashi's theme, how the humane individual copes and contests with an inhumane society.

In *Harakiri,* the emptiness of the samurai code of Edo Japan is symbolized by a suit of armor which appears throughout the film. It appears behind the opening credits as some sort of deity to be worshiped, later it is unceremoniously grabbed by Tsugumo as a shield and thrown across the room where it falls apart. Finally, it is again returned to its god-like status, whole, but very empty. This suit of armor belongs to the Iyi clan, the clan which, throughout Kobayashi's film, has acted in the most unsamurai-like fashion. It is they who treat Motome without the dignity he deserves and they who resort to muskets when fighting the superior warrior Tsugumo. Tsugumo, who has lost everything he loved, his daughter, grandson, Motome, even to some extent his samurai status, has nothing to lose by attacking the system which took it all from him. But Tsugumo embodies those values more than the hypocritical Iyi clan who can only claim to do so.

Kobayashi's films are antitraditional, with skillfully blended themes and styles. Although *Harakiri* is graphically violent, the scenes are composed with geometric grandeur. The story is told through a series of flashbacks which smoothly blend the past with the present. The stylized presentation continually builds tension while maintaining a deliberately heroic tempo which finally erupts with the ending battle. *Harakiri* went on to win a Special Jury Prize at the Cannes Festival in 1963.

High and Low (1963)
Tengoku to jigoku

1963 / Kurosawa Films for Toho. 143 min. B&W. *Director:* Akira Kurosawa. *Screenplay:* Ryuzo Kikushima, Hideo Oguni, Eijiro Hisaita and Akira Kurosawa. *Adaptation:* From the novel **King's Ransom** by Ed McBain. *Cinematography:* Asakazu Nakai and Takao Saito. *Art Direction:* Yoshiro Muraki. *Music:* Masaru Sato. *Sound:* Fumio Yanoguchi and Hisashi Shimonaga. *Lighting:* Ichiro Inohara. *Producer:* Tomoyuki Tanaka and Ryuzo Kikushima. Videotape: Pacific Arts. Film Rental: East-West Classics and Films Inc.

Toshiro Mifune *as Kingo Gondo.* Kyoko Kagawa *Reiko, his wife.* Tatsuya Mihashi *Kawanishi.* Yutaka Sada *Aoki, the chauffeur.* Tatsuya Nakadai *Inspector Tokuro.* Takashi Shimura *Director.* Susumu Fujita

Commissioner. Kenjiro Ishiyama *Detective Taguchi (also called Bo's'n).* Ko
Kimura *Detective Arai.* Takeshi Dato *Detective Nakao.* Yoshio Tsuchiyama
Detective Murata. Hiroshi Unayama *Detective Shimada.* Koji Mitsui
Newspaperman. Tsutomu Yamazaki *Ginji Takeuchi, the kidnapper.*

• Kingo Gondo is a modern-day businessman, president of the
National Shoe Company. He has come up through the ranks and believes
in making good shoes for low prices. At a meeting of executives at
Gondo's posh hilltop home in Yokahama, they inform him that there is
more profit to be made in making cheaper shoes and that there may be a
new president in the works. To save his job and the company, Gondo
mortgages everything he owns to come up with money to purchase enough
stock to give him control of the company. Just as he is about to cinch the
deal, however, fate steps in. A kidnapper abducts Senichi, the son of
Gondo's chauffeur. The kidnapper had meant to take Gondo's son, Jun,
but the two boys had changed outfits while playing cowboys and the
wrong boy taken. A ransom of 30 million yen is demanded.

At first Gondo refuses to pay the ransom since it would end his
career, but his chauffeur is a widower, and Senichi is his only child. Gondo
has known poverty, and he doesn't intend on giving up everything he has
worked for. However, Gondo realizes that if he uses his money to buy the
company, everyone will hate him and probably not buy his shoes because
he would be branded a child killer. Eventually Police Inspector Tokura
convinces him to pay the money hoping that the police can obtain enough
information to get it back and make an arrest. When the kidnapper
phones, Gondo agrees to pay, but demands to see the boy. Arrangements
are worked out by which Gondo will take the bullet train carrying briefcases containing the money. The police arrange one trap by hiding capsules
in the briefcases which will smell if they get wet, and will produce pink
smoke if burned.

On the train, Gondo receives a telephone call. He is told to look out
the window where he sees the boy at the foot of the bridge over the
Sakawa River (between Kozu and Atami). He is told to toss the briefcases
out the bathroom windows and not long afterward, Senichi is returned.
Now the police go into action. Gondo receives a great deal of press
coverage, and sympathy for him grows into national acclaim. Soon the
police learn the make and license number of the kidnapper's car. They
learn that Senichi was drugged with ether and that he could see Mt. Fuji
and the sea from where he was held. They even learn what trolley line runs
near the phone booth where the kidnapper calls from.

Eventually they find the kidnapper's accomplices, but it is too late,
they are dead of heroin overdoses. Suddenly, pink smoke is seen drifting
above the city. They are finally led to Takeuchi, a hospital intern. They
follow him through the back streets of Yokahama and witness him buying

heroin and using it to murder a woman by overdose. They follow Takeuchi
to his home in a squalid area just below Gondo's house. He is arrested and
all but 20,000 yen which was used to buy heroin is recovered of Gondo's
money. But it is too late to save Gondo. The kidnapper is tried and
sentenced to death, but he asks to see Gondo. Gondo, who has now
started his own small shoe business, goes to see Takeuchi in prison. The
two men face each other through the glass and wire walls and Takeuchi
rails at Gondo. He tells Gondo how he has lived in hell all his life and is
not afraid to go to hell now. He starts to shake, stands and clutches the
wire wall. Quickly, the visit ends when an iron shutter falls between them.

• Translated from the Japanese, the title of *High and Low* is really
Heaven and Hell. It is a theme reflected througout the film. To Takeuchi
living in the hell of the slums lying directly below, Gondo's gleaming
house seemed to sit on a hilltop heaven. Often throughout the film the
air-conditioned coolness of Gondo's house is contrasted with the heat of
other places like the police station and the kidnapper's room, where less
fortunate people live and work. Takeuchi, motivated by these economic
and class differences, becomes obsessed with retribution.

Kurosawa takes Ed McBain's police story and turns it not only into a
clever and suspenseful police procedural but also into a brooding morality
play in which good will win out over evil, but not without paying a price.
The villains in a Kurosawa film are never dehumanized. They may be evil
or filled with hatred, but they are still human beings. Kurosawa presents the
human sides of his criminals, invoking a degree of understanding for their
mind sets. But it will be the "good guys" who will carry the day. Gondo,
although he hesitates at first to pay the ransom, does so only because he
has known the poverty in which the kidnapper still lives and refuses to
return to it. He wrestles with the dilemma of losing everything but saving
a child. He has worked at the shoe factory for 30 years (he started when he
was 16), and has invested a large portion of his life in it. He is proud of
the fact that the company makes good shoes and rejects the idea of making
cheaper shoes which wear out and must be replaced often.

Businessmen, like government officials, in Kurosawa's films rarely fare
well. It was the merchants which caused all the problems in *Yojimbo,* corrupt businessmen and unknown government officials were behind the
problems of *The Bad Sleep Well,* and overcoming the immovable bureaucrats became Watanabe's mission in *Ikiru.* In keeping with Kurosawa's
humanism, however, Gondo will sacrifice his career to save his chauffeur's
only child. Inspector Tokuro, seeing Gondo's sacrifice as being noble, now
invokes his men to work hard to solve the case. (One side effect of the film
which Kurosawa could not have predicted was that suddenly many kidnapping attempts were made in Japan which were modeled after the one in
High and Low.)

High and Low (Akira Kurosawa, 1963). Three of the inspector's policemen stake out the hospital, waiting for the kidnapper (Tsutomu Yamazaki, seen through the window, would go on to earn rave reviews as the male lead in several of director Juzo Itami's films). (Photo courtesy of Toho Co., Ltd.)

Some critics feel that Kurosawa's modern heroes are not as powerful as those in his period films. That his humanistic themes are not as well presented in contemporary society as they are against a historic background. But, when Kurosawa delves into the causes and the nature of good and evil in men, his modern films often surpass his *jidai-geki*. When Kurosawa sets a film in the present, it is invariably about sickness or crime. Illnesses, like Watanabe's cancer, and crimes like *High and Low*'s kidnapping, are indicative of those elements in society which are destructive to man either physically, emotionally or morally. The kidnapper was a medical intern. Although he lived in the slums, it would seem that a brighter future awaited him. But his values were corrupted by his hatred; class conflict overwhelmed his morals.

However, things are rarely this simple in a Kurosawa film. When Gondo, the man who almost sacrificed a little boy for his own profits, visits Takeuchi, the kidnapper, in jail, he views him through glass. Gondo's image is superimposed over Takeuchi's. The men would seem to have more in common than would be obvious by the results of their actions. This startling image is not the only one in *High and Low*. One of the breakthroughs in the criminal investigation is achieved after Takeuchi throws away a briefcase the money was in. The case contained a capsule which if it were to get wet would produce a smell, and if burned would produce pink smoke. While the police watch out over the city of Yokahama from Gondo's house on the hill, there suddenly appears a pillar of pink smoke — the criminal must be nearby. For the viewer the revelation is just as startling, for Kurosawa purposely colors the smoke pink in what is otherwise entirely a black and white film.

High and Low is a stylish and entertaining film. Unfortunately, it would mark a start to the end of one of Kurosawa's most creative periods. He would make one more film, *Red Beard,* in 1965, before a five-year lull would set in.

Kwaidan (1964)
Kaidan

1964 / Bungei Production–Ninjin Club for Toho. 164 min. (also a 125-min. version). Color. *Director:* Masaki Kobayashi. *Screenplay:* Yoko Mizuki. *Adaptation:* From stories by Lafacadio Hearn. *Cinematography:* Yoshio Miyajima. *Art Direction:* Shigemasa Toda. *Music:* Toru Takemitsu. *Sound Effects:* Hideo Nishizaki. *Producer:* Shigeru Watasuke. Videotape: Video Yesteryear, Discount. Film Rental: Films Inc., Janus.

1. Rentaro Mikuni *as Samurai.* Michiyo Aratama *First wife.* Misako Watanabe *Second wife.*
2. Keiko Kishi *Yuki/and the Snow Woman.* Tatsuya Nakadai *Minokichi.* Mariko Okada *Minokichi's mother.*
3. Katsuo Nakamura *Hoichi.* Rentaro Mikuni *Samurai spirit.* Ganjiro Nakamura *Head priest.* Takashi Shimura *Priest.* Joichi Hayashi *Attendant.* Tetsuro Tamba *Yoshitsune.*
4. Kanemon Nakamura *Kannai.* Noboru Nakaya *Shikibu Heinai.*

● 1. *Black Hair (Kurokami):* A young samurai, indignant at his life of poverty, divorces his first wife and marries into a rich family. His new wife, however, proves to be a hard woman. The samurai achieves advancement and money, but his first wife's loving ways haunt his every thought. Eventually, when the samurai's term of office has expired, he returns to his first wife in Kyoto.

The samurai's first wife, who loved him very much, has been awaiting patiently his return to their poor home. She is young and unchanged and they spend the night together in the room in which they had spent their wedding night. The next morning, the samurai affectionately lifts the covers over which his wife's dark hair flows, only to find that she is now a shriveled skeleton and her hair is shocking white. The first wife has her revenge on her husband as he fights with the skeleton's hair and quickly ages him until, in a mad frenzy, he dies.

2. *The Woman of the Snow (Yuki-onna):* Two woodcutters, one young and one old, take refuge from a winter snow storm in a small ferryman's hut. They both fall asleep, but during the night the younger woodcutter, Minokichi, awakens when the doors blow open and a ghostly white woman glides into the room. He watches as the Snow Woman approaches the elder woodcutter, Mosaku, and breathes her icy breath over him. She is about to do the same to Minokichi when she is overcome by his youth and attractiveness. She promises to spare him as long as he never tells anyone about what he has seen. The next morning, Mosaku is dead, frozen, and Minokichi must be nursed back to health by his mother, all the time refusing to tell anyone what happened that night.

One day, a year later, Minokichi meets Yuki on the road. Her parents have died and she is going to Yedo to find work as a servant. Minokichi invites her for dinner and his mother quickly likes her and invites her to stay. Minokichi and Yuki marry and have three children. The older women in the area gossip about how Yuki has remained so young looking over the years and how she has been such a good wife that even her mother-in-law died praising her.

One night as Yuki sews kimonos and Minokichi makes sandals as gifts for the children, Minokichi glances at Yuki's face and suddenly sees the Snow Woman. He is shaken and tells her about that fateful night many years ago which he now believes was nothing more than a dream. But it was not a dream. Yuki was that Snow Woman. She rails at Minokichi for betraying her trust. She will not kill Minokichi, however, for the children's sake. Instead she runs out of the house and disappears into the snow. Minokichi is greatly saddened by the loss of the woman he loved and gently places the red sandals he made for her outside the door. Soon, they disappear.

3. *Hoichi the Earless (Miminashi Hoichi):* The episode begins with the story of the battle at Dan-no-ura where the Taira (or Heike) and Minamoto (or Genji) clans fought their last battle on March 24, 1185. In this battle, the Taira clan perished by drowning along with the infant emperor despite the efforts of the brave samurai warrior, Noritsune, who follows them into the water. The tale is told in Noh song, interspersed with re-enacted battle scenes and print pictures, and tells how the Taira clan has haunted the waters and shores of the Shimonoseki Channel for 700 years.

Hoichi, a blind and skilled storyteller who plays the biwa (a type of lute) and sings tales of the Taira clan, is invited by the head priest to live at the Amidaji Temple which was built near the site of the battle. One night when the head priest is away and while Hoichi is practicing his songs, he is approached by a shadowy warrior. The samurai tells Hoichi

Kwaidan (Masaki Kobayashi, 1964). Katsuo Nakamura plays Hoichi, the storyteller who is almost lured to his death by the ghostly Taira clan in the third of four tales. (Photo courtesy of Toho Co., Ltd.)

that his lord is staying nearby and wants to hear Hoichi's acclaimed stories of the Taira clan. Hoichi goes with the samurai and returns very late.

The next day he oversleeps, exhausted by his night-long storytelling. Because his complete Taira clan song takes many nights to recount, his disappearance from the temple occurs several nights in a row. Each day Hoichi grows paler and more exhausted. He is prevented from telling the head priest what is happening, however, because the samurai has warned him not to. That night, two of the priest's servants follow Hoichi out into the storm. They eventually find him playing for the ghostly Taira clan and bring him back to the temple.

The priest tells Hoichi who he has been performing for and warns him that should he obey the samurai's summons once more, they will possess him and tear him to pieces. To help him become invisible and impervious to the samurai, the priests write sacred texts all over Hoichi's body. But when the samurai returns, Hoichi discovers that the priests have forgotten to write text on his ears. They are the only part of his body the samurai can see. Hoichi refuses to go with the samurai, and as a result, the samurai rips off Hoichi's ears to present to his lord. Eventually Hoichi's story spread throughout the area and he becomes wealthy reciting the Taira songs for visiting noblemen.

4. *In a Cup of Tea (Chawan no naka):* On New Year's Day of 1679, Lord Nakagawa stops for a visit at the temple in Hongo. One of his guards, Kannai, sees a mysterious face reflected in a bowl of water he is about to drink. He throws the water away several times but the face always reappears. Finally Kannai just drinks the water. Later that night, while on guard duty, Kannai sees the man whose face was reflected in the bowl of water. Kannai attacks the man, Heinai, and wounds him, but Heinai disappears through the wall. Kannai rouses the guards, but they can find no one. The next night, three of Heinai's retainers call to say he is tending his wounds at a hot spring and that he will be back on the 16th to even the score. Kannai strikes at the three with his sword, but they keep disappearing and reappearing. Kannai believes he has killed them, but they reappear, surround Kannai and he begins to laugh hysterically.

Here the plot breaks off because the writer has not finished his story. It becomes clear that it is being told in flashback many years later. When the writer's publisher arrives looking for the manuscript, the writer is gone. The publisher waits for the writer, reads the story and ponders the consequences of swallowing a man's soul. The landlady, who was about to make tea for the publisher, suddenly screams. He walks to the large water bucket and sees the reflection of the writer in the water.

• Each region of Japan is steeped in its own history and legends. Add to them the influences of the Shinto religion which promotes ancestor worship as a means of insuring the prosperity and happiness of both the living and the dead, then one will find a difference between how ghosts are viewed in Japan as opposed to the West. Because there is no heaven or hell in the Japanese religious theology (neither Shinto nor Buddhist), ghosts (or *yurei*) are seen as the spirits of those who have died a terrible death, who have not undergone the ceremony during which their spirits travel on to join the spirits of their ancestors, and who must wander the earth forever. The other type of spirit which shares the earth with the people of Japan are those called *yokai* which are not ancestors, but are associated with a particular time or place.

Kwaidan is a collection of four "ghost" stories written by a Westerner, Lafacadio Hearn, in the early 1900s. Hearn's stories (highly regarded by the American master of weird tales, H.P. Lovecraft) are based on tales he collected from throughout the Japanese countryside and from *kaidan* (weird tales) previously recorded by the Japanese.

After seeing the acceptance of his film *Harakiri* (1962) at Cannes, Kobayashi decided to make a film which would not only appeal to an international audience, but which would also help introduce Western audiences to Japanese traditions and tales. ("Woman of the Snow" is often omitted from U.S. prints of *Kwaidan* and may even be shown separately.) The film was produced independently and took ten years of planning and one year of shooting to produce. When it was finished, it was the most expensive film ever made in Japan up until that time. The cast consisted of most of Toho's top actors and was filmed in a borrowed industrial plane plant.

There was a meticulous attention to detail in the film. Many of the articles used in the stories were authentic artifacts from the time depicted. In fact, many were national treasures which were lent to the filmmakers.

Although Kobayashi is usually known for his filmic theme of revolt against tradition, *Kwaidan* is more of a stylistic exercise than a movie with a message. The settings and lighting used in the stories are purposefully theatrical and emphasize the supernatural aura of each tale.

Kobayashi works slowly and has made relatively few films by Japanese standards. In the 1960s when audience attendance at the cinema was dropping, Kobayashi's serious movies didn't seem to fit in with an industry which turned more and more to making profitable pornography, violence and disaster movies. Unlike Ichikawa, he was not comfortable working in television where many directors turned during this time. He did, however, film an eight-part television show titled *Fossils (Kaseki)* about a Japanese industrialist who is diagnosed as having terminal cancer while on vacation in France. When he returns to Japan, he breaks with tradition and rescues his company from a crisis and also discovers his cancer can be cured. Kobayashi did the television epic only to use the footage he shot, edited down to theatrical feature length, and released it in 1975.

Few of Kobayashi's projects seem to make it to production. He spent three years editing *The Tokyo Trials (Tokyo Saiban)* which is more than four hours long and which was released in 1983 and is also known as *The Far East Court Martial.* This documentary film was edited down from U.S. World War II footage and film from the International Military Tribunal for the Far East. It is about the trial of Japanese war criminals, and unlike his earlier *Thick-Walled Room,* this time his film was well received. *Kwaidan* won the Special Jury Prize at the Cannes Film Festival in 1965.

Woman in the Dunes (1964)
Suna no onna

1964 / Teshigahara Productions. 123 min. B&W. *Director:* Hiroshi Teshigahara. *Screenwriter:* Kobo Abe. *Cinematographer:* Hiroshi Segawa. *Film Editor:* F. Susui. *Music:* Toru Takemitsu. *Producer:* Kiichi Ichikawa and Tadashi Ohono. Videotape: Corinth Films, Discount. Film Rental: Corinth, Filmic Archives/Reel Images, Kit Parker.

Eiji Okada *as The man.* Kyoko Kishida *The woman.*

• A man goes to the dunes to pursue his hobby, collecting insects, but accidentally misses the last bus to the city. A group of villagers tells him of a place he can spend the night. They take him to the edge of a sand pit at the bottom of which lives a widow. They lower him down on a rope ladder and the woman tries to make him comfortable for the night. To the man's surprise, when he goes to bed, the woman spends the night shoveling sand out of the pit and into buckets which the villagers above carry away. In the morning the man tries to leave but the villagers have removed the ladder. They intend to keep the man in the dune to help the woman with the endless job of saving her home. By saving her own home, she also prevents the entire village from being engulfed by the shifting and blowing sands.

The man rages at the woman and prevents her from her nightly duties. When the villagers discover this, they stop delivering supplies and water to the house. The man attempts to escape several times, and during one attempt runs into quicksand. The villagers pull him out and return him to the woman in the dune. Eventually, the man learns to love the woman and resigns himself to the role which the villagers have forced upon him. He even discovers a way to remove water from the sand through capillary action. When the woman develops problems during pregnancy and has to be removed quickly, the rope ladder is inadvertently left in place. The man chooses to stay in the dune, however, ostensibly to show the villagers how to harvest the water.

• Director Hiroshi Teshigahara was born in Tokyo in 1927 and studied painting at the Tokyo Art Institute where he expressed an interest in surreal painting. In the early 1950s he started directing short documentaries but, like Hani, Yoshida, and Oshima, soon realized that he had to break with the major companies that hired him and start out on his own. With the help of his father's money (his father was a famous *ikebana* "flower arrangement" master), he set up his own production company: Teshigahara Productions. In 1961 he released his first feature-length film, *The Pitfall (Otoshiana),* which combined elements of a documentary on labor conflicts with the popular Japanese *kwaidan eiga* (ghost film). It was based on a television script by Kobo Abe, an existentialist writer with whom Teshigahara was later to collaborate on *Woman in the Dunes.*

Taken from Abe's novel of the same name, *Woman in the Dunes* was made independently for about $100,000 — a modest amount even for films in the mid 1960s. It is a compelling allegory which can be viewed on several levels: as a surrealist love story, as exemplifying man's constant struggle against his environment, or as symbolic of man's role in society. The strongest argument could probably be made for the latter. The film's opening credits are superimposed over official seals, and in one scene the man is going through his wallet while the voice-over says, "One needs so many certificates . . . contracts, licenses, ID card, deed, permit registration, permit to carry, union card, letter of commendation, IOUs, draft card, temporary

Woman in the Dunes (Hiroshi Teshigahara, 1964). The sand plays as important a role in Teshigahara's allegorical film as does the woman (Kyoko Kishida, left) and the man (Eiji Okada).

permit, written consent, income certificate. . . ." Even the ending—a close-up of a missing person report in which the viewer finally learns the man's name (Jumpei Niki), and that he has been missing for seven years and is now listed as disappeared—underscores the man's loss of position in "real" society while the viewer knows he has just found another position in it. His loss of identity has resulted in his acceptance of another one.

Teshigahara effectively used extreme depth of focus shots to present man as a small interruption in the enormous landscape of the sand dunes while at the same time using extreme close-ups to make grains of sand seem as big, and as important as, the characters. Through the lens of cinematographer Hiroshi Segawa, and the high contrast lighting, it even becomes a third actor in the film. The sand, which would engulf the pair and eventually the village itself if not removed, is everywhere: sticking to sweaty skin, falling into eyes, building up on the food covers and blowing into clothing. It is even mimicked in the patterns of the woman's pants and blouses.

Woman in the Dunes is a tour de force for Kyoko Kishida and Eiji Okada. Okada was already familiar to Western audiences from his roles as the Japanese lover in Alain Resnais' *Hiroshima mon Amour* (1959) and from his appearance in *The Ugly American* (1963). Born in 1920, the handsome Okada studied economics at Keio University and in 1946 joined the Shinkyo Theater Group. By 1949 he had made his film debut and one year later appeared in Tadashi Imai's *Until the Day We Meet Again (Mata au hi made,* 1950). This was the film which was almost sent to Cannes instead of *Rashomon* until it was discovered that Toho was in such financial difficulties that they couldn't afford to have French subtitles put on the film. It was also the first Japanese film to feature a kiss. Long avoided, the kiss was done with a glass window between Okada and his love.

Woman in the Dunes brought Hiroshi Teshigahara his first international recognition. It took the Special Jury Prize at the 1964 Cannes International Film Festival, was nominated for an Academy Award for best foreign-language film, and was shown as one of five Japanese films at the second New York Film Festival along with Kenji Mizoguchi's *The Taira Clan,* Susumu Hani's *She and He,* and Kon Ichikawa's *Conflagration* and *Alone on the Pacific.* After the failure of his *Summer Soldiers (Natsu no heitai)* in 1972, Teshigahara retired from directing, although he does maintain an interest in experimental filmmaking. Separated from his second wife, actress Toshiko Kobayashi, Teshigahara began a second artistic career in pottery, and has received acclaim for his ceramics.

Tokyo Olympiad (1965)
Tokyo Olrmpikku

1965 / Toho. 165 min. orig. (also many other edited versions at various time lengths). Color. *Director:* Kon Ichikawa. *Screenplay:* Natto Wada, Yoshio Shirasaka, Shuntaro Tanikawa, Kon Ichikawa. *Cinematography:* Shigeo Hayashida, Kazuo Miyagawa, Shigeichi Nagano, Kinichi Nakamura, Tadashi Tanaka. *Art Direction:* Yusaku Kamekura. *Music:* Toshiro Mayuzumi. *Producer:* Suketaru Taguchi for the 13th Olympic Organizing Committee. Film Rental: R5/S8, Films Inc., Kit Parker.

• The only plot for this film is the one provided by the events, athletes and surroundings of the 1964 Summer Olympics in Tokyo. The film begins with a builder demolishing a wall and the grounds being cleared for new Olympic buildings. A voice-over tells of past Olympics and the Olympic flame is shown making its way to Tokyo and the athletes arriving at the airport. The film then covers the men's 100-meter race, women's high jump, shot-put and pole vault winners. After seeing Billy Mills win the 10,000-meter run, Ichikawa's cameras wait for the last man to cross the finish line.

Many other events are covered but one athlete, Ahamed Isa of Chad, is singled out to have his story told in isolation of the other events and athletes. More events follow, including the emotional women's volleyball finals, which were won by Japan, and a longer segment on the marathon. The film ends, appropriately, with the athletes all joining together at the closing ceremonies.

• Ichikawa, the director of such black comedy antiwar films as *The Burmese Harp* and *Fires on the Plain,* would seem to be a strange director for the Tokyo Olympic Film Committee to choose to film this event (actually, the committee's first choice was Kurosawa, whose budget demands they were not, however, willing to meet), but throughout his career, Ichikawa has been a director of eclectic subjects. Ichikawa has been a most adaptable director which can be advantageous in Japan where films are often just assigned to directors.

His early career was marked by light comedies, but he has also done dark melodramas like *The Heart (Kokoro, 1955),* contemporary juvenile delinquent films like *Punishment Room (Shokei no heya, 1956),* chilling psychological adaptations like *Conflagration (Enjo, 1958),* stories of sexual fixation like *Odd Obsession/The Key (Kagi, 1959),* avant-garde experiments like *An Actor's Revenge (Yukinoji henge, 1963),* gangster parodies like *The Wanderers (Matabi, 1973),* and even thrillers like *The Inugami Family (Inugami-ke no Ichizoku, 1976).*

As can be imagined, Ichikawa's edited coverage of this major sports event is anything but conventional. In keeping with his humanistic inclination, he concentrates on the athletes instead of the events of the Olympics. He effectively used telephoto close-ups for scenes such as audience reactions and occasionally puts each event into a human perspective by using slow motion. There are also the inevitable touches of Ichikawa humor. In a wildly celebratory crowd, we focus in on one woman grimacing. Her foot has just been stepped on. A British marathon runner virtually stops to say thank you at one of the tables offering the runners refreshments.

To capture the human element behind the demanding athletic endeavors Ichikawa used 164 cameramen supervised by renowned cameraman Kazuo Miyagawa and 1,031 cameras. For the marathon event alone he used 59 cameras and a staff of 250. Through many months of advanced planning he knew where he wanted the camera to be placed, but there was no telling what would happen in front of them. According to Ichikawa, some of the best scenes in the film were "absolutely fortuitous."

Ichikawa used many innovative techniques for what was expected to be just another sports film. Instead of relying on background music to cover live sound at the events, he used live, synch sound. It is said that to achieve this effect with the relatively unsophisticated microphones of the 1960s, he buried them in the track. The music he did use was provided by avant-garde composer Toshiro Mayuzumi, who later went on to score John Huston's *The Bible.*

Tokyo Olympiad (Kon Ichikawa, 1965). Focusing on the individuals instead of the events of the Olympics gave Ichikawa's documentary a humanism not often depicted in chronicles of sporting events. Depicted here is Ethiopia's Abebe Bikila, who won the marathon; cinematically he seems overwhelmed by the crowd, but in reality was oblivious to it. (Photo courtesy of R5/S8 and Toho Co., Ltd.)

By the time the event was over, Ichikawa had about 400,000 feet, or about 70 hours worth, of film to edit. (He supervised every cut and every sound cue himself.) The eventual cost was $1,000,000 in 1964 dollars. The original version (which many consider to be far superior to the severely edited one circulated) was seen only once—by the Olympic Organizing Board.

At first the Board was unsure what to think about Ichikawa's lyrical film until one member, politician Ichiro Kono, spoke up and said he was expecting something closer to Leni Riefenstahl's films. He had expected a more conventional documentary film and indicated that the film might be artistic but doesn't really record the event. The Committee even went so far as to ask Ichikawa if the film couldn't be done over their way. Ichikawa, typical of his wry humor, told them it was impossible since the "cast" had already gone home. The film was re-edited. At Cannes that year a 154-minute version was shown. This was the version which was begrudgingly released in Japan—to a very enthusiastic public response. In the U.S. the film was bought by a small sports-oriented company which cut it up once again and dubbed in narration (which Ichikawa had purposely avoided). Later, even footage that Ichikawa had cut out was added back in and the film released as the very pedestrian *Inspiration of the Century (Seido no kando,* 1966).

Ichikawa encountered difficulties with studios after his Olympic movie and especially with Daiei's Masaichi Nagata who suspended him earlier when he refused to direct *The Great Wall of China* as punishment for not making films with "happy endings." For a time he made documentaries and even did a short film in conjunction with Italy which featured their popular mouse puppet, Topo Gigio. In 1971 he returned to feature films with the romance *To Love Again* which seemed to lack Ichikawa's spirit. In 1973 he did *The Wanderers* and looked as if he was returning to his original style. He is still making films, his most recent being *The Makioka Sisters* (1983) and *Film Actress* (1987). Ichikawa also directed the "100-Meter Finals" portion of David Wolper's film of the 1972 Munich Games.

Red Beard (1965)
Akahige

1965 / Kurosawa Films for Toho. 185 min. B&W. *Director:* Akira Kurosawa. *Screenplay:* Ryuzo Kikushima, Hideo Oguni, Masato Ide and

Akira Kurosawa. *Adaptation:* From the novel by Shugoro Yamamoto. *Cinematography:* Asakazu Nakai and Takao Saito. *Art Direction:* Yoshiro Muraki. *Lighting:* Hiromitsu Mori. *Sound:* Shin Watarai. *Music:* Masaru Sato. *Producer:* Ryuzo Kikushima and Tomoyuki Tanaka. Videotape: Media Home Entertainment. Film Rental: Films Inc., Janus.

Toshiro Mifune *as Dr. Kyojio Niide (Red Beard).* Yuzo Kayama *Dr. Noboru Yasumoto.* Yoshio Tsuchiya *Dr. Handayu Mori.* Tatsuyoshi Ehara *Genzo Tsugawa.* Reiko Dan *Osuge, nurse-servant.* Kyoko Kagawa *The Mad Woman ("the Mantis").* Kamatari Fujiwara: *Rokusuke, the dying old man.* Akemi Negishi *Okuni.* Tsutomu Yamazaki *Sahachi.* Miyuko Kuwano *Onaka.* Eijiro Tono *Goheiji.* Takashi Shimura *Tokubei Izumiya.* Terumi Kiki *Otoyo.* Haruko Sugimura *Kin.* Yoko Naito *Nasae.* Ken Mitsuda *Yasumoto's mother.* Chishu Ryu *Yasumoto's father.* Yoshitaka Zushi *Chobo.*

• Arrogant Dr. Nobuo Yasumoto has studied Dutch medicine in Nagasaki for three years in order to become the shogun's doctor. He has been ordered to come to the Koishikawa Clinic which treats the poor. The head doctor at the clinic is Dr. Kyojo Niide, also known as Red Beard. Red Beard is stubborn, inconsiderate, proud, trusted by the rich and the Daimyo, and also a very good and caring doctor. Red Beard tells a shocked Yasumoto that he has been assigned to the clinic. Yasumoto refuses to accept the situation and will not treat patients, wear a uniform, follow clinic rules nor share his medical notes from his Dutch studies with Red Beard.

One of the first duties Yasumoto finally performs is to stay with an old man, Rokusuke, who is dying. This is Yasumoto's first view of death and it shakes him up. When Rokusuke's destitute daughter shows up, Yasumoto is touched by the gentle way she is handled by Red Beard. Another death is also watched over by Yasumoto. One of the clinic's patients, Sahachi, is a saintly man who even while ill continues to make wheels which he sells to buy fish and eggs for the other patients. When he is taken home to die, a mudslide uncovers a skeleton. It turns out to be that of Onaka, Sahachi's wife. He had loved her and lost her during an earthquake only to find her again, married to a man she had earlier been promised to. Onaka had visited Sahachi and arranged for a last embrace during which she killed herself with a concealed knife. Sahachi has buried her near him and spent the rest of his life living for others.

This convinces Yasumoto to become a clinic doctor. During a visit to a house of prostitution, Red Beard and Yasumoto find the madam beating a 12-year-old girl, Otoyo. Her mother had died in front of the house and the madam paid for her funeral. Now she is trying to make the girl "entertain" her guests. But the girl refuses. She has a high fever and compulsively scrubs floors until overcome by convulsions. Red Beard assigns Otoyo to be Yasumoto's first patient.

Yasumoto nurses the girl halfway back to health and out of her protective, fear-created cocoon, when he himself is overcome with illness. Otoyo further comes out of her shell when she nurses Dr. Yasumoto and when she befriends Chobo, an impoverished seven-year-old who steals gruel from the clinic kitchens to feed his family. As Yasumoto progresses in both his spiritual and medical education, it comes to pass that as of March he will achieve his original goal, becoming the shogun's doctor. But by now Yasumoto has inherited Red Beard's philosophy of life and decides to stay at the clinic.

• The story of *Red Beard* contains many more incidents than are imparted in this brief synopsis. Yasumoto meets many more people on his journey to enlightenment than are listed above, and each one helps him to take one more step on the road to becoming a good doctor not just in book knowledge, but in life as well.

Kurosawa, as usual, pays a good deal of attention to the details of the Tokugawa period in this beautifully textured film. Kurosawa had an exact replica of a charity hospital from the late Tokugawa period built as well as a complete town. He insisted that old wood and bricks be used, and the movie set became a tourist sight during the two years needed to make the film. When Otoyo runs into town to beg money to replace a bowl she has willfully broken, the almost unnoticed background is full of authentic touches like the shops which line the street and the samurai, fishermen and women who walk and shop there.

Just as important to Kurosawa's films are the many nuances of the senses which enhance a scene. During the flashback story of Sahachi meeting Onaka, a wind chime he has bought suddenly echoes throughout the market when a breeze stirs all the wind chimes. Later, as Yasumoto leaves the dead Sahachi, he too hears a wind chime. The past has been brought to the present.

One haunting scene revolves around the young thief Chobo. After his parents have poisoned the family, ostensibly because Chobo has disgraced them by stealing, they are brought to the clinic. Chobo's brothers die and it would seem that Chobo might also die. Just as Otoyo shouts out his name, it eerily echoes around the doctors. Out in the courtyard the kitchen maids are yelling Chobo's name down a well believing that they can call back Chobo's soul.

Kurosawa's perfectionism also extended to the weather. Since he couldn't order up the right weather from his art director like he did the town and hospital, Kurosawa was constantly waiting for the right conditions. This search for perfection in his films would cause Kurosawa many problems. The most immediate being a rift in the working relationship and friendship between Kurosawa and Toshiro Mifune. As the film continued to go over budget and fell further and further behind in its

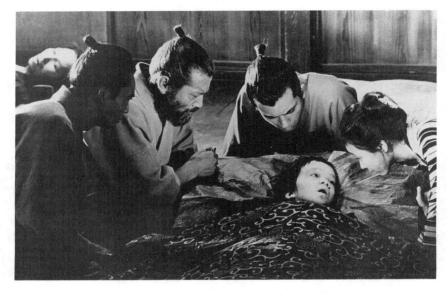

Red Beard (Akira Kurosawa, 1965). Toshiro Mifune (second from left) plays the compassionate doctor Red Beard, here seen tending Chobo (Yoshitaka Zushi), who has been poisoned along with the rest of his family after disgracing them by stealing. (Photo courtesy of Toho Co., Ltd.)

shooting schedule, Mifune found himself having to turn down many job offers, such as a profitable television series deal, not only because he was committed to Kurosawa's project, but also because he had to retain the beard he had grown for the part. When he was finally released, Mifune went on to appear in Western films like *Grand Prix* and *Shogun,* which Kurosawa did not approve of. Kurosawa felt that Mifune was undermining the image which the director had helped him build up over the years. As a consequence, the two never worked together again.

In *Red Beard,* East meets West. The character Red Beard (the name, by the way, was one applied to all Westerners during that period) wants to learn as much as possible about Western medicine. It's not that he thinks it is superior but that he wants to do everything in his power to alleviate the illnesses of his charges. Red Beard also realizes that sickness is not the only problem these people face. Their poverty and ignorance is also something he tries to battle. He does this not for personal gain, but because of the humanism of his heart.

In many respects *Red Beard* is a seminal statement of many of Kurosawa's themes. It also expands on Kurosawa's earlier *Drunken Angel.* In both there is an interest in illness and disease of both the body and soul which must be overcome and its relationship to poverty. In both there is a quest for the true self. One difference, however, is that the tone of the earlier film is more pessimistic, while the latter's is more optimistic. Illness was also a problem behind the scenes. During the two years of shooting Kurosawa became ill twice, Mifune and Kayama once each. But this did not keep Kurosawa from making a great film from novelist Yamamoto's work (Yamamoto also wrote *Sanjuro*).

Red Beard was a very successful film for Kurosawa, breaking many box office records in Japan. It also garnered critical acclaim in Japan, something which often eluded the director. In the West, however, it did not do as well, receiving mixed reviews and relatively few bookings, even though it won the Film Workers Union Special Award at the Moscow Film Festival and the San Giorgio Prize at the Venice Film Festival as well as many awards in Japan.

In 1966 Kurosawa signed a contract with producer Joseph E. Levine to go to the United States and work on several projects. (One project was a script written by Kurosawa which never came to fruition. It was about escaped convicts, and 20 years later, the Cannon Group would rewrite the script, keeping Kurosawa's name prominent and hire Russian emigré Andrei Konchalovsky to direct it. The convicts were played by Eric Roberts and Jon Voight and the film was titled *Runaway Train*.) Kurosawa was also engaged to direct the Japanese sections of the film about the bombing of Pearl Harbor, *Tora! Tora! Tora!* Not long afterward, he turned down the project. This angered many Japanese who were initially pleased that a Japanese director would be handling their sections of the film and do justice to the Japanese side of this historic event. Kurosawa, however, lost faith in the film, especially when he found out he would not have final cut on the film, something which he claimed was promised to him. For the next five years, Kurosawa would have a great deal of difficulty finding backing for his films.

Death by Hanging (1968)
Koshikei

1968 / Sozosha—Art Theatre Guild. 117 min. B&W. *Director:* Nagisa Oshima. *Screenplay:* Tsutomu Tamura, Mamoru Sasaki, Michinori Fukao and Nagisa Oshima. *Cinematography:* Yasuhiro Yoshioka. *Art Direction:* Jusho Toda. *Music:* Hikaru Hayashi. *Sound:* Akira Suzuki. *Editor:* Sueko Shiraishi. *Assistant Director:* Kiyoshi Ogakawara. *Producer:* Masayuki Nakajima, Tatsuji Yamaguchi and Nagisa Oshima. Film Rental: New Yorker.

Akiko Koyama *as The woman.* Yundo Yun *R.* Kei Sato *Warden.*
Fumio Watanabe *Education department chief.* Toshiro Ishido *Priest.* Hosei
Komatsu *Prosecutor.* Masao Adachi *Security department chief.* Mutsuhiro
Toura *Doctor.* Yoshio Tsuchiya *Rikichi.* Kuninori Kodo *Gisaku.* Nagisa
Oshima *Narrator.*

- The film's narrator asks, "Are you for or against the abolition of the
death penalty?" He recited the results of a recent poll indicating that 7
percent opposed its abolition, 16 percent favored it and 13 percent didn't
know. But for that 71 percent he offers an exact description of the death
house, last meal, official observers and actual events of a hanging. By this
time the actual execution of condemned prisoner "R." has begun.
Although prisoners usually die within 12 minutes, R. is still alive after 21½
minutes, his heart still beating. No one now knows what to do. Each
official is asked for a bureaucratic decision, but none can come up with a
proper and legal solution. The dilemma is further complicated when the
unconscious R. regains consciousness only to have amnesia. Now they can't
execute him because he is no longer the man convicted of the crimes of
forcible rape and premeditated murder of two women. R. does not accept
that he is R.
    In an attempt to jar his memory, the officers, guards and even the
doctor begin to re-enact R.'s crime. When that doesn't work, they next
begin to re-enact R.'s home life. R. is of Korean descent, was a devout
Catholic and had a mother who was deaf and dumb and a father who
drank up what little money the family had. While the story is acted out,
the death house walls are suddenly covered with newspapers just as if they
were the walls of a slum shack. Within the play-acting, R. plays himself.
When one of his little sisters asks for money for a school excursion, R.
takes them there in their imagination. But these home scenes are not a
part of the court record, and they are stopped by the education officer.
    Instead, R. and the officials leave the death house directly through the
real slums for Komatsugawa High School where R. supposedly killed one
of his victims. While R. is told how to commit the crime, R. doesn't do it
fast enough and the education officer steps in and completes the killing
for him. Back in the death house, the body of the young girl R. and the
education officer have killed lies in a casket. Some of the officials can see
the victim's body, while others cannot. Suddenly the education officer
worries about his part in this murder, but when he feels the corpse's hand,
it is warm. The girl gets up but it is no longer the victim. It is R.'s older
sister—a sister which the education officer insists R. doesn't have. Again,
some can see R.'s sister, and others can't.
    R.'s sister opposes capital punishment and is a great defender of
Korean pride and defamer of Japanese imperialism. When the prosecutor,
who cannot see her, decides she has entered the chamber without permis-

sion, she is hanged. In the next scene, however, R. and his sister lie beneath a Japanese flag in each other's arms. Around them the men are drinking and singing and reminiscing about wartime experiences. R. and his sister discuss R.'s feelings and thoughts and the role of an imagination which cannot satisfy desires. Now R. admits to the officials that he is R. They are pleased because now they can hang him, but R. says he is a different R. than they hung previously. He says that it is wrong to kill people and therefore it is wrong for anyone to execute him. While the prosecutor says it is the nation that wants to execute him, R. refuses to recognize the concept of "the nation." Consequently, the prosecutor sets R. free, but when he tries to walk out the door, he is met by a blinding light which the prosecutor indicates is his guilt. R. returns to the gallows and allows himself to be hanged. When the camera pans down to the swinging noose, it is empty. The narrator thanks all the officials for their participation in this execution and also thanks the audience for its part.

• After leaving Shochiku Studios, Oshima made *The Catch (Shiku, 1961)* independently and *The Revolutionary (Amakusa shiro tokisada, 1964)* for Toei. Eventually he began his own production company, Sozosha (Creative Company). When many prominent film personalities began creating their own companies, a critical turning point in the history of the postwar Japanese film industry was reached. The major studios went into a period of decline, and independent studios offered an oasis for experimental and personal filmmaking.

Under Sozosha's banner, Oshima made several politically provocative films, among them *Violence at Noon (Hakuchu no torima, 1966)* and *A Treatise on Japanese Bawdy Songs (Nihon shunka ko, 1967)*. No longer under the thumb of conservative studios, Oshima was free to fully explore his "revolutionary" proclivities. Oshima is a revolutionary in many respects. The filmmaking styles he employs are a revolt against the traditional methods used in Japanese films (not to mention those of Hollywood). It would be very difficult to find an "Oshima style." Every film is different, with Oshima choosing a style to match the film's subject, and each time seeming to come up with something innovative.

His film topics also make him a revolutionary as he presents himself as a forthright critic of the traditional values held by Japanese society. Through his films it is obvious that he distrusts those in power. While some label him a "leftist" director, Oshima declares that he is not a follower of the Japan Communist Party (or any party for that matter) and actually considers them just another part of the establishment. Social and political movements are often cameoed in the backgrounds of Oshima's films, but they are not necessarily the focus of the film.

Similarly, his plots are often based on true events, but are developed beyond mere fact in order to enhance their real meaning, their underlying causes and their social roots. *Death by Hanging* is based on the true story of a student of Korean descent who had difficulty finding a good job because of discrimination. He attended the Komatsugawa High School where he raped and killed two girls in 1958. His appeals exhausted, he was hanged in 1962. The real "R." was extremely intelligent and a collection of the letters he wrote while in prison was published. This attracted interest in the boy's personality and his place in Japanese society. Not long after the student's execution, Oshima wrote a realistic screenplay about him, but he never had the chance to make that film. Instead, by 1968, Oshima conjectured what would have happened if the boy hadn't died in the hangman's hands, and came up with the imaginative fictional plot for *Death by Hanging*.

Just as Oshima's imagination changed the reality of the student's hanging, similarly the distinction between reality and fantasy is distorted within the movie. The death house is in a secluded grassy area within prison walls, but when they go to re-enact the rape-murder on the high school roof, they leave through the death house's front door and step directly into the slums where R. lived. As the bumbling officials attempt to recreate R.'s actions to jar his memory, their actions take on more and more of a veneer of truth until finally they are totally thrust into reality of R.'s world. The supposedly sharp lines between reality and fantasy have become decidedly blurred.

In the process, the film also becomes a sketch of racial discrimination by the Japanese in general and the execution witnesses specifically. The film may have started out as a discourse on capital punishment, but it developed into something much more politicized than that. It became a polemic on Japanese discrimination against Koreans. While portraying R.'s family, one witness is told that since he is supposed to be a Korean, he should act more vulgarly. In many respects, it is the antics of these bureaucrats which provide a bitter and darkly black humor within this most political of films. The enthusiasm and striving for authenticity which the education officer brings to recreating R.'s life and crimes is often comical, but underneath it all is a grim depiction of the hypocrisy of the power structure.

Oshima makes effective use of the Japanese flag, a symbol of the state and its oppression, throughout this film (and many others). The court narrator sits behind a window with a flag of Japan behind him. The Korean R. and his "sister" lie beneath a Japanese flag while around them the history of Japanese atrocities against Koreans is retold. But Oshima holds out little hope for groups like the Koreans. Instead, he focuses on the frustrating inability of these smaller groups within society to make any changes while under the control of authorities who abuse their power and oppress individuals and whole segments of the population. By the end of the film, Oshima even comes to accuse the audience.

Oshima's films are always very personal expressions. From the choice of subjects to the choice of filming style, he is always in control. He uses his chosen medium to express his major themes, often sacrificing a commercial veneer (compounded by the necessary small budget of an independent studio) which could have gained him greater popularity. With *Death by Hanging,* however, Oshima finally gained a reputation in Europe and America when it was shown at Cannes (out of the festival) in 1968. Very few of his films had been seen outside Japan before this, but now he had caught their interest.

Nanami — The Inferno of First Love (1968)
Hatsukoi jigokuhen

1968 / Hani Productions — Art Theatre Guild. 108 min. (running time of some U.S. prints, 87 min.). Color. *Director:* Susumu Hani. *Screenplay:* Susumu Hani and Shuji Terayama. *Cinematography:* Yuji Okumura. *Music:* Akio Yashiro and Toru Takemitsu. *Producer:* Satoshi Fuji. Videotape: Video Yesteryear. Film Rental: Kit Parker.

Akio Takahashi *as Shun.* Kuniko Ishii *Nanami.* Koji Mitsui *Mr. Otagaki, Shun's stepfather.* Kazuko Fukuda *Mrs. Otagaki, Shun's stepmother.* Haruo Asanu *Algebra.* Minoru Yuasa *Ankokuji.* Ichiro Kimura *The psychiatrist.*

• Seventeen-year-old Shun and his girlfriend, Nanami, go to a hotel to make love, but Shun is so inexperienced that their attempts fail. Shun tells Nanami how he was abandoned by his mother when she remarried after his father died. He was raised by another couple. Shun's stepfather taught him the craft of metalworking, but also was attracted physically to him and molested the boy. Shun is very lonely and makes friends with a little girl, Momi, in a nearby park. One day, his attentions to Momi are seen by passers-by who interpret them as perversions. They chase him through the park, capture him and hold him for the police. As a consequence, Shun's stepmother takes him to see a psychiatrist. He is hypnotized for the session and tells of his stepfather's advances. The mother, angered, stops the session.

Nanami tells Shun of her life as a nude model for men who want to take pictures of her. Nanami has a crush on one of her regular customers,

Ankokuji. One of her jobs involves a sadomasochistic orgy at which a group of men take photographs. Shun follows her to this job and spies on her through a window. Later, during an outdoor photographic session, Nanami sees Ankokuji, with his wife and child and is disillusioned. She goes to look for him at the studio where she had participated in the photographed "orgy," but it is now a ballet studio.

Shun and Nanami take a trip to a university to see the amateur film about first love done by one of Nanami's friends, Algebra. It is obvious Nanami and Shun are out of place on the college campus. When they see the film, the couple takes the subject to heart and walks around the city. Realizing their love, they arrange to meet again at the hotel.

On his way there, however, Shun is approached by the men who arranged for the orgy, including Ankokuji. They want to know where Nanami is because they have arranged for a new photographic session. Shun obviously does not want Nanami to return to these men and he runs away from them. They chase him and, while dodging traffic on the busy street in front of their hotel, he is hit by a car and killed. Nanami looks out from her window and sees Shun lying in the street.

• Susumu Hani was born in Tokyo in 1926, the son of a historian. He started work as a journalist with the Kyoto News Agency in 1945. When a friend of his father's formed a photography division, Iwanami Productions, in 1952 as an adjunct of the Iwanami Shoten Publishing Company for which he was a manager, Hani joined. He worked primarily as an editor of still photography anthologies, but it was here that he learned many photography techniques which he would need when he turned to films. The company made a few industrial advertising films, and Hani was noticed by the educational ministry who wanted a short film about delinquents for new teachers who would deal with troubled children. The result was *Children in the Classroom*. Hani was now on the road to making a series of quality documentaries of short and medium length.

Hani's second film, *Children Who Draw (Eo kaku kodomatachi, 1955)* was financed by a sugar company which was organizing a drawing contest for children. The film won first prize (educational short division) at the Venice Film Festival and first prize (short film category) at the Cannes Festival in 1955. It also won the Robert Flaherty Award in 1957. In 1965 *Children Hand in Hand (Te o tsunagu kora, 1962)* won the Special Jury Prize for best direction at the Moscow Festival. In 1961 Hani graduated to making a semidocumentary feature, and his first dramatic film, with *Bad Boys (Furyo shonen)* which used nonprofessionals, real delinquents, to depict life at a reform school. Based on the book *Wings That Couldn't Fly* and with a budget of only $15,000, the film's "actors" improvised most of their dialogue.

While documentaries about children are at Hani's roots, another of his

Nanami—The Inferno of First Love (Susumu Hani, 1968). Chosen from hundreds of amateur applicants, director Hani finally chose Kuniko Ishii, left, to play Nanami and Akio Takahashi to play Shun, the star-crossed teenage lovers.

favorite topics and themes is the emergence of women within the male-dominated Japanese society. In 1963 he made *He and She (Kanojo to kare)* about a middle-class marriage in which a wife gains self-awareness through her kindness to a local rag-picker. In *Bride of the Andes (Andesu no hanayome, 1966)*, a mail-order Japanese bride is sent to Peru and, by relating to the South American Indians, she grows personally. For this last film, Hani, like many of his contemporaries, started his own production company, Hani Productions.

In 1960 Hani married actress Sachiko Hidari who has become well known for her depictions of traditional passive Japanese women who grow into strong, independent, contemporary women. Born in 1930, Hidari was a high school music and gymnastics teacher until she became an actress in 1952. In 1956 she left Nikkatsu Studios to work independently. Hidari started in Imamura's *The Insect Woman* in 1963 as well as her husband's *He and She* and *Bride of the Andes*.

In Paris, Hidari directed several short films and was both the producer and director of *Far Road* in 1977 about the harsh living conditions of Japan's railway workers. The film was chosen as part of the Museum of Modern Art and the Film Society's "New Directors/New Films" series in 1978.

Besides children and the role of contemporary women, director Hani was also very interested in people who have difficulty communicating with one another and that is the theme behind *Bwana Toshi (Bwana Toshi no uta,* 1966). Filmed in Kenya, Africa, *Bwana Toshi* tells the story of an ordinary Japanese man who lives there in isolation but overcomes it by learning to cooperate with the natives. In both *Bwana* and *Bride,* Hani has placed the Japanese in an alien environment in the hopes of discovering something more about "Japaneseness."

Quickly distinguishing himself as "the foremost psychologist of the Japanese cinema," his reputation was cemented with the release of *Nanami* in 1968. Focusing on how childhood traumas can affect adulthood, *Nanami* looks at the lives of two innocent 17-year-olds who, each being exploited in his/her own way, manages to find a temporary shelter in each others' arms.

Even when making theatrical features, Hani still uses his roots as a documentary filmmaker. He works on location and often uses handheld camera techniques. A stationary camera is an intrusive, passive observer for Hani. The amateur film the couple watches at the university was actually filmed by high school students Hani equipped with 8mm cameras. Hani also keeps in touch with his documentary background by using nonprofessional actors as much as possible. To cast the lead roles in *Nanami,* Hani placed advertisements in news magazines. More than 600 people responded to the ads. Both Akio Takahashi who plays Shun and Kuniko Ishii who plays Nanami were 19 years old but still looked like the innocent 17-year-olds Hani wanted. Their story is one of innocence discovering experience, of growing self-awareness overcoming childhood trauma, broken homes and alienation. But Hani holds little hope for the individual. Just as Shun is killed before consummating his adult love for Nanami, so too Hani thinks it is difficult for people to escape personal and societal problems. With a budget of only $32,000, *Nanami* was a big box office success in Japan. It went on to be exhibited at Cannes, but not before many scenes, such as the photographed orgy party, were cut.

Goyokin (1969)

1969 / Fuji Telecasting — Tokyo Eiga for Toho. 124 min. Color. *Director:* Hideo Gosha. *Screenplay:* Kei Tasaka and Hideo Gosha. *Cinematography:* Kozo Okazaki. *Art Direction:* Motoji Kojima. *Music:* Masaru Sato. *Executive Producers:* Sanezumi Fujimoto, Hideo Fukuda, Hideyuki Shino and Masayuki Sato. Film Rental: R5/S8.

Tatsuya Nakadai *as Magobei Wakizaka.* Tetsuro Tamba *Rokugo Tatewaki.* Kinnosuke Nakamura *Samon Fujimaki.* Isao Natsuyagi *Kunai.* Yoko Tsukasa *Shino.* Kunie Tanaka *Hyosuko.* Ruriko Asaoka *Oriha.*

• From the 17th to the late 19th centuries, the island of Sado produced gold which was owned by the Shogunate, the Japanese government at Edo. In the year 1831, in the area controlled by the Sabai clan, a young woman, Oriha, is returning home. When she enters her fishing village, however, there are no living people there, only scavenging crows.

Three years later, Magobei, a ronin samurai, has been reduced to working in a side show in Edo. His act is to perform exacting feats with his sword. After he has cut through a fish placed on the thighs of a samisen-playing woman, a man in the crowd confronts him by cutting the samisen strings one by one. The man challenges Magobei to a duel, but Magobei walks away.

Later a group of men attack the samurai who cut the samisen strings, thinking he was Magobei. The man, Samon, easily defeats them. Later, when Magobei approaches a watchtower, he is attacked. The men who ambush him are members of the Sabai clan, Magobei's clan. He kills all but one, but before he kills the final man, he flashes back to an event which occurred several years ago.

After the wreck of one of the ships carrying the shogun's gold, the Sabai clan, which was in great financial difficulty, had stolen the gold then slaughtered all witnesses, the inhabitants of the small fishing village. Magobei, a samurai with the Sabai clan, had ridden into the village, but too late to stop the massacre. Magobei protests the clan's actions to his brother-in-law, Rokugo Tatewaki, who is the clan's chamberlain. Tatewaki claims that the good of the 600 people in the Sabai clan is more important than the lives of a few fishermen. This does not placate Magobei who manages to extract a pledge from Tatewaki that no more killings will take place. Disillusioned by the happenings, Magobei leaves the clan and his wife, Shino, in protest.

Before killing his final ambusher, Magobei learns that the Sabai clan is again in financial trouble, and that Tatewaki is planning another gold theft and massacre. Magobei feels that the only way he can regain his own self-respect is to stop the massacre before it happens. Tatewaki, who had feared Magobei's interference, has sent these men out to kill him first.

On his way to the coast, Magobei has occasion to save the life of a woman who turns out to be Oriha. While she tells him her story, it is overheard by Samon. Samon proposes to Magobei that they blackmail the clan, but Magobei refuses. Samon is then hired by the clan which is now waiting to ambush Magobei when he enters clan territory. At the border, Magobei is attacked and greatly outnumbered. Samon, who has not taken part in the attack, watches and then comes to Magobei's aid. They are saved when Oriha tells gang members in a nearby area that a rival gang is trying to take over their territory. This group rushes into the battle, thinking the clansmen are a rival gang. At the same time, Samon, who turns out to be a shogunate spy, and Magobei slip away.

Goyokin (Hideo Gosha, 1969). Magobei Wakizaka (Tatsuya Nakadai, left), who has chosen humanism *(ninjo)* over social obligation *(giri),* fights his final duel in the snow with his fellow clansman Rokugo Tatewaki (Tetsuro Tamba). (Photo courtesy of R5/S8.)

The two are eventually captured in clan territory, however, and Samon and Magobei are bound, with Magobei suspended in a tree. The clan is in the process of arranging their next gold theft. They have put out the fire which acts as a lighthouse and tells ships where rocks are and have lit another which will cause them to wreck. Magobei miraculously manages to free himself and Samon when Tatewaki, still concerned about Magobei's interference, sends men back to kill them. While Magobei fights these men, Samon manages to put out the false "lighthouse" fire while Oriha has restarted the original one. The ship's captain, unsure of which is right, moves his ship back out to sea, and the clan's plans are foiled. The next day, on a snowy, bitingly cold night, Magobei and Tatewaki meet to fight their final duel. Magobei wins the fight, and, followed by his wife Shino, he walks off in the snow.

• Hideo Gosha (born in 1929) is noted as one of the masters of the Japanese action picture. He got his start in television, at first as a reporter, and later as the director of the *Three Outlaw Samurai* hit television series. In 1964 he made his theatrical debut with a film based upon his television series and which starred Tetsuro Tamba, who played Tatewaki in *Goyokin*.

Gosha would make his reputation creating samurai films that were innovative in style and powerful in content. *Goyokin*, which translates as "gold of the shogun," is an acknowledged masterpiece of the samurai genre. Filmed on location on Hokkaido, the most northern of Japan's islands, in the depths of winter, *Goyokin* is filled with beautiful scenes (this was Japan's first film in Panavision), perhaps none more so than the final battle. Shot at night (not day-for-night in which a simulated night effect is achieved through the use of filters, exposure and processing), the snowy area where Magobei and Tatewaki fight is adrift in snow and illuminated with fires which also burn for warmth. Nearby the sea storms and overhead, crows fill the sky.

Crows were also used effectively by Gosha in the opening sequences. When the young girl, Oriha, enters her village, there are dead crows awash on the shore and hanging from doorways, and live crows flying out at her from uninhabited buildings. Their chaotic actions combined with Gosha's dizzying camera work evokes a feeling of turmoil in the viewer. *Goyokin* is marked by scenes shot wildly with cameras panning, zooming and tilting. While in some scenes they help create a disorientation similar to that which Oriha must have felt upon entering her village, they also work to give scenes intensity and vitality.

The feeling of disorientation also applies to Magobei's position in a decaying society where traditions and values have become undermined. *Goyokin* is a samurai film which attacks its own origins and also eulogizes the passing of an era. Like Kobayashi's earlier *Harakiri*, *Goyokin* attacks the feudal code which had degenerated and forced an otherwise noble clan to steal and sacrifice innocent lives to save their own status. At the same time, through the character of Magobei (nobly played by Tatsuya Nakadai), it mourns the loss. At the end, Samon asks Magobei about the festive dance some masked village fishermen are performing. They are the fishermen whose lives Magobei has just saved by foiling the clan's plans and killing Takewaki. "Is it a life-saving dance?" Samon asks? "No," Magobei answers, foreseeing the future, "it is a funeral. A funeral for the samurai."

Kinnosuke Nakamura (b. 1932), who played Samon, comes from a strong Kabuki background. The son of a distinguished Kabuki actor, Nakamura made his own Kabuki debut when four years old. In 1952 he entered Toei and made his film debut. Nakamura would come to specialize in *chambaras* (sword-fighting films), films aimed at teenage audiences and in turn making him a teenage idol who in the 1950s received a record amount of fan mail.

Goyokin is a study in the *ninji-giri* conflict. Both Magobei and Tatewaki believe their actions to be just, Tatewaki following the path of giri putting loyalty to his clan above all else, while Magobei defies this in favor of the compassionate *ninjo* of humanism and justice. By abandoning his duty to the clan, Magobei has made himself an outcast, without lord or family.

Goyokin was coproduced by Toho Films and Fuji TV and was one of the last great samurai films. As the production team would indicate, the genre was headed for television. By the 1970s, the samurai genre was virtually extinct. *Goyokin* was released in the same year as Gosha's *Tenchu*, which starred Nakadai, Shintaro Katsu (of Zatoichi fame), and famed novelist Yukio Mishima who eerily commits *harakiri* on screen just one year before he actually did so in life. Although the samurai genre virtually died in the 1970s, Gosha continued to be committed to it, turning out *Bandits vs. Samurai* and *Hunters of Darkness*. Still quite active in the 1980s, Gosha started to expand his scope, turning out *Yoriko* and *Onimasa,* the latter the story of gangsters in Osaka between the years 1921 and 1940.

Boy (1969)
Shonen

1969 / Sozosha–Art Theatre Guild. 97 min. B&W and color. *Director:* Nagisa Oshima. *Screenplay:* Masataka Hara and Mamoru Sasaki. *Adaptation:* From an original idea by Tsutomu Tamura and Nagisa Oshima. *Cinematography:* Yasuhiro Yoshioka and Seizo Sengen. *Art Director:* Jusho Toda. *Music:* Hikaru Hayashi. *Sound:* Hideo Nishizaki. *Sound Effects:* Akira Suzuki. *Editor:* Sueko Shiraishi. *Assistant Director:* Kiyoshi Ogasawara, Yun-do Yun and Daiji Ozeki. *Producer:* Masayuki Nakajima and Takuji Yamaguchi. Film Rental: New Yorker.

Fumio Watanabe *Father.* Akiko Koyama *Stepmother.* Tetsuo Abe *Toshio, the boy.* Tsuyoshi Kinoshita *Little brother.*

• Toshio, a 10-year old boy, lives with his father, stepmother and three-year-old half brother. His father, an indolent, self-indulgent ex-soldier who claims to be disabled by war wounds, exploits his wife and young Toshio to earn a living for the family. He has devised a scheme in which his wife steps into the path of an oncoming automobile, pretends to be hit by the car and then procures a quick cash settlement from the driver. Eventually, Toshio is taught how to take over his mother's job, and the family moves from town to town plying their scheme and avoiding notice by the authorities. At first his father injects Toshio to simulate bruises, but eventually Toshio gets real bruises and injuries. Because the family never settles down, Toshio is an outsider in every community and has no real friends outside of his family. To escape, Toshio creates a fantasy world which includes a man from outer space, a messenger of justice.

Toshio used to live with his grandparents in Kochi, and one day he attempts to run away and rejoin them. Unfortunately, he hasn't enough money for the train fare to Kochi, so instead he buys a ticket to a closer location. He spends the night on the beach, then returns to his parents. When Toshio's stepmother becomes pregnant, his father wants her to have an abortion, but on the day she is to have the operation, she decides against it. Toshio sees her come out of the doctor's office and at first she is angry with him, but eventually she offers him a "compensatory bribe," a wristwatch, if he doesn't tell his father. She and Toshio share her secret and the two become closer.

By now, however, the police have learned of the family's activities and they are forced to fly north to Hokkaido. While there, Toshio's father and stepmother argue over whether or not to continue the scam. His father thinks they should lie low while his mother believes they should make as much money as possible as quickly as possible. They consider separating and discuss who should have custody of Toshio, the one capable of bringing in money. During one argument, Toshio's father throws the watch Toshio had been given by his stepmother, out into the snow. Toshio's little brother goes outside to retrieve it and strays onto the road where a jeep swerves out of the way to miss hitting him. The jeep occupants, an adult and a little girl, are killed in the accident. Toshio picks up the little girl's boot out of the snow. Later, when his father throws the boot out of the window, Toshio builds a snowman "from outer space" which they decorate with the boot and the watch which his little brother has been holding. Toshio tells his brother the snowman will right all wrongs and wipe out all bad men. But Toshio knows this isn't true, and begins to tear down the snowman.

Toshio's family again moves south but are soon apprehended by the police to whom Toshio admits that he saw the Hokkaido accident. When they show him a picture of himself and ask him to identify it, he says it is a man from outer space.

• Like *Death by Hanging,* Oshima once again turns to newspaper headlines for the basic plot of *Boy.* Oshima takes the story of people who lived by faking accidents and extorting money from drivers and turns it into a bitter statement about the condition of the Japanese family. The father in *Boy* is a stereotypical Japanese patriarch. He is hard, demanding and self-centered. He is the master of his house and anyone who dares to challenge his power meets with verbal or physical retaliation. When he

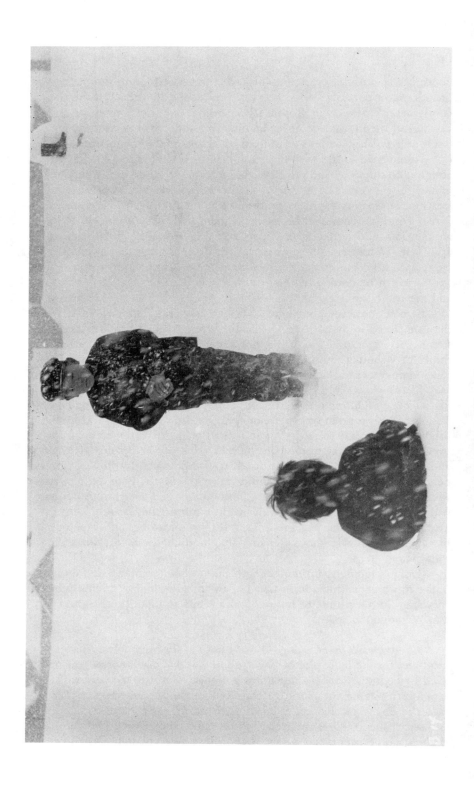

discovers his wife has not had an abortion, he beats her. When Toshio dreams of returning to his grandparents, his father seems to take delight in telling the poor boy that his grandparents were glad to be rid of him and that all his friends have forgotten him.

For Oshima, the power which the father exerts over his wife and children is symbolic of the authority the Japanese state exerts over its subjects. Toshio may hate the cheating scheme he is forced to participate in, but he is still intensely loyal to his parents. Similarly, individuals may dislike actions taken by the state, but they are still loyal patriots. As in *Death by Hanging,* the Japanese flag is again predominantly cameoed throughout the film, further cementing the symbolism between the father and the state as authority figures.

At the same time, the father is a victim of the state. He fought in World War II and carries scars (either real physical scars or just-as-real psychological wounds) from his dictated service. Unfortunately, the pain of these "wounds" are then passed on to the children. The fact that Toshio is called "boy" by his father is symbolic of his own ability to scar and Toshio's subservience in his father's eyes.

This compelling tale could be told with a great deal of sentimentality, but Oshima rejects any emotional superfluousness. Oshima does not pass any kind of moral judgment on Toshio and his family. Instead he treats the story with poignancy and lyricism. Oshima used a nonprofessional to play the role of Toshio. Tetsuo Abe was found in an orphanage and, after the film was completed, several crew members offered to adopt the young boy. Tetsuo, however, according to Oshima, refused and returned to the orphanage. Sadly, he had had enough bad experiences with "families."

Toshio seems to be an ordinary little boy caught in extraordinary circumstances. The character is played with a great deal of stoicism outwardly and finding refuge in his imagination inwardly. For most of the film, Toshio's face is totally impassive. (He only cries at the end when he sees his own picture.) But this blankness covers a great deal of pain. Unlike Western films, there is no happy ending for *Boy.* (In fact, happy endings are a rarity in Japanese films.) In Oshima's world the good guys rarely win, primarily because it is often difficult to distinguish them from the bad guys.

As usual, Oshima has chosen yet another style of filmmaking to tell the story of Toshio and his family. While shot primarily in color, there are occasional scenes done in black and white. The accident in which the young girl is killed is filmed without sound and in black and white and only when Toshio builds a snowman (in color) is the boot seen as bright red. Scenes are filmed with no logical endings to them, with jarringly

Boy (Nagisa Oshima, 1969). In the background is the "snowman from outer space who will come to earth to right all wrongs" that was built by Toshio (Tetsuo Abe) and which acts as a shrine for the boot of the little girl killed in an auto accident.

abrupt changes, and gaps in the continuity. Like its predecessors, *Boy* can be a difficult film to watch, but it is also innovative and challenging. This film marked Oshima's real film debut in the United States when it was shown at the Lincoln Center Film Festival in New York City. It became an international success, but at the same time, it began a period which marked a decline in Oshima's film output.

Double Suicide (1969)
Shinju ten no Amijima

1969 / Hyogensha–Art Theatre Guild for Toho. 104 min. B&W. *Director:* Masahiro Shinoda. *Screenplay:* Taeko Tomioka, Masahiro Shinoda and Toru Takemitsu. *Adaptation:* From the play by Monzaemon Chikamatsu. *Cinematographer:* Toichiro Narushima. *Music:* Toru Takemitsu. *Art Director:* Kiyoshi Awazu. Videotape: Sony. Film Rental: Films Inc., Janus.

Kichiemon Nakamura *as Jihei.* Shima Iwashita *Koharu/Osan.* Hosei Komatsu *Tahei.* Yusuke Takita *Magoemon.* Kamatari Fujiwara *Owner of the Yamatoya.* Yoshi Kata *Gosaemon.* Shizue Kawarazaki *Osan's mother.* Tokie Hidari *Osugi.*

• Jihei, a paper merchant in 18th-century Osaka, is desperately in love with the courtesan Koharu. He wants to purchase her contract but is prevented from doing so by the fact that he is already married and does not have enough money. His obsessive love has brought his business to ruin. Koharu also loves Jihei, but the impossibility of their love forces them to consider double suicide *(shinju)* as the only way to be together. His brother, Magoemon, a flour merchant disguised as a samurai, purchases Koharu's services. While Jihei listens nearby, Koharu begs the samurai to save her from Jihei's request to commit suicide. Jihei reveals himself and his brother reminds him of his social obligations to his wife. Thinking Koharu has betrayed him, Jihei renounces her. Magoemon collects the paper promises Jihei has made to Koharu and also a letter sent her by Jihei's wife, Osan.

An obnoxious merchant, Tahei, however, shames Jihei by spreading the news that he is on the verge of financial ruin. Tahei, who is also interested in purchasing Koharu's contract, has placed Jihei in the position of becoming shunned and distrusted by other merchants. In order for her husband to save face, Osan offers Jihei what money she has along with the

Double Suicide (Masahiro Shinoda, 1969). Shima Iwashita plays both the courtesan Koharu and the devoted wife Osan in Shinoda's film, which is marked by engrossing artifice and startling yet beautiful graphics.

family's best kimonos to pawn. Osan realizes that Koharu had only pretended not to want to commit suicide with Jihei because Osan had sent her a letter asking her to save her husband's life. By renouncing Jihei, Koharu has returned him to Osan. However, Koharu has also promised to kill herself rather than be redeemed by anyone other than Jihei. When rumors reach them that a merchant is planning to redeem Koharu, both

Osan and Jihei realize that she will soon commit suicide. To save her, they must come up with money.

When Osan's father hears the rumors, he assumes Jihei has not kept his promise to stay away from Koharu. Not listening to their reasons, he forcibly takes Osan away and demands a letter of divorce from Jihei. Osan struggles unsuccessfully against her father, desperately trying to tell him that she does not want a divorce. Jihei runs to Koharu who has indeed been purchased by Tahei. Realizing the hopelessness of their love, they run away. To escape the worldly entrapments which have duty-bound them at odds with their personal desires, they symbolically cut their hair, in essence, becoming a nun and a monk. They stumble along the banks of the river toward their destiny, suicide. Finally, Jihei kills Koharu with his sword and then hangs himself.

• In 1967 Nagisa Oshima became a partner with ATG (Art Theatre Guild), a company which began around 1961 primarily as a distribution and exhibition company. Oshima encouraged other directors to join along with him in making lower-budget films for which ATG would supply half the monetary backing and distribution through its theatres. Among those directors who joined, looking for more artistic freedom than they could find in the traditional studios, were Yoshishige Yoshida and Masahiro Shinoda who also started his own independent production company, Hyogensha (Express Company).

Shinoda (b. 1931), like Oshima and Yoshida, was a part of what is called the Ofuna (or Shochiku) New Wave of the 1960s, directors who were allowed to make relatively experimental films at Shochiku Studios at a time when it was not doing well. Shinoda attended Waseda University where he studied history. When his mother died, he was forced to find a job and answered a newspaper ad for an assistant director at Shochiku. Two thousand people applied for the job and eight were accepted, among them Shinoda and Oshima. As an assistant director Shinoda worked with Yasujiro Ozu and, upon Shochiku's taking a chance on its young directors, blossomed along with Oshima and Yoshida.

Shinoda was always interested in the popular theatre in Japan and especially in the works of Monzaemon Chikamatsu. Chikamatsu, often called the William Shakespeare of Japan, was an 18th-century *samurai* who became a social outcast when he turned to writing plays. In his works, the heroes were always *nimaime* (attractive but weak men who were susceptible to romantic entanglements) as opposed to *tateyaku* (the strong, silent samurai type). For this reason, his plays often appealed to the middle/merchant Japanese class.

Double Suicide, which is based on Chikamatsu's 1720 play *The Love and Suicide at Amijima (Shinju ten no Amijima),* is a most unusual film. It opens with the black-clad puppeteers *(kurokos)* of the popular Japanese

Bunraku theatre preparing their life-size puppets for a performance. As several men manipulate the puppets, the voice-over is that of a telephone conversation between the film's actual director, Shinoda, and actress Shima Iwashita discussing the location scouting for the final scene of the film. Shinoda is already creating a highly stylized and theatrical atmosphere that will not allow the viewer to passively flow with the plot.

Throughout the film the viewer is reminded of the artifice of the set-ting and the indebtedness to the Bunraku theatre. The *kurokos* are con-stantly in the background, watching the story evolve, facilitating or con-trolling a character's actions. They hover about scenes helping Magoemon tie Jihei's hands together, blowing out candles, removing the children from the stage, and eventually helping Jihei to hang himself. In effect, the actors have become puppets, and their actions and destiny are fatalistically out of their own control. The audience is kept from becoming emotionally involved with the story not only by the presence of the *kurokos,* but also by artificial sets with walls that are knocked down (or removed by the *kurokos*) and calligraphy (done by Shinoda's cousin, Toko Shinoda, one of Japan's leading abstract calligraphers) which is splashed artfully on the floor and walls.

One of Shinoda's favorite themes is the examination of the psychological underpinnings of Japanese society. In *Double Suicide* he examines the *ninjo-giri* (humaneness and love versus social obligations) conflict which is very common to the plots of Japanese stories. Jihei's duties to his family are in direct opposition to his love for Koharu. Shinoda, however, makes a very telling statement about Jihei's obsessive love for a woman other than his wife by having the same actress play both parts. Shinoda seems to be saying that not only is Jihei's love for Koharu illogi-cal, but also that society is responsible for offering Jihei no escape, sentenc-ing him and his love to doom.

In the final *michiyuki* (lovers' journey to death), both Jihei and Koharu cut their hair to symbolize their separation from the society that has necessitated their death — just as Buddhist monks and nuns cut their hair before entering the order to symbolize a similar separation. By dying as a monk and a nun Jihei and Koharu hope to find peace and enter heaven without family and without obligations.

Shima Iwashita (b. 1941), who plays both Osan and Koharu became an actress with Shochiku in 1955. She has worked with such notable direc-tors as Yasujiro Ozu and gave an impressive performance in his *An Autumn Afternoon* (1962) as the daughter who must choose between tak-ing care of her father and marriage. She has also appeared in Kobayashi's *Harakiri* (1962) and is married to *Double Suicide*'s director, Masahiro Shinoda. *Double Suicide* won the *Kinema Jumpo* "Best One" award, Japan's highest film honor.

Eros Plus Massacre (1969)
Erosu purasu gyakusatsu

1969 / Gendai Eigasha for Shibata. 202 min. (also a 185-min. version). *Director:* Yoshishige Yoshida. *Screenplay:* Masahiro Yamada and Yoshishige Yoshida. *Cinematography:* Motokichi Hasegawa. *Art Director:* Tsuyoshi Ishii. *Music:* Kei Chiyanagi.

Toshiyuki Hosokawa *as Sakae Osugi.* Morioko Okada *Noe Ito.* Yuko Kusunoki *Itsuko Masaoka.* Etishi Takahashi *Jun Tsuji.* Masako Yagi *Yasuko.* Kasuko Ineno *Akiko Hiraga.* Ejko Sokutai *Toshiko.* Daujaro Harada *Wada.*

• The plot of *Eros Plus Massacre* shifts between two stories, two sets of characters and two time periods. Oftentimes Yoshida blends the two into one, making a synopsis of the plot difficult. One story is set around the period of 1916 to 1923 and concerns Sakae Osugi, an anarchist and advocate of free love and the three women in his life, Yasuko, his wife, Itsuko Masaoka and Noe Ito. The other revolves around Eiko and her two lovers, Unema and Wada, and is set in the late 1960s.

Eiko is obsessed with studying the life of Noe Ito. At the start of the film she questions a young woman, Mako, whom she believes to be a daughter of Ito. Through her questions, Noe's story unfolds. Noe was married to Jun Tsuji, one of her teachers, but left him and their children to be Osugi's mistress.

The film flashes between the past and the present as Eiko appears in the Haneda Airport being seen off by Unema, a film director, followed by Eiko again questioning Mako in a studio then shifting to Noe walking along a beach then back to Mako. In a room of the Hotel Oriental, an impassive Eiko is making love to Unema while Wada sits on a sofa in the next room reading a newspaper. Afterwards, as Eiko showers, she caresses herself.

Osugi and Noe exit to a cherry grove. The cherry blossoms remind Osugi of January 24 three years earlier when 12 of his political comrades were executed in prison; Osugi and two others were spared. The cherry blossoms also recall the time Noe first arrived in Tokyo (she is in a kimono, her hair braided as would be a young country girl of the earth 20th century, but she arrived on the bullet train only to leave the station in a rickshaw). Noe has left her home and an impending wedding she does not want and gone to Tsuji's house. Noe replaces Akiko Hiraga as a journal editor and in the magazine's offices she is introduced to Osugi's mistress, Itsuko Masaoka. At Unema's studio, Unema directs a film using wire dolls as actors. Eiko and Wada watch one. A detective Hinoshiro comes in and tells Eiko that she is suspected of being a prostitute.

Back in 1916 Noe's husband, Tsuji, is sitting on the porch of a house, playing a flute. He and Noe discuss women's liberation and free love. In a dingy, dark hotel room, Eiko, also a believer in free love, tells the detective about the "prostitution crime" he suspects her of. She acts out the crime in detail, but seems to lose her identity at the same time.

Eiko and Wada dance and discuss that Wada has not slept with Eiko and his "psychological impotence." Suddenly Wada says a group of people is running towards them, but in reality there is no one there. In any event they run as if a group was coming and then pretend that a construction accident has happened. Wada plays a "reporter" interviewing "witness" Eiko. Wada describes in detail the carnage of the accident. Eiko runs off into the empty field, followed by Wada. The two fall on the ground, their bodies forming a cross.

Osugi and one of his mistresses, Itsuko, discuss the relationship which exists between Osugi and the three women in his life. He admits he loves them all. Osugi sees no problem with these relationships as long as three rules are followed: the three women must be economically independent, he must live separately from all three of them, each must respect the other's freedom, including sexual freedom.

In a coffee shop, Eiko and the detective discuss Eiko's "prostitution." Eiko tells him that there are two of her, an imaginary one who prostitutes and a real one talking to him now. He tells her that the prostitution ring has already been broken and that she should stop fantasizing.

Noe catches her husband Tsuji making love to his sister-in-law, Chiyoko. She goes to Osugi to tell him she is leaving. Itsuko fights with Noe and says she has true claim to Osugi because she is economically supporting both him and his wife. As Noe walks in the streets, she sees Osugi attacked by men with sticks. She reaches out for him but falls to the ground instead.

In Unema's studio, Eiko takes Wada's lighter and attempts to burn safety film hanging there. In the following darkness, Eiko switches on a projector and scenes of the great Kanato Earthquake are seen. Wada reads aloud from a book about Osugi and Noe which Eiko has. In Eiko's imagination Osugi and Noe are strangled by a pair of white-gloved hands in a military police station. Wada finishes reading and asks Eiko why she is so obsessed with these people from the past.

Finally the past and present fuse as Eiko interviews Noe. It is the day before the earthquake in which she will die. Eiko asks Noe what she thinks of the intervening 40 years, and the screen suddenly goes black. Flute music is heard and Noe's husband and son cross a field of tall grass. Noe tries to follow them. Three interpretations of the events which take place at the teahouse now follow, each separated by a flashforward to Unema's studio. In two of the versions, Osugi is stabbed by Itsuko (in one he seems to be bringing it about on purpose). In the third Itsuko imagines that she has stabbed Osugi, but it is Noe who actually does it. Back in the present, Wada tells Eiko that Osugi was not really murdered at the teahouse anyway. In another fusing of past and present, Eiko witnesses the real murder of Noe, Osugi and a young boy. Back again in Unema's studio in 1969, Unema hangs himself using rolls of film. Suddenly Eiko is taking pictures of Osugi, Itsuko and Noe with an old-fashioned camera. Eiko thanks them and she and Wada open the studio door and exit into bright sunlight.

• Yoshishige Yoshida (b. 1933) attended Tokyo University where he studied French literature. He started working for Shochiku Studios in 1955 as an assistant director to Kinoshita. When Shochiku decided to give its young directors a chance to make films without undergoing the usual long apprenticeship, Yoshida along with Shinoda and Oshima suddenly found themselves at the heart of what came to be called the Ofuna New Wave. Yoshida's films, which centered on alienation and isolation, soon caused him to fall out of favor with the studio.

As several other directors did, Yoshida left Shochiku in 1964 to start his own independent production company Gendai Eigasha (Modern Film Company). It was there that he made the film which brought him the most fame and which many feel to be exemplary of the Ofuna New Wave, *Eros Plus Massacre*. *Eros* is based on true events and real people. (In fact, the character of Itsuko was really named Ichiko Kamichika and she was still alive in 1969 when Yoshida made the film and insisted the director change her name and eliminate some of the scenes.) Yoshida's handling of the story, however, is not a historical one and he interprets the events in light of the society which evolved from them and existed in the late 1960s.

Yoshida tackles several subjects in this talky and disjointed yet very challenging and controversial film. Violence, freedom, sexuality, the impotence of modern love and the connection of past and present are all presented not only in dialogue but also through imagery within a scene and counterparted from one tightly edited scene to another. *Eros* was an innovative milestone for Japanese cinema and its amazingly complex and multilayered story makes it a rewarding, if difficult, film to watch.

Zatoichi Meets Yojimbo (1970)

1970 / Daiei (series taken over by Toho). 116 min. Color. *Director:* Kihachi Okamoto. *Screenplay:* Kihachi Okamoto and Tetsuro Yoshida. *Adaptation:* From an original story by Kan Shimozawa. *Cinematography:*

into a warm, lively woman. *Sandakan 8* was based on an original story written by feminist writer Tomoko Yamasaki. Its story of the exploitation of the helpless, poor young girls who forcibly were sent out at the beginning of the 20th century to help Japan with its colonization efforts, fits perfectly with Kumai's philosophy. Like Kobayashi, Kumai does not view individuals as being to blame for exploitation, but rather sees them as victims of the establishment. The bitterness one feels at the treatment of these women as exemplified by Osaki, reflected a rising (albeit slowly) Japanese feminist movement.

Kumai uses an intricate web of flashbacks to tell Osaki and Keiko's story. The film has several time frames, all interwoven throughout the film. There is Keiko in Borneo searching for proof of Osaki's stories. There are the scenes of Keiko and Osaki together at Osaki's house near Amakusa. And there are Osaki's flashbacks to her days as a *karayuki-san*. Even though it requires a more intellectual effort to follow the film's progress, Kumai—and more specifically, Tanaka's performance—create a highly charged and emotional response to the subject. Besides outstanding acting, *Sandakan 8* also contains beautiful cinematography which makes wonderful use of location shooting.

There are many psychologically memorable scenes in Kumai's film. Osaki's first "customer" as a prostitute is a callous native who thrusts his coin into Osaki's hand, locks the door, puts the key which is on a chain around his neck and proceeds to essentially rape her. During this scene, there is no sound. As he throws her on the bed, she drops the coin and all that can be heard is its bouncing on the wooden floor. In silence, Osaki endures her defilement while the key to her freedom dangles from the native's neck into her face.

When she kisses Hideo farewell when he goes on his trip, it is through the brothel's locked gate which symbolically and really separates them. He is free, she will never be. While Keiko lives with Osaki, she helps the woman rejuvenate her home, bringing in new floor coverings and replacing the paper in her *shoji* doors. While Osaki tells Keiko her story, she rejuvenates herself. Osaki's house becomes more livable, clean and open, and Osaki purges herself of the demons society has placed within her soul.

Sandakan 8 is not the only film about this segment of Japanese society and history which until recently has been hidden away. Shohei Imamura has done a compelling documentary, *Karayuki-san: The Making of a Prostitute* (1975), in which he lets one *karayuki-san*, Kikyuo, tell her story with a degree or nobility and forgiveness that is almost unfathomable. Later, in 1987, Imamura was to take this same topic and make the film *Zegen*.

In the Realm of the Senses (1976)
Ai no koriida

1976 / Oshima Productions. 105 min. Color. *Director:* Nagisa Oshima. *Screenplay:* Nagisa Oshima. *Cinematography:* Hideo Ito. *Art Direction:* Jusho Toda. *Music:* Minoru Miki. *Producer:* Anatole Dauman.

Eiko Matsuda *Sada*. Tatsuya Fuji *Kichi Zo*. Aoi Nakajima *Toku*. Taiji Tonoyama *Old beggar*. Kanae Kobayashi *Kikuryu, the old geisha*.

• Sada Abe works as a maid in an inn owned by Toku and her husband Kichi. One day Sada is insulted by Toku because Sada used to be a prostitute. Sada unsuccessfully attacks Toku with a knife and Kichi becomes fascinated with her. Later, while Sada is polishing the floors, Kichi sexually assaults her. The two become more and more drawn to each other, making love whenever they can. At one point they make love while Sada plays a musical instrument to keep Toku from suspecting what they're up to.

When Sada sees Kichi making love to his wife, she quits. Kichi, however, cannot let her go, and he abandons his wife to go with her. The two travel to a geisha house where they "get married." They consummate their new relationship by unabashedly making love in front of the geishas who proceed to "rape" the youngest with a bird dildo. Sada spends that happy and sleepless night continuously holding Kichi's penis. The next morning she tells him that a doctor once told her she is "hypersensitive," ready for sex all the time.

Sada must leave Kichi for a short time to "service" an old man who is a school principal and a city councilman. She plans on getting money from this old man on which the two of them can live. To keep him from going anywhere, Sada has taken his clothes and left him only her kimono. Sada is becoming more and more obsessed with Kichi and when she spies on him while he is with his wife, she threatens to cut off his penis with a carving knife. To try and stem her jealousy, Sada makes Kichi have sex with a 68-year-old geisha who so enjoys it that she completely loses control of herself.

Kichi desires to please Sada and suggests that the couple try to heighten their sexual excitement by strangling each other. At first Kichi tries to strangle Sada while they make love, but he can't stand to watch her suffer so he quits. Then Sada tries to strangle Kichi. They try this several times and Kichi even makes fun of Sada's attempts, asking if that is the best she can do. The next time, Sada ties his hands and Kichi tells her that his body is hers and she can do as she likes. Then, almost as a premonition, he tells her, "Don't stop in the middle. It hurts too much." This

In the Realm of the Senses. (Nagisa Oshima, 1976). Seized by U.S. Customs officials as obscene, Oshima's film about Kichi Zo (Tatsuya Fuji, left) and his infamous lover Sada Abe (Eiko Matsuda) still causes debate over whether it is pornography or art.

time Sada actually kills Kichi. But she is not ready to leave him, so she cuts off his penis as a keepsake. Sada wandered Tokyo for four days in 1936 before she was caught. The whole time she was in a state of ecstasy and held on to Kichi's organ.

• In the 1960s directors such as Tetsuji Takechi and Koji Wakamatsu started making revolutionary films which delved into the realm of sexual expression. These "eroductions" (erotic productions) were condemned for their obscene content which directly flaunted Japan's strict censorship laws, which refused to allow sexual organs, the sex act or even pubic hair to be shown in films. When Takechi's *Black Snow* (1965) was released, it and its studio, Nikkatsu, became the object of Japan's first obscenity trial.

Koji Wakamatsu is known for his "pink films." Similar to what Americans used to call blue movies, pink films are quickly made, low-budget, softcore pornography. Centering around sexual repression and antiestablishment sentiments, these films have found favor among students and blue collar workers, and, in a time (the 1970s) when attendance for mainstream films in Japan was dropping off, a triple bill of 70-minute pink movies could still pack a theatre. Typical of the new-found favor of sexploitation films is the way Nikkatsu Studios, which in 1971 was near bankruptcy, temporarily stopped operations only to start again several months later. Their new policy was to make only "roman porno" — romantic porno films.

In 1973 Nagisa Oshima abandoned his Sozosha production company and by 1975 had established Oshima Productions. His first production was the hardcore pornographic film, *In the Realm of the Senses,* based on the true story of Sada Abe. The story of Sada Abe's 1936 "crime" reached folkloric proportions among the Japanese people and had been filmed before, by Noboru Tanaka in 1975 as *A Woman Named Abe Sada.* Sada's obsessive love won her a great deal of public sympathy and when she was tried, she received the unusually light sentence of only six years imprisonment. When Oshima was approached by French producer Anatole Daumann to do a combined Japanese-French production, Oshima chose to do the story of Sada Abe. He shot the film in a closed studio in Japan (working 15-hour days, Oshima finished in 30 days), but had to send the film to France to be developed. Because of strict censorship in Japan, local laboratories would refuse to do it, or worse, the police would confiscate it. Also because of this censorship, Oshima was forced to travel to France to edit the film.

Originally the complete version of the film was only shown in countries without censorship. It ran for years in Paris, but had to be edited to various degrees before screening in other countries. When it finally played in Japan, it was "airbrushed" to blur all objectionable views. Although the censored film which played in Japan was no longer considered offending, it still became the center of an obscenity trial when the film's script and still photos from the film were published in book form. Oshima eventually won the case in 1982.

In the Realm of the Senses was chosen to be shown at the New York Film Festival in 1976, but it never made it. Before it could be shown, it was seized by customs officials as obscene material. The matter was settled and the film finally shown, but only after the festival was over. The film's explicit depiction of sexual obsession invoked polar reviews from audiences and critics. While many hailed it for being the first art film daring to show sex graphically, others condemned it as nothing more than pornography posing as art.

There is no doubt that Oshima does indeed portray sexual acts, many of which may be quite shocking, with a great deal of realism and eroticism. But Oshima's treatment of two people caught up in sexual obsession is not handled in the same way as pornography. For one thing, Oshima gives the couple a heroic and daring veneer befitting their legendary status while at the same time depicting them as doomed to a tragic end. Oshima is also at odds with normal pornography in the fact that it is the woman's pleasures which become the focus of the film and not the man's. In fact, it could be said that it is Kichi who is used as nothing more than a "sex object." Sada is not an oppressed woman in this film and there is an equality of sexuality exhibited.

Sexuality and eroticism is taken up again by Oshima in *Empire of Passion (Ai no borei,* 1978). Set in 1895, it tells of a wife who has an affair with another man. The two kill her husband, but are haunted by his ghost. (In what may be considered Oshima's answer to the scene in *Realm* where Sada castrates the dead Kichi, in *Empire* the woman's pubic hair is shaved off by her lover, making it impossible for her to return to her husband.) Oshima won the Best Director Award at the 1979 Cannes Film Festival for *Empire*. In 1973 Oshima became the host of a highly successful women's morning television program in Tokyo, *The School for Wives*. On the show he helped individual applicants with marital and social problems. He has also done game shows, fashion modeling and even commercials. In 1980 he was named the president of the Japanese Motion Picture Directors Association. The film industry's rebel had achieved legitimacy.

Vengeance Is Mine (1979)
Fukusho suruwa ware ni ari

1979 / Imamura Productions for Shochiku. 128 min. Color. *Director:* Shohei Imamura. *Producer:* Kazuo Inoue. *Screenplay:* Masaru Baba. *Adaptation:* Based on the book by Ryuzo Saki. *Cinematography:* Masahisa Himeda. *Editor:* Keiichi Uraoka. *Music:* Shinichiro Ikebe. Videotape: Sony. Film Rental: Kino International, Janus.

Ken Ogata *as Iwao Enokizu*. Rentaro Mikuni *Shizuo Enokizu, his father*. Chocho Mikayo *Kayo Enokizu, his mother*. Mitsuko Baisho *Kazuko Enokizu, his wife*. Mayumi Ogawa *Haro Asano*. Nijiko Kiyokawa *Hisano Asano*.

• On January 4, 1964, Iwao Enokizu is taken into police custody for the cold-blooded murder in October of 1963 of two men who collected money for the Japan Tobacco Monopoly Company. Enokizu has led the police on a chase throughout Japan and his story is told in flashback. Enokizu's father was a Christian fisherman from Goto whose boats were confiscated by the navy during the war. Because his father did not stand up for himself, Enokizu thought of him as a coward. From then on he became a discipline problem. His father bought an inn at Beppu and

Enokizu spent the war in a reformatory. He was in prison there for two years then, during the Occupation, worked as a translator for the army.

On the day Enokizu is to meet a woman his father has chosen to be his bride, Kazuko, Enokizu's girlfriend who is three months pregnant, shows up at the family's home. Enokizu marries her instead, even though she is a Buddhist and his family is Christian. Kazuko works in a spa with Enokizu's father, Shizuo, and his ill mother, Kayo. Enokizu's behavior does not improve with marriage, and in fact he again ends up in jail for fraud. Kazuko leaves home and gets a job in another spa in Ehime Prefecture. When Shizuo goes there to bring Kazuo home so his wife, Kayo, can see her grandchildren, there develops an attraction between Kazuko and her father-in-law. They stop themselves before it goes too far, but later, when Kazuko is serving one of her father-in-law's friends, Yasuda, he tries to rape her. When he tells her that Shizuo, whom she still admires, has arranged for the encounter to satisfy her sexually and make her happy, she stops struggling.

When Enokizu gets out of jail and finds out about the rape, he blackmails Yasuda. He uses this money to start a spree of fraud and murder throughout Japan. After Enokizu has murdered the two Japan Monopoly Company men, he boards the Honshu-Shikoku ferry and fakes his own suicide. He leaves a note for his father, wife and daughters, but no one believes he has really killed himself. While on the run, the one spot Enokizu returns to several times is the Asano Inn, where he poses as a professor and befriends the innkeeper, Haru, and her mother, Hisano. One day when Haru has come to Tokyo to visit "the professor," he takes her to the movies. There she sees a news bulletin about Enokizu being wanted by the police. Now she knows who he really is. When Enokizu returns to the Asano Inn, he murders Haru and Hisano and pawns their furniture and clothing. A prostitute he had hired while staying at the inn recognizes Enokizu on a television police bulletin, and when she sees him on the street she turns him in to the police.

Five years after Enokizu was arrested, his father and wife take his cremated remains to the top of a mountain to distribute them. When they attempt to throw his bones to the wind, however, they stop in midair. No matter who throws them, or how hard, the bones remain suspended.

• Shohei Imamura was born in 1926 in Tokyo, the son of a physician. He attended the best schools, but instead of attending the prestigious Tokyo University, he went to a technical school where he stayed until the war was over. After the war he attended Waseda University studying Western history.

He graduated in 1951 and went to work at Shochiku's Ofuna studios as an assistant director to Yasujiro Ozu and others. Imamura didn't care much for Ozu's directorial style and in 1954 left Shochiku for Nikkatsu

Vengeance Is Mine (Shohei Imamura, 1979). Shizuo Enokizu (Rentaro Mikuni) and his daughter-in-law Kazuko (Mitsuko Baisho) are attracted to one another despite their familial relationship and the shadow of the killer son/husband which binds them.

where he worked as an assistant to director Yuzo Kawashima. (Imamura collaborated on a book about Kawashima, *Life Is Only Goodbye,* in 1968.)

In 1958 Imamura made his directorial debut with *The Stolen Desire (Nusumareta yokujo).* Often considered to be a part of the Japanese "New Wave" along with Shinoda and Oshima, Imamura gained notice with his 1961 film, *Pigs and Battleships (Buta no gunkan),* about the black market which surrounded the United States naval base at Yokosuka. (This was a topic Imamura again approached with his documentary, *History of Postwar Japan as Told by a Bar Hostess,* 1970). The major difference between Imamura and the other "New Wave" directors is that he infuses his films with a degree of humor making them satiric political commentaries instead of the more serious tone usually associated with the movement.

In 1963 Imamura made *The Insect Woman (Nippon konchiku),* the story of one woman, Tome, from her origins in rural Tohoku through her life as a ruthless madam in Tokyo and back to Tohoku. Imamura, like Naruse and Mizoguchi, is often cited as a maker of films about women, but for Imamura, women are not self-sacrificing heroines. Instead, Imamura's women are survivors. They are strong, practical, earthy and usually from the lower classes and provincial in origins. These type of characters appear in *Intentions of Murder (Akai satsui, 1964)* and *The Profound Desire of the Gods (Kamigami no fukaki yokubo, 1968).*

Like many directors of the period, in 1965 Imamura formed Imamura Productions to make his own films. From 1970 to 1978 he "retired" from feature filmmaking, working mainly in television making documentaries such as *Karayuki-san* about the women sold into prostitution during Japan's colonial period. In 1975 Imamura founded and began teaching at the Yokohama Broadcast Film Institute, and in 1979 he again returned to the realm of feature films with the release of *Vengeance Is Mine*.

Vengeance Is Mine is an intricate and engrossing study of a cold-blooded murderer. Imamura weaves together a complex web of flashbacks to tell the story of remorseless killer Iwao Enokizu. Basically, flashbacks represent four different time periods or points of view: one is while Enokizu is in police custody, the second is during the police investigation, the third is while Enokizu is committing the murders and escaping from the police (which overlaps with the second), and the fourth is of Enokizu's life before the crimes.

While the murders Enokizu commits seem to have no motive (except possibly that of money), Imamura suggests that Enokizu killed people because he wasn't able to kill the one person he really hated, his father. As a consequence, because the people he murdered meant nothing to him, he was totally detached from them. Similarly, Imamura is just as detached from Enokizu and has created a disturbing but distant film. Imamura neither condemns nor justifies Enokizu's actions. Enokizu, and Imamura, know that he will be caught. A light pull-string in Enokizu's apartment is shaped like a noose. It waves back and forth in front of him while he counts the stolen money and listens on the radio for reports of his murders. This symbol is repeated near the Asano Inn. Just before he kills Haru and her mother, he sees a noose and a pair of hip-wader boots in a shed which looks like a man hanging in the gallows.

Vengeance only minimally contains the dark humor Imamura is known for. In the scene where Enokizu has murdered an elderly lawyer, he has difficulty keeping shut the doors of the wardrobe into which he has stuffed the man's body. After nailing and taping it shut, he vainly tries to strangle himself.

Vengeance Is Mine is based on Ryuzo Saki's "nonfiction novel" of the same name, and was inspired by actual events in the life of the infamous criminal Nishiguchi, who eluded police for 78 days and committed five murders in Kyushu, Hamamatsu and Tokyo. Imamura started *Vengeance* in 1976 and it was his first feature in almost a decade. It was a great commercial and critical success and it, along with his remake of *The Ballad of Narayama* in 1983, which won the Cannes Grand Prix, finally brought Imamura to world attention. Imamura was not well known outside Japan, probably because he had worked for small studios which did not actively pursue wider distribution. With these two films, however, Imamura retrospectives are now being shown and one of Japan's great postwar directors is achieving the status he deserves.

Foster Daddy, Tora! (1979)
Torajiro kamone uta

1980 / Shochiku. 96 min. Color. *Director:* Yoji Yamada. *Screenplay:* Yoji Yamada and Yoshitaka Asama. *Cinematography:* Tetsuo Takaba. *Art Direction:* Mitsuo Idegawa. *Music:* Naozomi Yamamoto. *Producer:* Kiyoshi Shimazo.

Kiyoshi Atsumi *as Tora.* Ran Ito *Sumire.* Chieko Baisho *Sakura.* Gin Maeda *Hiroshi, her husband.* Masami Shimojo *Tora's uncle.* Chieko Misaki *Tora's aunt.* Hisao Dazai *President.* Chishu Ryu *Temple priest.* Tatsuo Matsumura *Teacher Hayashi.*

• In an opening dream sequence, a young girl is in trouble but is saved by Tora. When Tora awakens, he begins his usual job as a traveling salesman. While in Hokkaido, Tora visits the grave of his old friend, Tsune. Tora has never been to the grave before and must find Sumire, Tsune's daughter, in order to locate it. Tsune tells Tora how she would like to get a job in Tokyo and finish high school. Tora, like in the dream, comes to Sumire's aid and brings her to Tokyo and gets her a job in the Toraya Tea Cake Shop run by his aunt and uncle.

Now that Sumire has a job, she tries with great difficulty to get accepted at night school. Tora is afraid Sumire might fail her exams and the good-hearted Tora tries to bribe her teacher. When Sumire's shyness makes it difficult for her to answer the oral part of her entrance exams, Tora yells out the answers for her and is thrown out of the room. When she finally is accepted, because they live in Katsushika, a lower-class area, Tora helps her to travel to and from night school. Tora waits outside her classroom and eventually is noticed by the teacher who invites him in to attend the class. But Tora is no student. He is constantly interrupting the class by digressing it with his stories or falling asleep and snoring loudly.

Sumire's mother, who had abandoned her daughter and husband years before because he was a drunken gambler, comes to Tokyo to visit her daughter for the first time since then. Sumire rejects her mother and sends her away, but Tora's sister, Sakura, persuades her to act like an adult. Sumire runs to her mother and the two embrace, reconciled. Another visitor from Sumire's past is her boyfriend. The two spend the night together, which greatly upsets the fatherly Tora. Even after the couple tell Tora that they plan to marry, he still feels as if Sumire has let him down. Again Sakura steps in to point out that Sumire is an adult and should be allowed to live her own life. Hurt, Tora again goes off on another sales trip.

As the family celebrates the new year holidays, a card comes from Tora with greetings and a wish for Sumire's happiness with her marriage. As Tora's thoughts drift out over the local river, one of Sumire's friends from the dried fish factory where she had worked comes up to him. She and several friends are going on an outing and invite Tora to come along. Tora accepts, and as the only man on the bus, he is surrounded by laughing women.

• While Hollywood has done its share to produce a proliferation of sequels, perhaps no country does it quite as well as the Japanese. The Japanese are very fond of series and have set them in the samurai past like *Zatoichi* or in contemporary times such as the very popular *Tora-san* series.

Tora's story began as a television series designed for actor Kiyoshi Atsumi who began his acting career as a vaudeville comedian. The show lasted one season, 26 episodes, and in the final episode, writer/director Yoji Yamada killed Tora with a snake bite. What Yamada hadn't counted on was the flood of protest letters and phone calls from viewers. As a consequence, Yamada convinced the producers to revive Tora, only this time as a theatrically released film. The first film, *It's Tough to Be a Man (Otoko was tsurai yo),* which is another name for the series, was released in 1969. It was such an instantaneous success that Shochiku demanded that Yamada make another three movies in only four months. Since then, two Tora-san pictures have been released each year, usually coinciding with the two major Japanese holidays of New Year and O-Ban (the Buddhist festival of the dead). He is a popular "hero" (the 40th film was released at the end of 1988) with whom the average Japanese person can identify and who has, almost singlehandedly, kept Shochiku Studios afloat.

Tora-san (whose "real" name is Torajiro Kuruma) is a husky, middle-aged itinerant street peddler who carries only one suitcase, containing his clothes. He always wears a garish suit with a wide sash, sandals *(zoris)* and a hat. He is at once funny and sad, a kindhearted, bumbling meddler reminiscent of times past when people had the time and innocent compassion to care for those who came into their lives, even in the most casual of ways. But Tora is also an inept, lazy loner. By being both funny and melancholy, Tora brings a bit of the Chaplinesque to the Japanese cinema. He is an everyman who can be a boorish lout one minute and an innocent child the next. He has never married and faces trouble at home by going on sales trips where he sells trinkets at Buddhist fairs. Tora is an anachronism in the rigid, tightly managed society of Japan, a throwback to an earlier time.

The plots to the Tora-san movies are almost always the same. Tora comes home to his family (his aunt, uncle, sister and brother-in-law) between sales trips. For some reason, they will "fight" and Tora again sets out on the road. There is a guest star in each film, and if it's a woman, Tora almost always falls in love with her, usually while out on the road. He then returns home with renewed purpose. But his love is doomed to remain unrequited and to send Tora once again back out on the road.

Director and Tora-san creator, Yoji Yamada was born in 1931, graduated from Tokyo University in 1954 and was one of the young directors who, along with Oshima, joined Shochiku. He did the usual stint as assistant director and scriptwriter and was given his first film as director in 1963. With the appearance of the Tora-san series, Yamada was catapulted into success. Yamada has done other films besides the Tora-san series, most notably *Where Spring Comes Late (Kazoku,* 1970*)* and *Yellow Handkerchief of Happiness (Shiawase no kiiroi hankachi,* 1977*)*. Although Yamada personally leans towards the Communist/socialist political philosophy, his films are not hard-edged treatises. He may depict the oppressed, but his presentation of their lives is softened by an attitude of family warmth and sincerity of action which realizes happiness for the individual. Yamada's people are ordinary citizens trying to cope with modern society and technology while cherishing the nostalgic virtues of a small-town or rural life.

Kagemusha (1980)

1980 / Toho. / a.k.a. "The Shadow Warrior." 162 min. Color. *Director:* Akira Kurosawa. *Screenplay:* Akira Kurosawa and Masato Ide. *Cinematography Supervisor:* Kazuo Miyagawa and Asakazu Nakai. *Cinematography:* Takao Saito and Masaharu Ueda. *Art Direction:* Yoshiro Muraki. *Music:* Shinichiro Ikebe. *Production Coordinator:* Inoshiro Honda. *Producer:* Akira Kurosawa and Tomoyuki Tanaka. *Assistant Producer:* Teruyo Nogami. Videotape: CBS Fox. Film Rental: 20th Century–Fox, Films Inc.

Tatsuya Nakadai *as Shingen Takeda and his double, the thief.* Tsutomu Yamazaki *Nobukado Takeda, his brother.* Kenichi Hagiwara *Katsuyori Takeda, Shingen's son.* Kota Yui *Takemaru Takeda, Shingen's grandson.* Hideo Murata *Nobuharu Baba.* Takayuki Shiho *Masatoyo Natio.* Shuhei Sugimori *Masanobu Kosaka.* Noboru Shimizu *Masatane Hara.* Koji Shimizu *Katsusuke Atobe.* Sen Yamamoto *Nobushige Oyamada.* Daisuke Ryu *Nobunaga Oda.* Masayuki Yui *Ieyasu Tokugawa.* Yasuhito Yamanaka *Ranmaru Mori.* Takashi Shimura *Gyobu Tagushi.* Mitsuko Baisho *Oyunokata.* Kaori Momoi *Otsuyanokata.* Akihiko Sugizaki *Noda Castle soldier.*

Toshiaki Tanabe *Kugutsushi.* Yoshimitsu Yamaguchi *Salt vendor.* Takashi Ebata *Monk.* Kumeko Otowa *Takemaru's nurse.* Kamatari Fujiwara *Doctor.*

• Shingen Takeda, his brother Nobukado and a thief sit together. Each looks very much like the other. Nobukado has saved the thief from execution because he greatly resembles Shingen, and having doubles is one of the ways in which Shingen seems to be everywhere, supervising all phases of the civil war he is fighting against two other powerful warlords, Nobunaga Oda and Ieyasu Tokugawa. All three men want to rule Japan and take the capital, Kyoto.

In 1572, Shingen marched on Kyoto, but Nobunaga and Ieyasu joined forces to stop him. They are repelled, and Shingen lays siege to Ieyasu's fortress, Noda Castle. However, it is not really Shingen in charge of the siege, but his lookalike brother, Nobukado. The castle has been surrounded for 20 days and the water supply cut off, but every evening, a lone flute player within the castle plays for all the soldiers. Shingen decides he will go to the castle to hear the flute, and while there, he is mortally wounded by a sniper. Realizing his death is near, Shingen orders that his death be kept a secret for three years and that the Takeda clan should not go to war during that time. When Shingen dies, the thief is brought in to play his double (his *kagemusha* or shadow warrior). When the thief visits Shingen's grandson, the young boy says it is not his grandfather. The thief wins him over, however, and the two become very close over the coming months.

Rumors abound about Shingen's death, and both Nobunaga and Ieyasu send out spies to try to find out the truth. When Shingen's son, Katsuyori, disobeys his father's last wishes and attacks Takatenjin Castle in May of 1574, the clan sends out Shingen's troops to protect his flank. They will obey Shingen's dying request not to fight, but hope Shingen's banners will protect Katsuyori, Shingen's son successfully seizes the castle and burns it, but enemy forces attack and the *kagemusha* Shingen is ordered to just sit in place, like a mountain. The enemy keeps attacking and retreating while all around the shadow warrior Shingen, men are shot. The enemy is trying to determine if it really is Shingen. Eventually the Takeda clan wins and returns to Katsuyori's manor.

One day, while playing with Shingen's grandson, the thief tries to ride Shingen's horse. When he is thrown, Shingen's mistresses run to his aid and discover the deception. The thief does not have Shingen's scar. Now the clan has no choice but to make the impulsive Katsuyori head of the clan. The thief is thrown out of the castle and an official funeral is held for Shingen.

Kagemusha (Akira Kurosawa, 1980). Tatsuya Nakadai deftly handles playing two physically identical but psychologically disparate roles of a great clan leader and a common thief. Here he is the mortally wounded Shingen Takeda. (Photo courtesy of Toho Co., Ltd.)

Now that he knows Ieyasu and Nobunaga are sure of Shingen's death, Katsuyori heads for Nagashino with 25,000 men. On his way there a bar of light appears in the sky. Clan elders say it is Shingen telling Katsuyori to stay at home and guard his castle, but he disregards their advice and on May 21, 1575, the battle of Nagashino is fought. It is a terrible battle for the Takeda clan. Nobunaga, who has adopted many modern concepts and inventions, has many riflemen who are ordered to shoot Takeda horses first. The Takeda clan cannot fight without horses. Eventually, all divisions of the Takeda army are gunned down and annihilated. The thief, who has come to care deeply for the clan, has been watching the carnage from nearby. He grabs a spear, but is immediately shot down.

• Even after the critical and box office success of *Red Beard* in 1965, Kurosawa had a great deal of difficulty in finding financing for his projects. The major Japanese studios either would not or could not back him (or many of their other renowned directors). One reason was that directors like Kurosawa would not make the kind of generic films the studio demanded. In 1970, Kurosawa, Keisuke Kinoshita, Kon Ichikawa and Masaki Kobayashi formed a production company called *Yonki no kai* (The Four Musketeers). The company's first (and only) production was Kurosawa's *Dodeskaden*. It was made in 28 days and was Kurosawa's first color film. The story of the intertwined lives of people living in a slum experimented with color even to the point where Kurosawa had the ground painted. It was a critical and commercial failure and the company was dissolved.

At this time Kurosawa was also having health problems and trouble with his eyesight. Filled with self-doubts and possibly facing the end of his career, Kurosawa chose "death before dishonor," and attempted suicide on December 22, 1971. Fortunately, the attempt was unsuccessful. Hearing of his plight, even schoolchildren wrote Kurosawa offering to finance his films.

Finding financing had become a considerable problem for directors like Kurosawa. He had become accustomed to budgets allowing him to make the quality of films he wanted: for perfectionists like Kurosawa, the films tended to be extremely costly. In 1975, Kurosawa was approached by the Russian company Mosfilm to make a film for them. Kurosawa accepted, and for the next several years, he kept up an exhausting schedule (and even suffered frostbite in his toes) to make *Dersu Uzala* in 1975. The film won an Academy Award for Best Foreign-language Film and was moderately successful in Japan, but it still failed to gain the financial backing Kurosawa needed in order to shoot the film he really wanted to make, *Ran*.

To earn money, Kurosawa was reduced to making whiskey commercials (for Suntory). As a dress rehearsal project in preparation for *Ran*, Kurosawa envisioned *Kagemusha*. The film is based on a true historical character who was thought to have had many doubles and an intriguing battle in which one army is totally destroyed while the other side was unscathed. But Kurosawa could find no financing for this project either. That is when Francis Coppola and George Lucas stepped in. They convinced Alan Ladd, Jr., at 20th Century–Fox to help finance *Kagemusha.* Coppola and Lucas would act as executive producers of the international version and Fox would have world-wide distribution rights (except in Japan). Fox would put up $1.5 million and Toho the remaining $4.5 million. With a $6 million budget, *Kagemusha* became the most expensive film ever made in Japan. It was also the first Japanese film distributed by and invested in by a foreign company.

Shintaro Katsu, of *Zatoichi* fame, originally was cast to play the dual role of Shingen and the thief. Katsu, as demanding an actor as Kurosawa was a director, ran headlong into conflict when on the set. One month into shooting, depending on which story one hears, Katsu either quit or was fired. Fox, worried about its investment, insisted on a name actor in the lead. Since Kurosawa and Toshiro Mifune were still on the outs with each other, Kurosawa called upon Tatsuya Nakadai.

Nakadai, who won great acclaim in Kobayashi's *The Human Condition* brought considerable skill to his dual roles. Even though dressed in identical clothing and makeup, Nakadai convincingly portrays Shingen as astute and discerning and the thief as raucous and unsavory. When the thief is called upon to become Shingen, Nakadai skillfully shows the thief's evolution. Though initially motivated by a desire to escape the gallows, the thief, in Nakadai's hands, becomes more than just Shingen's shadow, he gains confidence, he gains respect and he even gains love from Shingen's grandson. He is transformed from society's outcast to a man of character. Even when the clan dismisses him, he retains his loyalty to them. That is why the shock of the ending battle registers so heavily on his face, and why he dies, falling into the lake where Shingen is buried, reaching out to retrieve the clan banner floating there.

Kagemusha is a magnificent action film of epic proportions, made when one of the world's greatest directors was 70 years old. When Kurosawa had been looking for financing, he wondered if he'd ever get the film made and consequently spent his creative energies and many days preparing hundreds of drawings for the film. Focusing on colors, armor design, and the look of each scene, when the film finally began shooting, scenes were already "finished" and controlled by Kurosawa's pictures.

As a consequence, *Kagemusha* is a visually stunning film. The Takeda clan banner contains four characters, those for fire, forest, wind and mountain. Each character represents a different facet of the Takeda army. The horsemen are as swift as the wind, the lancers are as quiet as a forest, the cavalry is as fierce as a fire, and Lord Shingen is as immovable as a mountain. To emphasize this, Kurosawa dresses each division of the Takeda army in armor of different colors (either red or blue) and the lancers carry green banners. While full companies of men are shown in epic detail, Kurosawa never shows the battles. Instead the viewer hears the deafening gunfire and watches as the thief's face reflects the carnage on the field. What is shown is the terrible aftermath of the massacre: mounds of bloody and dead soldiers and horses. There are no heroics in *Kagemusha*'s war, only wasteful deaths.

Kagemusha became an international critical and commercial hit. While three of Japan's four major studios lost money in 1980, because of *Kagemusha*, Toho's profits increased by more than 50 percent. The film established a new box office record in Japan (2.7 billion yen or $10 million). It was nominated and won many awards including a nomination for an Academy Award for Best Foreign-language Film (*Moscoe Does Not Believe in Tears* was the winner) and was a co-winner of the Grand Prize at Cannes.

Muddy River (1981)
Doro no kawa

1981 / Kimura Productions. 105 min. B&W. *Director:* Kohei Oguri. *Screenplay:* Takako Shigemori. *Adaptation:* From the novel by Teru Miyamoto. *Cinematography:* Shohei Ando. *Art Direction:* Akira Naito. *Music:* Kuroudo Mori. *Lighting:* Tadaki Shimada. *Sound:* Hideo Nishizaki and Hiroyuki Hirai. *Producer:* Motoyasu Kimura. *Editor:* Nobuo Ogawa. Film Rental: New Yorker.

Nobutaka Asahara *as Nobuo.* Takahiro Tamura *Shinpei.* Yumiko Fujita *Sadako, Nobuo's mother.* Minoru Sakurai *Kiichi.* Makiko Shibata *Ginko.* Mariko Kaga *Kiichi and Ginko's mother.* Masako Yagi *Shinpei's first wife.* Gannosuke Ashiya *Shinoda, the horse cart man.* Reiko Hatsune *Tobacco-shop woman.* Keizo Kanie *Policeman.* Yoshitaka Nishiyama *Warehouse guard.* Taiji Tonoyama *Man on the festival boat.*

• Nobuo lives with his father and mother over the small restaurant they run in 1956 Osaka. A customer, Shinoda, says he's buying a used truck to replace the horse and cart he's been using to haul goods for the past ten years. Jokingly, he tells Nobuo he can have his horse when the truck comes. When Shinoda leaves, Nobuo follows him and watches as his cart becomes stuck in the mud on a bridge over the river. When the struggling horse is startled by a truck, the cart's contents fall on Shinoda and the cart rolls over him and kills him.

The next day, Nobuo sees another boy looking at Shinoda's abandoned cart. The boy, who is also nine years old like Nobuo, is named Kiichi and he lives on the riverboat which has just anchored across the river from Nobuo's family's restaurant. Also living on the riverboat is Kiichi's older sister, Ginko, and his mother who makes her living as a prostitute because her husband, a good boatman, was made to carry cargo during a storm and was killed. This is how she supports her family.

Kiichi and Ginko are invited to dinner with Nobuo's family. While there, Kiichi sings a song about the soldiers in Manchuria which his father used to sing when drunk. After returning from a trip to Kyoto to see Nobuo's father's dying first wife, Nobuo goes to the riverboat and sees Kiichi's mother for the first time. She's very proper and very pretty. As he leaves, he tells Ginko to come to the restaurant again. That evening Nobuo's father promises to take the boys to the festival at the shrine. Ginko takes a bath with Nobuo's mother and Kiichi hears his sister's rare laughter. When time for the festival comes, Nobuo's father has disappeared. The boys go alone. Nobuo's mother has given them each 50 yen and they can't decide what to spend it on. When they finally make up their minds, the money has been lost through a hole in Kiichi's pocket. They retrace their steps, but can't find the money.

Sadly they return home. Kiichi offers to show Nobuo a nest of crabs he's made. On the riverboat, Nobuo hears Kiichi's mother moaning on the other side of the boat while she is with a customer. To entertain Nobuo, Kiichi keeps soaking the crabs in kerosene then sets them afire. The crabs writhe in pain and Nobuo tells him to stop it. Nobuo follows a burning crab out onto the deck to help it and sees into the window where Kiichi's mother is having sex with a tattooed man. She also sees him. Nobuo leaves. At home it turns out that Nobuo's father had gone to see the ocean at Maizuru. That was where he landed when he returned from Korea. The next morning, Nobuo's mother sees the houseboat being towed away from its spot. Nobuo runs after it. At first he just whispers Kiichi's name but finally yells it. But there is no answer from the boat.

• Kohei Oguri's first film was, in many ways, a milestone. Oguri, born in 1945, studied screenwriting and, after graduating from college in 1968, became a freelance director, working with directors such as Masahiro Shinoda on *Double Suicide*. He wrote the script for *Muddy River* but had trouble finding financing. He took the script to the major studios, but, typical of the time, they were more interested in churning out quick and cheap double features about such topics as softcore pornography or the *yakuza* (Japanese gangsters). The great Japanese cinema of 30 years earlier which had given the world *The Seven Samurai* and *Ugetsu* was now an entrenched industry interested in making only the most common kinds of film. Only the best of its old-guard directors like Kurosawa or its proven

Muddy River (Kohei Oguri, 1981). Minoru Sakurai as Kiichi gives his sister Ginko (Makiko Shibata) a look of sympathy in this touching tale of a doomed friendship between two boys from different environments.

independents like Imamura, Hani and Oshima could find support for their projects. Most of Japan's newest talent was forced to find work in television or, like Oguri, on a freelance basis.

Oguri finally did find financial backing for his film in the form of Motoyasu Kimura, an iron factory owner with no film producing experience but a passion for making 16mm films. Kimura not only gave Oguri the $250,000 he needed to make the film but also complete artistic freedom. Oguri relied on experienced technical help. Cinematographer Ando worked with Imamura; sound man Nishizaki worked on *The Human Condition, Harakiri, Kwaidan* and *Boy;* and art director Naito worked with both Mizoguchi and Yoshimura. His adult actors were also professionals, but the children were not. Chosen from hundreds of non-professionals who auditioned for the part, the three chosen lived with Oguri before shooting started and during production.

Like the fifties he was recalling, Oguri returned to a conventional 1950s' style and shot the film in black and white. He captured the memories, images, feelings and tensions of childhood without becoming overly nostalgic. The story shows a journey of friendship and discovery, of experiences which cause a loss of innocence and which elicit maturity.

The muddy river of the title is the Aji River in Osaka, and it is a metaphor of Oguri's theme. As Oguri told Donald Richie, "At the spring the water is pure, but as it descends to the sea, as a stream and then as a river, it becomes more and more muddy. Yet this mud is also the essence of the river, which is, after all, made of both water and mud. In the same way, though a child may be as pure as spring water, it is the mud of humanity, the experience of living, of knowing happiness and sorrow, that nurtures him. This is what I wanted to celebrate in my film." *Muddy River* is also about discrimination. Nobuo's friend won't let Kiichi come to his house to watch television and Kiichi's mother asks Nobuo if his mother told him not to visit the houseboat. In fact, she is very grateful to Nobuo for the friendship he has shared with her children and indicates that it is rare. This theme would be explored more fully in *For Kayako,* Oguri's 1984 film about discrimination against Koreans living in Japan.

When *Muddy River* was completed (major shooting took only about 23 days), it ran into another problem. Just as the established major studios controlled film financing and production, they also owned most of the theatres in Japan and therefore also controlled distribution. There were very few places to show independent films in Japan unless a studio needed one to fill in a double-feature gap. Consequently the film was screened in small town halls for local groups. Soon this small film, which went beyond the mindless product usually expected from the Japanese studios, attracted the attention of critics and newspapers and large halls had to be rented. Eventually even Toei had to take notice of the rapidly snowballing acclaim garnered by the film and signed to distribute it nationally.

Muddy River proved to be commercially successful and gave a much needed boost to a virtually forgotten Japanese film genre, the *shomin-geki.* Oguri's success inspired a wave of new directors like Kichitaro Negishi (*Distant Thunder,* 1981) and Mitsuo Yanagimachi (*Himatsuri,* 1986). More importantly, the film's success indicated that the future of quality films in Japan seemed to belong entirely to independent producers like Kimura and directors like Oguri. *Muddy River* has a noteworthy wisdom and charm. It defied all odds in winning a great deal of international attention. It won the Silver Prize at the 1981 Moscow Film Festival and the Kinema Jumpo "best one" award. It was nominated in 1981 for a Best Foreign Film Academy Award.

The Ballad of Narayama (1982)
Narayama bushi-ko

1982 / Toei. 128 min. Color. *Director:* Shohei Imamura. *Screenplay:* Shohei Imamura. *Adaptation:* From the stories "The Ballad of Narayama"

and "Men of Tohoku" by Shichiro Fukazawa. *Cinematography:* Masao
Tochizawa. *Art Direction:* Tadataka Yoshino. *Lighting:* Yasuo Iwaki.
Music: Shinichiro Ikebe. *Sound:* Kenichi Benitani. *Editor:* Hajime Oka-
yasu. *Producer:* Goro Kusakabe and Jiro Tomoda. Film Rental: Kino International, Janus.

   Ken Ogata *as Tatsuehi.* Sumiko Sakamoto *Orin, his mother.* Takejo
Aki *Tamayan, his wife.* Tonpei Hidari *Risuke, his brother.* Seiji Kurasaki
Kesakichi, eldest son. Kaoru Shimamori *Tomekichi, youngest son.* Ryutaro
Tatsumi *Matayan, the old neighbor.* Junko Takada *Matsu.* Nijiko
Kiyokawa *Okane.* Mitsuko Baisho *Oei.* Shoichi Ozawa *Katsuzo.* Mitsuaki
Fukamizu *Tadayan.* Norihei Miki *Old salt dealer.* Akio Yokoyama *Amaya.*
Sachie Shimura *Amay's wife.* Masami Okamoto *Amay's son.* Fujio Tsuneda
Jinsaku. Taiji Tonoyama *Teruyan.*

   • The story is set about 100 years ago in a remote mountain village.
Sixty-nine-year-old Orin lives there with her two sons, Tatsuehi and
Risuke, and Tatsuehi's three children. Orin is a healthy and kind old
woman, but it is village law that when a person reaches the age of 70 he or
she must be taken to Mount Narayama where she will wait to die. Orin is
eager to make the journey, but first she must put her family in order. Just
after Tatsuehi's wife bore him a daughter, she died by falling off a cliff.
Now Orin needs to find a new wife for him before she can leave. Through
the salt seller, she learns of a new widow, Tamayan, who lives in a nearby
village. She makes arrangements for Tamayan to marry Tatsuehi. When
Tamayan arrives, Orin is pleased to note that she is a hearty and strong
woman. Orin likes her and helps her to feel at home, even showing her a
favorite spot to catch fish.
   Orin is very aware that the village is on the verge of making her a
social outcast because she is so healthy at her age. Even her grandson sings
the song calling Orin a demon because she has so many good teeth — a
situation Orin rectifies by painfully knocking two of them out. Tatsuehi
loves his mother and Orin tries to belay his reluctance to take her to
Narayama by telling him that his father was a coward because he ran away
rather than take his mother to Narayama.
   Kesa, Orin's grandson, brings his pregnant girlfriend, Matsu, to live
with the family. Matsu eats a lot without thinking of the welfare of the
other family members. She is also Amaya's daughter, and he has been
discovered to be a thief, stealing the undersized crops before they could be
harvested. As winter approaches, it becomes obvious that Matsu and her
baby will mean two more mouths to feed. When the villagers decide on
punishment for Amaya's family, Orin sends Matsu to her family with food.
That night the villagers bury Amaya's family alive.
   Orin now feels it is time for her to go to Narayama. She invites the
village elders to her home to receive instructions. The next morning, carry-

The Ballad of Narayama (Shohei Imamura, 1982). Ken Ogata stars as Tatsuehi in Imamura's more brutal version of the harsh realities underlying the popular folk tale about a village which must sacrifice its elders so the young may survive.

ing Orin on his back, Tatsuehi begins the journey. It is a taxing trip and Orin is not allowed to speak to her son. Reaching their goal, an eerie spot atop the mountain cluttered with human bones and crows, Tatsuehi leaves his beloved mother. On his return to the village, he comes upon a fellow villager and his old father, Mata, fighting on the path. Mata clings to life and had refused to make the trip to Narayama. Now his miserly son, who had refused to feed him and had kept him tied in his house, is forcing him to go to the mountain. The two struggle on the mountain path, however, and Mata is forced over the edge by his son.

In the quiet of the hillside, it begins to show—a portent of good luck. Tatsuehi, concerned for his mother, runs back to her. Orin, however, will not speak to him and the son returns to the village. Back home, Tatsuehi's son has brought a new woman into their home, and both she and Tamayan are wearing Orin's old clothes.

• Shohei Imamura, one of the best of the postwar Japanese directors, made an impression in the West with the release of *Vengeance Is Mine* in 1979. It was a dark and distant but nonetheless engrossing story of a remorseless murderer on the run in the 1960s. With *The Ballad of Narayama*, Imamura turns his attention on an old folktale to illustrate his favorite theme: that violence always lies just below the surface veneer of civilization. *Narayama* is not Imamura's first period film. That distinction belongs to the fascinatingly eccentric *Eijanaika* (1981) based on the historic events around the beginning of the Meiji Restoration and the overthrow of the shogun.

Imamura is often referred to as the "cultural anthropologist of the Japanese cinema." He shows a strong interest in the more primitive elements of Japanese society. In fact, most of his films attempt to discover the essence of "Japaneseness" by examining more primitive societies, those as much as possible untouched by civilization. That is where Imamura finds the most instinctual sides of Japanese culture, the superstitious and the irrational. Using these elements as his starting point, Imamura doesn't analyze but rather celebrates them as forming the source of the Japanese character. Believed to be a slow and exacting director, Imamura spends a lot of time researching and planning his films. He is known to do long interviews with source people not only to obtain information but also to secure regional accents, vocabularies, attitudes and feelings. Many of Imamura's films are set in remote regions of Japan and the director takes pride in shooting on location and recording sound directly. Such was the case with *Ballad*, which was filmed in a small, abandoned mountain village in the northern part of Nagano Prefecture.

This use of realism is the basic difference between Imamura's version of *The Ballad of Narayama* and that of Kinoshita done about 15 years earlier. Kinoshita's film purposely was very theatrical, Imamura's much more natural. In fact, Imamura makes a point of interweaving nature into his film. Constantly, animals mimic the lives of his characters. As Kesa and Matsu wrestle, snakes wrestle. As Kesa and Matsu make love, frogs copulate and birds build a nest. When the farmers plow their fields, a snake eats a mouse. When Amaya steals the village crops, a raccoon pillages a hen house. Even the spirit of Tatsuehi's dead father is represented by the wind.

In a way, it is nature which has caused the situation where the elders must be left on a mountaintop to die. It is a constant struggle for survival. When Tatsuehi shoots a rabbit, it is stolen by a hawk. In the winter snow thaw, the body of a dead baby boy becomes exposed. In this society, boys are just another mouth to feed, while girls can be sold. The villagers may seem cruel, but Imamura, by realistically showing life as it must have been, shows that they were necessary measures in a time when food was scarce, poverty the norm and survival selective. When Orin willingly chooses to go to the mountain, she is in essence choosing a heroic death, sacrificing herself for her family.

As bleak and as beautiful as Imamura has made his film, it also contains typical elements of Imamura humor, which means it is black and bawdy. Tatsuehi's unkempt brother, Risuke, is called "Stinky" for obvious reasons and spends most of the film trying to obtain a sexual partner. Ken Ogata, who plays Tatsuehi, the compassionate son, so sympathetically, also played the ruthless murderer in Imamura's *Vengeance Is Mine* and the title character in Paul Schrader's *Mishima*.

The Ballad of Narayama is one of the few Toei films to reach U.S. shores. Toei, one of Japan's five major film companies, began in 1949 as a film distributorship. In 1951 it merged with another small company to form the Tokyo Motion Picture Distribution Company, or Toei. Primarily known for mass-producing short, double-bill, period films, the company was also home for films by Tadashi Imai. Now it is known for its *yakuza* films. *The Ballad of Narayama* is a beautiful film with a strong and compelling story. It is impressively crafted and filled with the raw vitality usually associated with Imamura. At turns outrageous, perceptive, lusty and amusing, the film is both entertaining and haunting. It won the 1983 Cannes Film Festival Grand Prize.

Merry Christmas, Mr. Lawrence (1983)
Senjo no Merii Kurisumasu

1983 / Recorded Picture Company. 122 min. Color. *Director:* Nagisa Oshima. *Screenplay:* Nagisa Oshima and Paul Mayersberg. *Adaptation:*

From the novel, *The Seed and the Sower* by Sir Laurens van der Post. *Cinematography:* Toichiro Narushima. *Art Director:* Andrew Sanders. *Production Designer:* Jusho Toda. *Music:* Ryuichi Sakamoto. *Sound:* Tetsuya Okashi and Mike Westgate. *Editor:* Tomoyo Oshima. *Producer:* Jeremy Thomas. *Executive Producers:* Masato Hara, Eiko Oshima, Geoffrey Nethercott and Terry Glinwood. *Assistant Producer:* Joyce Herlihy. Videotape: MCA. Film Rental: Universal Classics.

David Bowie *as Major Jack Celliers.* Tom Conti *John Lawrence.* Ryuichi Sakamoto *Captain Yonoi.* Takeshi *Sgt. Hara.* Jack Thompson *Hicksley.* Johnny Okura *Kanemoto.* Allistair Browning *De Jong.* James Malcolm *Celliers' brother.* Chris Broun *Celliers at 12.* Yuya Uchida *Commandant of military prison.* Ryunosuke Kaneda *President of the court.* Takashi Naito *Lt. Iwata.* Tamio Ishikura *Prosecutor.* Rokko Toura *Interpreter.* Kan Mikami *Lt. Ito.*

• In a 1942 Japanese POW camp, Mr. Lawrence, the liaison officer, is suddenly called out by Sgt. Hara. Lawrence is to witness the punishment of a Korean guard, Kanemoto, who sodomized a Dutch prisoner, De Jong. The guard has been beaten and Lawrence fears what punishment will follow. When he hears the yells of Captain Yonoi who is practicing his swordfighting nearby, Lawrence calls out for him. Kanemoto steals a knife and attempts to commit harakiri, but Captain Yonoi appears and stops the proceedings.

Yonoi is called to the military prison in Batavia where a difficult prisoner, Jack Celliers, is on trial. Celliers and four men had parachuted into the area, attacked a troop transport, and then had surrendered. He claims the rest of his men are dead and that the only reason he surrendered is because the Japanese threatened to kill native villagers if he didn't. The Japanese, however, believe he has been leading native guerrilla troops. During the trial, it becomes evident that Yonoi is becoming attracted to Celliers.

Celliers is not a cooperative prisoner and he is beaten by the commandant and then is sent to face a firing squad, which shoots blanks. Celliers is sent to Yonoi's POW camp. When Yonoi learns that Lawrence and Celliers served together in Libya, he asks Lawrence for more information about him. Lawrence tells Yonoi that Celliers is called "straight foot" because he is a soldier's soldier. Yonoi demands from Hicksley, the commanding officer in charge of the POWs, the names of men who are experts in weapons and guns. Hicksley refuses and Yonoi threatens to replace him with another officer. The officer he has in mind is Celliers.

The camp officers are called out to witness Kanemoto's act of harakiri. The officers and De Jong refuse to watch the suicide, but when Kanemoto does it, De Jong screams out, bites off his own tongue and suffocates to death. The officers attempt to leave with De Jong, which Yonoi reads as a

Merry Christmas, Mr. Lawrence (Nagisa Oshima, 1983). An international production combining international talents features Western rock singer David Bowie as
Major Celliers and Japanese composer Ryuichi Sakamoto, who also wrote the film's
haunting score, as Captain Yonoi.

sign of disrespect. Yonoi says POWs are spiritually lazy and sentences them
all to 48 hours without food and drink (something he will do himself).
Celliers, who has been convalescing in the hospital, realizes that the patients cannot go that long without food and sneaks *manju* cakes into the
prison hospital hidden under red hibiscus flowers.

The cakes are discovered, and so is a radio. Yonoi has both Celliers
and Lawrence put into confinement. Lawrence, who is blamed for the
radio, is to be shot the next morning. Each tells the other about an important time in his life. Celliers recounts the story of his hunchbacked little
brother. His brother had a beautiful voice and made up songs to sing.
When his little brother goes off to school to join Jack, Jack doesn't inter-
vene during the school's psychologically brutal initiation in which his
brother's back is exposed and his singing ridiculed. His brother never sang
again, and Celliers has been carrying around the guilt of betrayal ever since.

That night, Christmas Eve, Sgt. Hara releases Lawrence and Celliers.
He has been drinking sake and calls himself Father Christmas. When Yonoi
finds out Lawrence has been released, he is angry with Hara until Hara
explains that he found out a Korean guard smuggled in the radio and has
released Celliers as well because he knows Yonoi wants him free.

When Yonoi again asks Hicksley for the names of the weapons expert and Hicksley again refuses, Yonoi demands the entire camp assemble and is angered when those in the hospital do not show up. He demands they come out, causing one patient's death. Yonoi is angered to the point of beheading Hicksley, but before he can bring his sword down on him, Celliers defiantly steps in between the two men. Enraged, Yonoi pushes Celliers aside, but he gets back up again and proceeds to kiss Yonoi on both cheeks. Yonoi attempts to kill Celliers, but is unable to do so. Instead, he has Celliers buried up to his neck and left out in the sun to die. That night, while Celliers still lives, Yonoi sneaks up to the buried man and cuts off a lock of his hair.

Four years later, in 1946, Lawrence arrives at the military prison where Sgt. Hara is to be executed. Yonoi has been executed after the war. Hara and Lawrence reminisce about their days together at the POW camp, and especially the night Hara called himself Father Christmas and saved Lawrence's life. Just as the Japanese thought they were right then, so the Allied powers think they are right now. As Lawrence leaves, Hara repeats words he said earlier, when he released Lawrence and Celliers from confinement, "Merry Christmas, Mr. Lawrence."

• *Merry Christmas, Mr. Lawrence* is Oshima's breakthrough film. Although it still tended to play at art houses, it did receive a wider degree of distribution in Universal's hands than any of his other films. Besides the backing of a large Hollywood studio, *Mr. Lawrence*'s popularity was also helped by the appearance of Western stars to draw in Western audiences. Tom Conti, who was winning rave reviews in *Reuben, Reuben* that same year, was a familiar name, as was Jack Thompson, who had appeared in a number of Australian films such as *Breaker Morant* that were released in America.

Although Oshima had originally wanted Robert Redford for the role of Celliers, the big draw for the film may have been the actor who did get the role, David Bowie. A popular rock and roll entertainer, Bowie was seen by Oshima in a commercial on Japanese television, and impressed, sent him the script.

Bowie is not the only rock and roller in the film: the prison commandant who leads the phony firing squad is Yuya Uchida who is a popular founding father of rock music in Japan and is known as the "Mick Jagger of Japan." (He would go on to write and star in the darkly amusing *Comic Magazine* with director Yojiro Takiata in 1986.) Takeshi, who plays the alternately brutal and friendly Sgt. Hara, and who also appeared in *Comic Magazine* as the *yakuza* killer, is most well known in Japan as a popular television comedian.

The exotic air which permeates the film is emphasized by the haunting music composed by Ryuichi Sakamoto, the actor who plays Captain

Yonoi and a popular recording artist in Japan. Both Sakamoto and Bowie
are similar in physical apearance (tall, thin and aesthetic-looking), and
both represent a spiritual person tormented by his own secret demon. For
Celliers, the demon is the guilt he feels over betraying his brother. For
Yanoi, it is the disgrace of not being given a military assignment in which
he can "die for his emperor" and the additional demon of Celliers to
whom he is strongly attracted.

Often called "the thinking man's *Bridge on the River Kwai*," *Merry
Christmas, Mr. Lawrence* is based on Laurens van der Post's novel *The
Seed and the Sower*. A South African who was assigned to Japan at the age
of 19 as a journalist, van der Post served in the British army during World
War II until taken captive and sent to a POW camp. His novel was condemned for its idealization of the Japanese when it was published in
England in 1951. It was published in Japan in 1978 and attracted Oshima's
attention. It is a story of the psychological struggle between love and hate
especially involving men who are not only from different cultures, but who
are also at war.

While repressed homosexuality and the cruelty of men at war (even
though there are no war scenes) are subtexts of the film, it is the
differences between the Japanese and the West that are most emphasized
throughout the film.

When Celliers is told at his trial that a Japanese soldier would commit
suicide before surrendering, Celliers simply replies that he is not Japanese.
It is a sentiment shared again later between Hara and Lawrence when Hara
says he would admire Lawrence more if he were dead and asks how he can
stand the shame of being a prisoner. Lawrence simply says that life is more
important.

Merry Christmas, Mr. Lawrence was filmed in New Zealand and in
Raratonga in the Cook Islands. It is beautifully photographed and was shot
in only two months with a minimum amount of retakes. (Oshima's speed
and efficiency exposed only 35,000 feet of film; it was said he edited in the
camera.)

Merry Christmas, Mr. Lawrence requires, like all of Oshima's films,
that the viewer invest time and effort into the viewing experience. (A factor many feel is unfortunately too difficult for American audiences.) But as
always, Oshima's films are worth the effort. *Lawrence* was a big hit in
Japan and, with its bigger budget, and outstanding acting and
photography, is more easily approached by Westerners than many of his
other films. It has finally brought Oshima an international and domestic
commercial success as well as the critical recognition he has always
enjoyed.

The Family Game (1983)
Kazoku geemu

1983 / Art Theatre Guild Production for Nikkatsu. 107 min. Color. *Director:* Yoshimitsu Morita. *Screenplay:* Yoshinori Kobayashi and Yoshimitsu Morita. *Adaptation:* From a novel by Yohei Honma. *Cinematography:* Yonezo Maeda. *Art Direction:* Katsumi Nakazawa. *Lighting:* Kazuo Yabe. *Sound:* Osamu Onodera. *Editor:* Akimasa Kawashima. *Assistant Director:* Shusuke Kaneko, *Producer:* Shiro Sasaki and Yu Okada. Videotape: Sony. Film Rental: Corinth, Circle.

Yusaku Matsuda *as Yoshimoto, the tutor.* Juzo Itami Mr. *Numata, the father.* Saori Yuki Mrs. *Numata, the mother.* Ichirota Miyagawa *Shigeyuki, the younger brother.* Junichi Tsujita *Shinichi, the older brother.*

• Shigeyuki Numata is not a good student. He feigns illnesses so he doesn't have to go to school, and when he does go he is a troublemaker. His grades are bad—he's the ninth from the bottom of his class. Because he's in the ninth grade, he will soon take the big exams to decide where he will go to school next. It looks as if he'll be going to Jingu High School instead of the better Seibu High School his older brother goes to.

To help Shigeyuki with his studies, his mother and father hire yet another tutor. The new tutor is a bit arrogant and very enigmatic. Mr. Numata offers the tutor a bonus of 10,000 yen for each rank his son goes up. When the tutor tells Shigeyuki to write down all the words in a story that he doesn't know, the boy just writes the word "twilight" over and over again in defiance. The tutor, who had sarcastically kissed the boy when he first arrived because he was "cute," now coldly hits the boy, giving him a bloody nose. When Shigeyuki doesn't show up for a tutoring lesson one day, his brother tells the tutor that he's in the book store. The tutur runs down to the store and wrestles him back to his room to study. Just the threat of a slap now makes Shigeyuki study.

One boy at Shigeyuki's school, Tsuchiya, enjoys bullying him. One day he and four of his friends beat Shigeyuki up. Shigeyuki drags home and demands his mother make his bed and stop talking to a neighbor who has come to her for advice on how to get her father-in-law's coffin down the high-rise apartment building's tiny elevator. When the tutor shows up, he wakes up Shigeyuki, and later takes him up on the rooftop and teaches him to box.

Shigeyuki's grades improve and now he can go to Seibu. The boy, however, has decided that it would be better to be at the top of Jingu than the bottom of Seibu. The tutor and his parents finally convince him to go to Seibu. When Shigeyuki passes his exams and is accepted into

The Family Game (Yoshimitsu Morita, 1983). Composed like a scene from the "Last Supper," the Numata family sits on each side of tutor Matsuda before the final food fight. From the left, Saori Yuki as the mother, Juzo Itami as the father, Yusaku Matsuda as the tutor, Ichirota Miyagawa as Shigeyuki and Junichi Tsujita as Shinichi.

Seibu, his parents have a celebratory dinner for him. While they eat, Mr. Numata discovers that his other son, Shinichi, has been cutting classes and is not only considering not going on to the state university, but is also thinking of dropping out of school. While the family calmly discusses this new crisis, the tutor has subtly started spilling and flinging food. As the discussion escalates, so does the food fight until finally the tutor ends up punching out the entire family. He leaves and the family is left to pick up the pieces of their dinner.

• At the beginning of the 1980s, Nikkatsu Studio did the same thing that Shochiku did in the 1960s—it promoted several young assistants to the rank of director without their undergoing a prolonged apprenticeship. Among them was self-taught filmmaker Yoshimitsu Morita. Morita was born in Tokyo in 1950 and graduated from Nippon University. Before joining Nikkatsu, he gained attention with his experimental 8mm film *Live in Chigasaki*. He made his first feature film, the comedy *Something Like Yoshiwara (No yo na mono, 1981)*, but it was followed by an unnoteworthy film vehicle for a popular singing trio at Toei Studios and several softcore "pink" movies at Nikkatsu with titles like *Love Hard, Love Deep.* While making these last films, Morita put together the technical crew which would continue to work with him.

The Family Game was one of the first original comedies to come out of Japan in decades. Comedies had been popular before World War II (Gosho's *The Neighbor's Wife and Mine.* Ozu's *I Was Born, But . . . ,*

Yamanaka's *Pot Worth a Million Ryo* and Mansaku Itami's *Kakita
Akanishi*) and even a few, a very few, were made in the golden age of the
1950s (Toyoda's *A Cat, Shozo and Two Women* and a few eccentric
Ichikawa films). But with *The Family Game*, the genre underwent a new
spurt. In the film, Morita seems to thoroughly enjoy tweaking middle class
values and veneers. The Numata family, while being well-off, also appears
to be directionless—except for one point. Their children *must* get a good
education. For them, this is the only way to obtain the best possible career
and "the better life." So obsessed are these middle class parents with their
son's gaining this passport to the future, that they think nothing of hiring
an unconventional and abusive tutor because at least he is effective. It
doesn't seem to matter that Shigeyuki may be getting an education devoid
of wisdom (his grades improve, but his attitude never does).

Morita's characters are sharply but sparsely sketched. In fact, one of the
most common ways in which he shows them—and the way each is introduced
at the start of the film—is around food. The father noisily slurps the yolks
out of his fried eggs, the tutor constantly gulps his drinks, the mother uses
tea breaks as an excuse to check up on her son and the tutor. It is no wonder
then that Morita uses the celebratory dinner for the tutor's final attack.

The family is always seated on one side of what appears to be a
Scandinavian-designed long, rectangular table. By seating them this way,
Morita emphasizes the apartment's crampedness (to have a private conversation, the mother and father must go downstairs and sit in the car). The
table makes serious discussions between family members extremely
difficult. (When the young neighbor seeks advice from Mrs. Numata she
asks permission to move her seat to the other side.) Even though each
member of the family eats with elbows in the other's way, they seem to
know very little about each other. In one scene the father is upset that his
egg yolk is too hard to be slurped. He chastises his wife who, after all their
years together, is surprised that this is how he always eats his eggs. When
the culminating food-fight dinner finally occurs, with the tutor seated in
the center of the family, the scene takes on the look of a "Last Supper."
And in a way it is, at least for the tutor. After the physical and emotional
upheaval of the food fight, Morita adds a final bit of sarcastic finger pointing. Although he has gotten Shigeyuki into the better high school, the
tutor hasn't really changed anything. The family continues on their
stuporous way right until the enigmatic end of the film in which the two
boys and their mother fall asleep while a helicopter hovers overhead.

Of interest in *The Family Game* is the cinematography. There is a
stark use of brilliant colors which are set off by many scenes' highly
geometric compositions. The final dinner is done in one long shot, with
the full table and its five diners in full view. What seems odd for a
Japanese film is that nature is almost completely missing. The closest
Morita gets is Shinichi's daydreaming sketches of trees and the field in which

Shigeyuki and Tsuchiya beat each other up. Instead we get a strong feeling of alienation with scenes filled with modern apartment buildings, Tokyo factories and the cold school building. Also of note in *The Family Game* is the actor who plays Mr. Numata. Juzo Itami is the son of the 1930s film director Mansaku Itami. Juzo Itami decided that he liked filmmaking so much that although he continued to act (see *MacArthur's Children*), he, too, became a director *(The Funeral, Tampopo* and *A Taxing Woman)*.

The Family Game won Japan's equivalent of an Academy Award for best picture of the year, Kinema Jumpo's Number One Film Award, in 1983 and garnered Morita many "best new director" awards. Morita went on to make *Sorekara* in 1986 based on the 1909 novel by Natsume Soseki and stars Yusaku Matsuda *(Family Game's* tutor*)* and Chishu Ryu, one of Yasujiro Ozu's favorite actors.

MacArthur's Children (1984)
Setouchi shonen yakyu dan

1984 / Shochiku. 117 min. Color. *Director:* Masahiro Shinoda. *Screenplay:* Tsutome Tamara. *Adaptation:* From the novel by Yu Aku. *Cinematography:* Kazuo Miyagawa. *Music:* Shinichiro Ikebe. *Editor:* Sachiko Yamaji. *Producer:* You-No-Kai and Masato Hara. Film Rental: Orion Classics. Video: Pacific Arts.

Takaya Yamuchi *as Ryuta.* Yoshyuki Omori *Saburo.* Shiori Sakura *Mume.* Masako Natsume *Komako.* Juzo Itami *The captain.* Shima Iwashita *Tome.* Hiromi Go *Masao Nahai.*

• World War II has just ended, and in a sixth-grade classroom, on the small Japanese island of Awaji, children are being instructed on how to edit their textbooks in accordance with Occupation directives. Two of the school children are Ryuta, who lives with his grandfather, the police chief, and Saburo, who runs away from school to protest the "loss of his country." New to the class is Mume, the daughter of a naval captain who may be considered a war criminal by the Allied forces and who has come to the island to cleanse his soul before his trial. The boys are taken with Mume and the captain and vow to protect them. Komako, the class' teacher, is a young widow; her husband, Masao was killed in the war. Her brother-in-law, Tetsuo, constantly makes advances to her, which she refuses. One day, however, he takes her against her will.

When the Americans arrive, they blow up the island's defenses and

MacArthur's Children (Masahiro Shinoda, 1984). The drastic impact of losing the war and the vast cultural changes caused by the Occupation are symbolized by a group of school boys in awe of a G.I.'s chewing gum.

immediately the American culture becomes manifest as children start asking for gum and candy from the soldiers. The boys meet a one-legged man who has been lurking on the island. He was wounded in the war and gives the boys a baseball inscribed "High School Championship 1937" which he wants them to take to Komako. The injured soldier turns out to be Masao, Komako's husband. Because Komako has been raped by Masao's brother and because Masao doesn't want to be a burden to his wife, he goes off and takes a clerical job in a shrine office.

In the meantime the captain has been declared a class B war criminal because he didn't rescue injured and drowning POWs and is taken off to prison. His ship, the *Nagato,* is used as a target during the Bikini A-bomb test. Eventually the captain is executed. Komako starts a baseball team for her students, the Kosaka Tigers, using handmade balls, mitts and bats. On a field trip Komako and her class visit the shrine where Masao works and they get back together. He returns to the island and cultivates flowers for sale. The children's baseball team is not a very good one. Before the American soldiers are to leave the island, however, it is proposed that there be a Japanese-American all-star game. In light of the captain's execution, the children see it as a grudge match. During the game, a dog runs away with the ball and evens the score. The children think of the dog as the spirit of Mume's father. The film ends with the children again in the classroom, only now they're learning English.

• After *Double Suicide,* the next Shinoda film to receive extensive distribution in the States was the haunting *Demon Pond.* A beautiful film mixing legend and reality with man's relationship to nature, *Demon Pond* took the astounding step of casting Tamasaburo Bando to play the dual role of the innocent Yuri and the sorceress Princess Shirayuki. What was so astounding was that Tamasaburo, as he is known in Japan, was, at the time, a 29-year-old female impersonator celebrated on the Kabuki stage.

For *MacArthur's Children,* Shinoda creates an entirely different type of film. Shinoda was only 14 when World War II ended. As a "MacArthur's child" himself, he directly experienced the Americanization of Japan. It was a development he brings to the screen in *MacArthur's Children* with humor, understanding and just a bit of resentment. It is a period and topic not easily dealt with in the Japanese cinema, with the possible exception of Kinoshita's *Twenty-Four Eyes.*

Shinoda's film was financed at a cost of $2,500,000 by Fuji Television. Although he hadn't envisioned a U.S. release for his film, it really is a story of the two cultures, one which imposed itself on the other, and one which resignedly acquiesced, if not actively embraced, the domination. Shooting on location on the island of Awaji and with a large and diverse cast (Iwashita is Shinoda's wife, Itami a fine director in his own right, and Go a popular rock singer), Shinoda weaves several story lines into an almost epic film. He captures all the emotions inherent in the defeat and occupation of his country from apprehension and sadness to disorder and loss. He even accepts the attraction many Japanese, especially the children, found in American ways. For Shinoda the Americanization of Japan probably had a more profound effect on his country than did the A-bomb.

There are many beautiful and symbolic scenes in *MacArthur's Children.* When the Americans blow up the island's armaments, the explosions are cut against the tombstone of a soldier killed on Guadalcanal, flowers trembling from the blast, and the badly wounded Masao. When the police officers bring Mume to her father for a final farewell, blossoms gently and sadly fall off the tree behind her. (Falling blossoms are often a representation of the Japanese philosophy of *mono no aware.*)

But the Occupation also had a dark side for Shinoda. When the soldiers think that the islanders are dirty, they are subjected to the indignity of being sprayed with DDT for lice. When Komako's brother-in-law overpowers her, it is with a definite parallel to the Occupation forces overpowering the people. And when Saburo's brother and sister arrive at school, they are in modern dress. They disrespectfully leave their shoes on and disrupt the class by throwing candy all over the floor, which the students (except the stoic Mume) scramble after. With the philosophy "Desire until you get it," Saburo's brother makes his living on the black market and at the expense of his own people.

As of the end of 1989, the most recent Shinoda film to be shown in America is 1986's *Gonza the Spearman.* Like *Double Suicide, Gonza* is an adaptation of a Bunraku puppet play (this time more realistically presented) and again takes on the subject of a tragic romance. The handsomely ambitious Gonza (Hiromi Go) is engaged to one woman while agreeing to wed another because it will provide a means of advancement for him. *Gonza* is a beautiful film (photographed by the legendary Kazuo Miyagawa) in which Shinoda reveals he is still a master of composition and story, and possibly the most mainstream of the directors to come out of the Shochiku New Wave.

The Crazy Family (1984)
Gyakufunsha kazoku

1984 / The Director's Company–Art Theatre Guild. 106 min. Color. *Director:* Sogo Ishii. *Screenplay:* Yoshinori Kobayashi, Fumio Kohnami and Sogo Ishii. *Adaptation:* From an original story by Yoshinori Kobayashi. *Cinematography:* Masaki Tamura. *Art Direction:* Terumi Hosoishi. *Lighting:* Mamoru Sato. *Music:* 1984. *Sound:* Shin Fukuda. *Editor:* Junnichi Kikuchi. *Producer:* Kazuhiko Hasegawa, Toyoji Yamane and Shiro Sasaki. Film Rental: New Yorker.

Katsuya Kobayashi *as Katsukuni Kobayashi, the father.* Mitsuko Baisho *Saeko, the mother.* Yoshiki Arizono *Masaki, the son.* Yuki Kudo *Erika, the daughter.* Hitoshi Ueki *Hisakuni, the grandfather.*

• It is November 2, and the Kobayashi family has moved into their new dream home in the suburbs. The two teenage children, Erika and Masaki, are very pleased finally to have rooms of their own. And Mrs. Kobayashi is so happy that she gift wraps herself in heart-decorated wrapping paper with a red bow for her husband. To remember the occasion, photographs are taken, but an ominous note is struck when Mr. Kobayashi writes in his diary that the family's "sickness" had worsened in their cramped flat and now he hopes they will all be "cured." As the family gets used to their new home, Mr. Kobayashi commutes to work and exercises and Mrs. Kobayashi delights in cooking in her new kitchen and tending her plants. Erika cultivates her two professional aims in her room by alternately acting the pop singer and the lady wrestler. Masaki, who is studying to retake his college entrance exams, spends all his time in his high-tech, information-laden room, where he constantly crams even to the point of stabbing himself in the thigh to stay awake.

Trouble stalks the house, however, the day Mr. Kobayashi discovers white ants (termites) on the dog Masaki found under the house and which his son believes was "destined" to belong to the family. In obsessive terror, Mr. Kobayashi begins an extensive extermination campaign. Further problems arrive in the form of Mr. Kobayashi's father. One day when Mr. Kobayashi returns home from work, he finds his drunken father and his friends excitedly applauding while Mrs. Kobayashi performs a strip tease. Mr. Kobayashi fears that the family sickness is returning.

When Grandpa decides to stay with his son in his new house, it suddenly seems very small. Consequently an expansion is planned — a basement room will be added through a hole in the living room floor. As construction (or better, destruction) continues, Mr. Kobayashi eventually discovers a nest of termites and also creates a geyser when he hits a water main. Chaos seems to be overtaking the house and its occupants and soon even Mr. Kobayashi is cracking. He gets up in the middle of the night, boards the windows and doors and attempts to poison his family with coffee laced with termite insecticide. The family catches on just in time, however, and each girds for battle with the other: Grandpa puts on his World War II uniform, Mother dresses in armor of pots and pans, Masaki becomes a samurai student, Erika resorts to her wrestler's know-how and father chases everyone with power tools. The ultimate family feud follows, with the entire house eventually coming down around them. In the end, the family is living out in the open, in the shadow of the expressway.

• Sogo Ishii was born in Fukuoka in 1957 and attended Nihon University, where he majored in film directing. His first film, the 8mm *Panic in the High School* (1976), was about a high school revolt and was made when he was 19. It was remade in 1978 on 35mm film. In 1980, Ishii established his reputation as a director popular with youth when he directed *Crazy Thunderbird,* an action-packed film about an outlaw. Ishii, who is a member of a rock band, also made rock videos. *The Crazy Family* was produced by The Director's Company, a filmmaking cooperative founded by and for young Japanese directors. The film's original title was *The Back-Jet Family,* which refers to an extremely dangerous aviation landing technique. When a disturbed Japan Air Lines pilot put his plane into Tokyo harbor using the back-jet technique the term was popularized to describe irrational behavior.

Yoshimitsu Morita's 1983 film *The Family Game* did not go far enough in lampooning modern Japanese family life for director Ishii and scriptwriter Yoshinori Kobayashi. Consequently the two came up with their extreme version of Morita's Numata family. *The Crazy Family* is a black comedy with absolutely no inhibitions. Morita's Numata family may have been the typical middle class Japanese family pushed just a bit into caricature for effect; Ishii's Kobayashi family, by contrast, are radical caricatures who have been pushed into the realm of the completely deranged.

Ran (1985)   257

Every member of this family eventually spirals downward into various depths of the "family sickness." But what is this sickness besides an excuse for a blackly hilarious movie? By moving the Kobayashis from a cramped apartment to a house with space which eventually becomes restricted and finally out into the open, Ishii would seem to imply that a lack of personal space is the cause of the illness. It would follow then that the methods employed by each family member to get as much of this space as possible and alleviate the social pressures caused by the closeness is the sickness. Masaki won't come out of his room and Erika won't share hers with her mother when Grandpa moves in. After the family murderously goes at each other, all decide (with the possible exception of Erika) that it would be best if the family got a fresh start by bringing down the entire house. Gleefully they take chainsaws to lintels and sledgehammers to walls. When we see them again, there are no walls. Living out in the open they appear to once again be a happy family living a "normal" life.

It is unusual to see such an anarchic film come out of Japan. Gone is the controlled acting and the classically perfect scene composition. In the place of ethnically inspired traditional Japanese music on the soundtrack, *The Crazy Family* employs what is modern and electronic (acknowledgement of Ishii's rock music and video background). Some critics have found *The Crazy Family* to be too tasteless to be funny (some audience members have walked out on the film), but when seen in conjunction with *The Family Game* it just seems like the next logical comic step.

The film is a low-budget production, but Ishii gets the best from his actors and their limited surroundings. The pressure-cooker tempo of the film builds nicely to the final showdown, and if the cartoon bizarreness can be kept in perspective then the laughs (and symbolism) are definitely there.

Ran (1985)

1985 / Greenwich Film Productions–Herald Ace, Inc. / a.k.a. "Chaos." 165 min. Color. *Director:* Akira Kurosawa. *Screenplay:* Akira Kurosawa, Hideo Oguni and Masato Ide. *Cinematography:* Takao Saito. *Art Direction:* Yoshiro Muraki and Shinobu Muraki. *Music:* Toru Takemitsu. *Producers:* Serge Silberman and Masato Hara. *Executive Producer:* Katsumi Furukawa. Videotape: CBS/Fox. Film Rental: Orion Classics.

The Crazy Family (Sogo Ishii, 1984). Never has a crazier family been captured on film than that of the Kobayashi's. From the left they are son Masaki (Yoshiki Arizono), grandfather Hisakuni (Hitoshi Ueki), father Katsukuni (Katsuya Kobayashi), mother Saeko (Mitsuko Baisho) and daughter Erika (Yuki Kudo).

Tatsuya Nakadai *as Hidetora Ichimonji*. So Terao *Tarotakatora Ishimonji*. Jinpachi Nezu *Jiromasatora Ichimonji*. Daisuke Ryu *Saburonaotora Ishimonji*. Mieko Harada *Lady Kaede*. Yoshiko Miyazaki *Lady Sue*. Peter *Kyoami*. Takeshi Nomura *Tsurumaru*. Hisashi Igawa *Kurogane*. Masayuke Yui *Tango*.

- After a boar hunt, Lord Hidetora Ichimonji and his three sons, Taro, Jiro and Saburo, dine on a hillside with lords Ayabe and Fujimaki. Each lord has an eligible daughter, but Hidetora has only one unmarried son, Saburo. Taro, the eldest is married to Lady Kaede, and Jiro, the middle son, to Lady Sue. Both women are daughters of lords Hidetora has beaten in battle. Hidetora is 72 years old and wants to retire from power, leaving his lands to his sons. Taro is chosen to lead, with Jiro and Saburo's help. Saburo, with the support of Hidetora's loyal retainer Tango, tells his father that it will never work. His honesty enrages his father, and both Saburo and Tango are banished. Lord Fujimaki follows Saburo. He appreciates Saburo's frankness and asks him to marry his daughter and stay at his castle.

Hidetora relinquishes the major part of his castle to Taro while planning on living in the keep himself. However, Hidetora's wives are insulted and Lady Kaede insists that Taro have his father sign a pledge in blood. Lady Kaede was originally from this castle and left it to marry Taro. Hidetora killed her father and brothers and her mother committed suicide. Now she is back and wants to be secure in her position. Insulted, Hidetora leaves Taro's castle and moves to Jiro's castle.

At Jiro's castle, things aren't much better. Jiro resents Taro's ascent to power and starts plotting to take it from him. His wife, Lady Sue, is also the victim of Hidetora's warring. Her castle was burned by Hidetora and her mother and father perished. Her brother was allowed to live, but his eyes were gouged out. When Jiro refuses to let his father's warriors inside the second castle, and suggests that his father return to Taro and apologize, Hidetora again leaves.

Seeking refuge at the third castle, Hidetora and his men are ambushed by Taro and Jiro's army. Hidetora attempts to defend himself, but his sword breaks. The remnants of his guards valiantly try to protect him, but they are slaughtered by the combined army. Hidetora's wives kill themselves, and his concubines surround Hidetora and are shot by bullets meant for him. Hidetora desperately looks for a dagger with which to commit seppuku, but there are none in the tower to which he has retreated. Flaming arrows stream through windows, and soon Hidetora is trapped in the burning building. Suddenly Hidetora emerges from the tower to face Jiro and Taro's army. He is emotionally drained by his ordeal, and verging on madness. Upon seeing him, the armies, stunned, back away and allow him to pass. Hidetora wanders on the plains until he is found by Tango and Kyoami, his court entertainer. He is taken to a nearby hut, only to find it inhabited by Lady Sue's blind brother, Tsurumaru.

In the chaos of the battle, Taro has been shot—supposedly by Hidetora's men, but in reality, by Jiro's confident, Kurogane. When Jiro takes over the first castle, Lady Kaede, Taro's widow, has a private audience with him. She threatens and then seduces Jiro and manages to maintain her position at the castle. However, she has no compunction about demanding the head of the one woman who could supplant her, Lady Sue.

Sue and her brother find out about the vengeful act, and run away to the shell of their former home. Tsurumaru has forgotten his flute, his only companion since his boyhood, and Sue returns to his hut for it. Within the same ruins, Hidetora walks accompanied by Kyoami, growing more and more insane. Saburo, the only son who really loved his father, now comes to rescue him. With his army, and Fujimaki's at the border, Saburo crosses the river. Jiro allows Saburo to take his father, planning on assassinating them when Saburo gives away his father's location. Saburo finds Hidetora, collapsed under a stone, quite mad. While the two reconcile, the battle begins and Saburo's riflemen fire at Jiro's horsemen from the protection of the forest. Jiro's men drop their banners and retreat and it would seem that Saburo has won. Saburo and Hidetora ride together on horseback, Hidetora restored to sanity. But the peace is shortlived, for a shot rings out and Saburo falls to a sniper's bullet. This is too much for Hidetora, and he too dies.

Back at Jiro's castle, Lady Sue's head is brought to Lady Kaede, but the clan is in ruins. This, it turns out, has been Lady Kaede's purpose all along, to destroy the Ichimonji clan which killed her family. Kurogane, angered, beheads her. At the ruins of Tsurumaru's family castle, Lady Sue's blind brother hesitantly walks along a wall. Coming abruptly to the end, he is startled and drops a scroll of the Amida Buddha, the symbol of compassion.

• *Ran* was a project Kurosawa had wanted to make for a long time. He had worked on it for almost a decade. The script was written by the early 1970s, years before the production of his previous film, *Kagemusha*. With an estimated budget of $12 million, however, Kurosawa had a great deal of difficulty finding a producer. Japanese studios found the story not only expensive to mount, but also too tragic in content, and passed on it. Initially, the French production studio Gaumont was interested in financing *Ran*. But when the French company cut back on its budget, Gaumont pulled out. Kurosawa then went on to make *Kagemusha* with the help of Francis Ford Coppola, George Lucas and 20th Century–Fox. But the connection with Gaumont brought together Kurosawa and French producer Serge Silberman (who did many of Luis Buñuel's later films). Eventually

Ran (Akira Kurosawa, 1985). Tatsuya Nakadai as Kurosawa's King Lear equivalent, Hidetora, begins on his path of madness after being betrayed by two of his sons.

Silberman, through his own Greenwich Film Production, took over the *Ran* project. He managed to interest Nippon Herald-Ace, a Japanese film-importing company, in the film and they guaranteed a $10.5 million loan. They also found support from Toho, which would distribute the film, and Fuji TV, which would get the broadcast rights.

Kurosawa originally forecast *Ran* to run three hours and cost $7 million, but Silberman realized this dollar amount was an underestimate. The script was cut to two hours and 15 minutes and a more realistic budget of $11 million was projected. A battle scene Kurosawa had wanted to film in the snowy mountains of Hokkaido would be less expensively shot in temperate Kyushu, and because of Kurosawa's international reputation, he was allowed to shoot at the historic Himeji and Kumamoto castles instead of building complete sets from scratch. Kurosawa did have to build one castle, the one he would burn down when Hidetora starts on his journey into insanity. Unlike the castle he built for *Throne of Blood* which had to be accurate in the most minute detail, the castle built for fiery destruction in *Ran* used molded plastic to simulate the rock foundation and plywood for the interiors. Normally Kurosawa shoots his scenes with three cameras, but for the castle burning, he took no chances and used five.

Ran required approximately 1400 extras and more than 200 horses (50 to 75 of them imported from the U.S. to augment those available in Japan). Approximately 1400 suits of armor had to be fabricated, their design personally supervised by Kurosawa and authentically replicating armor from the 16th century. Emi Wada, in charge of the costumes for army and horses, took three years to complete the job. Production began in June of 1984 and ended nine months later. Two sad events occurred for Kurosawa during this period: sound recordist Fumio Yanoguchi collapsed and died during filming, and Kurosawa's wife of almost four decades lost a long battle with cancer and died. When edited, *Ran* came in with a running time of two hours and 40 minutes. Kurosawa was under pressure to cut it, but it was shown as it was.

Ran obviously is not a straight translation of Shakespeare's *King Lear*. Instead it combines the central theme and plot with a historic figure named Morikawa from medieval Japanese history. Lear's Fool was transformed into Kyoami, also a kind of court jester. The character was played by a famous Japanese transvestite/entertainer, Peter. Peter followed in the footsteps of his famous father and studied the *Jiutamae,* the Noh form of dance, which he learned in his father's classes and of which he is an accomplished performer. An impressive actor, Peter was the first actor Kurosawa signed for *Ran*. One major difference between *Lear* and *Ran* is the transformation of the daughters into sons, and the presence of Taro's wife and Jiro's seductress, Lady Kaede. Functioning more as a Lady Macbeth, Lady Kaede plots not for the advancement of her husband or lover, but for the destruction of the clan which murdered her family. Contrasted to Lady Kaede is Lady Sue. Her family also was annihilated by Hidetora. Lady Sue however has renounced her anger and hatred in favor of a life committed to Buddhist principles.

To represent the three sons, Kurosawa has assigned a vibrant color to each (similar to the way in which he gave a different color to each segment of Shingen's army in *Kagemusha*). Taro, the eldest, is represented by yellow, Jiro, the middle son, with red, and Saburo, the youngest, with blue. During the confusion of battle, the viewer will always know which soldiers belong to whose army. Even when Lord Fujimaki's troops arrive to back up Saburo, they are assigned another color, white. While *Ran* is only Kurosawa's fourth color film, it is undoubtedly one of the most beautiful ever made. The colorful armies bring an aestheticism to brutal battle scenes which is underscored even more by the fact that Kurosawa has deleted all battle noises from the soundtrack. Instead there is the haunting music of Toru Takemitsu.

Kurosawa's camera is even more detached here than it was in *Kagemusha,* giving a god-like remote view of the endeavors which humans undertake. But this is not to underestimate the beauty of the film. As in *Throne of Blood,* Kurosawa uses nature superbly to enhance the mood of his film. When Tango and Saburo are banished, thunder rumbles from a once clear but still bright sky. The camera pans up to a huge dark cloud which is passing in front of the sun, a harbinger of the darkness which will soon descend on Hidetora's clan.

Ran opened at the First Tokyo International Film Festival, an event Kurosawa didn't attend. When it opened in the United States at the New York Film Festival, however, Kurosawa was there to receive a standing ovation and reviews comparing the film to some of the great epics in cinema history. *Ran* went on to garner the New York Film Critics Best Foreign Film Award but ran into initial trouble at the Academy Awards. Because Kurosawa had not appeared at Tokyo's very first Film Festival, the Japanese authorities responsible for nominating one of their country's films for consideration retaliated by nominating a film about Alzheimer's disease instead. Immediately, Kurosawa's banner was carried by United States directors such as Arthur Penn and Sidney Lumet who worked to get Kurosawa a Best Director nomination. He got the nomination, but lost the award to Sydney Pollack for *Out of Africa*. (Kurosawa, along with John Huston and Billy Wilder, presented the Best Picture Award that night in March of 1986 which also went to *Out of Africa*). *Ran* also garnered an unprecedented three Oscar nominations for Cinematography, Art Direction and Costume Design, winning only in the last category, a tribute to Emi Wada's work.

Kurosawa was 75 when he made *Ran,* and his sight failing. But the great director's career still didn't seem to be over. In 1989 plans were begun for a film titled *Dreams,* a semiautobiographical film which will again be aided by George Lucas and this time, another admirer, Steven Spielberg. Filming was scheduled to begin in January, with Lucas providing help with special effects and Spielberg providing financial backing and co-distribution with Warner Bros. On March 26, 1990, Akira Kurosawa's extraordinary work in films was recognized by the Academy of Motion Picture Arts and Sciences with an honorary lifetime achievement Academy Award.

There are many theories as to why Kurosawa's works are so popular in the West. Most of all, Kurosawa knows how to tell a great story. He is also a director of ideas and ideals which appeal to many cultures, and a director whose cinematic eye is virtually unfailing. Unfortunately, Kurosawa has had to pay for his appreciation by the West, often going unrecognized or unappreciated at home in Japan (as witnessed by his recent difficulty in finding financing wholly within Japan and his snubbing for an Oscar nomination for *Ran*). The first retrospective of Kurosawa's films was held in the U.S. in 1981, not in Japan. Kurosawa is a dynamically expressive and versatile director who easily ranks among the world's greatest. With his control of script, camera and editing, he is a true auteur able to work in many genres, periods, and styles. Fortunately, it is not necessary to share Kurosawa's cultural background to be moved by his films, but through the accessibility of his films, Kurosawa has possibly opened up Japanese culture to the West more than any other film director.

Himatsuri (1985)

1985 / Gunro, Seibu Saison Group and Cine Saison Co., for Shibata. / a.k.a. "Fire Festival." 120 min. Color. *Director:* Mitsuo Yanagimachi. *Screenplay:* Kenji Nakagami. *Cinematography:* Masaki Tamura. *Art Direction:* Takeo Kimura. *Lighting:* Hitoshi Takaya. *Music:* Toru Takemitsu. *Sound:* Yukio Kubota. *Editor:* Sachiko Yamaji. *Assistant Director:* Yusuke Narita. *Executive Producer:* Kazuo Shimizu. Videotape: Lorimar. Film Rental: Kino International.

Kinya Kitaoji *as Tatsuo.* Kiwako Taichi *Kimiko.* Ryota Nakamoto *Ryota.* Norihei Miki *Yamakawa.* Rikiya Yasuoka *Toshio.* Junko Miyashita *Sachiko, Tatsuo's wife.* Kin Sugai *Tatsuo's mother.* Sachiko Matsushita *Tatsuo's sister.* Masako Yagi *Tatsuo's sister.* Aoi Nakajima *Kimiko's sister.* Kenzo Kaneko *Her husband.* Aiko Morishita *The nursery school teacher.*

• In Nigishima, Tatsuo makes his living as a lumberjack. He is a womanizing, rough man who takes delight in hunting. Ryota, a 19-year-old tree cutter, idolizes Tatsuo and learns from him how to make animal traps and helps to take care of Tatsuo's hunting dogs. The village is a seaside one and there are plans underway to build a marine park there. Tatsuo does not approve of the park and he is holding up development because his house lies in the way, and he does not intend to sell. When a fuel oil spill kills fish in the fisherman's nursery they begin to suspect Tatsuo. There is a longstanding conflict in the area between the mountain people and the sea people. Since Tatsuo is a mountain person, the fishermen who want the marine park distrust him.

One day, Kimiko. Tatsuo's old girlfriend, returns to the village because the bar she owns in nearby Shingu is in debt. She plans on working at her sister's bar until she can get enough money to return. Even though he is married and has two sons, Tatsuo and Kimiko have an affair. Tatsuo is constantly acting against tradition. On a hunting trip he shoots monkeys, which is forbidden, and he even swims in sacred waters. After a second oil spill, fishermen discover oil containers near Tatsuo's home, reinforcing suspicions of his guilt to sabotage the marine park.

Yamakawa, the local land broker, uses the occasion of the 17th anniversary of Tatsuo's father's death and the gathering of the family, to pressure them into selling their land. Yamakawa is also attracted to Kimiko and lends her 600,000 yen. Now that she has enough money, Kimiko returns to Shingu.

While Tatsuo is in the forest chopping down trees, it begins to rain heavily. The other lumberjacks take cover, but not Tatsuo. He seems to commune with nature and after embracing a giant tree, it stops raining, but strong breezes begin. As if being spoken to by the *kami* (Shinto gods),

Himatsuri (Mitsuo Yanagimachi, 1985). In a film that blends Shintoism with the problems of progress, Kinya Kitaoji (Tatsuo) challenges the *kami* by swimming in sacred water.

Tatsuo suddenly says he understands. The town's annual *himatsuri* (fire festival) is a rite of purification and a celebration to drive out evil spirits. Tatsuo, now reborn to nature, attacks some men who are starting the fire without waiting for the sacred flame. They are eventually stopped and the sacred flame arrives. The next day, as the teacher walks Tatsuo's sons to his home, they suddenly hear gun shots. The boys run into the house and see their family dead. But they think it is a game and pretend to hide from their father. He finds them, and shoots them too. Propping the butt of his shotgun against the floor, he puts the barrel to his chest and pulls the trigger one more time. In the hatchery, oil bubbles up for another fish kill.

* Mitsuo Yanagimachi was born in rural Ibaragi in 1944. He graduated from Waseda University, where he received a liberal arts degree. He decided to turn his talents to filmmaking and started as a production assistant, a job he held for five years. In 1974 he formed his own independent production company, Gunro Films. His first feature was *God Speed You! Black Emperor,* a documentary on motorcycle gangs. It was filmed in

16mm but was picked up by Toei which blew it up to 35mm and distributed it—a first for a major film company. From the motorcycle gang he chose on "actor," Yuji Honma, to star in his next film, *The Map of a Nineteen-Year-Old Boy* (1979). The film, about a youth who gradually loses his grip on reality, won a great deal of attention at the 1980 Cannes Film Festival and commenced Yanagimachi's reception into the international film world.

Farewell to the Land (1982), Yanagimachi's third film, was financed and distributed by Yanagimachi himself and presages the director's concern about changing rural areas, a theme central to *Himatsuri*. When the Seibu department store decided to expand its activities into the area of culture (they also promoted art exhibits and went into publishing), they chose Yanagimachi to direct the first feature film they would produce, *Himatsuri*. This film, like Imamura's *Vengeance Is Mine*, was inspired by actual events. But unlike *Vengeance*, *Himatsuri* does not attempt to recount the experience factually or to justify it or psychoanalyze it. In 1980, a villager in Kumano, an area south of Osaka, murdered his family before committing suicide. That is the headline Yanagimachi turned into a highly personal statement.

The Kumano area of Japan is also a center of the ancient Japanese religion of Shintoism. In Shinto, the spirits of the gods manifest themselves within nature. These gods *(kami)* are found in places like trees, rocks, rivers and fire. Ancestor worship and rituals, especially those of purification, are critically important in Shinto and are performed at set times. One of these is the *himatsuri* or fire festival. Considering Japan's Shinto roots, it is difficult to fathom why so few directors incorporate it into their films. Although Shintoism was used by the military powers during World War II to enforce the emperor's divinity and march the nation into battle, and it is viewed with a degree of distrust for that reason, it is still a fairly significant part of Japanese thinking.

Yanagimachi uses Shintoism to interpret the murder/suicide at Kumano. Tatsuo boasts that he has made love to the mountain goddess and the gods "speak" to him through the sudden rustling of the wind through the trees. (Imamura used the same symbolism in his *Ballad of Narayama* when Tatsuehi's dead father is represented by a billowing tree.) Nature, the embodiment of Shintoism, is a palpable reality in Yanagimachi's film.

And the relationship and conflict between man and nature is Yanagimachi's central theme. Man, in the name of progress, is invading Kumano and unthinkingly desecrating nature. Rapidly, roads cut swaths through ancient forests and marine parks threaten sacred waters. The truly advanced towns, notes land broker Yamakawa, might even get a nuclear power station. *Himatsuri,* therefore, is also a tale of conflicts between ancient traditions and modern demands. When Kimiko makes love to

Tatsuo, she remembers back to a time when they were young, 1959, and the Kisei Honsen railway line opened up the area and brought with it the first tastes of modernization. Kimiko, herself, is in one sense a study in this conflict. When she comes back to Nigishima she comes in a small boat. She wears a traditional kimono when she arrives (as she does when she leaves by train and once when she prays for prosperity and meets and wins over Yamakawa whom she will bilk of money), but she is a modern bar hostess who normally dresses the part.

The main character of Tatsuo is an enigmatic one. He is thoughtless and brutal. While he makes his living from nature cutting down trees and hunting, he also seems to be unusually indifferent toward his environment. On the one hand he refuses to sell his family's land to make way for a marine park and the ensuing tourists, while at the same time he thinks nothing of killing the prohibited monkeys. When the oil slicks are discovered, the conflict between the mountain people (Tatsuo) and those who make a living from the sea makes Tatsuo a prime suspect and eventual scapegoat.

During the rainstorm in the forest, it is as if Tatsuo is purified of his past sins against nature. Now he will avenge the gods by offering a blood sacrifice to restore the nature's harmony. His actions, though they may never stop the advance of modernization, are a statement against these influences.

The viewer has witnessed Tatsuo's brutality throughout the film, but the murders and Tatsuo's shotgun harakiri, come as a complete surprise. Critics have interpreted the murders and suicide in several ways, and this fact attests to the director's unusual neutrality. The events depicted in *Himatsuri* are emotionally electrifying, but their violence is shown in a way that can only be described as nonjudgmental. That is why they are so difficult to interpret. Yanagimachi doesn't allow us the privilege of knowing if he approves or disapproves of Tatsuo's sacrifice. He simply tells us what happened. For some, this could make *Himatsuri* a difficult film. For all it is a challenging film. When Yanagimachi decided to reject working for Japan's larger studios and not make the formula films they demanded, he chose instead to make his own pictures, his own way. To take the course of the independent filmmaker meant restricted budgets and questionable distribution. But it has worked for him as it did for Kohei Oguri and a few other talented directors.

Himatsuri is breathtakingly photographed and excellently captures the spiritual essence and physical beauty of the area and Yanagimachi's themes. It was an ambitious film for an independent filmmaker and was the first Yanagimachi film to be released in the United States, premiering at the 23rd New York Film Festival. When shown at the Locarno Film Festival, it won the Silver Leopard Award.

Comic Magazine (1986)
Komikku zasshi nanika irani

1986 / M&R Film. 120 min. Color. *Director:* Yojiro Takita. *Screen-play:* Yuya Uchida and Isao Takagi. *Adaptation:* From headlines in sensa-tionalistic magazines of 1985. *Cinematography:* Yoichi Shiga. *Art Director:* Minoru Oshiwa. *Lighting:* Masao Kanazawa. *Editor:* Masatsugi Sakai. *Music:* Katsuo Ono. *Sound:* Takashi Sugisaki. *Assistant Director:* Heikichi Fujiwara. *Producer:* Yutaka Okada. Film Rental: Cinecom International.

Yuya Uchida *as Toshiaki Kinameri.* Yumi Asou *Girlfriend.* Beat Takeshi *Yakuza killer.* Hiromi Go *George.* Rikiya Yasuoka *Man at drink-ing bar.* Tsurutaro Kataoka *Gigolo.* Kazuyoshi Miura *Himself.* Seiko Mat-suda *Herself.*

• Kinameri is a reporter for the "gossip" Towa television show "Today." He is known for his "Narita (airport) reports" where he asks departing and arriving celebrities for "one word, please." He presses an actress at the airport about her affair with a scriptwriter and performs an adversarial interview with Kazuyoshi Miura, a man suspected of murdering his wife and implicated in the death of his mistress, after pursuing him to a bar. At a production meeting, Kinameri is told to sacrifice his own privacy for the sake of audience empathy and to go out and cover more scandals. He is sent to Kobe to cover a *yakuza* power struggle and even ends up interviewing the mob boss' son while he plays baseball. When a young girl is found murdered in a "love hotel," Kinameri insists on inter-viewing the mourning mother at the funeral even to the point of telling her something she didn't know, that her 14-year-old daughter was a pros-titute.

One of Kinameri's assignments is to cover the wedding of actress Seiko Matsuda. He tries interviewing her over her intercom, stakes out her house and tries to get inside by taking the place of the delivery person with her dry-cleaning (who also turns out to be a reporter). The only thing he can go on the air with is a videotape of Matsuda's bedroom window behind which she is happily singing. To get more, he climbs a utility pole outside her house, but is arrested by the police. After bribing the police to let him go, Kinameri tries to cover the wedding but is kept out by security guards.

With no coverage of the wedding, the television show's sponsors are annoyed and Kinameri is "demoted" to the 10:50 p.m. report show. Here Kinameri does "eye-witness reports," covering such things as the Mon Mon Bar, where all the customers are tattooed, and live-sex shows. He reports on the porn movie industry by taking a part in one, and on gigolos by attending their school and becoming one for the night. Kinameri is coming to dislike this form of journalism in which he is so adept. He wants to be given more serious assignments and asks his producer to let him cover the suspect gold sales of the Kinjo Trading Company. He is turned down, but Kinameri still follows the story.

While Kinameri is at a stakeout at the apartment of a Kinjo Trading Company executive, Nagata, with numerous other reporters, two hired *yakuza* killers show up. They break into the apartment, and with all cameras clicking, proceed to kill Nagata. At first Kinameri watches along with the other reporters, but finally is moved to action and jumps into the apartment where he too is stabbed by the killers. When he emerges wounded from the apartment, Kinameri finds himself the victim of the unrelenting reporters. In effect, he has become a "celebrity." His response to all their questions is to say, in English, that he doesn't speak Japanese.

• Director Yojiro Takita was born in 1955 and came to filmmaking quite by accident. When a neighbor introduced him to Ken Mukai, one of Japan's most recognizable "pink film" directors, Takita, at 20, signed on as his assistant director. After five years, he was given his first film to direct. He soon established a reputation as something of an "auteur" within the realm of softcore porn films and even won prizes and critical attention with them. With *Comic Magazine,* Takita has made his first legitimate theatrical feature.

Almost more important than Takita to *Comic Magazine* is Yuya Uchida, who conceived of the idea to make a film based on the sensational news headlines of 1985, helped write the screenplay, produced the film and starred in it as Kinameri. Uchida originally made a name for himself in the world of rock and roll as a concert producer and performer. He has recorded four albums, opened for the Beatles when they toured the Orient, and is known alternately as the "Granddaddy of Japanese Rock 'n' Roll" and the "Mick Jagger of Japan." As an in-joke, a bar patron at the beginning of the film repeatedly tells Kinameri that he knows nothing of rock and roll. (Hiromi Go, who plays the gigolo George, is also a rock star who has turned to the films appearing in *MacArthur's Children* and *Gonza the Spearman.*) Uchida has appeared in other films before *Comic Magazine,* most notably in Nagisa Oshima's *Merry Christmas, Mr. Lawrence.*

Comic magazines are scandal sheets sold in Japan which specialize in bad taste. They prey on Japan's obsession with violence, sex and scandal. In this film Takita and Uchida take the magazines to the airwaves and center the story on a reporter well versed in this type of media excess. Kinameri seems totally devoid of any journalistic ethics and his actions eventually blur the line of distinction between reporting and creating the news. It becomes increasingly difficult to decide what's real and what isn't. All of the events depicted in *Comic Magazine* were based on real

Comic Magazine (Yojiro Takita, 1986). Yuya Uchida as television reporter Kinameri with his ever-present microphone, interviews members of the Pussycat Club Girls.

experiences. Many of the figures in the film are actually the people from the headlines. Five days after the scene in which Kinameri interviews Miura, Miura actually was arrested. The murder of the fraudulent gold dealer (while recreated in the movie) was actually caught by reporters and television cameras and transmitted all over the world, causing a great deal of discussion over journalistic ethics. (The killer in *Comic Magazine* is played by popular Japanese comedian Beat Takeshi, who also appeared in Oshima's *Merry Christmas, Mr. Lawrence.*)

Comic Magazine is an intelligent film which poses some interesting questions about journalism for Japan as well as the United States. Where does the freedom of the press end? What is the public entitled to know? What about a person's right to privacy? Just trying to figure out which came first, the public's demand for entertaining and exciting news or the media's method of providing "thrill reports" to indulge this demand, is not easily answered. This film, however, takes dark delight in pointing the finger of guilt at the media which exploits these popular appetites for the sake of ratings and profits.

The character of Kinameri is a composite of several popular Japanese reporters who are out to get any story which is sensational or embarrassing. While Kinameri's job, with its lapse in journalistic integrity, would not make him seem so, he is in essence a wandering "hero," filled with unmet ambitions. Symbolic of these ambitions are the scenes sprinkled through the film of Kinameri's fantasy of pitching baseballs to various people in his life in an empty stadium. By the end of the film, after Kinameri has taken a stand against the passive coverage of events, he is again in the baseball stadium where he unzips his pants and surprisingly pulls out the ever-present microphone which he then smilingly pitches to the camera. Kinameri is a dogged reporter who proves the axiom that when it comes to show biz reporting, "no one does it like the Japanese." He is a political science graduate who admires and to some extent emulates America's Woodward and Bernstein. When his boss tells him to "go after scandals and keep pushing hard," he does exactly that. He is a passive observer of the events he captures on film. He is solemn-faced, unemotional and uninvolved. Even his name, Kinameri, is phonetically similar to "camera," and basically that is what he is, a human camera lens. Through Kinameri, Uchida and Takita show us ourselves.

Comic Magazine is a very contemporary film depicting a chaos which lies beneath the outward calm of Japanese society. When combined with a few other Japanese films of the 1980s like *The Family Game, The Crazy Family* and *Tampopo* it would seem that social satires, some of the blackest sort, are the genre of choice in the modern Japanese cinema.

To Sleep so as to Dream (1986)
Yume miruyoni memuritau

1986 / Eizo Tanteisha Production for Shibata. 81 min. B&W. *Director:* Kaizo Hayashi. *Screenplay:* Kaizo Hayashi. *Cinematography:* Yuichi Nagata. *Art Direction:* Takeo Kimura. *Music:* Hidehiko Urayama, Yoko Kumagai, Moe Kamura and Morio Agata. *Sound:* Akihiko Suzuki. *Lighting:* Tatsuya Osada. *Editor:* Yuichi Nagata and Kaizo Hayashi. *Make-up:* Mika Yoshida and Hikaru Sikihata. *Sword Fight Supervisor:* Tsuneo and Tatsuo Nakamoto. *Producer:* Kaizo Hayashi. Film Rental: New Yorker Films.

Moe Kamura *as Bellflower.* Shiro Sano *Uotsuka.* Koji Otake *Kobayashi.* Fujiko Fukamizu *Madame Cherryblossom.* Yoshio Yoshida *Matsunosuke, the director.* Akira Oizumi, Morio Agata and Kazunari Ozasa *The three magicians.* Shunsui Matsuda *Akagaki, the benshi.* Tsuneo

To Sleep so as to Dream (**Kaizo Hayashi, 1986**). **Moe Kamura (seated) who plays Bellflower cradles the head of the intrepid detective played by Shiro Sano in this homage to Japan's silent serials and detective movies. (Photo courtesy of New Yorker Films.)**

and Tatsuo Nakamoto *The white masks.* Kyoko Kusajima *Old lady in the comb shop.*

• With the whir of a projector as the only sound, a swordfight from an old Japanese movie serial from 1915 is seen. In it a woman is about to be carried off by the men of the White Mask. To her rescue comes the Black Mask, whose identity is just about to be revealed when the film suddenly breaks. An old woman, Madame Cherryblossom, has been watching the film.

Uotsuka, a detective, and his sidekick, Kobayashi, are hired by an emissary from Madame Cherryblossom, to find her daughter, Princess Bellflower, who has supposedly been kidnapped by a gang of double-dealers masquerading under the name of M. Pathe & Co. The Pathe gang is asking one million yen in ransom and seems to delight in leaving obscure clues for Uotsuke to ponder in the best Sherlock Holmes tradition. After solving many clues and following many leads, Uotsuke ends up in a restaurant which suddenly transforms itself into a movie theatre. There they see Princess Bellflower who begs them to "Save me from this endless story." The key to the mysterious kidnapping evidently lies in an incomplete 1915 film, *The Eternal Mystery,* the production of which was aborted by a police raid. According to Article 12, it was illegal for women to appear in films. The old woman, Madam Cherryblossom, was the young actress in that film, playing the part of Princess Bellflower, and it is the ending to the film which has been symbolically "kidnapped." With the help of Uotsuka, the end of the film is finally played out in Madam Cherryblossom's parlor and her "daughter" is set free.

• The above plot description does not begin to do justice to the magic of Hayashi's tribute to early filmmaking. *To Sleep so as to Dream* is not quite a silent film, and yet is also not really a sound film. Audiences can hear a telephone ring, but not the voices answering it. There are no voices, but plenty of sound effects. No background music, but a tape recording of a simple song (written by Moe Kamura, who plays Bellflower) provides a tantalizing clue. Shot on a low budget and in 16mm, the film's style also defies labeling. Scenes from *The Eternal Mystery* attempt to recreate the jumpy and stiff filmmaking methods of early *chambara* serials, while the solving of the kidnapping is more representative of film styles used to make Japanese detective films of the 1920s. These are both silent film genres, but both are different, and each is beautifully captured by Hayashi. In fact, so good is he at recreating these styles that initially it appears that he has actually used silent film footage until it becomes obvious that he has not.

Hayashi was born in 1957 in Kyoto where he attended Ritsumeikan University. With no experience in films and no usual internship as an assistant director, Hayashi came to Tokyo to make films. At 29, he made his very first, *To Sleep so as to Dream*. Like Hayashi himself, most of the staff and actors he used in his first film are relatively new to the screen, with several major exceptions. Fujiko Fukamizu, who plays Madame Cherryblossom, was a major star of the 1930s. She retired in 1947 and her appearance in *To Sleep so as to Dream* is her first film in 38 years. Similarly, Kyoko Kasajima, after appearing in Mizoguchi's *Utamaro and His Five Women* and *Life of Oharu* (as did Akira Oizumi, the magician), retired in 1960 only to re-emerge in Hayashi's film 25 years later. But perhaps most unusual is the appearance of Shunsui Matsuda who plays Akagaki, the *benshi*. Matsuda made his "film debut" in 1927, but not as an actor. He was in many ways bigger than that, he was a *benshi*. Plying his trade right until the end of the silent era in Japan in 1938, Matsuda actively works to preserve the silent films he explained to audiences as a younger man.

Just as the *benshi* became outmoded when sound movies became accepted, so too did the history of the *onogatas* or *oyamas,* men who impersonated women, in all the female roles. Taking its lead from Kabuki theatre, it was considered an affront to public decency for a woman to actually appear in films or on stage. It was a tradition soon challenged. Although Hayashi has the first woman appearing on film in 1915, it actually took place in 1918 when Norimasa Kaeriyama made *The Glow of Life.* The gain in popularity of women in films reached an impasse when Nikkatsu studios decided to hire actresses. Seeing the demise of their professional hold on films, the *onagatas,* led by soon-to-be director Teinosuke Kinugasa, went out on an unsuccessful strike.

Hayashi treats the history of Japanese films with great tenderness and humor in *To Sleep so as to Dream.* He fuses several styles of filmmaking and several generations of filmmakers into an impressive first film which evokes an enchanted world where reality and movie magic can easily merge.

Tampopo (1987)

1987 / Itami Productions. / a.k.a. "Dandelion." 117 min. Color. *Director:* Juzo Itami. *Screenplay:* Juzo Itami. *Cinematography:* Masaki Tamura. *Art Direction:* Takeo Kimura. *Lighting:* Yukio Inoue. *Music:* Kunihiko Murai. *Sound:* Fumio Hashimoto. *Editor:* Akira Suzuki. *Costumes:* Emiko Kogo. *Food Designer:* Izumi Ishimori. *Graphic Designer:* Kenichi Samura. *Casting:* Kosaburo Sasaoka. *Assistant Director:* Kazuki Shiroyama. *Producers:* Juzo Itami, Yasushi Tamaoki and Seigo Hosogoe. Film Rental: New Yorker Films.

Tsutomu Yamazaki *as Goro.* Nobuko Miyamoto *Tampopo.* Koji Yakusho *Man in white suit.* Ken Watanabe *Gun.* Rikiya Yasuoka *Pisken.* Kinzo Sakura *Shohei.* Mampei Ikeuchi *Tabo.* Yoshi Kato *Master of ramen making.* Shuji Otaki *Rich old man.* Fukumi Kuroda *Mistress of the man in the white suit.* Setsuko Shinoi *The rich old man's mistress.* Yoriko Doguchi *Girl catching oysters.* Masahiko Tsugawa *Supermarket manager.* Motoo Noguchi, Yoshihei Saga, Tsuguho Narita, Adio Tanaka, Choei Takahashi *Company executives.* Toshimune Kato *Young company employee.* Isao Hashizume *Waiter.* Akira Kubo *Rude owner of the competing ramen shop.* Saburo Satoki *Owner of the efficient ramen shop.* Mario Abe *Owner of the ramen stand.* Hitoshi Takage *Owner of the ramen shop in Chinatown.* Takao Futami *His neighbor.* Akio Yokoyama *Chinese ramen chef.* Masato Tsujimura *Small bum.* Ei Takami *Thin bum.* Gilliark Amagasaki *Bum with long face.* Norio Matsui *Fat bum.* Noboru Sato *Bum with red nose.* Tadakazu Kitami *Dentist.* Kyoko Oguma *Lady owner of the soba shop.* Toshiya Fujita *Man with toothache.* Izumi Hara *Old lady who pinches everything in the supermarket.* Hisashi Igawa *Man who runs to see dying wife.* Kazuyo Mita *Dying wife.* Nobuo Nakamura *Old con man.* Naritoshi Hayashi *Con man who is being conned.* Ryutaro Otomo *Master of ramen eating.* Mariko Okada *Teacher of table manners.*

• A gangster in a white suit and his "moll" are seated in a theatre, preparing to watch a film. While his henchmen prepare a sumptuous

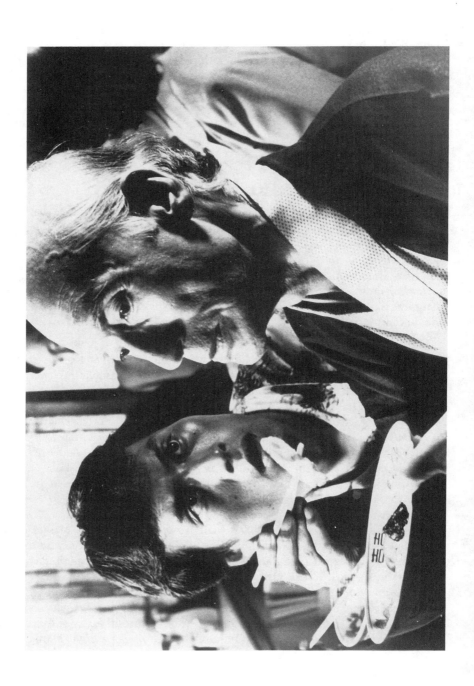

buffet for him to eat, he addresses the audience with his opinions about theatre-eating etiquette such as no eating of noisy curry-flavored potato chips. He then settles back to watch the movie.

Goro is a milk truck driver and his partner, Gun, reads aloud to him from a book on appreciating *ramen* noodles as they drive towards Tokyo. The book so whets the men's appetites that they decide to stop at the nearby Lai Lai Noodle Restaurant. The proprietress of the restaurant is Tampopo. Goro and Gun try bowls of Tampopo's *ramen* and are not impressed. Sitting nearby is a drunken admirer of Tampopo's, Pisken, an interior contractor. When Goro tells Pisken to be quiet, he and his pals beat Goro up and leave him unconscious. Goro awakens the next morning, with Tampopo tending to his wounds.

Tampopo realizes Goro is a *ramen* epicure, and asks his opinions on her cooking. He diplomatically declares that her noodles "have sincerity but lack guts." Tampopo is inspired by Goro and decides she would like to make truly good *ramen,* since the store is the only way she has of supporting herself and her son. She asks Goro to help her save her failing business and find the perfect noodle and soup recipe. In exchange for this, not only will Goro then have a restaurant where he will always be able to find delicious noodles, but Tampopo will also keep special pickles just for him. Goro accepts the challenge and the two go and search for the perfect noodle recipe and soup stock. Goro puts Tampopo through a grueling training regimen, which includes timing her so that she can serve the perfect *ramen* within three minutes. Goro rounds up a group of *ramen* masters who stalk other chefs, and even resorts to bribery to obtain the perfect recipe. When they get near the completion of their mission, the name of the noodle shop is changed to "Tampopo's Noodles," and Pisken volunteers to revamp the restaurant's interior.

When all declare Tampopo's noodles to be perfection, the shop is reopened and soon has crowds of customers lining up outside. Goro, realizing his "mission" has been accomplished, boards his truck, and rides off into the sunset.

• Director Juzo Itami was born in Kyoto in 1933, the son of another film director, Mansaku Itami, who worked in the 1930s making successful films about ronin (masterless samurai) whose historical context commented on the current period of the depression. His father died in 1946, when Juzo was 12. Itami has had an interesting and extremely varied career. He has been a welterweight boxer, a band organizer, a commercial designer, a magazine editor and a translator (of the works of William Saroyan and Peter Shaffer). Itami has worked as a reporter and a chat-show host on

Tampopo (Juzo Itami, 1987). Ken Watanabe (left) as Goro's truck-driving partner Gun, watches expectantly to see if Ryutaro Otomo, who plays the *ramen* master, approves of Tampopo's latest dish.

Japanese television. His efforts, whether they're a travelogue or a documentary, are marked by their imaginative presentations and intellectual humor. Also among Itami's long list of achievements is the fact that he has authored witty essays, many of which have been collected in books: *Diary of Boredom in Europe (Yoroppa taikutsu nikki,* 1974), *Hey, Women! (Onnatachi Yo!,* 1975), *Stranger Than Fiction (Shosetsu yori ki nari,* 1976) and *Anthology of Japanese Small Talk (Nihon seken banashi taikei,* 1979). Itami's essays are not about weighty problems, but diverting and amusing tracts about unimportant matters.

In 1960 he made his debut as an actor in *The Phony University Student (Nise daigakusei),* but his performance didn't attract much attention. The first real notice was taken of Itami's unique acting style when he appeared in Nagisa Oshima's *A Treatise on a Japanese Bawdy Song (Nihon shunkako,* 1967). He has since had a successful career as an actor, appearing as the father in Morita's *The Family Game* in which he won several acting awards, as he did for Ichikawa's *The Makioka Sisters (Sasemeyuki,* 1983). He also appeared as the naval captain in Shinoda's *MacArthur's Children* (1984), was in Ichikawa's *I Am a Cat* and even has appeared in Nicholas Ray's *55 Days at Peking* (1963) and Richard Brook's *Lord Jim* (1964). In 1984 Itami wrote and directed *The Funeral (Ososhiki).* He had wanted to make films for a long time and had spent many hours in theatres studying them. The idea for *The Funeral* originated at the real funeral of his wife's father. The film takes what could be a somber subject and treats it with a light hand. It deftly comments on the Japanese rigid ceremonial traditions (the young couple learns "the rules" by watching a videotape on proper behavior) and went on to win many Japanese film awards. Although *The Funeral* was made before *Tampopo,* it was released in the States only after the successful run of the latter film.

Tampopo (which translates as "dandelion," but which goes by its Japanese name in the States) was released in 1986 and if not inspired by, it certainly employed Itami's background acting in and directing Japanese television commercials for a food-product company. Made with money Itami raised himself, the film cost $1.6 million and is based on a wonderfully original concept which at the same time employs deliciously lampooned cinematic clichés. "Spaghetti Westerns" were popularized by Sergio Leone in the 1960s with films like *The Magnificent Seven* and *A Fistful of Dollars,* all take-offs of Akira Kurosawa films. Now director Juzo Itami introduces the *"ramen* Western." The hero, Goro, wears a dark cowboy hat and boots and has perfected his best Clint Eastwood squint. In a typical plot for a Western, he comes riding into town in a milk truck complete with horns on the rooftop. This reserved stranger, complete with comical sidekick, finds a widow in trouble, helps her, falls in love with her, but cannot bring himself to settle down with her. Instead, like Shane, he rides off. (There are other genres running deeply in Itami's litany, however.) In the tradition of the best samurai movie, the *sensei* (teacher) must pass down the proper rituals and knowledge to his student. As in *Rocky*, Tampopo, the underdog, must work and train to beat the odds. And intercut throughout the film is a typical character straight out of a *yakuza* movie.

Tampopo is presented in an ingenious free-form style. The synopsis above really describes only one-half of the film. For darting in and out of Tampopo and Goro's story are a myriad of sketches which, although they really have nothing to do with the main plot, are nonetheless just as much about food. It is the creativity and humor of these digressions that makes *Tampopo* entertaining and inventive. Among these highly amusing cinematic detours is a man with a painfully abscessed tooth who leaves the dentist's office only to maliciously offer a child (who wears a sign around his neck from his parents indicating that he only eats natural foods) an ice-cream cone. Then there is the old lady who runs around a supermarket squeezing everything: Camembert cheese, a peach, bread, rolls, while pursued by the manager armed with a fly swatter. Dignified corporate executives, perplexed by the menu in a posh French restaurant, won't admit their ignorance and all order the same item only to be upstaged by an inept young colleague who orders with perfect knowledge of French cooking. Nearby, a group of yuppie women take a course in how to eat spaghetti without slurping. There is a dying woman who gets out of her deathbed to make her family one more meal, bums who nostalgically recall a 1980 Bordeaux wine, and one bum who sneaks into a restaurant kitchen to make a perfect and fluffy rice omelet. The gangster *(yakuza)* and moll who introduced the film show up regularly. In one scene they erotically kiss and pass a raw egg between their mouths again and again and again. The eating scenes involving these two put the famous eating scene in *Tom Jones* to shame.

These scenes are skillfully inserted into the story of Tampopo and Goro. Often the camera will follow one character into a scene only to pick up a character from the next which it then follows. Before the old lady with a food-pinching fetish enters the grocery store, for instance, the camera, which has pulled back for an exterior shot of Tampopo's store, finds her sneaking around Tampopo's and follows her. When Goro has Tampopo do stretching exercises after jogging, the businessmen with a date at the French restaurant come up behind them and the camera follows them.

After the successes of *The Funeral* (about death) and *Tampopo* (about food), Itami next tackled money in the two-part film, *A Taxing Woman (Marusa no onna, 1987)*. It is a highly entertaining, analytical action film which was released just as the Japanese government was debating tax reform. Although Itami's films all center on a different topic, they all seem to have sex as the underlying theme. In fact, sex, as seen through Itami's characters, has been usurped by their individual obsessions. And it is their obsessions which form their characters. Their obsessions in Itami's hands become the wellspring of everything that is intriguing and zany in human behavior.

Many of the actors in *Tampopo* have had distinguished careers in Japan and appear in this film only in cameos. In a way, it is quite a vote of confidence in Itami as a filmmaker. One veteran, Ryutaro Otomo, who plays a *ramen* master, died during the film's shooting. Tsutomu Yamazaki, who plays the gourmet truck driver, Goro, has appeared in all three of Itami's films. He was born in Matsudo City, Chiba Prefecture, in 1936. In 1956 he joined the Haiyuza Theater Company as a trainee and graduated in 1959. At that time he joined the Kumo Company which he left in 1976. His first screen appearance was in Kihachi Okamoto's *The University Scamps (Daigaku no sanzokuktachi)* in 1960. Unusual for "beginning" screen actors, Yamazaki was very selective about the roles he took. His reputation was established when he portrayed the kidnapper in Kurosawa's *High and Low (Tengoku to jigoku)*. He has also appeared in Kurosawa's *Red Beard* and *Kagemusha*. Yamazaki has also worked in television as well as on the stage and screen, and in 1984 he received numerous acting awards for his roles in Itami's *The Funeral* and Shuji Terayama's *Farewell to the Ark (Saraba hakobune)*.

Of special interest is actress Nobuko Miyamoto, the hard-working Tampopo. She was born in Otaru City in Hokkaido in 1945. In 1964 she started as a trainee with the Bungakuza Theatre. In 1972 she became an independent actress. Her first film appearance was in Nagisa Oshima's 1967 *A Treatise on Japanese Bawdy Songs,* in which Juzo Itami also appeared. In 1969, Itami and Miyamoto were married and since then she has had the leading role in all four of his films, winning several acting awards for her appearance in *The Funeral.* They have two sons, the youngest of which, Mampei, appears as Tampopo's son Tabo.

Itami's touch is light, possibly the lightest of all the Japanese directors at the close of the 1980s. With Japan's newest cinematic wave being represented by Morita's *The Family Game,* Takita's *Comic Magazine* and Ishii's *The Crazy Family* as well as the works of Itami, it would seem that irreverent satire comes easily to this generation (although Itami is the oldest). As Itami has explained, his generation is more than just Japanese. It has been greatly influenced by the West. As a consequence, his generation of directors can step back and view Japanese society as if from the point of view of a very knowing outsider.

Directors like Itami are helping to bring about another flowering of the Japanese film industry. While they may have sacrificed many of those traits traditionally associated with Japanese films (love of nature, leisurely stories, beautiful scene composition), it is because they are the product of a different generation, making films for different audiences. Their films have a more universal appeal which, if given the chance, can attract larger audiences than their earlier counterparts ever did. This universality could help to introduce more viewers to the experience of Japanese films. And once they have laughed with Itami they may be more inclined to cheer with Kurosawa, sigh with Ozu or be intrigued with Ichikawa.

Chronology of Major Japanese Historic Periods

8000–300 B.C.   *Jomon period*
Neolithic period named for a type of pottery found near Tokyo.

300 B.C.–A.D. 300   *Yayoi period*

300–552   *Tomb period*

552–710   *Age of Reform*
 552–645   *Asuka epoch*
 645–710   *Hakuho epoch*
In A.D. 552 Buddhism and Chinese writing were introduced to Japan.

710–784   *Nara period*
 mid-8th c.   *Tempyo epoch*
The first permanent capital was built in Nara. The nation experienced a
flowering of Buddhist architecture and art.

794–1185   *Heian period*
The capital was moved from Nara to Nagaoka, where it remained for only ten
years. It was then moved to Kyoto, which was called "Hein-kyo," Capital
of Peace.
 mid–late 9th c.   *Jogan epoch*
 10th–late 11th c.   *Fujiwara epoch*
Power was taken from the emperor ("tenno") by the powerful Fujiwara
family, whose daughters married successive emperors. It was an age of great
scholars and writers. By the end of this period, clan warfare had broken out.

1185–1333   *Kamakura period*
The Minamoto Clan emerged strongest from the civil wars and their leader,
Yoritomo, was created shogun. A military government, or "bakufu," was
established in Kamakura. Various Buddhist sects, like Zen, arose.

1333–1336   *Kemmu Restoration*
Civil war again broke out, with Emperor Godaigo (1288–1339) trying to regain
power from the bakufu.

1336–1573   *Muromachi (Ashikaga) period*
late 14th–early 15th c.   *Kitayama epoch*
latter 15th c.   *Higashiyama epoch*
Ashikaga Takauji (1305–1358) regained control from the emperor and
established his power base in the Muromachi district of Kyoto. Shoguns
Yoshimitsu (1358–1408) and Yoshimasa (1436–1490) were great patrons of the
arts. The period ended with more civil war between feudal lords, "Daimyo."
In 1542, the Portuguese come to Japan, bringing Christianity and firearms.

1568–1600   *Age of Unification*
Oda Nobunaga (1534–1582) began unification of Japan, deposing the last
Ashikaga shogun, but was assassinated before finishing. He was succeeded by
Toytomi Hideyoshi (1536–1598), who finished the job. A period of great
feudal architecture and art followed.

1600/1615–1867   *Tokugawa (Edo) period*
Ieyasu Tokugawa defeated Hideyoshi's son at the great battle of Sekigahara
(1600) and wiped out his family at the siege of Osaka Castle (1615). A long
period of peace followed in which the merchant class flourished and all
foreigners were expelled, and Japan became isolated from the rest of the
world. In 1853 Commodore Perry demanded the reopening of Japan and in
1858 a treaty with the United States was signed.

1868–1911   *Meiji period*
In 1867 the shogun resigned and power was returned to the emperor, thus
ending feudalism in Japan. The capital was moved from Kyoto to Tokyo and
the country underwent modernization. In 1889 a constitution was adopted.
Japan went to war with China over Korea in 1894–1895, and with Russia over
Manchuria in 1904–1905.

1912–1925   *Taisho period*
Japan entered World War I on the side of the Allies and after the war was
given German possessions in China and the Pacific.

1926–1989   *Showa period*
In 1932 Japan conquered Manchuria and in 1937 armed conflict arose with
China. The Pacific War began in 1941 with Japan's bombing of Pearl Harbor.
Atomic bombs are dropped on Hiroshima and Nagasaki in August of 1945 and
World War II ended. American Occupation of Japan (1945–1951) and postwar
constitution established in 1947. Japan rebuilds itself and grows into a finan-
cial world power.

1989–   *Heisei period*
Emperor Hirohito died January 7, 1989, and with him the Showa period.
His son Akihito became emperor and thus began the Heisei period.

Directory of
Video and Film Sources

There are many distributors of Japanese films both on 16mm and 35mm film and on videotape. This guide is current through late 1989, but titles are often added and deleted from a company's list as rights to films (theatrical and non-theatrical) expire. Be advised that several titles are considered to be in the public domain. By not being protected by copyright, anyone can reproduce them. As a consequence, transfer quality (especially on videotape) may vary considerably from company to company.

Balzac Video. 1253 Tanager Lane, West Chester PA 19382. (215) 431-2171. VIDEOTAPES: *Early Spring* (Ozu, 1956), *Late Spring* (Ozu, 1949), *Lower Depths* (Kurosawa, 1957), *Saga of Anatahan* (Von Sternberg, 1953), *Sanshiro Sugata* (Kurosawa, 1943), *Sisters of the Gion* (Mizoguchi, 1936), *Story of the Last Chrysanthemum* (Mizoguchi, 1939), *Taira Clan Saga* (Mizoguchi, 1955). FILMS: *Drunken Angel* (Kurosawa, 1948), *Saga of Anatahan* (Von Sternberg, 1953), *Sansho the Bailiff* (Mizoguchi, 1954).

Cinecom International. 1250 Broadway, New York NY 10001. (212) 239-8360. FILMS: *Comic Magazine* (Takita, 1986).

Circle Releasing Corporation. 1 Westin Center, 2445 M St. N.W., Suite 225, Washington DC 20037. (202) 331-3838. FILMS: *The Family Game* (Morita, 1984)—theatrical rentals, *The Go Masters* (Sato and Ji-Shun, 1983)—theatrical rentals.

Connoisseur Video Collection. 8455 Beverly Blvd., Suite 302, Los Angeles CA 90048. (213) 653-8873. VIDEOTAPES: *The Burmese Harp* (Ichikawa, 1956), *Floating Weeds* (Ozu, 1959). *No Regrets for Our Youth* (Kurosawa, 1946), *Onibaba* (Shindo, 1964), *The Pornographers* (Imamura, 1966), *A Taxing Woman* (Itami, 1988).

Corinth Films. 34 Gansevoort Street, New York NY 10014. (212) 463-0305. VIDEOTAPES: *Woman in the Dunes* (Teshigahara, 1964). FILMS: *The Family Game* (Morita, 1984), *The Go Masters* (Sato and Ji-Shun, 1983), *Woman in the Dunes* (Teshigahara, 1964).

Discount Videotapes. P.O. Box 7122, Burbank CA 91510. (818) 843-3366.
VIDEOTAPES: *The Island* (Shindo, 1961), *Kwaidan* (Kobayashi, 1964), *Sanjuro*
(Kurosawa, 1962), *Ugetsu* (Mizoguchi, 1953), *Woman in the Dunes* (Teshigahara,
1964), *Yojimbo* (Kurosawa, 1961).

East-West Classics. 1529 Acton St., Berkeley CA 94702. (415) 526-3611.
FILMS: *Chushingura [47 Ronin]* (Inagaki, 1962), *Floating Clouds* (Naruse, 1955),
Flowing (Naruse, 1956), *High and Low* (Kurosawa, 1963), *A Human Bullet*
(Okamoto, 1968), *The Insect Woman* (Imamura, 1963), *Intentions of Murder* (Ima-
mura, 1964), *Late Chrysanthemums* (Naruse, 1954), *No Regrets for Our Youth*
(Kurosawa, 1946), *Onibaba* (Shindo, 1963), *Onimasa* (Gosha, 1983), *Pigs and Bat-
tleships* (Imamura, 1961), *The Pornographers* (Imamura, 1961), *Profound Desire of
the Gods* (Imamura, 1968), *Sound of the Mountains* (Naruse, 1954), *Snow Country*
(Toyoda, 1957), *Tokkan* (Okamoto, 1975), *When a Woman Ascends the Stairs*
(Naruse, 1960).

Embassy Home Entertainment. 1901 Ave. of the Stars, Los Angeles CA 90067.
(213) 553-3600. VIDEOTAPES: *Dersu Uzala* (Kurosawa, 1980), *Dodeskaden*
(Kurosawa, 1970), *Fires on the Plain* (Ichikawa, 1959), *Gate of Hell* (Kinugasa,
1953), *The Golden Demon* (Shima, 1953), *Odd Obsession* (Ichikawa, 1959),
Rashomon (Kurosawa, 1951), *Samurai (Trilogy)* (Inagaki, 1955–6), *Sanjuro* (Kurosawa, 1962), *The Seven Samurai* (Kurosawa, 1954), *Street of Shame* (Mizoguchi,
1956), *Ugetsu* (Mizoguchi, 1953), *Wild Geese [The Mistress]* (Toyoda, 1953),
Yojimbo (Kurosawa, 1962).

Filmic Archives / Reel Images. The Cinema Center, Botsford CT 06404-0386.
(203) 261-1920. FILMS: *Drifting Weeds* [elsewhere known as *Floating Weeds*] (Ozu,
1959), *Drunken Angel* (Kurosawa, 1948), *The Men Who Tread on the Tiger's Tail*
(Kurosawa, 1945), *Sansho the Bailiff* (Mizoguchi, 1954), *The Seven Samurai*
(Kurosawa, 1954), *Ugetsu* (Mizoguchi, 1953), *Woman in the Dunes* (Teshigahara,
1964), *Yojimbo* (Kurosawa, 1961).

Films Incorporated. [1] 5547 N Ravenswood Ave., Chicago IL 60640, (312)
878-2600; (800) 878-2600 outside Illinois. [2] 35 S. West St., Mount Vernon
NY 10550, (914) 667-0800; (800) 223-6246 outside N.Y. FILMS: *The Assassination*
(Shinoda, 1964), *Bad Boys* (Hani, 1960), *The Bad Sleep Well* (Kurosawa, 1960),
Brothers and Sisters of the Toda Family (Ozu, 1941), *The Burmese Harp* (Ichikawa,
1956), *Bwana Toshi* (Hani, 1965), *A Cat, Two Women, and One Man* (Toyoda,
1956), *The Crucified Lovers* (Mizoguchi, 1959), *Dersu Uzala* (Kurosawa, 1975),
Dodeskaden (Kurosawa, 1970), *Double Suicide* (Shinoda, 1969), *Drunken Angel*
(Kurosawa, 1948), *Fires on the Plain* (Ichikawa, 1959), *Floating Weeds* (Ozu, 1959),
The Forty-Seven Ronin (Mizoguchi, 1942), *Gate of Hell* (Kinugasa, 1953), *Harakiri*
(Kobayashi, 1962), *High and Low* (Kurosawa, 1963), The Human Condition
(Kobayashi, 1959), *I Live in Fear* (Kurosawa, 1955), *Ikiru* (Kurosawa, 1952),
Kagemusha (Kurosawa, 1980), *Kwaidan* (Kobayashi, 1964), *The Lower Depths*
(Kurosawa, 1957), *The Men Who Tread on the Tiger's Tail* (Kurosawa, 1945),
Muddy Waters (Imai, 1953), *Night Drum* (Imai, 1958), *Odd Obsession* (Ichikawa,
1960), *Ohayo* (Ozu, 1959), *The Only Son* (Ozu, 1936), *Osaka Elegy* (Mizoguchi,
1936), *Page of Madness* (Kinugasa, 1926), *Passing Fancy* (Ozu, 1933), *Rashomon*
(Kurosawa, 1950), *Rebellion* (Kobayashi, 1967), *Red Beard* (Kurosawa, 1965),
Samurai Spy (Shinoda, 1965), *Samurai (Trilogy)* (Inagaki, 1955–6), *Sanjuro*
(Kurosawa, 1962), *Sanshiro Sugata* (Kurosawa, 1943), *Sansho the Bailiff* (Mizoguchi,
1954), *Scandal* (Kurosawa, 1950), *Seven Samurai* (Kurosawa, 1954), *She and He*

(Hani, 1963), *Sisters of the Gion* (Mizoguchi, 1936), *Stray Dog* (Kurosawa, 1949), *Street of Shame* (Mizoguchi, 1956), *Tales of the Taira Clan* (Mizoguchi, 1955), *There Was a Father* (Ozu, 1942), *Throne of Blood* (Kurosawa, 1957), *Tokyo Olympiad* (Ichikawa, 1965), *Twenty-Four Eyes* (Kinoshita, 1954), *Twilight in Tokyo* (Ozu, 1957), *Ugetsu* (Mizoguchi, 1953), *Wild Geese [The Mistress]* (Toyoda, 1953), *Yojimbo* (Kurosawa, 1961).

International Historic Films. P.O. Box 29035, Chicago IL 60629. (312) 436-8051. VIDEOTAPES: *Throne of Blood* (Kurosawa, 1957), *The Men Who Tread on the Tiger's Tale* (Kurosawa, 1954), *The Seven Samurai* (Kurosawa, 1954; 140 min. version).

Janus Films. 888 Seventh Ave., New York NY 10106. (212) 753-7100. (Through contractual agreements, many Janus films are handled by other distributors listed in this appendix.) FILMS: *The Assassination* (Shinoda, 1964), *The Bad Sleep Well* (Kurosawa, 1960), *The Ballad of Narayama* (Imamura, 1983), *Being Two Isn't Easy* (Ichikawa, 1962), *The Brothers and Sisters of the Toda Family* (Ozu, 1941), *Double Suicide* (Shinoda, 1969), *Drunken Angel* (Kurosawa, 1948), *Early Summer* (Ozu, 1951), *Face of Another* (Teshigahara, 1966), *Fires on the Plain* (Ichikawa, 1959), *Floating Weeds* (Ozu, 1959), *The Forty-Seven Ronin, Parts I and II* (Mizoguchi, 1942), *Gate of Hell* (Kinugasa, 1953), *The Golden Demon* (Shima, 1953), *Harakiri* (Kobayashi, 1962), *The Hidden Fortress* (Kurosawa, 1958), *The Human Condition, Parts I, II and III* (Kobayashi, 1959), *I Live in Fear* (Kurosawa, 1955), *Ikiru* (Kurosawa, 1952), *Kill!* (Okamoto, 1968), *Kwaidan* (Kobayashi, 1964), *The Lower Depths* (Kurosawa, 1957), *The Men Who Tread on the Tiger's Tail* (Kurosawa, 1945), *Night Drum* (Imai, 1958), *Odd Obsession* (Ichikawa, 1960), *Ohayo* (Ozu, 1959), *The Only Son* (Ozu, 1936), *Osaka Elegy* (Mizoguchi, 1936), *Passing Fancy* (Ozu, 1933), *The Phantom Horse, Rashomon* (Kurosawa, 1950), *Red Beard* (Kurosawa, 1965), *Samurai (Trilogy)* (Inagaki, 1955–6), *Samurai Spy* (Shinoda, 1965), *Sanjuro* (Kurosawa, 1962), *Sanshiro Sugata* (Kurosawa, 1943), *Scandal* (Kurosawa, 1950), *The Seven Samurai* (Kurosawa, 1954), *The Sisters of the Gion* (Mizoguchi, 1936), *The Story of the Last Chrysanthemum* (Mizoguchi, 1939), *Stray Dog* (Kurosawa, 1959), *Street of Shame* (Mizoguchi, 1956), *Sword of Doom* (Okamoto, 1967), *There Was a Father* (Ozu, 1942), *Three Outlaw Samurai* (Gosha, 1942), *Throne of Blood* (Kurosawa, 1957), *Twenty-Four Eyes* (Kinoshita, 1954), *Twilight in Tokyo* (Ozu, 1957), *Ugetsu* (Mizoguchi, 1953), *Vengeance Is Mine* (Imamura, 1979), *Wild Geese [The Mistress]* (Toyoda, 1953), *Women of the Night* (Mizoguchi, 1948), *X from Outer Space* (Nihomatsu, 1967), *Yojimbo* (Kurosawa, 1961).

Kino International Corporation. 333 West 39th St., Suite 503, New York NY 10018. (212) 629-6880. FILMS: *The Ballad of Narayama* (Kinoshita, 1958), *The Ballad of Narayama* (Imamura, 1983), *Ballad of Orin* (Shinoda, 1979), *Eijanaika* (Imamura, 1981), *The Emperor's Naked Army Marches On* (Hara, 1987), *Gonza the Spearman* (Shinoda, 1986), *Himatsuri* (Yanagimachi, 1984), *I Lived, But...* (Inoue, 1983), *Karayuki-San* (Imamura, 1975), *She Was Like a Wild Chrysanthemum* (Kinoshita, 1955), *Vengeance Is Mine* (Imamura, 1979), *Violence at Noon* (Oshima, 1966).

Kit Parker. 1245 Tenth St., Monterey CA 94930-3692. (408) 649-5573. FILMS: *Being Two Isn't Easy* (Ichikawa, 1962), *Drunken Angel* (Kurosawa, 1948), *Empire of Passion* (Oshima, 1978), *Fires on the Plain* (Ichikawa, 1959), *Floating Weeds*

(Ozu, 1959), *Godzilla vs. Megalon* (Fukuda, 1976), *The Island* (Shindo, 1961), *The Men Who Tread on the Tiger's Tail* (Kurosawa, 1945), *Mothra* (Honda, 1961), *Nanami: Inferno of First Love* (Hani, 1968), Rickshaw Man (Inagaki, 1957), *Sansho the Bailiff* (Mizoguchi, 1954), *Tokyo Olympiad* (Ichikawa, 1965), *Ugetsu* (Mizoguchi, 1953), *Woman in the Dunes* (Teshigahara, 1964).

Kuzui Enterprises. 220 Fifth Ave., New York NY 10001. (212) 708-9400. FILMS: *The Typhoon Club* (Somai, 1985).

Media Home Entertainment (Cinémathèque Collection). 5730 Buckingham Parkway, Culver City CA 90230. (213) 216-7900; (800) 421-4509 outside California. VIDEOTAPES: *Hidden Fortress* (Kurosawa, 1958), *Ikiru* (Kurosawa, 1952), *Red Beard* (Kurosawa, 1965), *Throne of Blood* (Kurosawa, 1957).

New Yorker Films. 16 West 61st St., New York NY 10023. (212) 247-6100. FILMS: *An Actor's Revenge* (Ichikawa, 1963), *An Autumn Afternoon* (Ozu, 1962), *Boy* (Oshima, 1969), *The Ceremony* (Oshima, 1971), *The Crazy Family* (Ishii, 1984), *Cruel Story of Youth* (Oshima, 1960), *Dear Summer Sister* (Oshima, 1972), *Death by Hanging* (Oshima, 1968), *Demon Pond* (Shinoda, 1980), *Diary of a Shinjuku Thief* (Oshima, 1969), *Early Spring* (Ozu, 1956), *Enjo* (Ichikawa, 1958), *Equinox Flower* (Ozu, 1958), *The Flavor of Green Tea over Rice* (Ozu, 1952), *A Full Life* (Hani, 1962), *The Funeral* (Itami, 1984), *A Geisha* (Mizoguchi, 1953), *I Was Born, But...* (Ozu, 1932), *The Idiot* (Kurosawa, 1951), *Late Autumn* (Ozu, 1960), *Late Spring* (Ozu, 1949), *The Man Who Left His Will on Film* (Oshima, 1970), *Muddy River* (Oguri, 1981), *My Love Has Been Burning* (Mizoguchi, 1949), *Night and Fog in Japan* (Oshima, 1960), *Princess Yang Kwei Fei* (Mizoguchi, 1955), *A Promise* (Yoshida, 1986), *The Record of a Tenement Gentleman* (Ozu, 1947), *Sorekara* (Morita, 1986), *A Story of Floating Weeds* (Ozu, 1934), *The Sun's Burial* (Oshima, 1960), *Tampopo* (Itami, 1986), *A Taxing Woman* (Itami, 1987), *Tokyo Story* (Ozu, 1953), *To Sleep so as to Dream* (Hayashi, 1986), *Utamaro and His Five Women* (Mizoguchi, 1946). VIDEOTAPE: *Tokyo Story* (Ozu, 1953).

Orion Classics. 711 Fifth Ave., New York NY 10022. (212) 758-5100. FILMS: *MacArthur's Children* (Shinoda, 1984), *Ran* (Kurosawa, 1985).

Pacific Arts. 50 North La Cienega Blvd., Suite 210, Beverly Hills CA 90211, (213) 657-2233; (800) 538-5856 outside California. VIDEOTAPES: *High and Low* (Kurosawa, 1963), *Irezumi* (Takabayashi, 1982), *MacArthur's Children* (Shinoda, 1985).

Prestige Film Corporation. 18 E. 48th St., Suite 1601, New York NY 10017. (212) 888-2662. FILMS: *Irezumi* (Takabayashi, 1982).

R5/S8 Presents. 1028 Poplar Dr., Falls Church VA 22046. (202) 452-1717. FILMS: *Dark Hair* (Kurisaki, 1988), *Film Actress* (Ichikawa, 1987), *Goyokin* (Gosha, 1969), *The Hidden Fortress* (Kurosawa, 1958), *Horse* (Yamamoto, 1941), *Love Suicides at Sonezaki* (Kurisaki, 1981), *The Makioka Sisters* (Ichikawa, 1983), *The Men Who Tread on the Tiger's Tail* (Kurosawa, 1945), *The Most Beautiful* (Kurosawa, 1944), *One Wonderful Sunday* (Kurosawa, 1947), *Sanshiro Sugata, Parts 1 and 2* (Kurosawa, 1943 and 1945), *Tokyo Olympiad—uncut* (Ichikawa, 1964), *Zatoichi Meets Yojimbo* (Okamoto, 1971). VIDEOTAPE: *The Makioka Sisters* (Ichikawa, 1983).

Republic Pictures Home Video. 12636 Beatrice St., Los Angeles CA 90066. (213) 306-4040. *Tampopo* (Itami, 1987), *The Funeral* (Itami, 1984).

Sony Video Software Company. 1700 Broadway, New York NY 10019. (212) 757-4990. (Note: In 1988 Sony, in conjunction with the Japan Society, started releasing four quality Japanese films every three months. This program continued into 1989. The titles listed below were those available as of this writing. More titles may be available. Teaching modules based on these films are also available. Modules center around topics such as "Japanese Society Through Film: The Family" and "Japanese Literature on Film" and include three videotapes and two teaching guides.) VIDEOTAPES: *The Bad Sleep Well* (Kurosawa, 1958), *Double Suicide* (Shinoda, 1969), *Early Summer* (Ozu, 1951), *The Family Game* (Morita, 1983), *The Forty-Seven Ronin, Parts I and II* (Mizoguchi, 1941–42), *The Go Masters* (Sato and Ji-Shun, 1983), *The Human Condition, Parts I, II and III* (Kobayashi, 1959–61), *Mother* (Naruse, 1952), *Osaka Elegy* (Mizoguchi, 1936), *Sanshiro Sugata* (Kurosawa, 1943), *Sansho the Bailiff* (Mizoguchi, 1954), *Stray Dog* (Kurosawa, 1949), *Twenty-Four Eyes* (Kinoshita, 1954), *Vengeance Is Mine* (Imamura, 1979).

Video Action. 708 W. First St., Los Angeles CA 90012. (213) 687-8262; (800) 422-2241 outside California. VIDEOTAPES: *Rickshaw Man* (Inagaki, 1958), *Red Lion* (Okamoto, 1969), *Sandakan No. 8* (Kumai, 1975), *Station* (Furuhata, 1981), *Zatoichi Meets Yojimbo* (Okamoto, 1970).

Video Yesteryear. P.O. Box C, Sandy Hook CT 06482. (203) 426-2574; (800) 243-0987 outside Connecticut. VIDEOTAPES: *Gate of Hell* (Kinugasa, 1953), *The Island* (Shindo, 1961), *Ghidra, the Three-Headed Monster* (Honda, 1965), *Kwaidan* (Kobayashi, 1964), *Life of Oharu* (Mizoguchi, 1952), *Nanami—Inferno of First Love* (Hani, 1968), *Ugetsu* (Mizoguchi, 1953), *Yojimbo* (Kurosawa, 1961).

The Voyager Company (The Criterion Collection). 1351 Pacific Coast Hwy., Santa Monica CA 90401. (213) 451-1383. LASERDISCS: *Rashomon* (Kurosawa, 1950), *The Seven Samurai* (Kurosawa, 1954). (The Voyager Company also has non-theatrical rights for group presentations of videotapes for several Janus film titles. Contact Voyager for information.)

Miscellaneous Secondary Distributors

Many of the above businesses do not handle direct sales of their titles. The following distributors offer many of the above titles at one location.

Festival Films
2841 Irving Ave. S.
Minneapolis MN 55408
(612) 870-4744

Tamarelle
110 Cohasset Stage Rd.
Chico CA 95926
(916) 895-3429
(800) 356-3577 outside CA

Video Action
708 W. First St.
Los Angeles CA 90012
(213) 687-8262
(800) 422-2241 outside CA

Video Clubs

These are businesses which offer videotapes for rent through the mail. Through them, Japanese films available on videotapes are accessible to anyone, no matter where they live. Not all films are available on videotape, and not all videotapes are available through each club. Costs vary; write or phone for information.

Evergreen
213 W. 35th St.
New York NY   10001-4204
(212) 714-9860
(800) 225-7783 outside NYC

Facets Multimedia, Inc.
1517 W. Fullerton Ave.
Chicago IL   60614
(312) 281-9075

Home Film Festival
P.O. Box 2032
Scranton PA   18501-9952
(800) 633-FILM in PA
(800) 258-FILM outside PA

Miscellaneous Addresses for Japanese Films

Japan Film Library Council
Ginza-Hata Building
4-5, 4-chome, Ginza, Chuo-ku
Tokyo 104 Japan
(03) 561-6719

Kawakita Memorial Film Institute
Ginza-Hata Building
4-5, 4-chome, Ginza, Chuo-ku
Tokyo 104 Japan
011-813-561-3627

Museum of Modern Art/
   The Toho Collection
11 W. 53rd St.
New York NY   10019
(212) 708-9400

Pacific Film Archives
University Art Museum
2625 Durant St.
Berkeley CA   94720
(415) 642-1412

Shochiku Films of America
8230 Beverly Blvd.
Los Angeles CA   90048
(213) 653-7003

Toho Co., Ltd.
Two Century Plaza, Suite 490,
2049 Century Park E.
Los Angeles CA   90067
(213) 277-1081

Glossary

Benshi During silent films—and even into the period of talkies—Japanese theatres used narrators *(benshi)* to explain stories to audiences. (Also known as *katsuben.*)

Bunraku The theatre form in Japan which uses puppets manipulated by men *(kuroko)* dressed totally in black working in full view of the audience.

Bushido The code of conduct for a samurai in feudal Japan. It emphasized loyalty, courage, plain living and suicide *(seppuku)* before dishonor.

Chambara Film featuring sword fighting—usually refers to a plot revolving around the samurai.

Edo Feudal-era (1600–1868) name for present-day Tokyo.

Eroductions Films which are erotic productions.

Geisha "Arts person." Trained in song and dance, geishas were usually indentured to a specific establishment, which used them until their debts were paid off. It was not unusual for a poor family to sell daughters as geishas.

Gendai-geki One of the two largest genres of Japanese movies, encompassing films about contemporary Japanese life—usually set in the period after 1868 (see *Meiji Restoration* below) and evolving out of the *Shimpa* theatre.

Giri Obligation, loyalty or duty usually incurred after receiving favors or help. Often in conflict with *ninjo.*

Haha-mono Mother films; she is usually depicted as suffering and self-sacrificing.

Heian In 800–1200, this was the name given to present-day Kyoto.

Isshoku Ippan "A meal and a night's lodging": A general plot in which a man accepts hospitality and becomes overwhelmingly obligated to pay back the favor.

Jidai-geki One of the two largest genres of Japanese movies—period costume films. Usually set prior to the Meiji Restoration.

Josei Eiga A woman's film, usually sentimental and emphasizing romance and mother-love. Often associated with the "Ofuna flavor" of the Shochiku studios.

Junbungaku Movement The "pure literature" movement.

Kabuki   Live stage entertainment from the 1600s featuring highly stylized dialogue and acting interspersed with singing and dancing.

Kaidan   (Sometimes: *kwaidan*) Ghost story.

Keiko Eiga   Leftists "tendency films" of the 1930s.

Kodan   Historical stories of heroic warriors recited by a storyteller. When watching films based on these stories the audiences already knows the plot.

Kokutai   Japanese national spirit.

Meiji Restoration   Name given to the reign of Mutsuhito (1868–1912), the Japanese emperor restored after the fall of the Tokugawa shogunate. During this time, Japan became a world power (including territorial expansion) and absorbed Western knowledge and technology.

Michiyuki   In stories featuring *shinju* (double suicide), this is the lovers' journey to their death.

Migawari   Plot in which one person takes another's place.

Mono no aware   Acceptance of the inherent sadness of life, of the transience of all earthly things.

Nimaime   "Second": Kabuki actor given second billing. He is usually handsome, pure of heart, a lover. He is kind and gentle to the heroine.

Ninja   One who practices ninjitsu, which consists of the arts such as weaponry needed to achieve covert political intrigue. They are usually shown dressed entirely in black.

Ninjo   "Humaneness": Feelings and emotions such as romantic love and compassion. Often in conflict with *giri*.

Noh   A stage drama developed in the 14th century primarily for the enjoyment of the warrior classes. Usually chanted dialogue and masks, it is more reserved than kabuki.

O-Namida Chodai Eiga   "Tears, please, films": Tearjerker films often measured by Japanese critics as one-, two-, or three-handkerchief pictures.

Onnagata   Male actors who specialize in female roles. Also referred to as *oyama*.

Oyabun-Kobun   "Gang boss and underling": Plot in which the underling's loyalty is compromised, the boss killed and the underling put in the position of avenging him.

Pinku movies   "Pink" films is the term used by the Japanese to describe what the West often refer to as "blue" movies—low budget, short films featuring softcore pornography.

Rensa-Geki   "Chain drama": With the advent of films, *shimpa* troupes would sometimes film outdoor scenes and project them onto a stage behind the actors or show them alternately with the live action.

Roman Porno   Romantic porno films.

Ronin   "Man on the wave": A masterless samurai. Unemployed, his position has usually been brought about by the fall from favor or death of his lord.

Rumpen Mono Film genre featuring plots about, in Marxist terms, the "lumpen proletariat," or the working class.

Seppuku (Also referred to as *harakiri*) Ritual suicide performed by samurai, usually to prevent dishonor.

Shakai Mono Social genre films.

Shimpa "New school": A form of stage entertainment developed during the Meiji period in contrast to Kabuki. Usually consists of slow-paced, sentimental domestic dramas.

Shingeki Modern drama. Text and technique mainly imported from the West; aimed at realism.

Shinju The act of double suicide, traditionally considered to be the ultimate protest and an expression of spiritual union.

Shomin-Geki Films about the common people and lower middle class life.

Shoshimin-Geki Films in which the scope of action and emotion is scaled down. Plots center around family life and the everyday events they go through. Usually presented with some humor, there is nonetheless a pervasive and passive acceptance of the general sadness of life.

Sure Chiga "To brush past someone": The scene where two people just miss meeting.

Taiyozoku "Sun tribe": A genre of films about juvenile delinquency.

Tateyaku "Standing character": Actor who is the main lead in Kabuki drama. He plays noble, idealized samurai warriors, intelligent, strong-willed, determined. He puts loyalty to his lord above love of a woman. He is true to *bushido*.

Tendency films Films which carried the message to fight against a certain accepted social condition.

Tokugawa Shogunate (1614–1868) During this period, Japan was only nominally ruled by the emperor, who resided at Kyoto. Power actually rested in the hands of the military dictators of the Tokugawa family who resided in Edo (present-day Tokyo). When the Tokugawas could not expel the foreigners from Japanese soil, they lost control of the government, which returned to the emperor (see *Meiji Restoration*). This period is characterized by a rigidly feudalistic social structure (with a growing merchant class), political isolationism, relative peace, and a flourishing of the arts.

Tsuma-Mono A film centering on the wife as an individual.

Yakuza (From the numbers 8 "ya," 9 "ku" and 3 "sa" which lose if they come up in dice) A Japanese gangster usually associated with gambling and prostitution. Organized in a manner similar to the Mafia, *yakuza* have strict codes they must follow and are often depicted with their elaborate tattoos. In the early 1960s, an entire film genre developed featuring *yakuza*.

Select Bibliography

Books on Japanese Films and Directors

Allyn, John. *Kon Ichikawa: A Guide to References and Resources.* Boston: G.K. Hall, 1985.
   Contains a biographical background of director Kon Ichikawa, a critical survey of his films and a section with credits, notes and synopses of the films up to 1980. Also contains an annotated bibliography of works written about and by Ichikawa.

Anderson, Joseph L., and Richie, Donald. *The Japanese Film: Art and Industry.* Rutland, Vt.: Charles E. Tuttle, 1959.
   An indispensable work about the Japanese film industry. An in-depth historical look at the industry, its major artists and technical people as well as the studios. Contains illustrations, bibliographies and special chapters on directors and actors as well as charts of the major companies and director/student relationships.

Andrew, Dudley, and Paul Andrew. *Kenji Mizoguchi: A Guide to References and Resources.* Boston: G.K. Hall, 1981.
   The Andrews present a biography of Mizoguchi followed by a filmography complete with plot summaries, credits, listings of reviews and notes on awards. Also contains a comprehensive bibliography of most written works on Mizoguchi.

Barret, Gregory. *Archetypes in Japanese Film.* Selinsgrove, Pa.: Susquehanna University Press, 1989.
   An interesting study of the symbolization of the main characters within Japanese films such as the loyal retainer and the tormented lord; the *yakuza* hero; the vengeful spirit; and the prodigal son, the forgiving parent and the self-sacrificing sister. Also contains a section comparing Japanese archetypes with those of the West.

Bock, Audie. *Japanese Film Directors.* Tokyo: Kodansha International, 1978.
   An enlightening look at ten Japanese directors (Mizoguchi, Ozu, Naruse, Kurosawa, Kinoshita, Ichikawa, Kobayashi, Imamura, Oshima and Shinoda), their lives and careers. Contains abbreviated filmographies with plot summaries.

_____. *Mikio Naruse: A Master of the Japanese Cinema.* Chicago: Film Center of the School of the Art Institute, 1984.

This 32-page booklet was written and edited by Bock to be used in conjunction with a Naruse retrospective. As of this writing, it is the only work available exclusively on this relatively unknown but important Japanese film director. The booklet contains an introduction to Naruse's work and style, an interview about Naruse with one of his primary actresses, Hideko Takamine, an inteview with Kihachi Okamoto who worked as Naruse's assistant director, a film-by-film writeup of the 25 films in the retrospecitve, a chronological Naruse fimography and a bibliography.

Bordwell, David. *Ozu and the Poetics of Cinema*. Princeton, N.J.: Princeton University Press, 1988.

Bordwell's book analyzes and explains Ozu's films. The first part discusses Ozu's career and biography and presents his "poetics" (how films are put together and how they generate desired effects). The second part evaluates existing Ozu films by examining their plots, offering comments and presenting "theory as practiced."

Burch, Noel. *To the Distant Observer: Form and Meaning in the Japanese Cinema*. Berkeley: University of California Press, 1979.

A scholarly study of Japanese film aesthetics, hampered by excessive use of semiotic terminology which makes this book slow going for anyone unfamiliar with semiology.

Desser David. *Eros Plus Massacre: An Introduction to the Japanese New Wave Cinema*. Bloomington: Indiana University Press, 1988.

The only English language book exclusively about Japanese films from the 1960's "New Wave" which challenged cinematic conventions. Strong on film analysis and explanation.

_____. *The Samurai Films of Akira Kurosawa*. Ann Arbor, Mich.: UMI Research Press, 1983.

Desser introduces the reader to many aspects of Japanese culture (such as language) and history which play a part within the genre of the samurai film. After discussing the elements of various types of samurai films, Desser addresses Kurosawa's samurai films in particular.

DeVos, George A., and Audie Bock. *Themes in Japanese Society as Seen Through the Japanese Film*. Berkeley: Pacific Film Archive, 1974.

A study guide published to accompany the PBS television series which gives historic and cultural background for the 13 films presented. Also includes brief plots for these films.

Erens, Patricia. *Akira Kurosawa: A Guide to References and Resources*. Boston: G.K. Hall, 1979.

Erens offers a biographical background for Kurosawa, a critical overview of his work, a film-by-film synopsis with credits and notes, and a bibliography for writings through 1977.

Grilli, Peter. *Japan in Film: A Comprehensive Annotated Catalog of Documentary and Theatrical Films in Japan*. New York: Japan Society, 1984.

An annotated catalogue of films about and from Japan, both theatrical releases and documentaries. Entries contain credits and brief synopsis along with distributor information.

Japan Society. *Japan at War: Rare Films from World War II*. New York, 1987.

Booklet published in conjunction with the Japan Society's 24-film retrospective on films made in Japan between 1937 and 1947. The Society also has a 15-page symposium report on the topic.

_____. *Kurosawa: A Retrospective*. New York, 1981.
Booklet published in conjunction with the Japan Film Center's 26-film retrospective of Kurosawa's work. Contains an introduction by Peter Grilli, extensive quotes from critics, directors and actors, a biography by Audie Bock, "Kurosawa's Heroes and Japanese Tradition" by Tadao Sato, translated excerpts from an interview with Kurosawa, and write-ups on the featured films.

_____. *A Tribute to Toshiro Mifune: 40 Great Films Starring Japan's Greatest Actor*. New York, 1984.
Booklet published in conjunction with Mifune retrospective presented at the Japan Film Center. Contains a filmography as well as film notes and a biography by David Owens.

Kurosawa, Akira; Hideo Oguni and Ide Masato. *Ran*. Boston: Shambhala, 1986.
While waiting for production to begin on *Ran*, Kurosawa drew many pictures to communicate to his staff his personal vision of the film. Since the younger Kurosawa had intended to become a painter, this published version of the movie script along with Kurosawa's vivid illustrations offer a picturesque insight into Kurosawa's art both on the screen and on paper.

_____. *The Seven Samurai: A Film by Akira Kurosawa*. Translated by Donald Richie. New York: Simon and Schuster, 1970.
Based on the 160-minute version of the Toho script as well as viewings of Japanese, American and British prints of the film, Richie has compiled an as-complete-as-possible-for-the-time script of *Seven Samurai*.

_____. *Something Like an Autobiography*. Translated by Audie E. Bock. New York: Vintage Books, 1983.
Engrossing translation of Kurosawa's autobiography from his early years through the release of *Rashomon*. Also includes a section titled "Some Random Notes on Filmmaking."

McDonald, Keiko I. *Cinema East: A Critical Study of Major Japanese Films*. East Brunswick, N.J.: Associated University Presses, 1983.
Taking 12 masterpieces on the Japanese cinema *(Rashomon, Woman in the Dunes, Double Suicide, Red Beard, Harp of Burma, Ugetsu, Death by Hanging, Throne of Blood, Eros Plus Massacre, Tokyo Story, Twenty-Four Eyes* and *Odd Obsession)*, McDonald devotes an entire essay to each. Similar to a literary criticism, she discusses plots in detail as well as an analysis of each's structure, symbolism, and atmosphere as appropriate.

_____. *Mizoguchi*. Boston: Twayne Publishers, 1984.
McDonald approaches Mizoguchi's films in relationship to the various stages he went through in his life. By analyzing many scenes from his existing films this Japanese-born author offers an invaluable English guide through Mizoguchi's films. Includes a filmography and selected bibliography.

Mellen, Joan. *Voices from the Japanese Cinema*. New York: Liveright, 1975.
Mellen interviews 15 people important to the Japanese cinema from Akira Kurosawa to Mme. Kashiko Kawakita, distinguished for aiding in the distribution of Japanese films abroad.

_____. *The Waves at the Genji's Door: Japan Through Its Cinema*. New York: Pantheon, 1976.
While taking a feminist approach to Japanese films, Mellen puts them into a "historical, social and political" context in an attempt to make them more accessible to a Western audience.

Morris, Peter. *Mizoguchi Kenji*. Ottawa: Canadian Film Institute, 1967.
This monograph contains several sections. The first is "The Cinema of Mizoguchi" by Peter Morris, which introduces the director's themes, style and the sources for his films. The second is "Mizoguchi: Life and Times" by Donald Richie and Joseph Anderson, which is based on their *Sight and Sound* article from Autumn 1955 (see the Article Bibliography below). The third, "Mizoguchi: Three Statements," reprints three interviews from the 1950s. "According to Mizoguchi" is the final entry and it contains letters between Mizoguchi and his scriptwriter Yoda about the film *Ugetsu*. Also includes an annotated filmography and limited bibliography.

Owen, David. *Mizoguchi: The Master*. New York: Japan Society, 1981.
Booklet published in conjunction with a retrospective of Mizoguchi's films shown at the Japan Film Center in New York. Contains brief synopses of the director's films with introductions by Peter Grilli and Dudley Andrew.

Provinzano, Linda, ed. *Films in the Collection of the Pacific Film Archive, Volume I:* Daiei Motion Picture Co., Ltd., Japan, 1979.
The Pacific Film Archives, one of the finest collections of Japanese films in America, has put out this informative catalog of a small part of their holdings. Entered alphabetically (by their Japanese titles), movie listings contain cast and credit information along with a short plot synopsis, an even shorter criticism, bibliographic references, subject headings and a general statement of the archive's print condition. The catalog also contains a glossary and name, title and subject indices.

Richie, Donald, ed. *The Films of Akira Kurosawa*. Berkeley: University of California Press, 1970.
In-depth look at Akira Kurosawa's film career in a film by film study. Includes biographical information on the director; an outline of each story, its characters and treatment; and technical and production notes. There is a filmography which contains credits, a bibliography and many photographs.

_____. *Focus on Rashomon*. Englewood Cliffs, N.J.: Prentice-Hall, 1972.
Several books are available which contain a partial or complete script for the film *Rashomon* as well as essays and reviews of this historically important film and the two Ryunosuke Akutagawa stories on which it is based. Richie has edited at least two of these books. [Also see Richie's *Rashomon* below]. These books offer both redundant entries as well as entries particular only to its version. Several of the redundant essays can be found in their original form within the books mentioned in this bibliography (i.e. essays from Mellen's *The Waves at the Genji's Door* and Richie's own *The Films of Akira Kurosawa*). This edition contains only an excerpt of the script, but also includes an overview of Kurosawa by Akira Iwasaki and "An Afternoon with Kurosawa" by R.B. Gadi.

_____. *Japanese Cinema: Film Style and National Character*. Garden City, N.Y.: Anchor, 1971.
First published as *The Japanese Movie,* this expanded version examines the underpinnings, philosophical and cultural, of Japanese society which are reflected in their films and gives them their unique world view.

_____. *Japanese Experimental Film: 1960–1980*. New York: American Federation of Arts, 1981.

In 1980 the A.F.A. asked Richie to develop a film series based on Japan's experimental movies. This program for that 20-film retrospective contains brief biographies of the directors and plot summaries and an extensive introduction by Richie on the history of the Japanese experimental film movement.

_____. *The Japanese Movie: An Illustrated History.* Tokyo: Kodansha International, 1966.
Fascinating and very readable introduction to the history of Japanese films which includes interesting trivia and many photographs.

_____. *Japanese Movies.* Tokyo: Japan Travel Bureau, 1961. [See Richie's *Japanese Cinema,* above.]

_____. *Ozu.* Berkeley: University of California Press, 1974.
In-depth look at the career and films of the most Japanese of all Japanese directors. Discusses Ozu's themes, characters, visual style and editing. Contains a bibliography and a biographical filmography.

_____, ed. *Rashomon.* New Brunswick, N.J.: Rutgers University Press, 1987.
Similar to *Focus on Rashomon* [see above], also by Richie, this edition is the latest update. It contains *Rashomon*'s credits, cast and a continuity script, as well as reviews, essays and the original Ryunosuke Akutagawa stories on which the film is based. Added to this most recent edition are essays by, among others, Audie Bock (translator of Kurosawa's autobiography) and an excerpt from that book, *Something Like an Autobiography,* offering Kurosawa's own insights into this important film.

Sato, Tadao. *Currents in Japanese Cinema.* Translated by Gregory Barrett. Tokyo: Kodansha International, 1982.
A collection of Sato's essays mostly drawn from his 12-year-old work *Nihon eiga shisho shi (History of Intellectual Currents in Japanese Films).* An interesting but uneven collection, the essays take a popular approach to film and present a very personal view of the art. The first English-language book about Japanese film by a Japanese critic.

Silver, Alain. *The Samurai Film.* Woodstock, N.Y.: Overlook Press, 1983.
The samurai film, one of the most popular among Western audiences, is discussed in great detail. Silver approaches the subject from both a historical standpoint and a cinematic one. With an extensive chapter on Hideo Gosha, the book covers several classics in the genre in detail and includes a bibliography and detailed filmography.

Svensson, Arne. *Screen Series: Japan.* New York: A.S. Barnes, 1971.
Helpful and fact-filled encyclopedia-like book which alphabetically lists important films and biographies of important directors, actors and actresses. Good for information prior to 1970. Indexed.

Tucker, Richard. *Japan: Film Image.* London: Studio Vista, 1973.
This book begins with a brief history of Japanese films then discusses several directors in terms of their special Japaneseness and their social and cultural influences.

Books with References to Japanese Films and Directors

Brandon, James R., ed. *The Performing Arts in Asia.* Paris: Unesco: 1971.
Contains two essays on Japanese films: "The Japanese Film Industry" by Jean de Baroncelli and "Japanese Film Exhibits Abroad" by Kashiko Kawakita. The

first addresses the decline in quality of Japanese films and the attempts by directors to find creative freedom. The second discusses retrospective packages of Japanese films receiving distribution in the West.

Braudy, Leo, and Morris Dickstein, eds. *Great Film Directors: A Critical Anthology.* New York: Oxford University Press, 1978.
Contains "Kurosawa and His Work" by Akira Iwasaki (reprinted article form the Jan.-March 1965 *Japan Quarterly*), "The Seven Samurai" by Tony Richardson (reprinted from spring 1955 *Sight and Sound*), "The Seven Samurai" by Donald Richie (from his *The Films of Akira Kurosawa*).

Buruma, Ian. *Behind the Mask: On Sexual Demons, Sacred Mothers, Transvestites, Gangsters, Drifters and Other Japanese Cultural Heroes.* New York: Meridian, 1984.
An insightful exploration of Japanese cultural traditions and popular attitudes which form the basis of the Japanese character. Examines the social facade and its internalized underpinnings especially as manifested in social endeavors such as in the theatre and in film.

Cameron, Ian. "Nagisa Oshima." In *Second Wave.* New York: Praeger, 1970.
Cameron's article on Nagisa Oshima is one of eight essays written by various authors in this book about filmmakers who experimented and found new ways to use film to express their own personal views of reality. In-depth plot analysis of three of Oshima's films: *The Catch, Diary of a Shinjuku Thief* and *Boy.*

Cowie, Peter, ed. *International Film Guide.* New York: A.S. Barnes; annual.
Offers a yearly look at the Japanese film industry focusing on expenditures, profits, overall production, and a list of important titles for that year. Also occasionally contains profiles of specific Japanese directors with filmographies. Those covered have included Oshima, Kurosawa, Imamura, Ichikawa and others.

Dissanayake, Wimal, ed. *Cinema and Cultural Identity: Reflections on Films from Japan, India and China.* Lanham, Md.: University Press of America, 1988.
Contains five essays on Japanese films: "Viewing Japanese Film: Some Considerations" by Donald Richie, "The Destiny of Samurai Films" by Michitaro Tada, "Japanese Film Genres" by Audie Bock and "The Multilayered Nature of the Tradition of Acting in Japanese Cinema" and "Change in the Image of Mother in Japanese Cinema and Television" by Tadao Sato.

Ellis, Jack C. *A History of Film.* Englewood Cliffs, N.J.: Prentice-Hall, 1985.
Section on Japan begins with *Rashomon* winning at Cannes then discusses the major differences which make Japanese films unique. Covers several films and directors in detail, and others very briefly.

Encyclopedia of Japan. Tokyo: Kodansha, 1983.
Comprehensive, multivolume encyclopedia about many facets of Japanese life. Also includes entires on Japanese film history as well as directors, actors and actresses.

Gedlud, Harry M., ed. *Film Makers on Film Making: Statements on Their Art by Thirty Directors.* Bloomington: Indiana University Press, 1967.
Essay and interview with Akira Kurosawa ("Japan's Poet Laureate of Film" from *Show Business Illustrated,* April 1962).

Heath, Stephen, and Patricia Mellencamp, eds. *Cinema and Language.* Los Angeles: American Film Institute, 1983.

Contains the following chapters: "Mizoguchi and the Evolution of Film Language" by David Boardwell (an examination of the 1930's works of Kenji Mizoguchi in terms of construction of film style especially in relationship to Andre Bazin's theory of deep focus and découpage), "Approaching Japanese Film" by Noel Burch (a technical article on the linguistic and cultural problems encountered in a study of Japanese films by foreigners), and "Kabuki, Cinema and Mizoguchi Kenji" by Don Kirihara (an examination of how Kabuki and cinema meet in Kenji Mizoguchi's *The Story of the Last Chrysanthemum*).

Hibbett, Howard, ed. *Contemporary Japanese Literature: An Anthology of Fiction, Film and Other Writing Since 1945.* New York: Alfred A. Knopf, 1977.
Contains "Ozu Yasujiro" by Kogo Noda, which is the complete written text of Ozu's film *Tokyo Story* along with a short introduction to Ozu, and "Kurosawa Akira" by Shinobu Hashimoto and Hideo Oguni, which is the written text of Kurosawa's film *Ikiru* with a short introduction to Kurosawa.

Hirano, Kyoko. "Japan." In *World Cinema Since 1945,* edited by William Luhr. New York: Ungar, 1987.
Approximately 40 pages of Luhr's book are devoted to an overview of Japanese films and the Japanese film industry since 1945. Good for anyone wanting a fast, readable introduction to the subject which is heavy on names and titles.

Holmes, Winifred. *Orient: A Survey of Films Produced in Countries of Arab and Asian Culture.* London: British Film Institute, 1959.
Contains cast and credit listings as well as a brief plot synopsis of approximately 35 Japanese films from the 1950s.

Houston, Penelope. "The Major Industries." In *The Contemporary Cinema.* Baltimore: Penguin Books, 1963.
A general discussion of Japanese and Indian films as discovered by British audiences and critics.

Jorgens, Jack J. *Shakespeare on Film.* Bloomington: Indiana University Press, 1979.
This book about how Shakespeare's plays have been translated to film contains a section titled "Defining *Macbeth:* George Schaefer, Orson Welles and Akira Kurosawa," which compares the three directors' film adaptations.

Leyda, Jay, ed. *Film Makers Speak: Voices of Film Experience.* New York: Da Capo Paperback, 1977.
Contains short quote excerpts from various sources on the following directors: Ichikawa, Imai, Kobayashi, Kurosawa, Mizoguchi, Ozu and actor Chishu Ryu.

Manvell, Roger. *Shakespeare and the Film.* New York: Praeger, 1971.
Contains a chapter on Kurosawa's *Macbeth, Throne of Blood,* which includes an interview with Kurosawa by Tadao Sato in which the director discusses the elements of the Noh theatre used in the film.

Meyers, Richard; Amy Harlib, and Bill and Karne Palmer. *Martial Arts Movies.* Secaucus, N.J.: Citadel Press, 1985.
Contains sections on Bruce Lee, China, Hong Kong and American martial arts films and a section on Japan titled "Samurai Swordsman and Karate Killers." It offers a brief background of the samurai and the films which portray them including several successful series such as "Zatoichi," "Son of Black Mass," and "Band of Assassins."

Mintz, Marilyn. *The Martial Arts Film.* New York: A.S. Barnes, 1978.
  While there is no specific section on Japanese films, this book is liberally
  sprinkled with information on martial arts films made in Japan.

Murray, Edward. "Ikiru." In *Ten Film Classics; A Re-viewing.* New York: Frederick
  Ungar, 1978.
  A shot-by-shot analysis of Kurosawa's film *Ikiru.*

Phillips, Baxter. *Swastika: Cinema of Oppression.* London: Lorrimer, 1976.
  Contains a section on "The Cinema of Hirohito," which is brief on text but
  contains some good stills from rarely seen Japanese films.

Polan, Dana B. *The Political Language of Film and the Avant-Garde.* Ann Arbor,
  Mich.: UMI Research Press, 1985.
  "Oshima's Political Art" section is basically a reprint of Polan's "Politics as Process in Three Films by Nagisa Oshima," which appeared in the fall 1983 edition of *Film Criticism.*

Reader, Keith. "Inscrutability and Reproduction—Four Major Japanese Directors."
  In *Cultures on Celluloid.* London: Quartet Books, 1981.
  Reader examines how "history, ideology and sub-culture emerge in a country's
  cinema." (Refer to entries on Ozu, Kurosawa, Mizoguchi and Oshima in the
  Japanese section.)

Richie, Donald. *Different People.* New York: Kodansha International, 1987.
  Richie offers brief but intimate glimpses into the lives of approximately 50
  Japanese people he has encountered while living there. From the film world he
  presents Setsuko Hara, Akira Kurosawa, Toshiro Mifune, Hiroshi Momma,
  Chishu Ryu, Sessue Hayakawa, Kon Ichikawa, Isuzu Yamada, Shintaro Katsu,
  and Nagisa Oshima. Also includes Sada Abe after her release from jail (see *In
  the Realm of the Senses*).

_____. "Mono No Aware: Hiroshima in Film." In *Film: Book 2, Films of Peace
  and War,* edited by Robert Hughes. New York: Grove Press, 1962.
  Discussion of various Japanese films about atomic weapons and their aftermath
  from the "sober and honest" *Hiroshima* (1953) through the virtually comic
  Carmen's Pure Love (1952), and even including the monsters *Godzilla* (1954)
  et al. Interesting mention of Resnais' *Hiroshima Mon Amour* and the mistakes
  it made which amused Japanese audiences.

Rhode, Eric. *A History of the Cinema from Its Origins to 1970.* London: Penguin
  Books, 1976.
  Section on Japan offers an abbreviated history of Japanese films primarily
  focused around major directors.

Roud, Richard, ed. *Cinema: A Critical Dictionary: The Major Filmmakers.* Two
  volumes. London: Secker and Warburg, 1980.
  Includes critical essays on "Akira Kurosawa" and "Nagisa Oshima and Japanese
  Cinema in the 60s" by Noel Burch, "Kon Ichikawa" and "Teinosuke
  Kinugasa" by John Gillett, and "Kenji Mizoguchi" and "Mikio Naruse" by
  Donald Richie.

Schrader, Paul. *Transcendental Style in Film: Ozu, Bresson, Dryer.* Berkeley:
  University of California Press, 1972.
  An analysis of the films of Yasujiro Ozu in terms of how he reflects the
  transcendent.

Stephenson, Ralph. *The Animated Film*. New York: A.S. Barnes, 1973.
Contains section discussing the major figures in Japanese animation: including Yoji Kuri, Taku Furukawa, Sadao Tsukioka, Taiji Yabushita and Kimio Yabuki.

Wood, Robin. *Personal Views: Explorations in Film*. London: Gordon Fraser, 1976.
One of the last entires in this subjective book is an expanded version of an article Wood wrote for *Film Comment* (March-April 1973) titled "The Ghost Princess and the Seaweed Gatherer." Focusing primarily on Mizoguchi's *Ugetsu* and *Sansho Dayu*, Wood discusses the director's distinctive camera style and scene composition.

Young, Vernon. *On Film: Unpopular Essays on a Popular Art*. Chicago: Quadrangle Books, 1972.
Essays on film, arranged chronologically, discusses characteristics of Japanese films with references to Japanese directors Ichikawa, Kurosawa, Ozu, Teshigahara, and cinematographer Miyagawa.

Periodical Articles

American Cinematographer. "Kon Ichikawa at the Olympic Games." (Nov. 1972): 1265 + .
Technical information on Ichikawa's coverage of the 100-meter finals at the 1972 Olympics in Munich. Ichikawa was one of several directors David Wolper employed to cover the event.

American Film Institute. "Dialogue on Film: Masahiro Shinoda." *American Film* (May 1985): 10–13.
Interview with Shinoda which explains how he got into film, the philosophy of the "Ofuna New Wave" directors, his work with Ozu on *Tokyo Twilight*, and the use of violence in his films.

Anderson, Joseph L. "History of Japanese Movies." *Films in Review* (June/July 1953): 277–290.
Detailed overview of the development of Japan's films and film industry.

————. "Japanese Film Periodicals." *Quarterly of Film, Radio and Television* (Summer 1955): 410–423.
An overview of periodicals published in Japan for its legions of film lovers from those publishing scripts to "Kinema Jumpo" (in its 925th issue in 1955) to fan magazines.

————. "Japanese Swordfighters and American Gunfighters." *Cinema Journal* (Spring 1973): 1–21.
A discussion of the traditions and development of samurai films.

————. "The Other Cinema." *Sight and Sound* (March 1951): 452–453.
Postwar developments in the Japanese film industry.

————. "Seven from the Past." *Sight and Sound* (Autumn 1957): 82–87.
A short history of the Japanese cinema before World War II and a discussion of the films *Crossroads, I Was Born, But...*, *Sisters of the Gion, Humanity and Paper Balloons* and *Five Scouts*.

————. "Where the Silver Screen Has Turned to Gold." *Theatre Arts* (March 1954): 80–83 + .

Written from a very limited viewpoint, the article sees *Rashomon* as a good
beginning for Japanese films to break away from Western influences and start
out on its own.

_____, and Loren Hoekzema. "The Spaces in Between: American Criticism of
Japanese Films." *Wide Angle* (1977): 2–7.
A brief look at the problems of Western critics viewing Japanese films in terms
of cultural differences.

_____, and Donald Richie. "The Films of Heinosuke Gosho." *Sight and Sound*
(Autumn 1956): 76–81.
A biographical account of Gosho's life and career with a fascinating description
of the filming of Japan's first sound film, *The Neighbor's Wife and Mine*. Also
discusses the "pure literature" movement, sentimentality in Japanese films, and
Gosho's working techniques.

_____, and _____. "Kenji Mizoguchi." *Sight and Sound* (Autumn 1955):
76–81.
Interesting biography of Mizoguchi which also discusses his strengths and
evolution as a filmmaker, his working style and his approach to films. One of
the first English-language articles on Mizoguchi. (Reprinted in Morris'
monograph *Kenji Mizoguchi*.)

Anderson, Lindsay. "Two Inches Off the Ground." *Sight and Sound* (Winter
1957–58): 131–133 + .
British director Anderson examines the "action" in Japanese films from the
Western-like Kurosawa to the more traditional Ozu and compares them to the
narrow Western definition.

Barr, Stephen H. "Reframing Mizoguchi." *Film Criticism* (Fall 1983): 79–85.
Analysis of Mizoguchi's 1951 film *Miss Oyu* with special attention to the director's movement of the camera.

Bazerman, Charles. "Time in Play and Film: *Macbeth* and *Throne of Blood*."
Literature and Film Quarterly (Fall 1977): 333–337.
Compares the use of time in the play by Shakespeare and the film by
Kurosawa based on it.

Belton, John. "The Crucified Lovers of Mizoguchi." *Film Quarterly* (Fall 1971):
15–19.
A Story from Chikamatsu is analyzed in relationship to Mizoguchi's themes
and styles.

Bernardi, Joanne R. "Catching a Film Audience Abroad." *Japan Quarterly* (July-
Sept. 1985): 290–295.
Comprehensive historical analysis of the distribution of Japanese films abroad.

Blue, James. "Susumu Hani Interview." *Film Comment* (Spring 1969): 24–45.
Offers a biographical sketch in Hani's own words as well as an in-depth discussion of how he started in films, his personal style of filmmaking, working with
non-professionals, and the background of his films *Bad Boys, Children in the
Classroom, Children Who Draw*, and *Nanami—Inferno of First Love*. Includes
filmography and list of writings.

Bock, Audie. "Ozu Reconsidered." *Film Criticism* (Fall 1983): 50–53.
Bock examines the film style of "the master of the mundane" with wit and a
look at some of Ozu's more unusual cinematic texts, such as symbolic
Americana sprinkled into his films and his "bathroom" humor.

Branigan, Edward. "The Space of Equinox Flower." *Screen* (Summer 1976): 74–105.
Analysis of the poetic use of space in Ozu's films and how it is achieved. A very technical article.

_____. "Subjectivity Under Siege—From *8 1/2* to Oshima's *The Story of the Man Who Left His Will on Film.*" *Screen* (Spring 1978): 7–69.
An in-depth analysis which compares the subjectivity and objectivity in the narrative of the characters in the Fellini and Oshima films of the title.

Bucher, Felix. "Akira Kurosawa and Hiroshi Teshigahara." *Camera* (Sept. 1966): 50–55.
A study of the two directors with analysis of how "Western" Kurosawa is.

Burnett, C. Ewan. "Japanese Cinema." *Cinema Papers* (June-July 1980): 181–183 + .
Burnett interviews the West's foremost authority in Japanese films, Donald Richie. Primary focus of the interview is the current [1980] health of the industry, the situation with independent production companies, censorship, and a prediction for the future.

Burr, H.A. "Two-Sword Hombres." *Atlantic* (Oct. 1954): 104–105.
A brief and superficial look at samurai movies with a comparison to Hollywood Westerns.

Business Week. "For Japan's Films, a Hard Choice." (Feb. 11, 1956): 114.
At a time when Japanese films were making inroads into Western markets, this article suggests that the industry may have to choose between cashing in on this success with "quick" films or making quality films.

Butcher, Harold. "Japan Goes to the Movies." *Travel* (April 1935): 51–53 + .
First-person account of attending the movies in Japan and a visit to Shochiku studios.

Cameron, Ian. "Interview with Oshima." *Movie* (Winter 1969–70): 7–15.
See Ian Cameron entry in the "Books with References to Japanese Films and Directors" bibliography section above.

Cameron, Julia. "Inside Kurosawa: Insights from Japan's Cinema Master." *Chicago Tribune* (Oct. 6, 1985): Section 13, 4 + .
Article presents biographical information on Kurosawa and background on his film career upon the release of *Ran* at the New York Film Festival. Kurosawa gives his opinions on the Japanese film industry, the internationalism of film and how his own films are made.

Casebier, Allan. "Images of Irrationality in Modern Japan: The Films of Shohei Imamura." *Film Criticism* (Fall 1983): 42–49.
Casebier examines irrationality ("instinct," "emotional response" and "other human responses independent of language") in Imamura's films *A Man Vanishes, Intentions of Murder* and *Profound Desire of the Gods.*

_____. "Oshima in Contemporary Theoretical Perspective." *Wide Angle* (Number 2, 1987): 4–17.
Introduction to Oshima for an issue of *Wide Angle* devoted entirely to that director.

Chekhonin, B. "A Few Stones from a Glass House: Kurosawa's Troubles in Big Bad Hollywood." *Atlas* (March 1970): 59–61. Reprint of an *Izvestiya* [Soviet] article on the problems Kurosawa had in Hollywood with creative freedom.

Clayburn, Peter. *Chambara. Sight and Sound* (Summer 1964): 123.
Discussion of the popularity of the ninja in Japanese films, which comprised the subject matter of one-third of the produced *chambara* films.

Cohen, Jules. "A Season of Japanese Films." *Film Society Review* (January 1968): 12–16.
Illustrated. Recent Japanese films shown in the United States at the Museum of Modern Art. Reference Kurahara, Yoshida, Kawabe, Masamura and Hani.

Cohen, Robert. "Mizoguchi and Modernism." *Sight and Sound* (Spring 1978): 110–118.
Cohen examines modernism as represented in the point-of-view structures of Mizoguchi's films. He surveys editing, cultural impact and motifs in the director's films.

Coleman, J. "Ichikawa." *New Statesman* (Aug. 12, 1966): 236.
Personal analysis of the attraction of Ichikawa's films and cinematic techniques.

Conant, Theodore. "Anti-American Films in Japan." *Films in Review* (Jan. 1954): 8–11.
Discusses the influence of post–Occupation leftist unions on the anti–American content in some Japanese films. Mentions two by Akira Kurosawa before he left the "Progressive" movement.

Cott, Jonathan. "The Art of Ozu." *Rolling Stone* (April 13, 1972): 74.
An introduction to Ozu's films and style for those who needed background information before seeing the retrospective organized by Donald Richie for the Museum of Modern Art.

Cunningham, R.R. "The Japanese Cinema Today." *Sight and Sound* (Spring 1948): 16–18.
Discusses the changing character of Japanese movies since the influences of the West and especially under the post–World War II Occupation. Looks at the characteristics of films produced in 1948.

Davis, D. William. "Back to Japan: Militarism and Monumentalism in Prewar Japanese Cinema." *Wide Angle* (Volume 11, Number 3, 1989): 16–25.
A discussion of a period in Japanese filmmaking in which Western influences were cast aside in favor of glorified Japanese traditions.

Desser, David. "Kurosawa's Eastern 'Western'; *Sanjuro* and the Influence of *Shane*." *Film Criticism* (Fall 1983): 54–65.
Desser's analyses of *Sanjuro* in which he compares Kurosawa's narrative style to that in George Steven's *Shane* and makes a case for cross-culturalization.

_____. "Toward a Structural Analysis of the Postwar Samurai Film." *Quarterly Review of Film Studies* (Winter 1983): 25–41.
Stating that there is a difference in the samurai films of the 1950s and those of the 1970s, Desser elaborates on the genre basics and its indications of the culture which created it.

Deverall, Richard L-G. "Red Propaganda in Japan's Movies." *America* (Nov. 14, 1953): 172–174.
In the wake of the Occupation's pro-union stance, Communism grew within the Japanese film industry and Deverall discusses several films which he feels are spreading extreme anti–Western messages.

Durgnant, R.E. "Oriental Notebook." *Sight and Sound* (Oct.-Dec. 1954): 79–84.
An illustrated overview of several lesser films made and shown in Japan during 1954.

Falk, Ray. "Introducing Japan's Top Director." *New York Times* (Jan. 6, 1952): Section 2, p. 5.
A short introduction to Kurosawa upon the opening of *Rashomon* in New York—the first post–World War II Japanese film to do so.

Film. "Oshima." (Spring 1970): 4–6.
Illustrated, brief film-by-film article on six Oshima films: *Naked Youth, The Sun's Burial, Night and Fog in Japan, The Catch, Pleasures of the Flesh* and *Violence at Noon.*

————. "Yasujiro Ozu." (Spring 1963): 8–9.
The author briefly introduces Ozu's films and divides them into three categories ("studies of social injustice, portraits of family life and groups of people living together, and social studies in which the hero perseveres amidst the forces of injustice and illegality").

Film Journal (Oct. 1958).
Entire issue is on Japanese films with two articles by Richie, two by Kirby and one by Shindo (see below). There is also an introduction ("Not Only the Paintings on Silk" pp. 2–4), an "Index to the Films of Akira Kuroswa" pp. 22–28, and an "Alphabetical List of Notable Japanese Films" pp. 38–40.

Films and Filming. "Personality of the Month: Akira Kurosawa." (Nov. 1957): 5.
Offers a brief biography and overview of Kurosawa's career.

Freiberg, Freda, and Susan Stewart. "Making Sense of Japan." *Cinema Papers* (March 1987).
The authors discuss retrospectives of Japanese films they have seen in France and in Australia with emphasis on the differences in audiences between the two countries and the problems in presenting them in Australia.

Gerlach, John. "Shakespeare, Kurosawa and Macbeth." *Literature and Film Quarterly* (Fall 1973): 352–359.
An analysis of the point of view of the Macbeth/Washizu character in *Throne of Blood.*

Gibney, Frank. "The Teeming World of Japanese Films." *Show* (July 1962): 56–57 + .
Introductory article of several within the magazine which looks at Japanese films. (See also entries for West and Sklarewitz.)

Gillett, John. "Coca Cola and the Golden Pavilion." *Sight and Sound* (Summer 1970): 153–156.
Diary of Gillett's trip to Japan to attend Expo 70 and its film festival to do research meetings with Ichikawa and Kurosawa.

————. "Japanese Notebook." *Sight and Sound* (Winter 1972–73): 27–30.
Short interview with Mizoguchi screenwriter, Hisakazu Tsuji, on his visit to London in which he reminisces about working with Mizoguchi. Also discusses the newly discovered print of Kinugasa's *Page of Madness.* References Gosha, Imamura, Yamada and Kobayashi.

Greenspan, Roger. "Mizoguchi and Ozu: Two Masters from Japan." *New York Times* (July 9, 1972).

Although both directors had died by the time this article was written, Greenspan introduces the films *The Princess Yang Kwei Fei* and *Late Spring* which were just showing in New York at the time.

Grilli, Peter. "The Old Man and the Scene: Notes on the Making of *Ran*." *Film Comment* (Oct. 1985): 48 + .
Grilli traveled to Japan to meet with Kurosawa during the making of *Ran*. The article discusses the film's financing and logistics as well as a dinner with Kurosawa and the film's cast, including Peter.

Haberman, Clyde. "Zen and the Art of Noodle Making." *The New York Times* (May 24, 1987): Section 2, page 1 + .
Analysis of *Tampopo* along with an interview with its director, Juzo Itami, in which his personal background and the film's background are discussed.

Harrington, Clifford. "Japanese Filmmaking Today." *Films in Review* (March 1957): 102–107.
A look at Japanese film industry as it existed in 1957. Reference *Export of Women* directed by Yutaka "Jack" Abe and Nikkatsu Studios.

Hart, Henry. "New York's Japanese Film Festival." *Films in Review* (March 1957): 97–101.
Films produced in Japan with government assistance.

―――. "The Second Japanese Film Festival." *Films in Review* (March 1958): 125–128.
Showings of Japanese films sponsored by production studios.

Harvey, Stephen. "Setsuko Hara." *Film Comment* (Nov.-Dec. 1974): 34.
Setsuko Hara, star of several Ozu films, is highlighted in this short article about her career and the type of characters she played.

Heath, Stephen. "Added Attraction: The Question Oshima." *Wide Angle* (1977): 48–57.
Discusses the relationship between sex and politics in the cinema with emphasis on Oshima's *In the Realm of the Senses*.

High, Peter B. "Kihachi Okamoto: An Interview." *Wide Angle* (1977): 25–27.
Okamoto discusses his war films, his nontraditional film hero and actor Tatsuya Nakadai.

―――. "Oshima: A Vital Sexualis on Film." *Wide Angle* (1978): 62–71.
This article tackles the connection between sexuality (especially repressed sexuality) and violence in Oshima's films. Also contains a brief history of the *roman poruno* and "pink" films and references Shindo and Imamura.

―――. "The War Cinema of Imperial Japan and Its Aftermath: An Introduction." *Wide Angle* (1977): 19–21.
A general introduction to the directors, films and factors involved in making Japan's propaganda films of World War II.

Hirano, Kyoko. "MacArthur's Children: An Interview with Masahiro Shinoda." *Cineaste* (1986): 51.
On the release of *MacArthur's Children*, Shinoda expresses his views of the Occupation forces and the transformation of Japanese society after their defeat in World War II. (Also includes a review of *MacArthur's Children*.)

Hoaas, S. "Shohei Imamura." *Cinema Papers* (Sept.-Oct. 1981): 336–341 + .

Interview with Imamura which presents his view of his work and his film philosophy. Provides interesting background information on the filming of *The Ballad of Narayama, Vengeance Is Mine* and *Eijanaika.*

Hoberman, J. "Rebel Rouser." *Village Voice* (Oct. 18, 1983): 62.
An introduction to Oshima and his films brought about by a retrospective showing at the Japan Society in New York City.

————. "That Sirkian Feeling." *Village Voice.* (Oct. 23, 1984): 57–60.
An overview of Naruse's career and film style occasioned by the release of a 25-film retrospective.

Iwabuchi, Masayoshi. "Japanese Cinema, 1961." *Film Culture* (Spring 1962): 85–88.
With several Japanese lists of the 10 best films of 1961, Iwabuchi discusses the state of the industry with emphasis on directors Kinoshita, Oshima, Hani, Imamura, Kobayashi and Matsuyama.

————. "Japan's Idealists." *Films and Filming* (Jan. 1960): 31.
Looks at how Japan's film industry approaches World War II films, specifically Jukichi Unos' *Iwo Jima* and Kobayashi's *The Human Condition.*

————. "1954 in Japan." *Sight and Sound* (Spring 1955): 202–205.
Review of feature, independent and documentary films released in Japan for 1954.

Iwasaki, Akira. "Documentary Story: The Occupied Screen." *Japan Quarterly* (July-Sept. 1978): 302–322.
Interesting personal view of the newsreels' role (especially the Nihon Film Company) under the censorship of the Allied Occupation government.

————. "Honourable Movie-Makers." *Sight and Sound* (Winter 1937–38): 194–197.
One of the earliest articles to introduce the Japanese film industry to Western audiences. It discusses history, influences, studios, film genres, and the coming of sound (the last, strangely enough, without once mentioning the *benshi*). Abridged from the *Japanese Cinema Year Book.*

————. "The Japanese Cinema." *Film* (Nov.-Dec. 1956): 6–10.
Brief discussion of the most important and unexported Japanese films.

————. "Kurosawa and His Work." *Japan Quarterly* (Jan.-March 1965): 59–64.
Discusses how Kurosawa seems different from other Japanese directors and how his work fuses the East with the West.

Japan Quarterly. "Films: Phoenix or Flop?" (April-June 1972): 129–131.
A look at Japan's declining film production caused by the spread of television, and a plea for more quality films.

————. "People in the Spotlight: Oshima Nagisa." (April-June 1982): 212–214.
Biography of director Nagisa Oshima with an attempt to understand his "rebelliousness." Special reference to *In the Realm of the Senses.*

————. "Pure, Sweet and Slightly Dangerous—Japanese Actresses." (April-June 1983): 169–172.
Brief profiles of Yukio Toake, Keiko Matsuzaka, Kiwako Taichi and Naoko Otani.

Jarden, G.W. "All Godzilla's Children." *(Crawdaddy) Feature* (April 1979): 56–59.

Although heavily illustrated with photos from Japanese "monster films," this article is really about the making of a Japanese Western starring two female pop singers known as Pink Lady.

Johnson, W. "Ichikawa and the Wanderers." *Film Comment* (Sept.-Oct. 1975): 16–21.
An examination of the disparity and development in Ichikawa's film styles and subject matter. Although the article is supposed to be about his film *The Wanderers,* it only discusses that film briefly at the end of the article.

Kaminsky, Stuart. "The Samurai Film and the Western." *Journal of Popular Film* (Fall 1972): 313–324.
A comparison of two genres of film which come from different cultural backgrounds but which share many common traits and many subtle differences. Special analysis of *The Seven Samurai* and *The Magnificent Seven.*

Kauffmann, Stanley. "Across the Pacific." *New Republic* (Feb. 3, 1986): 28.
Column discusses Teshigahara and Mitsuo Yanagimachi (with special references to his film *Himatsuri*) after Kauffmann met them in Tokyo.

Kehr, Dave. "The Last Rising Sun." *Film Comment* (Sept.-Oct. 1983): 32–40.
Article presents a brief biography of Shohei Imamura and a chronological account of his films and their themes.

_____. "Samurai Lear: Akira Kurosawa's *Ran* Emerges from the Fog of Japanese Commercial Cinema." *American Film* (Sept. 1985): 20 + .
Kehr, on hand during the shooting of the castle burning sequence in Kurosawa's *Ran,* offers background on the film's financing and history, and information on actor Peter. Kehr also touches upon the status of films in Japan and the making of *Himatsuri* and *Godzilla '85.*

Kinder, Marsha. "*Throne of Blood*: A Morality Dance." *Literature and Film Quarterly* (Fall 1977): 339–345.
Comparison of Shakespeare's play to the film *Throne of Blood* by Kurosawa.

Kirby, Gordon. "The Japanese Cinema: Impressions of a Visitor." *Film Journal* (October 1958): 15–18.
Personal reflections by Mr. Kirby upon the type of films he saw and witnessed being filmed while on a three week visit to Japan.

_____. "Who's Who in the Japanese Cinema." *Film Journal* (October 1958): 29–37.
A selected directory of actors, actresses, directors, writers and technicians working in Japanese films. Entries vary in length and detail but usually include personal background and notable films.

Knee, Adam. "Criminality, Eroticism and Oshima." *Wide Angle* (No. 2, 1987): 47–59.
Knee sees the characters in Oshima's films who suffer because they "part from society" as "requisite to any personal freedoms" and consequently central to many Oshima films. Special emphasis is given to *Merry Christmas, Mr. Lawrence.*

Knight, Arthur. "Season in the Sun." *Saturday Review* (Feb. 13, 1960).
Comments on Thomas J. Brandon's experiment in bringing Japanese films to New York.

Koch, Carl. "Japanese Cinema." *Close Up* (Dec. 1931): 296–299.
    Use of *benshi* at showing of Japanese film to a Japanese audience in Berlin.
    Refers to Katsumi.

Komatsu, Hiroshi, and Charles Musser. "Benshi Search." *Wide Angle* (1987).
    A Western view of the effect of the historic *benshi* (film narrator) upon seeing
    a contemporary performance by one during Griffith's film *Orphans of the
    Storm*. Includes a sample of image/voice-over script and an interview with
    Shunsui Matsuda who teaches the art of the *benshi*.

Konshak, Dennis J. "Space and Narrative in *Tokyo Story*." *Film Criticism* (Spring
    1980): 31–40.
    Analysis of Ozu's unique style of film construction especially as it relates to the
    use of space.

Kuroda, Toyoji. "A Japanese Film History." *Variety* (May 13, 1981): 259 + .
    A concise overview of the history of Japanese films with emphasis on the
    industry, exhibition and legislation and not on personalities or specific films.

Leach, James. "Mizoguchi and Ideology: Two Films from the Forties." *Film
    Criticism* (Fall 1983): 66–78.
    While some critical analyses of Mizoguchi's films center on the director's per-
    sonal political opportunism and psycho-sexual problems, Leach examines *The
    Loyal 47 Ronin* and *My Love Is Burning* in terms of loyalty, opportunism and
    traditional values.

Lehman, Peter. "The Act of Making Films: An Interview with Nagisa Oshima."
    Wide Angle (Number 2, 1982): 56–61.
    One of the few English language interviews with Oshima. It offers insight into
    what Oshima thinks of his films' styles, sexuality, and violence. Also indicates
    his views of Western film directors.

————. "Oshima: The Avant-Garde Artist Without an Avant-Garde Style." *Wide
    Angle* (Number 2, 1987): 18–31.
    Examines *In the Realm of the Senses* in relationship to the more standard por-
    nographic film and looks at the experimental film styles Oshima uses.

Leyda, Jay. "Films of Akira Kurosawa." *Sight and Sound* (Oct.-Dec. 1954):
    74–78 + .
    Leyda offers a biography of Kurosawa and an explanation of his films at a time
    when Kurosawa was still relatively unknown. Includes a synopsis of several
    films.

Life. "Exquisite New Films from Japan." (Nov. 15, 1954): 89–90 + .
    Color pictures from and brief text about *Gate of Hell, Golden Demon*, and
    Ugetsu.

Lindstrom, Siegfried F. "The Cinema in Cinema-Minded Japan." *Asia* (Dec. 1931):
    768–775 + .
    Wonderfully illustrated discussion of moviegoing in Japan as well as their pro-
    duction methods and a history of their industry.

Lopate, Phillip. "A Taste for Naruse." *Film Quarterly* (Summer 1986): 11–21.
    An introduction to Naruse for Western audiences who had not been exposed
    previously to many Naruse films. Delves into the special quality of his films,
    both in plot and acting styles.

McCarthy, Todd. "Oshima's Japanese Candor as to Directors of West and Orient."
    Variety (April 9, 1980): 15.

Description of the major contributions of Oshima in the realm of Japanese films and a look at his, at the time, newest venture, a film based on *The Seed and the Sower* which was to become *Merry Christmas, Mr. Lawrence.*

McCormick, Ruth. "Ritual, the Family and the State: A Critique of Nagisa Oshima's *The Ceremony.*" *Cineaste* (Nov. 1974): 20–27.
Brief introduction to Oshima's life and work with emphasis on his major themes and his film style as presented in *The Ceremony.* Followed by an interview with Oshima in which he discusses popular and critical acceptance of his films and the influence of the American Occupation on Japan and his films.

_____, and Bill Thompson. "Feminism in the Japanese Cinema: An Interview with Sachiko Hidari." *Cineaste* (Spring 1979): 26–29.
Intriguing interview with one of the few Japanese actresses who have managed also to become directors. Hidari, wife of Susumu Hani and star of several of his films, discusses her upbringing, her film *The Far Road* and women as portrayed in Japanese society.

McDonald, Keiko. "Form and Function in Osaka Elegy." *Film Criticism* (Winter 1982): 35–44.
Analysis of Mizoguchi's film in terms of point of view and theme development.

_____. "Kinji Fukasaku: An Introduction." *Film Criticism* (Fall 1983): 20–32.
Interesting analysis of the themes and contributions of Kinji Fukasaku, primarily a "B" movie director who specializes in *yakuza* genre films. McDonald also shows the difficult interrelationship between directors and the major Japanese studios and producers they work for.

_____. "Milieu in Yojimbo." *Literature and Film Quarterly* (Number 3, 1980): 188–196.
Analysis of Kurosawa's *Yojimbo* from the unique point of view of its re-creation of historical setting through realistic imagery, the clash of three character types, and a cinematography used to express visual irony.

_____. "Symbolism of *Odd Obsession.*" *Literature/Film Quarterly* (Number 2, 1979): 60–66.
Examines Kon Ichikawa's film *Odd Obsession* in relationship to how time is emphasized.

McKegney, Michael. "New Tales of the Taira Clan." *Village Voice* (August 5, 1971): 51.
Analysis of Mizoguchi's film with respect to narrative and tone.

McVay, Douglas. "The Rebel in a Kimono." *Films and Filming* (July 1961): 9–10 + and (Aug. 1961): 15–16 + .
In this two-part article, McVay analyzes *Rashomon* and why Kurosawa is popular in the West.

McWilliams, Dean. "The Ritual Cinema of Yukio Mishima." *Wide Angle* (1977): 34–43.
An analysis of Yukio Mishima's film *The Rite of Love and Death* in relation to his short story, "Patriotism," on which it is based.

Malcomson, Scott L. "Mitsuo Yanagimachi." *Film Criticism* (Fall 1983): 12–19.
Examination of independent filmmaker Yanagimachi's themes of "conflict between tradition and modernity, destruction of nature, the dislocation and alienation of modern Japanese life, and the difficulties of cultural self-definition."

Mancia, Adrienne Johnson. "Woman in the Dunes." *Film Comment* (Winter 1965): 55–63.
Analysis and review of both the book and film *Woman in the Dunes*. This issue of *Film Comment* also contains a review by Kirk Bond (pp. 64–65) and "A Conversation with Two Japanese Film Stars," Kyoko Kishida and her husband Noboru Nakaya.

Mayberry, Ruth. "He's the Pure Artist." *American Film* (April 1982): 50.
Mayberry interviews Donald Richie about the problems Kurosawa had in obtaining financing for *Kagemusha* and his rift with Mifune.

Milne, Tom. "Flavor of Green Tea over Rice." *Sight and Sound* (Autumn 1963): 183–186 + .
Discusses the characteristic style of an Ozu film with special attention to *An Autumn Afternoon*.

———. "The Skull Beneath the Skin." *Sight and Sound* (Autumn 1966): 185–189.
Illustrated analysis of the heroes and humanism in the movies of Kon Ichikawa. Film overview.

Miner, Earl Roy. "Japanese Film Art in Modern Dress." *Quarterly of Film, Radio and Television* (Summer 1956): 436–442.
A first view of Japanese contemporary films. Reference *Inn at Osaka*, *The Echo*, *Their First Trip to Tokyo* (a.k.a. *Tokyo Story*), *Wheat Whistle* and *Ikiru*.

Mitchell, Greg. "Kurosawa in Winter." *American Film* (April 1982): 46–51.
This article shows a director at the end of his career. It offers background information on both Kurosawa the person and Kurosawa the filmmaker. It presents the director's comments on the making of his newest film, *Ran*, and the problems he has had procuring financing for his films.

Miyagawa, Kazuo. "Japanese Cameraman: Kazuo Miyagawa." Interviewed by Max Tessier and Ian Buruma. *Sight and Sound* (Summer 1979): 188–189.
Famed cinematographer Miyagawa comments about working with Mizoguchi and the art which effected his film's scene compositions.

Nakamura, Haruji, and Leonard Schrader, translator. "The Uniqueness of Kon Ichikawa: A Translated Symposium." *Cinema* (Fall 1970): 30–31.
Notes from question-and-answer symposium attended by Ichikawa. Discusses his styles and themes with special references to *Being Two Isn't Easy*, *Revenge of Yukinojo* and *The Sin*.

New York Times Magazine. "Pearl Harbor, Japanese View." (Nov. 13, 1960).
Production photos of the making of the film *Storm over the Pacific*.

New Yorker. "Documentary Fantasist." (April 10, 1965): 35–36.
Description of Hiroshi Teshigahara, who was in New York making a documentary about prizefighter Jose Torres.

Newsweek. "Eloquent Silence." (Sept. 10, 1962): 104.
Plot synopsis and review of *The Island* along with biography of Kaneto Shindo.

———. "Industry: Beauty from Osaka." (Oct. 10, 1955): 116.
Article on a visit to New York and Hollywood by Machiko Kyo and Masaichi Nagata.

————. "Japan: The 'Rackheed' Scandal." (June 7, 1976): 45.
Filming of the fictional movie *The Barren Zone* by director Satsuo Yamamoto and its relation to the Lockheed scandal.

————. "Monster-san." (Oct. 19, 1964): 110.
Discusses the popularity of monster films and the making of the film *The Biggest Fight on Earth*.

————. "Outdoing *Olympia*." (Sept. 21, 1964): 106.
Article on Ichikawa's making of *Tokyo Olympiad* and a comparison to Leni Riefenstahl's *Olympia*.

————. "Samurai to Shomin-Geki." (May 11, 1970): 96 + .
Article introducing the 90-film retrospective of Japanese films put together by Donald Richie.

————. "Seven Bullets." (March 9, 1964): 84.
Newsweek contends that with the showing of Kurosawa's *Stray Dog* out of chronological order, it is difficult to judge the development of the director's style.

Noriega, Shon. "Godzilla and the Japanese Nightmare: When Them! Is U.S." *Cinema Journal* (Fall 1987): 63–77.
A sociohistoric reading of the Godzilla films with emphasis on how the Japanese approach this genre reflects their relationship to nuclear weapons.

Nygren, Scott. "The Pacific War: Reading, Contradiction and Denial." *Wide Angle* (No. 2, 1987): 60–70.
Discusses Oshima's television documentary *The Greater East Asia War (Kai toa senso*, 1968) in context of "contemporary considerations of the war and its ideological representations." Also discusses the 1944 animated feature *Momotaro umi no shimpei*.

————. "Reconsidering Modernism: Japanese Film and the Postmodern Context." *Wide Angle* (Vol. 11, No. 3, 1989): 6–15.
This heavily technical article discusses rereading Japanese films in light of cross-cultural influences between that country and the West.

Oberbeck, S.K. "Samurai to Shomin-Geki." *Newsweek* (May 11, 1970): 96–98.
Review of the Museum of Modern Art's Japanese film series. Put together by Donald Richie, the series, which consists of 90 films, spans almost 50 years and covers most of the great directors.

Ogino, Yasushi. "Before Daybreak." *Close Up* (Dec. 1931): 290–295.
Analysis of Kinugasa's films. Illustrated.

————. "Japan as Seen in Films." *Close Up* (Dec. 1933): 353–360.
Protest that the Japan shown in films abroad—both those made in Japan and those made in the West which depict Japan—does not represent the country as it is today, but caters to foreign prejudices based on feudal relics.

————. "Japanese Film Problems: 1932." *Close Up* (March 1933): 61–66.
Discusses the dearth of film criticism and the problems of making sound films in Japan. Refers to Kinugasa's *Chushingura* and director Sadao Yamanaka.

Osamu, Takahashi. "Brilliant Shadows: Ozu Yasujiro (1)." *Japan Quarterly* (July-Sept. 1984): 269–277. "Brilliant Shadows: Ozu Yasujiro (2)." (Oct.-Dec. 1984): 435–444.
Two-part article on Ozu written by one of his assistant directors. Contains interesting behind-the-scenes stories illuminating Ozu's directing style while

Osamu worked with him on *Tokyo Story* as well as introspective insights on the film after finally seeing it several years later in Paris.

Ozaki, Koji. "Popular Entertainments of Japan." *Atlantic* (Jan. 1955): 148–151.
Discusses status of moviegoing in Japan since the success of *Rashomon* and other films in the West.

Pally, Marcia. "A Conversation with Kurosawa." *Saturday Review* (Jan.-Feb. 1986): 87–88.
Brief biography of Kurosawa with a few quotes on his style and message occasioned by the release of *Ran* in New York.

Paul, Alan. "Alan Paul from Tokyo." *Film Comment* (Sept. 1978): 8 + .
Discusses conditions in the Japanese film industry in the late 1970s, foreign funding and hints at the changes to come. References Shochiku Studios.

Peary, Gerald. "Akira Kurosawa: Japan's Existential Cowboy Looks West and Thinks East." *American Film* (April 1989): 80–82.
An introduction to the films of Kurosawa with an emphasis on video availability.

People Weekly. "Akira Kurosawa." (Dec. 23, 1985): 42 + .
Photo of Kurosawa with short article on the director upon the release of *Ran*.

Petric, Vlada. "*A Page of Madness:* A Neglected Masterpiece of the Silent Cinema." *Film Criticism* (Fall 1983): 86–106.
An in-depth analysis of Teinosuke Kinugasa's expressionistic film which some critics dismiss as "an overrated curiosity." Petric offers a comprehensive scene-by-scene study and explains the qualities which the author feels raise the film to the level of a masterpiece.

Polan, Dana. "Politics as Process in Three Films by Nagisa Oshima." *Film Criticism* (Fall 1983): 33–42.
Treatise concerns how Oshima deals with tradition, cultural innovation and political progress.

Prouse, Derek. "Report from Japan." *Sight and Sound* (Summer 1958): 218.
Brief discussion of Japanese film industry. Expresses a desire for Western views of Japanese films and references Imai.

Rayns, Tony. "Tokyo Stories." *Sight and Sound* (Summer 1981): 170–176.
Interviews with Kurosawa about *Kagemusha,* his early training under Yamamoto and the impact of *Rashomon;* and with Oshima, especially about *In the Realm of the Senses* and *Empire of Passion.*

Reischauer, Edwin O. "Japanese Film." *TV Guide* (Jan. 18, 1975): 10–12.
Introduction to the PBS series which presented 13 Japanese films to American audiences. Discusses the two types of films viewers will see, swashbucklers and contemporary social dramas.

Rhode, Eric. "Ugetsu Monogatari." *Sight and Sound* (Spring 1962) 97–99.
Discussion of the narrative of *Ugetsu* and Mizoguchi's "classical" realism.

Richardson, Tony. "Seven Samurai." *Sight and Sound* (Spring 1955).
See Leo Braudy entry in the "Books with References to Japanese Films and Directors" bibliography section above.

Richie, Donald. "The Clashing Twain." *Film Journal* (Nov. 1959): 18–21.
Many Japanese films are based on Western literary works, and Richie examines what changes are made for these adaptations.

_____. "Dostoevsky with a Japanese Camera." *Horizon* (July 1962): 42.
Biography with a discussion of Kurosawa's filmic style in relation to his love of
Dostoevsky's works.

_____. "Eight Takes Are Just Fine for Japan's Director Itami." *Far Eastern
Review* (March 10, 1988): 46.
Interesting description of working techniques of Juzo Itami while working on
the second part of *A Taxing Woman*.

_____. "Face of 63." *Films and Filming* (July 1963): 15–18 + .
Richie takes a studio-by-studio look at the then declining conditions within
the Japanese film industry with attention to the rise of independent production companies and the works of Ichikawa, Kurosawa, Kobayashi, Hani and
Teshigahara.

_____. "Honour All Round." *Films and Filming* (Dec. 1964): 55.
Richie addresses the status of the five big film industries as they begin to work
with independent production companies.

_____. "Japanese Cinema." *Cinema Papers* (June-July 1980): 181–183 + .
Richie gives an in-depth examination of the state of the Japanese film
industry, the loss of talented directors, the dearth of film critics not directly
paid by the industry, and foreign financing.

_____. "Japan: The Younger Talents." *Sight and Sound* (Spring 1960): 78–81.
Richie examines five directors (Ichikawa, Kobayashi, Hani, Yasushi Nakahira
and Yasuzo Masumura) who have come up through the film industry and
achieved varying degrees of success.

_____. "Kurosawa on Kurosawa (Parts I and II)." *Sight and Sound* (Summer-
Autumn 1964): 108–113 and 200–203.
Offers Kurosawa's observations and personal comments on his films from his
first, *Sanshiro Sugata,* to *Sanjuro.* Most of the article is repeated within
Richie's book *The Films of Akira Kurosawa.*

_____. "The Later Films of Yasujiro Ozu." *Film Quarterly* (Fall 1959): 18–25.
Richie discusses the "Japaneseness" of Ozu's films from their restrained style to
his lack of camera movement.

_____. "Notes for a Definition of the Japanese Film." *Performance* (April 1972):
20–30.
A concise and well thought out description of those traits which Richie feels
are the essence of Japanese films and how they compare to Western films.

_____. "Notes on Mitsuo Yanagimachi— A New Japanese Director." *Film
Criticism* (Fall 1983): 7–11.
Richie discusses Yanagimachi's films in terms of their themes, their point of
view, and the director's neutrality.

_____. "A Personal Record." *Film Quarterly* (Fall 1960): 20–30.
Interesting but brief interviews with various film personalities and Richie's per-
sonal recollections of them. References Kurosawa, Toyoda, Yoshimura,
Mifune, Mishima, Kinoshita, Matsuyama, Hidari, and Hani.

_____. "Poetic Metaphor in the Japanese Film" *Film Journal* (October 1958):
5–9.
An examination of the poetic devices used within Japanese movies such as
their use of intercutting scenes of nature.

_____. "Red Beard." *Film Quarterly* (Fall 1965): 14–25.
Analysis of the film *Red Beard*. An abridged chapter from his book *The Films of Akira Kurosawa*.

_____. "*The Several Sides of Ichikawa.*" *Sight and Sound* (Spring 1966): 84–86.
Richie, as usual, provides the Western reader with insight and many good quotes in this analysis of the multifaceted films of Ichikawa, from the light comedies, to the darker tales. Mentions *The Burmese Harp* and *Odd Obsession*.

_____. "Sex and Sexism in the Eroduction." *Film Comment* (Jan.-Feb. 1973): 12–17.
In 1973, when attendance at movies in Japan was very low, one type of film could still pack theatres, soft-core pornography. Richie examines the essentials of these "eroductions" in light of strict Japanese censorship and what it says about the psychological assumptions of its audiences.

_____. "The State of the Japanese Film." *Japan Quarterly* (April-June 1983): 176–179.
Typically insightful Richie article discusses the cause for the decline in quality of the Japanese film and the rise of independent productions as a possible avenue for the revitalization of the Japanese cinema.

_____. "A Talk with Shiro Toyoda." *Film Journal* (Oct. 1958): 11–14.
This article offers insights into the way Toyoda makes his films, from his regard for the actors to his use of storyboards. Also includes a filmography.

_____. "The Unexceptional Japanese Film." *Films in Review* (June-July 1955): 273–277.
Looks at the fact that what is popular in Japan is not necessarily popular abroad — heavily emotional stories, for example.

_____. "Yasujiro Ozu: A Biographical Filmography." *Film Comment* (Spring 1971): 4–17.
Brief background information on many of Ozu's films. Eventually became the back part of Richie's book *Ozu*. (See initial "Books" bibliography section above.)

_____. "Yasujiro Ozu: The Syntax of His Films." *Film Quarterly* (Fall-Winter 1963–64): 11–16.
A stylistic analysis of Ozu's films for viewers who will be seeing any of his five films which were then touring the United States. Richie examines Ozu's grammar, structure, editing, and tempo.

_____, and Joseph Anderson. "Traditional Theatre and Film in Japan." *Film Quarterly* (Fall 1958): 2–9.
Influence of Kabuki, Noh and other theatrical forms on Japanese film content and style.

Rosenbaum, Jonathan. "Ozu." *Film Comment* (Summer 1972).
Upon the screening of eight Ozu films in Paris, Rosenbaum compares many Ozu shots to shots in Western works and, superficially, Ozu's style to Western directors' styles such as that of Sirk.

Ryu, Chishu. "Yasujiro Ozu." *Sight and Sound* (Spring 1964): 92.
Reminiscences of Ozu by Chishu Ryu, the leading actor in almost all of Ozu's postwar films.

Sabatier, Patrick. "Japan's Walt Disney." *World Press Review* (Dec. 1980): 60.
Article on Chiaki Imada who founded in 1965 Toei Doga, the world's leading producer of cartoons.

Sarris, Andrew. "Films in Focus." *Village Voice* (June 24, 1971): 57.
Sarris discusses the poor state of Japanese film criticism for American audiences. References *Princess Yang Kwei Fei* and acts as a rebuttal to Anderson and Richie, who dismiss the film.

Sato, Tadao. "The Art of Yasujiro Ozu." *Wide Angle* (1977): 44–49.
Sato examines the cinematic style of Ozu from his camera placement to the placement of actors within a scene.

_____. "The Comedy of Ozu and Chaplin: A Study in Contrast." *Wide Angle* (1979): 50–53.
An examination of Ozu's comic style with comparisons made to the works of Chaplin.

_____. "The Everyday Films of Itami Juzo." *Japan Quarterly* (July-Sept. 1987): 291–294.
Biography of Itami with a look at his first three films *(The Funeral, Tampopo,* and *A Taxing Woman),* the successes of which indicate Itami may be symptomatic of a new vigor in the Japanese cinema.

_____. "On Kenji Mizoguchi." *Film Criticism* (Spring 1980): 2–16.
In 1965 Michel Mesnil published *Mizoguchi Kenji* (Paris: Seghers, 1965) as a part of the *Cinéma d'aujourd'hui* series in which he claimed that Mizoguchi was virtually unappreciated in Japan until the West "discovered" him. As a part of the book, Sato was allowed to defend Japan and dispute Mesnil's theory. The appendix is here reprinted with an introduction by Dudley Andrew.

_____. "Oshima and Bowie: Culture Shock." *American Film* (Sept. 1983): 26–32.
A look at the making of *Merry Christmas, Mr. Lawrence.* Also includes interviews with David Bowie (by Ruth McCormick) and Nagisa Oshima ("Oshima: Sex, Militarism and Empire").

_____. "Rising Sons." *American Film* (Dec. 1985): 58 + .
Introduction to young filmmakers Yoshimitsu Morita, Kohei Oguri, Shinji Somai and Mitsuo Yanagimachi.

_____. "War as a Spiritual Exercise: Japan's 'National Policy Films'." *Wide Angle* (1977): 22–24.
Introduction to propaganda films made in Japan during World War II which had to work through the wartime bureaucracy and censorship of the Home Ministry and the Media Section of the Army.

Schecter, Leona Protes. "World War II on Japanese Screens." *Films in Review* (March 1957): 108–110.
Analysis of the documentary *Thus Fought Japan.*

Schorer, Mark. "Japan's Delinquents: Children of the Sun and Moon." *Reporter* (Oct. 18, 1956): 35–37.
Interview with Shintaro Ishihara, writer of many *taiyozoku* ("sun family" or "sun tribe") stories which were made into films like *Season of the Sun, The Punishment Room* and *Crazed Fruit.*

Schrader, Paul. "Yakuza-Eiga, a Primer." *Film Comment* (Jan.-Feb. 1974): 9–17.
Director Schrader *(Mishima),* who also wrote the screenplay for *The Yakuza,*
examines the evolution of the *yakuza* (gangster) film in terms of themes, genre
conventions and style. It also includes an overview of those personalities
strongly associated with this genre: Actors Ken Takakura, Koji Tsurta, Junko
Fuji, Hideki Takahashi and directors Tai Kato, Kosaku Yamashita, Singehiro
Ozawa, Masahiro Makino, Norifumi Suzuki, Kinji Fukasaku and Tomu
Uchida.

Sewell, Dorita. "The Japanese Film as a Storytelling." *Wide Angle* (1982): 56–61.
Article discusses the basic differences between the narrative structure within
Japanese and Western films with the West emphasizing reflections of reality
and the Japanese as a story being told to them within a social context.

Shindo, Tak. "Japanese Film Music." *Film Journal* (Oct. 1958): 21.
Discusses the use of Westernized music within Japanese films and also
delineates several traditional Japanese musical instruments used.

Shio, Sakanishi. "Dilemma of Japanese Film World." *Japan Quarterly* (April-June
1955): 219–223.
Profile of Masaichi Nagata, Daiei's head of production, and Japanese films sent
abroad.

Silberman, Robert. "Masahiro Shinoda, Hiromi Go and the Performing Self." *Wide
Angle* (1988): 24–31.
Go, a popular Japanese rock star, does a video, *Allusion,* directed by Shinoda.
The 45-minute-long videotape, which was also released as a theatrical short,
sold 20,000 copies in 1985 and consisted of eight songs.

Silver, Alain. "Samurai." *Film Comment* (Sept.-Oct. 1975): 10–15.
Silver's article predates his book, *The Samurai Film,* but offers an interesting
in-depth look at the historical origins, legends, code of ethics and filmic evolution of the samurai. Includes an interesting and informative chart of "narrative
and character motifs in the postwar samurai film."

Silverstein, Norman. "Kurosawa's Detective-Story Parables." *Japan Quarterly* (July-
Sept. 1965): 351–354.
A look at Kurosawa's detective films *(Stray Dog* and *High and Low)* with an
eye to their moral Christian teachings.

Sipe, Jeffrey. "Death & Taxes: A Profile of Juzo Itami." *Sight and Sound.* (Summer
1989): 186–189.
Itami discusses the influences on his film style, his film successes, his childhood
and his family.

Sklarewitz, Norman. "White Villains Wanted: $8.33 a Day." *Show* (July 1962):
63 + .
Often used to play villains in Japanese films, the author discusses the problems
and pay of Westerners cast in these parts.

Sports Illustrated. "Triumph in Cannes." (May 31, 1965): 17.
Column indicates what a surprise Ichikawa's *Tokyo Olympiad* was at the
Cannes Film Festival.

Stanbrook, Alan. "The Break with the Past." *Films and Filming* (March 1960):
9–11 + .
First part of a history of the Japanese film with emphasis on the industry. Part
II is titled "Oriental Talent."

————. "On the Track of Hiroshi Shimizu." *Sight and Sound* (Spring 1988): 122–125.
Stanbrook examines the style, humor and humanism of director Hiroshi Shimizu, whose films, many of which are about children, are not well known in the West.

————. "Oriental Talent." *Films and Filming* (April 1960): 13–14 + .
Second part of an overview of the Japanese film with a special emphasis on the major filmmakers and films of the 1950s. Part I is titled "Break with the Past."

————. "Tokyo's New Satirists." *Sight and Sound* (Winter 1987): 54 + .
A look at the re-emergence of humor in the Japanese cinema of the 1980s. Examines Yoshimitsu Morita, Sogo Ishii, Juzo Itami, Kaizo Hayashi and Yojiro Takita.

Steele, Robert. "Japanese Underground Film." *Film Comment* (Fall/Winter 1967): 74–79.
Japanese independent filmmakers and their films.

Stokes, Henry Scott. "Mishima, a Movie and Nakasone." *Japan Quarterly* (Jan.-March 1984): 49–54.
Provides background information on Yukio Mishima and discusses the limitations placed on Paul Schrader who was about to do his film *Mishima* and the indifference of the Japanese public to the project.

Strauss, Bob. "Director: Juzo Itami." *Premiere* (June 1988) 25–26.
Interview with Itami in which he discusses his working style and his theories of why his films work.

Strauss, Harold. "My Affair with Japanese Films." *Harper's* (July 1955): 54–59.
A G.I.'s account of watching off-limits Japanese films during the Occupation. Offers a view of Daiei's Kyoto studio, Mizoguchi making *Chikamatsu,* a comparison of Japanese film and art and the use of color, and an interview with Kurosawa. An interesting historical viewpoint, even if it does at times conflict with currently accepted fact.

Takahashi, Osamu. "Brilliant Shadows: Ozu Yasujiro (1)." *Japan Quarterly* (July-Sept. 1984): 269–277. "Brilliant Shadows: Ozu Yasujiro (2)." (Oct.-Dec. 1984): 435–444.
Two-part personal account of working as Ozu's assistant director on *Tokyo Story* and the personal relationship between the two men.

Thomas, Kevin. "Film Did Only So-So in Japan, Director Says." *Los Angeles Times* (June 24, 1987): Part VI, 1 + .
Profile of director Juzo Itami upon the U.S. release of his film *Tampopo.*

————. "Kurosawa Retrospective: Films that Won the West." *Los Angeles Times* (Jan. 9, 1983): Calendar, 16.
To introduce a Kurosawa retrospective being offered at the L.A. County Art Museum, the article offers a biography of the director and a discussion of the importance of his films.

Thompson, Kristin. "Notes on the Spatial System of Ozu's Early Films." *Wide Angle* (Number 1, 1977): 8–18.
A sequel to and extension of the article Thompson did with Bordwell in *Screen* which was prompted by the fact that more works of Ozu had now been seen.

_____, and David Bordwell. "Space and Narrative in the Films of Ozu." *Screen* (Summer 1976): 41–73.
One of the first attempts to define and analyze Ozu's work against a mirror of the "classical Hollywood cinema." To examine the relationship and logic between space and narrative style.

Time. "Japanese Apocalypse." (Sept. 21, 1962): 90.
Review of Kurosawa's *Yojimbo* plus a biography of the director and a discussion of his working techniques.

_____. "The Rising Sun Is Blue." (Nov. 5, 1965): 93.
Japanese industry turns to "eroductions" to fight television. Mentions 18-year-old actress Takako Uchida.

_____. "Sequel Mania." (Jan. 17, 1983): 67.
While Hollywood was putting out sequel after sequel, none could match the record of Yoji Yamada's Tora-san series, which in that year numbered 30 films.

_____. "Stirrings amid Stagnation." (Aug. 1, 1983): 82–83.
With the release of Imamura's *The Ballad of Narayama*, Oshima's *Merry Christmas, Mr. Lawrence* and others, the article discusses the past "golden age," the current industry difficulties and hopes for the future.

_____. "The Sword Swingers." (Nov. 8, 1954): 104 + .
Aiming for the export of Japanese films to the U.S., Masaichi Nagata sees a comeback for Japanese moviemakers.

_____. "Zen Commandments." (Aug. 11, 1961): 37.
The making of *The Life of Buddha*.

Trumbull, Robert. "Rising Star of Japan." *New York Times Magazine* (April 24, 1955): 25.
Biography and an examination of the career of actress Machiko Kyo.

Turim, Maureen. "Signs of Sexuality in Oshima's Tales of Passion." *Wide Angle* (No. 2, 1987): 32–46.
Examines the sexuality and shifts in titles for Oshima's two films *In the Realm of the Senses* and *Empire of Passion* as they are released for French and English audiences.

_____, and John Mowitt. "Thirty Seconds Over—Oshima's the War of Tokyo or The Young Man Who Left His Will on Film." *Wide Angle* (1977): 34–43.
Discusses the method of presentation within Oshima's *The Man Who Left His Will on Film*.

Variety. "Shinoda's *MacArthur's Children* Recalls Aftermath of 1945 Defeat." (May 29, 1985): 86.
Shinoda offers his insights to his latest film and how it reflects his own childhood.

_____. "Shochiku—Special Report." (March 4, 1987): 48 + .
An extensive collection of articles on Shochiku, Japan's oldest continuous major film company, from its history to its plans for the future.

_____. "Tora-san Special." (Dec. 21–27, 1988):41 + .
Upon the release of the fortieth entry in the Tora-san film series, *Variety* has a special section containing several articles devoted to this most beloved character.

Venables, E.K. "The Cinema in Japan." *Sight and Sound* (Autumn 1933): 87–88.
An interesting, though a bit condescending personal view of what it was like
to go to a Japanese movie theatre in the 1930s.

Vernac, Eric. "Mourning a Lost Identity." *World Press Review* (April 1980): 60.
Quick overview of Japanese directors with notes on their styles.

West, Anthony. "The Art of Akira Kurosawa." *Show* (July 1962): 58–62.
West explains how Kurosawa is a "Western" director and how his films, even
though they may be period films, reflect a contemporary theme.

Wharton, Lawrence. "*Godzilla* to *Latitude Zero:* The Cycle of the Technological
Monster." *Journal of Popular Film* (Winter 1974): 30–38.
Superficial analysis of nuclear technology as represented in monster movies.

Willis, Don. "Yasujiro Ozu—Emotion and Contemplation." *Sight and Sound*
(Winter 1978–79): 44–49.
Since so many of Ozu's films do not rely on plot to engage an audience, Willis
examines the role of emotions invoked and the handling of scenes which
appear static but are filled with subtle meaning.

Wolf, Barbara. "Detectives and Doctors." *Japan Quarterly* (Jan.-March 1972):
83–87.
Although Kurosawa is known best in the West for his period films, most of his
modern stories center on detectives or doctors, sickness or crime. Wolf
examines these films.

Wollenberg, H.H. "The Situation in Japan." *Sight and Sound* (Summer 1946): 65.
Superficial description of the status of the Japanese film industry after the war
and under the Occupation.

Yakir, Dan. "The Warrior Returns." *Film Comment* (Nov.-Dec. 1980): 54–57.
Fascinating interview with Kurosawa about the production background of
Kagemusha, its place among samurai films, and its style of presentation.

Yates, Ronald E. "Japan's Everyman." *Chicago Tribune* (April 16, 1989): Section
13, page 28.
Illustrated article on Yoji Yamada and his most famous and enduring creation,
the Tora-san series.

Yoshiyama, Tats. "The Benshi." *Film Comment* (Spring 1964): 34–36.
Combines historical research and personal recollection of a theatre in Hawaii
which used *benshis* for its Japanese audiences.

_____. "Japanese Film Director: Noboru Nakamura." *Cinema and Television
Digest* (Winter 1966–67): 15–18.
While a very prolific director, Nakamura is little known outside of Japan
because he primarily produces films for Japan's ever-changing, double-billed
theatre program.

_____. "Susumu Hani: Report and Interview." *Cinema and Television Digest*
(Spring 1966): 7–9.
Hani comments on the simplicity of his films, on his filming techniques and
his use of nonprofessional actors.

Young, Vernon. "Japanese Film: Inquiries and Inferences." *Hudson Review* (Fall
1955): 20–21.

Attempt to clarify basic Western misconceptions about Japanese films. Reprinted in Young's *On Film: Unpopular Essays on a Popular Art* and in *Focus on Rashomon*. (See initial Book bibliography section above.)

_____. "Reflections of the Japanese Film." *Arts Digest* (Aug. 1955): 20–21. Discussion of the essence of Japanese films through examples like *Rashomon*, *Ugetsu* and *Gate of Hell*.

Zambrano, Ana Laura. *"Throne of Blood:* Kurosawa's *Macbeth."* *Literature and Film Quarterly* (Summer 1974): 262–274. Historic analysis of the use of art in *Throne of Blood* and the foundations of the Japanese aesthetic tradition.

Zeman, Marvin. "The Artistry of Ozu." *Film Journal* (Fall-Winter 1972): 62–73. Although Zeman starts out attempting to explain Ozu's style in terms of Japanese art, his enthusiasm for Ozu's films causes him to digress into scene summaries and explanations without returning to his original thesis. Contains a filmography and selective bibliography.

Index